Risks, Innovations, and Corporate Social Responsibility in Finance and Accounting

Maizaitulaidawati Md Husin
https://orcid.org/0000-0002-2789-8274
Universiti Teknologi Malaysia, Malaysia

Muslim Amin
Azman Hashim International Business School, Universiti Teknologi Malaysia, Malaysia

Haliyana Khalid
Azman Hashim International Business School, Universiti Teknologi Malaysia, Malaysia

Nor Aiza Mohd Zamil
https://orcid.org/0000-0002-0121-5914
Universiti Teknologi Malaysia, Malaysia

Mustafa Nourallah
https://orcid.org/0000-0002-3321-3366
Mid Sweden University, Sweden

IGI Global
Scientific Publishing
Publishing Tomorrow's Research Today

Vice President of Editorial	Melissa Wagner
Director of Acquisitions	Mikaela Felty
Director of Book Development	Jocelynn Hessler
Production Manager	Mike Brehm
Cover Design	Jose Rosado

Published in the United States of America by
IGI Global Scientific Publishing
701 East Chocolate Avenue
Hershey, PA, 17033, USA
Tel: 717-533-8845 | Fax: 717-533-7115
Website: https://www.igi-global.com E-mail: cust@igi-global.com

Library of Congress Cataloging-in-Publication Data

LCCN: 2025032418 (CIP Data Pending)
ISBN13: 979-8-3373-5047-9
Isbn13Softcover: 979-8-3373-5048-6
EISBN13: 979-8-3373-5049-3
British Cataloguing in Publication Data
A Cataloguing in Publication record for this book is available from the British Library.

Table of Contents

Detailed Table of Contents

This chapter examines the strategic integration of corporate social responsibility (CSR) and carbon offsetting within financial and accounting practices, highlighting their role in sustainable value creation. CSR has shifted from primarily philanthropic activities to a core component of corporate strategy, particularly regarding environmental responsibility. This chapter draws on empirical research and real-world cases to explore carbon footprint measurement, selection of offset projects, accounting treatments, and ESG reporting, as well as their influence on managerial decision-making. Findings suggest that well-designed carbon offset programs, supported by credible verification, robust governance, and transparent reporting, can enhance stakeholder confidence and long-term organizational value. However, challenges such as fragmented carbon markets, greenwashing concerns, and risks related to the permanence of offsets highlight the importance of clearer standards and stronger regulatory oversight to ensure that carbon offsetting delivers climate benefits.

This study has provided a comparative analysis of the performance of mutual fund with a focus on three categories: Index Funds, Large Cap Funds, and Balanced Advantage Funds for both private and public sector AMCs. The study assessed 24 selected schemes to assess risk-adjusted returns and market association of schemes based on key financial metrics such as Sharpe Ratio, Treynor Ratio, Standard Deviation, and Beta for a 3-year period (2021-2024). The study found that public sector funds such as UTI and SBI do well in passive categories such as Index Funds while private sector funds such as HDFC and ICICI Prudential significantly outperform public sector funds in active categories with better risk-adjusted returns. The statistical analysis

I study the importance of Fintech investment on Environmental, Social, and Governance (ESG) performance score and on ESG risk rating (i.e., the bank's economic risk driven by ESG factors) of 342 investment banks, and whether the impact is greater or less during the Covid years. I find that Fintech investment does have a significant positive impact on ESG performance score. I also find that Fintech investment does have significant positive impact on governance (G) score, but insignificant impact on E score and S score. The findings indicate that Covid does have a significant impact on ESG risk rating, although Covid does not have significant impact on ESG performance, regardless of Fintech investment levels. There is a positive relationship between Fintech investment and ESG performance during both Covid and non-Covid years, with little variation in intensity. Additionally, the impact of Fintech investment on ESG performance is stronger for banks with smaller investment sizes. Lastly, Fintech investment has greatest positive effect on ESG performance when made through private equity.

This study explores the factors influencing the adoption of green banking among young adults in India, drawing on the Theory of Planned Behaviour. Key determinants include environmental concern, social factors, perceived behavioural control, subjective norms, and attitude toward behaviour. The moderating role of effort expectancy is also examined. Based on data from respondents aged 18–35, the findings provide practical insights for banks to develop targeted strategies that encourage green banking practices among youth.

Preface

In today's challenging world, companies' survival and growth are highly influenced by rapid technological and environmental changes. Innovation is a survival strategy that unlocks transformation, while calculated risk-taking is fundamental to developing new, necessary solutions and overcoming market, geopolitical, or operational challenges. This book, entitled 'Risks, Innovations, and Corporate Social Responsibility in Finance and Accounting', meets the demand of the current accounting and finance landscape for a comprehensive, innovative approach and mechanism, while promoting ethical, sustainable business that positively impacts society and the environment. In this book, the chapters are compiled to meet the theme and are timely and relevant to readers in the field.

CHAPTER OVERVIEW

In Chapter 1, the authors examine the sustainability context by synthesising how carbon offsetting is integrated into corporate sustainability strategies, financial decision-making, and accounting systems (such as IFRS and US GAAP). It discusses the methodological requirements for high-quality offsets, the theoretical drivers behind their adoption, and how technologies like AI and blockchain can enhance transparency and mitigate greenwashing. This chapter is important and current, especially because ESG management is critical to drive sustainable growth.

Chapter 2 compares the performance of mutual fund schemes managed by public- and private-sector Asset Management Companies (AMCs). The chapter focuses on specific fund categories while incorporating structural attributes like Net Asset Value (NAV) and expense ratios. This chapter contributes distinct findings regarding where public and private funds excel, which offers a practical guide for decision making, especially for investors.

Chapter 3 also covers the sustainability context by analysing the impact of green bonds on banks' profitability. Specifically, the chapter examines how the issuance of green bonds affects the financial performance and ESG scores of major Indian banks, underscoring the importance of strong asset management and competent governance in this field.

Chapter 4 explores how FinTech innovations (such as the India Stack, UPI, and mobile banking) and government policies (such as the PM SVANidhi scheme) are bridging the gap in financial inclusion for underserved populations. The chapter focuses specifically on the socio-economic dynamics of Indian street vendors and their transition into the formal digital economy. This chapter presents the current state of financial inclusion, FinTech innovation, and digital public infrastructure in India.

In Chapter 5, the authors evaluate the stock market performance of banks, NBFCs, and fintech companies. Specifically for Initial Public Offerings (IPOs), the authors separate performance into short- and medium-term post-listing periods, reflecting the company's success in the financial sector.

Chapter 6 brings together the sustainability and ESG reporting topics linked to corporate financial performance. In this chapter, the authors discussed how Stakeholder and Legitimacy theories explain corporate motivations for sustainability disclosures and their subsequent impact on financial outcomes. It highlights that high-quality, transparent reporting generally correlates with positive financial performance. This chapter provides valuable information, especially to readers whose interests lie in sustainability and the company's performance.

In Chapter 7, the authors cover the topic of FinTech investments and relate it to ESG performance and ESG risk ratings in the context of global investment banking. Focusing on the impact of FinTech investment on overall ESG performance across both COVID-19 and non-COVID-19 years, the authors note that the pandemic period significantly reduced ESG risk ratings. This chapter covers the current ESG topics that are always critical to stakeholder groups, including investors, regulators, and issue-focused parties.

Chapter 8 covers green banking, sustainable finance and consumer behaviour of young adults. It investigates the factors driving the adoption of eco-friendly banking practices (such as paperless services and green loans) among youth by examining subjective norms, environmental concerns, and perceived behavioural control. This chapter brings the phycological perspective to explain human behaviour.

In Chapter 9, the authors cover the fields of financial behaviour, investor psychology, artificial intelligence (AI) in finance, and digital decision-making. In this chapter, the authors analyse how changing digital and AI-powered contexts influence investors' financial behaviour and evaluate the connection of financial beliefs, attitudes, and goals, finding that in the AI era.

Overall, this book combines theoretical foundations with practical applications, offering valuable contributions to both scholars and practitioners. Academicians and students will find this book beneficial, while policymakers and practitioners will find it interesting, as it covers a wide range of current topics in accounting and finance.

Maizaitulaidawati Md Husin
Universiti Teknologi Malaysia, Malaysia

Muslim Amin
Azman Hashim International Business School, Universiti Teknologi Malaysia, Malaysia

Haliyana Khalid
Azman Hashim International Business School, Universiti Teknologi Malaysia, Malaysia

Nor Aiza Mohd Zamil
Universiti Teknologi Malaysia, Malaysia

Mustafa Nourallah
Mid Sweden University, Sweden

Chapter 1
Strategic CSR and Carbon Offsetting in Financial and Accounting Practices

Soleiman Mohammadi Limaei
http://orcid.org/0000-0001-6379-6120
Department of Economics, Geography, Law, and Tourism, Mid Sweden University, Sweden

ABSTRACT

This chapter examines the strategic integration of corporate social responsibility (CSR) and carbon offsetting within financial and accounting practices, highlighting their role in sustainable value creation. CSR has shifted from primarily philanthropic activities to a core component of corporate strategy, particularly regarding environmental responsibility. This chapter draws on empirical research and real-world cases to explore carbon footprint measurement, selection of offset projects, accounting treatments, and ESG reporting, as well as their influence on managerial decision-making. Findings suggest that well-designed carbon offset programs, supported by credible verification, robust governance, and transparent reporting, can enhance stakeholder confidence and long-term organizational value. However, challenges such as fragmented carbon markets, greenwashing concerns, and risks related to the permanence of offsets highlight the importance of clearer standards and stronger regulatory oversight to ensure that carbon offsetting delivers climate benefits.

1. INTRODUCTION

Corporate Social Responsibility (CSR) has evolved from a voluntary philanthropic activity into a strategic and financially material component of corporate governance,

DOI: 10.4018/979-8-3373-5047-9.ch001

risk management, and disclosure practices. Contemporary CSR frameworks encompass community engagement, responsible labor governance, ethical supply-chain oversight, environmental stewardship, and transparent sustainability reporting—each now central to maintaining corporate legitimacy and long-term value creation (Carroll & Shabana, 2010; Kolk, 2016). Within financial and accounting domains, CSR considerations increasingly shape investment appraisal, influence risk-adjusted decision-making, and reinforce disclosure obligations as firms respond to heightened regulatory scrutiny and stakeholder expectations. Recent empirical evidence demonstrates that high-quality environmental and carbon disclosures significantly enhance environmental, social, and governance (ESG) performance and firm value, particularly when supported by green innovation and strong regulatory environments (Wen & Kang, 2025; He et al., 2025; Zhou et al., 2025). Parallel research shows that carbon credit schemes can positively influence financial performance when embedded within robust CSR strategies and governance structures, underscoring the growing integration of climate finance instruments into corporate decision-making (Martielli et al., 2025; Salvi et al., 2025).

Carbon offsetting has become a central mechanism within environmental CSR, enabling organizations to compensate for residual greenhouse gas emissions through investments in certified reduction or removal projects. When applied credibly, carbon offsetting supports corporate climate accountability while contributing to global mitigation objectives (World Bank, 2023). As voluntary carbon markets expand, carbon credits have become increasingly intertwined with ESG reporting, sustainability accounting, and enterprise-wide risk management systems, reinforcing the need for rigorous verification, accurate carbon accounting, and transparent disclosure (Badgley et al., 2021; Zetterberg et al., 2021). However, recent analyses highlight persistent integrity challenges in voluntary carbon markets—including non-additionality, leakage, permanence risks, and double counting—that can undermine the credibility of offset claims and inflate reported climate benefits (ICVCM, 2024; SBTi, 2024; Salguero, 2025).

Empirical evidence further suggests that the climate effectiveness of corporate offsetting remains ambiguous. Large-scale studies show that voluntary credit use often does not correlate with measurable emissions reductions (European Commission, 2011) unless paired with substantial internal decarbonization efforts (Stolz & Probst, 2025). This finding aligns with broader concerns about greenwashing, as firms with high emissions sometimes produce extensive ESG disclosures without corresponding improvements in environmental performance (Bolognesi et al., 2025; Siddique et al., 2026). Legal and regulatory scrutiny has intensified accordingly. Courts and consumer protection authorities increasingly challenge misleading "carbon neutral" and "net-zero" claims, as illustrated by the Nuremberg Fürth Regional

Court's ruling against Adidas's "climate neutral by 2050" claim for failing to clarify its reliance on offsets (Climate Case Chart, 2025; European Commission, 2023).

Despite these challenges, firms continue to adopt carbon offsets as part of broader sustainability strategies. Qualitative research shows that organizations often integrate offsets as the final step in climate strategies, motivated by legitimacy, competitiveness, and stakeholder expectations, though concerns about additionality and trust remain (Schmuck et al., 2025). At the same time, regulatory and standard-setting initiatives—such as the Carbon Data Open Protocol (CDOP), the Integrity Council for the Voluntary Carbon Market (ICVCM) Core Carbon Principles, and the updated Science Based Targets initiative (SBTi) Corporate Net-Zero Standard—are strengthening expectations for transparency, harmonized data, and credible emissions tracking prior to credit use (ICVCM, 2024; SBTi, 2024).

Taken together, emerging evidence suggests that the effectiveness of carbon offsetting within CSR and financial practice depends on three interrelated conditions: (1) the integrity and quality of offset projects, which determine whether credits represent real and additional emissions reductions (ICVCM, 2024; Salguero, 2025); (2) the integration of offsets within governance-anchored sustainability strategies aligned with broader emissions management goals (Schmuck et al., 2025; Kochar et al., 2025); and (3) transparent, standardized accounting and reporting systems that link climate action to financial performance and stakeholder accountability (Zhou et al., 2025; Frankel et al., 2025). By synthesizing contemporary offset quality frameworks, regulatory developments, and empirical evidence on disclosure quality and financial outcomes, this paper clarifies the conditions under which carbon offsetting can enhance—rather than undermine—corporate climate responsibility and long-term value creation. Real-world case studies illustrate both exemplary practices and common pitfalls, contributing to the advancement of credible, transparent, and accountable carbon offset use within financial and accounting practice.

This chapter adopts a conceptual and integrative literature review approach. Rather than conducting a systematic or meta-analytic review, it synthesizes insights from accounting, sustainability, and finance literatures to examine how carbon offsetting is conceptualized, implemented, and reported within corporate ESG strategies. Selected examples and policy references are used illustratively to ground the discussion in current practice.

2. BACKGROUND

2.1 Evolution of CSR in Finance

CSR has experienced a profound transformation over the past century, evolving from a primarily philanthropic and voluntary activity into a strategic and increasingly institutionalized component of corporate governance, finance, and accounting (Aguinis & Glavas, 2012; Aslaksen et al., 2021). Early CSR practices, prevalent from the 1920s through the mid-twentieth century, were largely framed around ethical obligations and corporate citizenship, emphasizing charitable contributions, community engagement, and compliance with legal norms (Carroll, 1999; Moura-Leite & Padgett, 2011). During this period, CSR initiatives were generally decoupled from core business strategy and financial decision-making and were often perceived as discretionary expenditures rather than investments capable of generating tangible economic value (Shmelev & Gilardi, 2025; Thamara et al., 2025).

A growing body of literature shows that the evolution of CSR has been neither linear nor universal, unfolding instead in context-dependent stages influenced by institutional quality, stakeholder pressures, and regulatory environments (Campbell, 2007; Matten & Moon, 2008). Early CSR scholarship identifies a philanthropic phase (1920s–1950s), characterized by charitable giving and community engagement, followed by a transitional period in the 1960s and 1970s, when firms began applying traditional management functions to social responsibilities (Bowen, 1953; Carroll, 1999). The most significant shift occurred in the 1980s and 1990s, as CSR became increasingly integrated with strategic management and reconceptualized from a primarily ethical obligation to a performance- and value-oriented business practice (Lee, 2008; Carroll & Shabana, 2010; Aguinis & Glavas, 2012; Li & Sasaki, 2024; Lebbar & El-Aroui, 2025).

By the 1990s, firms increasingly recognized that integrating social and environmental considerations into business operations could generate long-term financial benefits, strengthen stakeholder trust, and mitigate operational, reputational, and regulatory risks (Campbell, 2007; Matten & Moon, 2008). Grounded in stakeholder theory (Freeman & McVea, 2005) and the resource-based view of the firm (Barney, 1991), CSR was reframed as a potential source of competitive advantage, enhancing intangible assets such as legitimacy, corporate culture, and organizational resilience (Bowen, 1953; Porter & Kramer, 2006). This reconceptualization marked a critical shift in how CSR was evaluated within finance, moving from a perception of cost or constraint to a strategic investment with value-creation potential (Campbell, 2007; Aguinis & Glavas, 2012).

Since the early 2000s, CSR has become more deeply embedded within corporate strategy, governance structures, and financial systems, particularly in developed economies (Matten & Moon, 2008; Campbell, 2007). Contemporary CSR emphasizes the triple bottom line, stakeholder accountability, and shared value creation, positioning sustainability initiatives as integral to core business models rather than peripheral or symbolic activities (Porter & Kramer, 2006; Lee, 2008). Empirical evidence indicates that effective CSR integration can generate tangible benefits, including cost efficiencies, reputational gains, improved risk management, and enhanced competitive advantage, especially when aligned with performance measurement systems and managerial decision-making processes (Aguinis & Glavas, 2012; Ioannou & Serafeim, 2015; Ashrafi et al., 2020; Dzage & Szabados, 2024).

The institutionalization of CSR has been further reinforced by the proliferation of formal governance and reporting mechanisms (Matten & Moon, 2008; Campbell, 2007). Global sustainability frameworks—such as the Global Reporting Initiative (GRI) and the UN Global Compact—as well as the expansion of socially responsible investment (SRI) funds, have facilitated greater standardization in the measurement and disclosure of non-financial performance (Kotsantonis et al., 2016; Itan et al., 2025). ESG metrics have become essential tools for investors seeking to assess long-term risks and opportunities beyond traditional financial statements, enhancing transparency, reducing information asymmetry, and supporting more forward-looking valuation and decision-making practices (Eccles et al., 2014; Ioannou & Serafeim, 2014; Friede et al., 2015).

Following the 2008 global financial crisis, CSR became more explicitly linked to risk management, financial stability, and corporate accountability. High-profile governance failures and ethical lapses exposed the limitations of purely financial performance metrics, prompting regulators, investors, and rating agencies to demand greater transparency and oversight of ESG-related activities (Lins et al., 2017). Empirical research from this period shows that firms with stronger CSR performance experienced lower downside risk, greater stakeholder loyalty, and superior resilience during periods of market stress (Albuquerque et al., 2019). Moreover, evidence suggests that firms focusing on financially material ESG issues—those most relevant to their industry and operational context—outperform peers that pursue broad but unfocused CSR strategies (Khan et al., 2016; Ioannou & Serafeim, 2014; Yang et al., 2025).

Despite this broad trend toward strategic integration, the literature emphasizes that CSR evolution remains highly contingent on institutional context (Ahen & Amankwah-Amoah, 2018; Qureshi, 2025). In developed economies characterized by strong regulatory frameworks, transparent governance, and active stakeholder engagement, CSR has largely progressed toward genuine strategic integration and long-term value creation (Waked et al., 2025). In contrast, in developing economies marked by institutional voids and weak enforcement mechanisms, CSR frequently remains predominantly philanthropic or symbolic, with firms often filling gaps in public services rather than driving structural social or environmental change (Shakil et al., 2025). In such contexts, multinational corporations may exploit weak governance to define CSR in ways that prioritize reputational legitimacy while avoiding substantive operational or structural impact.

In recent years, CSR has become increasingly embedded in financial and accounting practices as sustainability considerations are mainstreamed across global capital markets. Institutional investors now routinely integrate ESG data into valuation models, capital allocation decisions, and stewardship activities, while firms leverage CSR frameworks to guide sustainable investment, enterprise risk management, and strategic planning (Bolton & Kacperczyk, 2021; Zairis et al., 2024; Vaihekoski & Yahya, 2025). Research in climate finance further demonstrates that environmental performance—particularly exposure to carbon risk—is increasingly reflected in asset pricing, underscoring the growing financial materiality of CSR-related information (Krueger et al., 2020; Pata et al., 2024; Huang et al., 2025).

At the accounting level, CSR's evolution has accelerated the integration of non-financial information into mainstream reporting and assurance processes (De Villiers et al., 2021). Climate risk, human capital, and governance quality are now disclosed alongside traditional financial results, reflecting heightened regulatory and stakeholder expectations (Pratama et al., 2024; Tharsika, 2025). The establishment of the International Sustainability Standards Board (ISSB) and the issuance of International Financial Reporting Standards (IFRS) Sustainability Disclosure Standards (S1 and S2) represent critical milestones in embedding sustainability information within globally comparable financial reporting systems (IFRS Foundation, 2023; Zdolšek & Taškar Beloglavec, 2023). These standards set out general requirements for the disclosure of sustainability-related risks, opportunities, governance, strategy, and financial effects that are decision-useful for investors (Deloitte, 2023; ICAEW, 2023). Reinforcing this integration, research shows that aligning sustainability and financial disclosures improves transparency, comparability, and accountability in corporate reporting, and represents a paradigm shift in how firms communicate ESG performance alongside financial outcomes (van Wyk & Els, 2023).

Importantly, the evolution of CSR from philanthropic activity to strategic business practice parallels broader shifts in how firms conceptualize environmental responsibility, including climate change mitigation (Carroll & Shabana, 2010; Matten & Moon, 2008; Lee, 2008). Just as early CSR initiatives were often symbolic and discretionary, contemporary climate strategies—such as carbon offsetting—risk reproducing philanthropic logics when implemented in weak institutional settings or without robust governance, accounting, and verification mechanisms (Ahen & Amankwah-Amoah, 2018; Haque & Islam, 2017; De Villiers et al., 2021). Conversely, when embedded within strong governance frameworks, transparent accounting systems, and credible performance measurement regimes, such instruments can function as strategic tools aligned with long-term value creation and risk management (Ioannou & Serafeim, 2015; Deloitte, 2023; Zdolšek & Taškar Beloglavec, 2023).

Overall, CSR evolution should be understood as a set of institutionally contingent trajectories rather than a universal progression (Campbell, 2007; Qureshi, 2025). This perspective provides a critical foundation for analyzing carbon offsetting within financial and accounting practice, clarifying why offsets may reinforce strategic sustainability in some contexts while degenerating into symbolic or greenwashing practices in others (Lee & Raschke, 2023; Tang et al., 2025).

2.2 Carbon Offsetting

Carbon offsetting enables organizations to compensate for greenhouse gas (GHG) emissions by financing projects that reduce or remove emissions elsewhere (Broekhoff et al., 2019; UNFCCC, 2024). Offsets are particularly relevant for emissions that are technologically or economically difficult to eliminate in the short term (Kallbekken & Sælen, 2011). A foundational principle of offsetting is additionality, which requires that credited emission reductions would not have occurred in the absence of the offset project or associated financial incentive (Gillenwater, 2012; Schneider et al., 2019). By linking environmental performance with financial accountability, carbon offsetting has become an increasingly prominent component of corporate sustainability strategies (Cames et al., 2016; Broekhoff et al., 2019). Recent empirical research indicates that voluntary carbon credit schemes can positively influence firm financial performance when embedded within a clear CSR strategy and strong corporate governance practices, suggesting that offsets can contribute to value creation when strategically managed (Choi & Lee, 2024; Yang et al., 2025). However, evidence also shows that offsets alone may have limited effects on actual emission reductions compared to direct internal decarbonization measures, underscoring ongoing debates about the effectiveness of offsetting in corporate climate strategies (Calel & Dechezleprêtre, 2016; Stolz & Probst, 2025).

Types of Offset Projects

Carbon offset projects typically fall into four broad categories:

1. *Nature-based projects*, including reforestation, afforestation, and avoided deforestation, which sequester carbon in ecosystems (Li & Zhang, 2024).
2. *Renewable energy projects,* such as solar, wind, and hydropower, which displace fossil fuel-based energy generation (Huber et al., 2024).
3. *Carbon capture and removal technologies,* including direct air capture and Bioenergy with Carbon Capture and Storage (BECCS) (Zetterberg et al., 2021).

4. *Energy efficiency projects*, such as industrial process upgrades and clean cookstove initiatives, which reduce energy consumption and associated emissions (Kochar et al., 2025).

To minimize the risks of over-crediting and greenwashing, project selection should adhere to recognized standards and protocols that ensure transparency, environmental integrity, and independently verified additionality (Broekhoff et al., 2019).

Offsets in Carbon-Pricing Systems

Offsets play a critical role in carbon-pricing mechanisms, complementing cap-and-trade or carbon-tax schemes. They allow verified reductions from unregulated sectors to be credited toward compliance obligations or tax liability reduction (Broekhoff et al., 2019; World Bank, 2023). Offsets contribute to mitigation by:

- Expanding the range of reduction opportunities and enhancing the cost-effectiveness of mitigation strategies (Broekhoff et al., 2019).
- Increasing the political and economic feasibility of carbon-pricing policies by lowering compliance costs (Zetterberg et al., 2021).
- Extending coverage to sectors not directly regulated, such as land use, forestry, or decentralized energy systems (IPCC, 2022).
- Enabling cost-effective mitigation in regions or sectors where direct abatement would be financially or technically challenging (UNFCCC, 2020).

The integrity and climate effectiveness of offsets depend on rigorous monitoring, reporting, and verification systems, strong governance, and robust additionality assessments to prevent risks such as non-permanence, leakage, or over-crediting (Broekhoff et al., 2019; Gillenwater, 2012).

Some regulatory carbon markets limit the use of offsets. For example, under the Regional Greenhouse Gas Initiative (RGGI, 2023), offset credits may cover only 3.3% of a source's compliance obligation. By integrating offsets into ESG reporting and sustainability accounting under proper standards and verification regimes, firms can demonstrate accountability, manage reputational and environmental risk, and contribute meaningfully to global mitigation efforts (Broekhoff et al., 2019; Lewis & Tietenberg, 2020; Zetterberg et al., 2021).

2.3 Theoretical Framework: Explaining CSR and Carbon Offsetting in Financial and Accounting Practice

Understanding the role of carbon offsetting within CSR and financial decision-making requires a robust theoretical foundation. While carbon offsetting is often presented as a technical or market-based climate instrument, its adoption, reporting, and perceived legitimacy are fundamentally shaped by organizational behavior, institutional environments, and governance structures (DiMaggio & Powell, 1983; Suchman, 1995). This section integrates four complementary theoretical perspectives—stakeholder theory, legitimacy theory, institutional theory, and agency theory—to explain why firms adopt carbon offsetting, how it is operationalized within financial and accounting systems, and under what conditions it contributes to genuine sustainability outcomes rather than symbolic compliance (Dowling & Pfeffer, 1975; Freeman & McVea, 2005; Lakhani & Herbert, 2022).

2.3.1 Stakeholder Theory and Carbon Offsetting

Stakeholder theory posits that firms must manage relationships with a diverse set of stakeholders—including investors, regulators, customers, employees, and civil society—whose expectations influence corporate strategy and performance (Freeman & McVea, 2005). In the context of climate change, carbon offsetting has emerged as a mechanism through which firms signal environmental responsibility to external stakeholders, particularly where direct emissions reductions are costly or technologically constrained.

From a financial perspective, stakeholder pressure increasingly manifests through ESG ratings, sustainable finance requirements, and investor stewardship activities. Institutional investors, for example, integrate climate-related disclosures into valuation models and portfolio allocation decisions, incentivizing firms to demonstrate credible emissions management strategies (Krueger et al., 2020; Bolton & Kacperczyk, 2021). Carbon offsets thus function as a visible and quantifiable response to stakeholder expectations, allowing firms to claim progress toward climate commitments while maintaining operational flexibility.

However, stakeholder theory emphasizes the heterogeneity of stakeholder expectations, as different groups exert varying pressures on firms to provide meaningful climate and environmental disclosures (Haque & Islam, 2017). While some stakeholders prioritize rapid emissions reductions regardless of method, others—particularly NGOs, regulators, and courts—closely scrutinize the integrity and credibility of offset claims, motivating firms to enhance transparency in ESG reporting (Frankel et al., 2025). This divergence helps explain why carbon offsetting can improve corporate reputation for certain audiences while simultaneously increasing reputational and legal risk when offsets are perceived as low quality or misleading (Lee & Raschke, 2023; Siddique et al., 2026). Consequently, transparent accounting, rigorous disclosure, and independent assurance are essential for maintaining stakeholder trust (Bolognesi et al., 2025).

2.3.2 Legitimacy Theory and Symbolic versus Substantive Action

Legitimacy theory provides further insight into the strategic use of carbon offsetting. Firms operate within a "social contract" that requires their activities to be perceived as consistent with societal norms and expectations (Suchman, 1995). Climate change has become a core dimension of this contract, rendering carbon-intensive firms particularly vulnerable to legitimacy challenges.

Carbon offsetting can serve as a legitimacy-restoring mechanism, especially in sectors where absolute emissions reductions are difficult to achieve in the short term. By purchasing offsets, firms may seek to demonstrate alignment with societal climate goals and maintain access to capital, markets, and political support. Yet legitimacy theory also distinguishes between symbolic actions—designed primarily to influence perceptions—and substantive actions that materially alter environmental outcomes (Suchman, 1995; Delmas & Burbano, 2011).

Empirical evidence suggests that carbon offsetting often occupies an ambiguous space between these two forms of action (Stolz & Probst, 2025). While some firms integrate offsets as a residual measure within comprehensive decarbonization strategies, others rely on offsets to justify "net zero" claims without commensurate internal mitigation. This distinction is critical in accounting and reporting contexts, as symbolic offset use increases the risk of greenwashing, misrepresentation, and regulatory sanction, as illustrated by recent litigation over climate neutrality claims (Climate Case Chart, 2025). Legitimacy theory therefore underscores the importance of disclosure quality, methodological transparency, and assurance in determining whether offsets enhance or undermine corporate legitimacy.

2.3.3 Institutional Theory and the Role of Regulatory Context

Institutional theory emphasizes how organizational behavior is shaped by formal regulations, normative standards, and peer practices within specific institutional environments (DiMaggio & Powell, 1983). Carbon offsetting practices vary significantly across jurisdictions, reflecting differences in regulatory stringency, market maturity, and enforcement capacity.

In highly institutionalized settings—such as the European Union—firms face coercive pressures from sustainability disclosure regulations (e.g., CSRD, IFRS S1/S2) and normative pressures from professional accounting bodies and ESG rating agencies (Conca, et al., 2020). These forces encourage more rigorous emissions accounting and constrain opportunistic use of offsets. By contrast, in jurisdictions with weaker regulatory oversight, firms may face fewer barriers to adopting low-quality offsets, reinforcing concerns about over-crediting and market fragmentation (Salguero, 2025).

Mimetic pressures drive firms to adopt carbon offsetting by imitating peers perceived as sustainability leaders. While this can accelerate climate-related practices, it may also encourage symbolic actions if disclosure is prioritized over real impact. Institutional theory explains why offsetting can spread globally yet result in uneven climate outcomes, highlighting the need for standardized rules and strong governance (Conca, et al., 2020).

2.3.4 Agency Theory and Governance of Carbon Offsetting

Agency theory focuses on conflicts of interest between managers (agents) and shareholders (principals), particularly where information asymmetries allow managerial discretion (Jensen & Meckling, 1976). Carbon offsetting introduces such discretion into sustainability strategy, as managers may choose offsets over capital-intensive abatement projects to meet short-term targets or reputational goals.

From an accounting standpoint, the classification and valuation of carbon credits create opportunities for earnings management, selective disclosure, or underreporting of climate-related risks. Without strong governance and assurance mechanisms, offsets may be used to obscure underlying emissions exposure rather than mitigate it (Ding et al., 2025). Empirical studies show that the financial benefits of carbon credits are more pronounced in firms with strong governance structures, suggesting that effective oversight aligns offset use with long-term value creation rather than managerial opportunism (Martielli et al., 2025).

Agency theory therefore reinforces the role of boards, audit committees, and external auditors in overseeing carbon accounting practices. Integrating offsets into enterprise risk management systems, linking executive compensation to verified emissions reductions, and subjecting sustainability disclosures to independent assurance can mitigate agency problems and enhance credibility (Ding et al., 2025; Bolognesi et al., 2025).

2.3.5 Integrative Implications for Finance and Accounting

Taken together, these theoretical perspectives illustrate that carbon offsetting is not merely a technical climate solution, but a governance-sensitive financial instrument embedded in broader CSR and accounting systems (Di Vaio et al., 2024). Stakeholder expectations drive adoption, legitimacy concerns shape disclosure, institutional contexts condition quality, and governance structures determine effectiveness (Conca et al., 2021). For finance and accounting professionals, this implies that the value of carbon offsets depends less on their nominal volume and more on their integration within transparent, well-governed, and theory-consistent sustainability strategies (Zhou et al., 2025).

3. CSR INTEGRATION IN FINANCE AND ACCOUNTING

3.1 ESG Reporting

ESG reporting enables stakeholders to assess corporate sustainability performance. Accountants quantify environmental impacts, integrate these metrics into financial statements, and ensure compliance with frameworks (World Bank, 2023). Transparent ESG reporting supports responsible investment decisions and aligns financial performance with sustainability objectives.

3.2 Sustainable Investments

Sustainable finance instruments—including green bonds, sustainability-linked loans, and ESG-focused investment funds—channel capital toward projects with measurable environmental and social benefits. Carbon credits function as tradable instruments within this ecosystem, supporting compliance obligations and voluntary sustainability commitments while carrying financial value (Kochar et al., 2025).

3.3 Risk Management

CSR initiatives introduce opportunities and risks, including regulatory penalties, reputational damage, and operational disruptions. Carbon offset projects mitigate these risks by demonstrating proactive sustainability engagement. Financial managers and accountants integrate CSR into risk management frameworks, assessing both financial and non-financial implications (Badgley et al., 2021).

4. CARBON OFFSETTING IN PRACTICE

4.1 Methodologies

Carbon footprint measurement provides the foundation for corporate offsetting strategies, enabling firms to identify, quantify, and prioritize emissions for mitigation (Li & Zhang, 2024; UNFCCC, 2024). Offsets are particularly relevant for emissions that are technologically or economically difficult to eliminate in the short term (Kallbekken & Sælen, 2011; Haya et al., 2023). A foundational principle of offsetting is additionality, which requires that credited emission reductions would not have occurred in the absence of the offset project or associated financial incentive (Gillenwater, 2012; Schneider et al., 2019). By linking environmental performance with financial accountability, carbon offsetting has become an increasingly prominent component of corporate sustainability strategies.

Emissions are typically categorized into three scopes:

- *Scope 1:* Direct emissions from sources owned or controlled by the organization.
- *Scope 2:* Indirect emissions from purchased electricity, heat, or steam.
- *Scope 3:* All other indirect emissions occurring in the value chain, including upstream and downstream activities, which often represent the largest share of a firm's total carbon footprint (Gillenwater, 2012; Kallbekken & Sælen, 2011).

Once the carbon footprint is assessed, firms select offsets based on corporate sustainability objectives, applicable verification standards, and cost-effectiveness (Broekhoff et al., 2019; Cames et al., 2016).

4.1.1 Key Methodological Considerations for High-Quality Offsets

- *Additionality:* Ensuring that emission reductions would not have occurred without the offset project (Gillenwater, 2012; Schneider et al., 2019).
- *Permanence:* Guaranteeing that emission reductions are long-lasting and not reversed in the future (Ruseva et al., 2017).
- *Avoidance of Double Counting:* Ensuring that the same emission reduction is not claimed by multiple actors or jurisdictions (Schneider et al., 2019).
- *Co-Benefits:* Assessing additional environmental or social benefits, such as biodiversity preservation or local community development, which can enhance stakeholder value and legitimacy (Cames et al., 2016; UNFCCC, 2024).

4.1.2 Accounting Treatment of Carbon Offsets

Accounting treatments for carbon offsets vary depending on firm policies and reporting frameworks. Carbon credits may be:

- Capitalized as assets if they are expected to generate future economic benefits,
- Expensed as CSR-related expenditures if they are primarily aimed at reputational or compliance objectives.

Different accounting frameworks provide guidance on recognition, measurement, and disclosure:

- *IFRS:* Typically treats carbon credits as intangible assets if acquired for trading or compliance purposes; disclosure should follow IFRS S1/S2 sustainability standards.
- *US GAAP (Generally Accepted Accounting Principles):* May treat carbon credits as inventory or expense depending on whether they are held for trading or used to offset emissions.
- *Emerging ISSB standards:* Focus on integrating ESG-related assets and liabilities into financial reporting to improve transparency and decision-usefulness.

Transparent reporting, independent verification, and alignment with international standards such as ISO 14064, Gold Standard, or Verified Carbon Standard (VCS) are essential for maintaining credibility and stakeholder trust (Gallego Álvarez et al., 2016; Cheung, 2023; Syam et al., 2024).

4.1.3 Strategic Integration

By integrating these methodologies and accounting practices, firms can strategically link carbon offsetting to broader sustainability and financial objectives, ensuring that offsets contribute meaningfully to both emissions' reduction and corporate value creation rather than serving merely symbolic purposes (Hatalis, 2024).

4.2 Carbon Offsetting: Project Types, and Case Studies

4.2.1 Offset Project Types

Offset projects provide tangible mechanisms through which firms can meet their climate commitments. Selecting high-quality projects requires consideration of additionality, permanence, verification standards, and alignment with corporate sustainability objectives (Gillenwater, 2012; Cames et al., 2016). Common project types include:

- *Renewable Energy Projects:* Investments in wind, solar, hydro, and biomass energy generation reduce reliance on fossil fuels and lower scope 2 emissions. These projects are often recognized under global standards such as the Verified Carbon Standard (VCS) and Gold Standard (Broekhoff et al., 2019; Utgård & Gaustad, 2024).

- *Forestry and Land Use Projects:* Afforestation, reforestation, and avoided sequester carbon deforestation while contributing to biodiversity and ecosystem restoration. Robust monitoring, reporting, and verification (MRV) systems are critical to ensure permanence and prevent leakage (Calel & Dechezleprêtre, 2016; Cames et al., 2016).
- *Energy Efficiency Projects:* Industrial process upgrades, building retrofits, and clean cookstove initiatives reduce energy consumption and associated emissions. These projects deliver immediate and verifiable reductions while offering social co-benefits such as improved health and productivity (Kochar et al., 2025).
- *Methane and Other GHG Reduction Projects:* Capturing methane from landfills, wastewater treatment plants, or agricultural operations prevents potent greenhouse gases from entering the atmosphere, providing high global warming potential (GWP) reduction per unit of investment (Schneider et al., 2019; Anderson & Bernauer, 2016).

4.2.2 Selection Criteria

Firms typically evaluate offsets using a combination of environmental, financial, and strategic considerations:

- *Credibility and Verification:* Projects should be certified under recognized standards and subject to rigorous monitoring, robust MRV systems to ensure credible, transparent, and replicable emission reductions (Li & Zhang, 2024).
- *Cost-Effectiveness:* Projects are assessed for price per ton of CO_2-equivalent reduced relative to internal abatement options (Lewis & Tietenberg, 2020; Utgård & Gaustad, 2024).
- *Strategic Alignment:* Projects should reinforce corporate sustainability objectives, including community development, supply chain resilience, and brand reputation (Calel & Dechezleprêtre, 2016; Ajayi et al., 2025).
- *Risk Mitigation:* Consideration of permanence, leakage, and regulatory or reputational risk ensures offsets support long-term corporate credibility (Yang & Park, 2025).

By carefully selecting offsets that meet these criteria, firms can integrate carbon compensation into a broader sustainability strategy, ensuring that offsets complement internal mitigation measures rather than substitute for them.

4.2.3 Case Studies

4.2.3.1 National Bank of Kuwait (NBK) Green Bond (2024–2025)

NBK issued a USD 500M green bond under its Sustainable Financing Framework, receiving independent verification from S&P Global Ratings and UNFCCC-accredited consultants. The allocation included renewable energy and green buildings, demonstrating ESG integration, transparent reporting, and CSR alignment in financial practices (NBK, 2025).

Theoretical Integration: This case illustrates Stakeholder Theory, as NBK responds to investor and regulatory expectations for credible ESG commitments, and Institutional Theory, as external verification reflects normative and coercive pressures shaping organizational behavior.

4.2.3.2 Reforestation Project in South America:

A manufacturing firm implemented verified reforestation offsets under VCS standards, incorporating community-based land management. Due diligence ensured additionality, conservative baselines, and long-term permanence monitoring, improving both environmental credibility and CSR value (Broekhoff et al., 2019; Utgård & Gaustad, 2024).

Theoretical Integration: The project highlights Legitimacy Theory, emphasizing substantive action that aligns with societal expectations for genuine environmental impact, and Agency Theory, by demonstrating governance and oversight mechanisms that reduce managerial discretion and ensure accountability in CSR implementation.

4.2.3.3 Blockchain-Based Carbon Tracking Pilot (Project Carbon, 2021)

A consortium of global banks launched a blockchain platform to improve transparency, traceability, and price discovery for voluntary carbon credits. This technological innovation strengthened ESG integration and accountability in voluntary carbon markets (East & Partners, 2021).

Theoretical Integration: This pilot illustrates Stakeholder Theory, enhancing trust and engagement among investors, regulators, and other stakeholders through transparent reporting, and Agency Theory, by mitigating information asymmetry and strengthening governance oversight in corporate sustainability practices.

4.3 Voluntary vs. Compliance Carbon Markets

Voluntary carbon markets allow firms to purchase carbon credits beyond regulatory requirements, enabling companies to offset emissions as part of corporate sustainability initiatives. Compliance markets, on the other hand, are driven by mandatory emission reduction obligations under frameworks such as the EU Emissions Trading System (ETS) or the California Cap-and-Trade Program (Lewis & Tietenberg, 2020). Understanding the distinction helps contextualize corporate offset decisions and the strategic use of carbon credits in both regulated and voluntary environments, providing insight into market dynamics and corporate sustainability strategies.

4.4 Accounting and Reporting Considerations

4.4.1 International Accounting Frameworks

4.4.1.1 IFRS

Under IFRS, carbon credits may be recognized as intangible assets if they are expected to generate future economic benefits. Offsets purchased for compliance obligations are usually recorded as inventory or a liability if obligations exist, while voluntary offsets for CSR purposes are typically expensed (IASB, 2022; Gallego Álvarez et al., 2016). Disclosure is guided by IAS 1 and IAS 38, with additional narrative on climate-related risks encouraged by IFRS S1/S2 standards (ISSB, 2023).

4.4.1.2 US GAAP

In the US, accounting treatment depends on the nature of the credit and the firm's intent. Carbon credits can be capitalized as intangible assets if they provide measurable future benefits or expenses when used to meet voluntary or regulatory targets (FASB, 2024). Disclosure requirements include relevant risk factors and contingent liabilities under ASC 450 and environmental reporting guidelines.

4.4.1.3 Emerging ISSB Standards

ISSB standards focus on sustainability-related disclosures, including quantitative reporting of carbon liabilities and offsets. Firms are encouraged to provide forward-looking information, scenario analyses, and accounting policy notes to reflect the financial implications of carbon management activities (ISSB, 2023).

4.4.2 Industry-Specific Considerations

4.4.2.1 High-Emission Industries

Industries such as aviation, energy, and heavy manufacturing face complex offsetting requirements due to significant Scope 1 and 2 emissions. Accounting practices may differ based on regulatory obligations, contractual commitments, and market mechanisms. For example, energy companies often classify carbon allowances as inventory or derivative assets if tradable, while airlines may record compliance-related offsets as liabilities until surrendered (Hatalis, 2024; Syam et al., 2024).

4.4.2.2 Corporate Reporting Implications

Firms need to integrate carbon accounting into broader financial reporting, including sustainability reporting frameworks such as GRI, CDP, or TCFD. Proper classification, consistent measurement, and transparent disclosure are essential to maintain credibility with investors, regulators, and stakeholders (Cheung, 2023; Gallego Álvarez et al., 2016).

4.5 Technological Trends in Carbon Offsetting

Emerging technologies are increasingly transforming carbon offsetting practices by enhancing transparency, verification, and measurement accuracy. These technologies not only improve corporate sustainability reporting but also help mitigate risks such as greenwashing and accounting inconsistencies.

4.5.1 Blockchain for Transparency

Blockchain is being piloted in voluntary carbon markets to enhance the traceability and credibility of carbon credits. By creating immutable records of carbon credit issuance, ownership, and retirement, blockchain ensures that credits are not double-counted and are verifiable by multiple stakeholders (Kan & Delina, 2025). Platforms leveraging blockchain, such as Project Carbon, demonstrate how digital ledgers can reduce transaction friction, improve auditability, and increase stakeholder trust.

4.5.2 Artificial Intelligence (AI) for ESG and Greenwashing Detection

AI applications are now being deployed to automate ESG data collection, detect inconsistencies in sustainability reporting, and identify patterns indicative of greenwashing. Machine learning algorithms analyze corporate disclosures, social media, and regulatory filings to flag discrepancies or exaggerated claims regarding emissions reductions (Alshareef, 2025). By integrating AI into carbon accounting, firms can strengthen decision-making and demonstrate compliance with both voluntary and regulatory standards.

4.5.3 Satellite and Remote Sensing for Carbon Measurement

Satellite monitoring and remote sensing technologies provide high-resolution, near-real-time data for carbon measurement in nature-based projects, particularly forestry and land-use initiatives. Multi-spectral and radar imagery allow for the assessment of forest cover, biomass changes, and carbon sequestration, while also detecting leakage or permanence issues (Li et al., 2025; Tay et al., 2025). These tools enable verification of carbon credits and improve the reliability of corporate reporting on offset projects.

5. CHALLENGES, RECOMMENDATIONS, AND FUTURE DIRECTIONS

5.1. Challenges

Key challenges in carbon offset implementation and ESG reporting include greenwashing risks, verification and permanence concerns, administrative complexity, and difficulties integrating offsets into accounting systems (Gillenwater, 2012; Vinayak, 2025). Measurement and data quality remain significant hurdles in carbon offset implementation, particularly for nature-based projects that have traditionally relied on manual surveys, inconsistent baseline assumptions, and limited remote sensing data—all of which can produce inaccurate or incomparable emissions estimates (Trencher et al., 2024; Jaffer et al., 2024), although emerging satellite monitoring and blockchain platforms are improving transparency and traceability (Kan & Delina, 2025). Market fragmentation across multiple registries, inconsistent methodologies, and delayed reporting further impede comparability and verification (Yang & Park, 2025). Permanence and reversal risks, such as wildfire, pest infestations, or political instability, threaten the durability of carbon sequestration, while leakage—displacement of emissions to other locations—can negate intended benefits (Vinayak, 2025). Furthermore, systemic integrity issues in voluntary carbon markets—such as inconsistent verification methodologies, baseline manipulation, leakage, and double counting—undermine the credibility of many offset credits and can result in widespread overestimation of climate benefits (Haya et al., 2023; Salguero, 2025).

5.2. Recommendations

Table 1 presents important recommendations to address challenges in ESG reporting and carbon offset implementation. Each challenge is paired with actionable measures, responsible stakeholders, and expected outcomes. The table highlights practical steps to improve transparency, comparability, and environmental impact, supporting the adoption of global sustainability standards and high-quality carbon offsets.

Table 1. Recommendations to Improve ESG Reporting and Carbon Offset Implementation

Recommendation	Action/Measure	Responsible Stakeholders	Expected Outcome
Harmonize ESG and carbon accounting	Develop standardized methodologies and align rating/reporting frameworks	ESG rating agencies, regulatory bodies, standard-setters (IFRS, ISSB)	Improved comparability and reliability of sustainability metrics. **Note:** IFRS S1/S2 are sustainability disclosure standards issued by the ISSB under the IFRS Foundation to integrate ESG into corporate reporting (Berg et al., 2022; Pratama et al., 2024)
Strengthen verification and monitoring	Use satellite data, blockchain, and third-party audits for real-time tracking	Carbon registries, auditors, project developers	Reduced risk of over-crediting, leakage, and reversal; higher credibility of carbon credits (Trencher et al., 2024; Kan & Delina, 2025)
Integrate sustainability disclosures into financial reporting	Embed ESG data in IFRS S1/S2-aligned corporate reports	Corporations, finance teams, accountants	Enhanced decision-usefulness of ESG information; improved financial materiality (Pratama et al., 2024)
Leverage AI and advanced analytics	Automate ESG data collection, reporting, and assurance processes	Technology providers, corporations, auditors	Higher-quality ESG disclosures, reduced information asymmetry, improved transparency (Alshareef, 2025)
Promote governance and assurance mechanisms	Implement robust internal controls, risk management, and assurance frameworks	Boards, audit committees, regulators	Greater accountability, trust, and stakeholder confidence in sustainability performance (Khatri et al., 2025)
Address market fragmentation	Foster collaboration across registries, adopt global standards	Industry associations, ICVCM, standard-setters	Harmonized voluntary carbon markets, consistent verification, better comparability. **Note:** ICVCM = Integrity Council for the Voluntary Carbon Market, which sets global quality benchmarks (Vinayak, 2025; Yang & Park, 2025)
Mitigate permanence and leakage risks	Establish risk buffers, insurance pools, jurisdictional projects	Project developers, insurers, regulators	Durable climate benefits; reduced likelihood of offset reversals or emissions displacement (Vinayak, 2025; Haya et al., 2023)

The recommendations in Table 1 provide a structured roadmap for addressing important challenges in ESG reporting and carbon offset implementation. Harmonizing accounting frameworks and voluntary carbon markets enhances comparability and reliability, while robust verification, monitoring, and risk mitigation strategies safeguard environmental integrity. Integrating ESG disclosures into financial reporting, leveraging AI and advanced analytics, and strengthening governance frameworks improve transparency, decision-usefulness, and stakeholder trust. Together, these measures support the adoption of high-quality carbon credits, credible sustainability reporting, and effective implementation of global standards such as IFRS S1/S2, enabling organizations to achieve both environmental and financial objectives.

Table 2 summarizes key CSR and carbon offset activities alongside their accounting, reporting, and strategic implications, providing a practical overview of how sustainability initiatives translate into financial and reporting outcomes.

Table 2. Linking CSR and Carbon Offset Activities to Accounting and Reporting Elements

CSR / Carbon Offset Activity	Accounting Implications	Reporting & Disclosure Considerations	Strategic / Financial Impact
Purchase of voluntary carbon credits	Recognized as intangible assets or expensed depending on use; fair value vs. cost accounting	Disclose recognition, measurement basis, and assumptions; report volume and retirement status	Supports sustainability claims; affects financial statements; may enhance investor trust
Internal emission reduction projects	Capitalized if expected to provide future economic benefit (e.g., energy efficiency CAPEX); operational expenses otherwise	Disclose capital investments, expected emissions reduction, and cost-benefit analysis	Reduces long-term carbon liability; impacts ROI and cost of capital
Integration of offsets into corporate ESG strategy	Linked to CSR budget, incentive plans, or strategic initiatives	Include in ESG disclosures and sustainability reports; align with IFRS S1/S2 metrics	Strengthens stakeholder legitimacy and reputational capital; may affect firm valuation
Verification and certification of offsets (e.g., third-party audits)	Costs recognized as operating expenses; assurance fees may be separately reported	Disclosure of verification standards, audit scope, and outcomes	Enhances credibility; reduces greenwashing risk; improves market confidence
Technology-enabled monitoring (AI, blockchain, satellite)	Capitalization of software/hardware investments or expensing depending on use	Report methodology for emission tracking, data reliability, and risk management	Improves transparency, data quality, and ESG reporting integrity
Sector-specific offset strategies (aviation, energy, manufacturing)	Industry-specific treatment may affect asset recognition, inventory, or expense classification	Disclose sectoral approach and compliance with regulatory standards	Enables benchmarking, strategic decision-making, and targeted risk management
Governance & internal control mechanisms	Oversight costs may be expensed; risk provisions recognized for potential liabilities	Disclosure of internal controls, audit committees, and board oversight	Strengthens accountability, reduces legal and reputational risk

5.3. Future Research Directions

Future research should address critical gaps in ESG measurement, carbon market integrity, and the integration of sustainability disclosures into financial and accounting systems. Empirical evidence shows that methodological divergence among ESG rating providers weakens the reliability and comparability of corporate sustainability signals (Berg et al., 2022). At the same time, systemic quality issues in voluntary carbon markets reveal that a majority of offsets retired by large corporate buyers carry high risks of not delivering real and additional emissions reductions (Trencher et al., 2024), indicating that firm-level purchasing choices may perpetuate low-quality credits and undermine climate mitigation efforts. Historical studies also highlight over-crediting risks in compliance settings (Badgley et al., 2021). Advances in AI-enabled ESG disclosure show promise for enhancing transparency, while the recent issuance of IFRS Sustainability Disclosure Standards S1 and S2 has opened new frontiers for integrating sustainability information within corporate reporting systems (Pratama et al., 2024; Alshareef, 2025). Collectively, these developments point to several key research priorities: improving data integrity and comparability in ESG and carbon accounting; assessing the financial materiality of high-quality sustainability disclosures; evaluating governance and assurance mechanisms under emerging global standards; and exploring how AI and advanced analytics can support rigorous implementation of integrated reporting frameworks.

6. CONCLUSION

CSR and carbon offsetting are critical tools for linking environmental sustainability with corporate value and stakeholder trust. Effective implementation requires rigorous verification, transparent reporting, and alignment with recognized standards, supported by governance mechanisms and technological solutions such as AI, blockchain, and satellite monitoring. Harmonizing ESG disclosures with global frameworks, including IFRS S1 and S2, enhances comparability, reliability, and financial materiality.

Carbon offsetting strategies should be integrated with internal decarbonization efforts, taking into account trade-offs between short-term costs, long-term transition risks, and the overall effectiveness of emission reduction measures. Linking CSR and offset activities to accounting and reporting practices, such as asset recognition, expense treatment, risk disclosure, and assurance, strengthens both financial accountability and stakeholder confidence.

Forward-looking considerations highlight that evolving regulatory frameworks, market reforms, and sustainability reporting standards will continue to shape corporate strategies, requiring adaptive governance and proactive risk management. By embedding high-quality offsets into strategic decision-making and aligning them with broader sustainability and financial objectives, firms can achieve measurable emissions reductions, advance ESG performance, and contribute substantively to global climate mitigation efforts.

REFERENCES

Aguinis, H., & Glavas, A. (2012). What We Know and Don't Know About Corporate Social Responsibility: A Review and Research Agenda: A Review and Research Agenda. *Journal of Management, 38*(4), 932–968. DOI: 10.1177/0149206311436079

Ahen, F., & Amankwah-Amoah, J. (2018). Institutional voids and the philanthropization of CSR practices: Insights from developing economies. *Sustainability (Basel), 10*(7), 2400. DOI: 10.3390/su10072400

Ajayi, A. D., Hayo, L., Iliya, J. P., & Hasegawa, H. (2025). Exploring voluntary carbon markets as a tool for sustainable agriculture in Nigeria: Opportunities and challenges. *Scientific African, 29*, e02923. DOI: 10.1016/j.sciaf.2025.e02923

Albuquerque, R., Koskinen, Y., & Zhang, C. (2019). Corporate social responsibility and firm risk: Theory and empirical evidence. *Management Science, 65*(10), 4451–4469. DOI: 10.1287/mnsc.2018.3043

Alshareef, M. N. (2025). Artificial intelligence-enhanced environmental, social, and governance (ESG) disclosure quality and financial performance. *Sustainability, 17*(16), 7421. DOI: 10.3390/su17167421

Anderson, B., & Bernauer, T. (2016). How much carbon offsetting and where? Implications of efficiency, effectiveness, and ethicality considerations for public opinion formation. *Energy Policy, 94*, 387–395. DOI: 10.1016/j.enpol.2016.04.016

Ashrafi, M., Magnan, G. M., Adams, M., & Walker, T. R. (2020). Understanding the conceptual evolutionary path and theoretical underpinnings of corporate social responsibility and corporate sustainability. *Sustainability (Basel), 12*(3), 760. DOI: 10.3390/su12030760

Aslaksen, H. M., Hildebrandt, C., & Johnsen, H. C. G. (2021). The long-term transformation of the concept of CSR: Towards a more comprehensive emphasis on sustainability. *International Journal of Corporate Social Responsibility, 6*(11), 11. Advance online publication. DOI: 10.1186/s40991-021-00063-9

Badgley, G., Freeman, J., Hamman, J. J., Haya, B., Trugman, A. T., Anderegg, W. R. L., & Cullenward, D. (2021). Systematic over crediting in California's forest carbon offsets program. *Global Change Biology, 28*(4), 1433–1445. DOI: 10.1111/gcb.15943 PMID: 34668621

Barney, J. (1991). Firm resources and sustained competitive advantage. *Journal of Management, 17*(1), 99–120. DOI: 10.1177/014920639101700108

Berg, F., Kölbel, J. F., & Rigobon, R. (2022). Aggregate confusion: The divergence of ESG ratings. *Review of Finance*, *26*(6), 1315–1344. DOI: 10.1093/rof/rfac033

Bolognesi, E., Burchi, A., Goodell, J. W., & Paltrinieri, A. (2025). Stakeholders and regulatory pressure on ESG disclosure. *International Review of Financial Analysis*, *103*, 104145. DOI: 10.1016/j.irfa.2025.104145

Bolton, P., & Kacperczyk, M. (2021). Do investors care about carbon risk? *Journal of Financial Economics*, *142*(2), 517–549. DOI: 10.1016/j.jfineco.2021.05.008

Bowen, H. R. (1953). *Social responsibilities of the businessman*. Harper & Row.

Broekhoff, D., Gillenwater, M., Colbert-Sangree, T., & Cage, P. (2019). *Securing climate benefit: A guide to using carbon offsets*. Stockholm Environment Institute & Greenhouse Gas Management Institute. https://www.offsetguide.org

Calel, R., & Dechezleprêtre, A. (2016). Environmental policy and directed technological change: Evidence from the European carbon market. *The Review of Economics and Statistics*, *98*(1), 173–191. DOI: 10.1162/REST_a_00470

Cames, M., Harthan, R. O., Füssler, J., Lazarus, M., Lee, C. M., Erickson, P., & Spalding-Fecher, R. (2016). *How additional is the Clean Development Mechanism? Analysis of the application of current tools and proposed alternatives* (Study prepared for DG CLIMA). Öko-Institut. https://ec.europa.eu/clima/system/files/2017-04/clean_dev_mechanism_en.pdf

Campbell, J. L. (2007). Why would corporations behave in socially responsible ways? An institutional theory of corporate social responsibility. *Academy of Management Review*, *32*(3), 946–967. DOI: 10.5465/amr.2007.25275684

Carroll, A. B. (1999). Corporate Social Responsibility: Evolution of a Definitional Construct. *Business & Society*, *38*(3), 268–295. DOI: 10.1177/000765039903800303

Carroll, A. B., & Shabana, K. M. (2010). The business case for corporate social responsibility: A review of concepts, research and practice. *International Journal of Management Reviews*, *12*(1), 85–105. DOI: 10.1111/j.1468-2370.2009.00275.x

Cheung, H. (2023). Non-monetary double-entry carbon accounting method for entities in emission trading systems. *Journal of Cleaner Production*, *422*, 138475. DOI: 10.1016/j.jclepro.2023.138475

Choi, S. U., & Lee, W. J. (2024). Financial statement comparability and environmental, social, and governance (ESG) performance. *Sustainability (Basel)*, *16*(18), 7993. DOI: 10.3390/su16187993

Climate Case Chart. (2025). *Deutsche Umwelthilfe v. Adidas*. Retrieved December 14, 2025, from https://www.climatecasechart.com/non-us-case/deutsche-umwelthilfe-v-adidas

Conca, L., Manta, F., Morrone, D., & Toma, P. (2021). The impact of direct environmental, social, and governance reporting: Empirical evidence in European-listed companies in the agri-food sector. *Business Strategy and the Environment, 30*(4), 1080–1093. DOI: 10.1002/bse.2672

de Villiers, C., Kuruppu, S., & Dissanayake, D. (2021). A (new) role for business in society and the emergence of CSR accounting. *Journal of Business Research, 131*, 598–609. DOI: 10.1016/j.jbusres.2020.11.066

Delmas, M. A., & Burbano, V. C. (2011). The drivers of greenwashing. *California Management Review, 54*(1), 64–87. DOI: 10.1525/cmr.2011.54.1.64

Deloitte. (2023). *Heads up — Global sustainability disclosure standards converge: ISSB finalizes IFRS S1 and S2*. Deloitte Accounting Research Tool. Retrieved December 17, 2025, from

Di Vaio, A., Zaffar, A., Chhabra, M., & Balsalobre-Lorente, D. (2024). Carbon accounting and integrated reporting for net-zero business models towards sustainable development: A systematic literature review. *Business Strategy and the Environment, 33*(7), 7216–7240. DOI: 10.1002/bse.3863

DiMaggio, P. J., & Powell, W. W. (1983). The iron cage revisited: Institutional isomorphism and collective rationality in organizational fields. *American Sociological Review, 48*(2), 147–160. DOI: 10.2307/2095101

Ding, T., Zhou, Y., & Chen, L. (2025). Non-financial factors and financial returns: The impact of linking ESG metrics to executive compensation on corporate financial performance. *Sustainability (Basel), 17*(22), 10220. DOI: 10.3390/su172210220

Dowling, J., & Pfeffer, J. (1975). Organizational Legitimacy: Social Values and Organizational Behavior. *Pacific Sociological Review, 18*(1), 122–136. DOI: 10.2307/1388226

Dzage, E. J., & Szabados, G. N. (2024). The relationship of corporate social responsibility with business performance—A bibliometric literature review. *Sustainability (Basel), 16*(7), 2637. DOI: 10.3390/su16072637

East & Partners. (2021, July 12). *"Project Carbon" offset platform launched by global bank consortium*. Retrieved December 17, 2025, from https://eastandpartners.com/news/project-carbon-offset-platform-launched-by-global-bank-consortium/

Eccles, R. G., Ioannou, I., & Serafeim, G. (2014). The impact of corporate sustainability on organizational processes and performance. *Management Science*, *60*(11), 2835–2857. DOI: 10.1287/mnsc.2014.1984

European Commission. (2011, October 7). *Progress towards achieving the Kyoto objectives* (COM(2011) 624 final; SEC(2011) 1151 final). Retrieved December 18, 2025, from https://eur-lex.europa.eu/legal-content/EN/TXT/?uri=CELEX%3A52011DC0624

European Commission. (2023). *Green claims: New criteria to stop companies from making misleading claims about environmental merits of their products and services.* Directorate-General for Environment. Retrieved December 18, 2025, from https://environment.ec.europa.eu/topics/circular-economy/green-claims_en

FASB. (2024). *Proposed Accounting Standards Update: Environmental credits and environmental credit obligations (Topic 818) [Exposure draft]*. FASB. https://www.fasb.org

Frankel, R., Kothari, S. P., & Raghunandan, A. (2025). The economics of ESG disclosure regulation. *Review of Accounting Studies*, *30*(4), 3218–3253. DOI: 10.1007/s11142-025-09900-9

Freeman, R. E., & McVea, J. (2005). A stakeholder approach to strategic management. The Blackwell handbook of strategic management, 183-201. doi:DOI: 10.2139/ssrn.263511

Friede, G., Busch, T., & Bassen, A. (2015). ESG and financial performance: Aggregated evidence. *Journal of Sustainable Finance & Investment*, *5*(4), 210–233. DOI: 10.1080/20430795.2015.1118917

Gallego-Álvarez, I., Martínez-Ferrero, J., & Cuadrado-Ballesteros, B. (2016). Accounting treatment for carbon emission rights. *Systems*, *4*(1), 12. DOI: 10.3390/systems4010012

Gillenwater, M. (2012). *What is additionality? Part 1: A long-standing problem* (Discussion Paper No. 001). Greenhouse Gas Management Institute. Retrieved December 20, 2025, from https://ghginstitute.org/wp-content/uploads/2015/04/AdditionalityPaper_Part-1ver3FINAL.pdf

Haque, S., & Islam, M. A. (2017). Stakeholder pressures on corporate climate change-related accountability and disclosures: Australian evidence. *Business and Politics*, *17*(2), 355–390. DOI: 10.1017/S1369525800001674

Hatalis, M. (2024). Greenwashing or going green? An empirical analysis of the drivers and the effects of carbon offsets and renewable energy certificates on firm performance. *American Journal of Management, 24*(2), 7108. Advance online publication. DOI: 10.33423/ajm.v24i2.7108

Haya, B. K., Alford-Jones, K., Anderegg, W. R. L., Beymer-Farris, B., Blanchard, L., Bomfim, B., Chin, D., Evans, S., Hogan, M., Holm, J. A., McAfee, K., So, I. S., West, T. A. P., & Withey, L. (2023). *Quality assessment of REDD+ carbon credit projects*. Berkeley Carbon Trading Project. Retrieved December 17, 2025, from https://gspp.berkeley.edu/research-and-impact/centers/cepp/projects/berkeley-carbon-trading-project/REDD+

He, P., Chen, Q., & Chen, L. (2025). The impact of ESG on corporate value under the 'Dual Carbon' goals: Empirical evidence from Chinese energy listed companies. *Energies, 18*(18), 4811. DOI: 10.3390/en18184811

Huang, P.-C., Mirza, N., Umar, M., & Horobet, A. (2025). Impact of environmental double materiality on firm valuation: Evidence from the EU. *International Review of Economics & Finance, 103*, 104461. DOI: 10.1016/j.iref.2025.104461

Huber, E., Bach, V., & Finkbeiner, M. (2024). A qualitative meta-analysis of carbon offset quality criteria. *Journal of Environmental Management, 352*, 119983. DOI: 10.1016/j.jenvman.2023.119983 PMID: 38183915

ICAEW. (2023). *ISSB issues first sustainability disclosure standards. ICAEW Insights.* Retrieved December 17, 2025, from https://www.icaew.com/insights/viewpoints-on-the-news/2023/jun-2023/issb-issues-first-sustainability-disclosure-standards

IFRS Foundation. (2023). *IFRS Sustainability Disclosure Standards S1 and S2.* IFRS Foundation. Retrieved December 21, 2025, from https://www.ifrs.org/news-and-events/news/2023/06/issb-issues-ifrs-s1-ifrs-s2/

Ioannou, I., & Serafeim, G. (2014). The impact of corporate social responsibility on investment recommendations: Analysts' perceptions and shifting institutional logics. *Strategic Management Journal, 36*(7), 1053–1081. DOI: 10.1002/smj.2268

IPCC. (2022). *Climate Change 2022: Mitigation of Climate Change*. Cambridge University Press., DOI: 10.1017/9781009157926

Itan, I., Sylvia, S., Septiany, S., & Chen, R. (2025). The influence of environmental, social, and governance disclosure on market reaction: Evidence from emerging markets. *Discover Sustainability, 6*(1), 347. DOI: 10.1007/s43621-025-01085-0

Jaffer, S., Dales, M., Ferris, P., Swinfield, T., Sorensen, D., Message, R., Keshav, S., & Madhavapeddy, A. (2024). Global, robust and comparable digital carbon assets *(arXiv:2403.14581v2)* [Computer science—Cryptography and security]. DOI: 10.1109/ICBC59979.2024.10634343

Jensen, M. C., & Meckling, W. H. (1976). Theory of the firm: Managerial behavior, agency costs and ownership structure. *Journal of Financial Economics, 3*(4), 305–360. DOI: 10.1016/0304-405X(76)90026-X

Kallbekken, S., & Sælen, H. (2011). Public acceptance for environmental taxes: Self-interest, environmental and distributional concerns. *Energy Policy, 39*(5), 2966–2973. DOI: 10.1016/j.enpol.2011.03.006

Kan, C., & Delina, L. L. (2025). Unlocking the transformative potential of blockchain to enhance transparency and efficiency in voluntary carbon markets for a sustainable energy transition. *Energy Research & Social Science, 126*, 104177. DOI: 10.1016/j.erss.2025.104177

Khan, M., Serafeim, G., & Yoon, A. (2016). Corporate sustainability: First evidence on materiality. *The Accounting Review, 91*(6), 1697–1724. DOI: 10.2308/accr-51383

Khatri, I., Giskås, P. E., Kyrrø, A. K., & Kjærland, F. (2025). Corporate governance mechanisms and non-financial disclosure quality: Evidence from sustainability committee, external CSR assurance, and stakeholder engagement. *International Review of Financial Analysis, 107*, 104645. DOI: 10.1016/j.irfa.2025.104645

Kochar, R., Kalsie, A., & Deka, N. (2025). Voluntary carbon markets (VCMs) in a nutshell: A systematic review based on the empirical evidence from across the globe. *Journal of Cleaner Production, 522*, 146261. DOI: 10.1016/j.jclepro.2025.146261

Kolk, A. (2016). The social responsibility of international business. *Journal of World Business, 51*(1), 23–34. DOI: 10.1016/j.jwb.2015.08.010

Kotsantonis, S., Pinney, C., & Serafeim, G. (2016). ESG integration in investment management: Myths and realities. *The Bank of America Journal of Applied Corporate Finance, 28*(2), 10–16. DOI: 10.1111/jacf.12169

Krueger, P., Sautner, Z., & Starks, L. T. (2020). The importance of climate risks for institutional investors. *Review of Financial Studies, 33*(3), 1067–1111. DOI: 10.1093/rfs/hhz137

Lakhani, L., & Herbert, S. L. (2022). Theoretical frameworks applied in integrated reporting and sustainability reporting research. *Suid-Afrikaanse Tydskrif vir Ekonomiese en Bestuurswetenskappe, 25*(1), a4427. DOI: 10.4102/sajems.v25i1.4427

Lebbar, H., & El-Aroui, M.-A. (2025). CSR performance in global context: Institutional determinants in developed, developing, and emerging economies. *Social Responsibility Journal*, 1–23. DOI: 10.1108/SRJ-04-2025-0386

Lee, M.-D. P. (2008). A review of the theories of corporate social responsibility: Its evolutionary path and the road ahead. *International Journal of Management Reviews, 10*(1), 53–73. DOI: 10.1111/j.1468-2370.2007.00226.x

Lee, M. T., & Raschke, R. L. (2023). Stakeholder legitimacy in firm greening and financial performance: What about greenwashing temptations? *Journal of Business Research, 155*(Part B), 113393. DOI: 10.1016/j.jbusres.2022.113393

Lewis, L., & Tietenberg, T. (2020). *Environmental economics and policy* (7th ed.). Routledge.

Li, B., Liu, S., Liu, D., Fan, Z., Qu, Z., Yao, S., Su, X., & Wang, L. (2025). Using Sentinel-2A and Landsat 8 imagery to assess changes in forest carbon storage. *Scientific Reports, 15*(1), 37489. DOI: 10.1038/s41598-025-21607-0 PMID: 41145783

Li, J., & Sasaki, M. (2024). Political embeddedness and corporate social responsibility (CSR) in a state-led developing country: Evidence from China. *Asian Business & Management, 23*(4), 597–621. DOI: 10.1057/s41291-023-00256-z

Li, L., & Zhang, D. (2024). Forest carbon offset protocols in compliance carbon markets. *Forest Policy and Economics, 165*, 103253. DOI: 10.1016/j.forpol.2024.103253

Lins, K. V., Servaes, H., & Tamayo, A. (2017). Social capital, trust, and firm performance during the financial crisis: The value of corporate social responsibility. *The Journal of Finance, 72*(4), 1785–1824. DOI: 10.1111/jofi.12505

Martielli, F., Battisti, E., Gonzalez-Cruz, T. F., & Salvi, A. (2025). Carbon credits and financial performance: Exploring the moderating role of CSR strategy and corporate governance practices. *Research in International Business and Finance, 77*(Part B), 102919. DOI: 10.1016/j.ribaf.2025.102919

Matten, D., & Moon, J. (2008). "Implicit" and "explicit" CSR: A conceptual framework for a comparative understanding of corporate social responsibility. *Academy of Management Review, 33*(2), 404–424. DOI: 10.5465/amr.2008.31193458

Moura-Leite, R. C., & Padgett, R. C. (2011). Historical background of corporate social responsibility. *Social Responsibility Journal, 7*(4), 528–539. DOI: 10.1108/17471111111117511

NBK. (2025). *Green Bond Allocation & Impact Report 2025*. NBK. Retrieved December 17, 2025, from https://www.nbk.com/dam/jcr%3A0c178f5f-223a-407f-8656-a14be484f8e2/green-bond-report-2025.pdf

Pata, U. K., Si Mohammed, K., Serret, V., & Kartal, M. T. (2024). Assessing the influence of climate risk, carbon allowances, and technological factors on the ESG market in the European Union. *Borsa Istanbul Review*, *24*(4), 828–837. DOI: 10.1016/j.bir.2024.04.013

Porter, M. E., & Kramer, M. R. (2006). Strategy and society: The link between competitive advantage and corporate social responsibility. *Harvard Business Review*, *84*(12), 78–92. PMID: 17183795

Pratama, A., Dewi, N., Sofia, P., Muhammad, K., & Megawati, L. R. (2024). Sustainability reporting ecosystem and IFRS S1 and S2: How accounting research can assist its implementation. *Journal of Ecohumanism*, *3*(4), 3101–3129. DOI: 10.62754/joe.v3i4.3830

Qureshi, N. (2025). The growing significance of corporate social responsibility: From ethical obligation to strategic imperative. *International Journal for Multidisciplinary Research*, *7*(3), 1–5. DOI: 10.36948/ijfmr.2025.v07i03.48259

RGGI. (2023). *CO_2 allowance program overview*. Retrieved December 24, 2025, from https://www.rggi.org/

Ruseva, T., Marland, E., Szymanski, C., Hoyle, J., Marland, G., & Kowalczyk, T. (2017). Additionality and permanence standards in California's Forest Offset Protocol: A review of project and program level implications. *Journal of Environmental Management*, *198*, 277–288. DOI: 10.1016/j.jenvman.2017.04.082 PMID: 28477569

Salguero, R. A. F. (2025). *Effectiveness of carbon pricing and compensation instruments: An umbrella review of the empirical evidence* (arXiv:2512.06887) [Preprint]. arXiv. 2512.06887

Salvi, A., Martielli, F., Battisti, E., Forliano, C., & Kumar, S. (2025). Climate change management and companies' financial performance: Exploring the moderating role of carbon credits. *Research in International Business and Finance*, *75*, 102785. DOI: 10.1016/j.ribaf.2025.102785

SBTi. (2024). *Corporate Net-Zero Standard: Updated guidance*. Retrieved December 22, 2025, from https://sciencebasedtargets.org/net-zero

Schmuck, D., Andersson, H., & Mark-Herbert, C. (2025). Corporate motives for financing carbon offsets: A case study of Swedish corporations. *Journal of Cleaner Production*, *520*, 146049. DOI: 10.1016/j.jclepro.2025.146049

Schneider, L., Duan, M., Stavins, R., Kizzier, K., Broekhoff, D., Jotzo, F., Winkler, H., Lazarus, M., Howard, A., & Hood, C. (2019). Double counting and the Paris Agreement rulebook. *Science*, *366*(6462), 180–183. DOI: 10.1126/science.aay8750 PMID: 31601755

Shakil, A. K. M. A. Z., Hossain, M. M., Khan, M. M., Noyon, S. I., & Ripon, M. B. (2025). A systematic review of corporate social responsibility practices in emerging markets. *Business and Social Sciences*, *3*(1), 1–9. DOI: 10.25163/business.3110211

Shmelev, S. E., & Gilardi, E. (2025). Corporate environmental, social, and governance performance: The impacts on financial returns, business model innovation, and social transformation. *Sustainability (Basel)*, *17*(3), 1286. DOI: 10.3390/su17031286

Siddique, M. A., Karim, S., Haque, M. R., & Mia, P. (2026). The truth behind sustainability claims: Examining carbon risk, ESG disclosures, and greenwashing. *International Review of Financial Analysis*, *109*, 104735. DOI: 10.1016/j.irfa.2025.104735

Stolz, N., & Probst, B. (2025). The negligible role of carbon offsetting in corporate climate strategies. *Nature Communications*, *16*(1), 7963. Advance online publication. DOI: 10.1038/s41467-025-62970-w PMID: 40931031

Suchman, M. C. (1995). Managing legitimacy: Strategic and institutional approaches. *Academy of Management Review*, *20*(3), 571–610. DOI: 10.2307/258788

Syam, M. A., Djaddang, S., Adam, A., Merawati, E. E., & Roziq, M. (2024). Carbon accounting: Its implications on accounting practices and corporate sustainability reports. *International Journal of Economics and Financial Issues*, *14*(4), 178–187. DOI: 10.32479/ijefi.16333

Tay, C., Jovani-Sancho, A. J., Yulianti, L., Evans, C., Callaghan, N., Jaya, A., Salman, R., Zheng, Y., Susilo, S., Dohong, S., & Yun, S.-H. (2025). Satellite radar advances carbon emissions accountability over tropical peat. *Communications Earth & Environment*, *6*(1), 971. DOI: 10.1038/s43247-025-02926-6

Thamara, S. D., Andriani, N., & Syarif, M. (2025). Integration of CSR and ESG into corporate strategies in realizing social-environmental accountability: Systematic literature review. *East African Journal of Multidisciplinary Research*, *4*(11), 5407–5416. DOI: 10.55927/eajmr.v4i11.461

Tharsika, K. (2025). *A systematic review of IFRS sustainability standards*. Institute of Certified Management Accountants of Sri Lanka. Retrieved December 27, 2025, from http://repo.lib.jfn.ac.lk/ujrr/handle/123456789/11599

Trencher, G., Nick, S., Carlson, J., & Johnson, M. (2024). Demand for low-quality offsets by major companies undermines climate integrity of the voluntary carbon market. *Nature Communications*, *15*(1), 6863. Advance online publication. DOI: 10.1038/s41467-024-51151-w PMID: 39127784

UNFCCC. (2020). *The Paris Agreement and carbon markets.* Retrieved December 19, 2025, from https://unfccc.int/process-and-meetings/the-paris-agreement

UNFCCC. (2024). *What is offsetting?* UN Climate Neutral Now. Retrieved December 19, 2025, from https://offset.climateneutralnow.org/aboutoffsetting

Utgård, J., & Gaustad, T. (2024). Carbon emission reductions and offsets: Consumer perceptions of firm environmental sustainability. *Journal of Cleaner Production*, *470*, 143300. DOI: 10.1016/j.jclepro.2024.143300

Vaihekoski, M., & Yahya, H. (2025). Environmental, social, and governance (ESG) and firm valuation: The moderating role of audit quality. *Journal of Risk and Financial Management*, *18*(3), 148. DOI: 10.3390/jrfm18030148

van Wyk, M., & Els, G. (2023). The relevance of integrated reporting in future standard setting of the International Sustainability Standards Board. *Frontiers in Sustainability*, *4*, 1218985. Advance online publication. DOI: 10.3389/frsus.2023.1218985

Vinayak. (2025, May 21). Why carbon offsets matter: Understanding the science behind credible credits. *Switch Climate Tech.* Retrieved December 17, 2025, from https://switchclimatetech.com/blog/why-carbon-offsets-matter

Waked, S. S., Alturki, K. H., & Yamani, A. (2025). How governance and CSR reporting shape emission outcomes: A firm-level study from BRICS countries. *Sustainability (Basel)*, *17*(17), 8040. DOI: 10.3390/su17178040

Wen, Q., & Kang, H. (2025). Research on the impact of carbon information disclosure on corporate ESG performance: Evidence from China's manufacturing industry. *Sustainability (Basel)*, *17*(20), 9272. DOI: 10.3390/su17209272

World Bank. (2023). *World Bank (IBRD) Green Bonds — FY22 Impact Report.* Retrieved December 19, 2025, from https://treasury.worldbank.org/en/about/unit/treasury/impact/impact-report

Yang, D., & Park, H. (2025). Integrity challenges in carbon markets: Comparing UNFCCC and voluntary REDD+ verification in the Amazon Biome. *Environmental Science & Policy*, *169*, 104080. DOI: 10.1016/j.envsci.2025.104080

Yang, S. S., Huang, J.-W., Chen, H.-Y., & Tsay, M.-H. (2025). Detecting corporate ESG performance: The role of ESG materiality in corporate financial performance and risks. *The North American Journal of Economics and Finance*, *76*, 102370. DOI: 10.1016/j.najef.2025.102370

Zairis, G., Liargovas, P., & Apostolopoulos, N. (2024). Sustainable finance and ESG importance: A systematic literature review and research agenda. *Sustainability (Basel)*, *16*(7), 2878. DOI: 10.3390/su16072878

Zdolšek, D., & Taškar Beloglavec, S. (2023). *"The 2023's new and the fresh": The International Sustainability Disclosure Standards*. In *Proceedings of the International Scientific Conference on Economy, Management and Information Technologies (ICEMIT 2023)* (Vol. 1, No. 1). DOI: 10.46793/ICEMIT23.205Z

Zetterberg, L., Johnsson, F., & Möllersten, K. (2021). Incentivizing BECCS—A Swedish case study. *Frontiers in Climate*, *3*, 685227. Advance online publication. DOI: 10.3389/fclim.2021.685227

Zhou, X., Wang, X., Fei, X., Liu, W., Xie, B.-C., & Zhao, J. (2025). Carbon disclosure effect, corporate fundamentals, and net-zero emission target: Evidence from China. arXiv. 2508.17423

Chapter 2
Risk Return Analysis of Mutual Fund Schemes in Public and Private AMC Companies

Chandrashekhar Durgesh Reddy
Chandigarh University, India

Amandeep Kaur
Chandigarh University, India

Manjit Kour
http://orcid.org/0000-0003-1043-3187
Chandigarh University, India

Ramanjeet Singh
http://orcid.org/0000-0001-7424-7039
Chandigarh University, India

ABSTRACT

This study has provided a comparative analysis of the performance of mutual fund with a focus on three categories: Index Funds, Large Cap Funds, and Balanced Advantage Funds for both private and public sector AMCs. The study assessed 24 selected schemes to assess risk-adjusted returns and market association of schemes based on key financial metrics such as Sharpe Ratio, Treynor Ratio, Standard Deviation, and Beta for a 3-year period (2021-2024). The study found that public sector funds such as UTI and SBI do well in passive categories such as Index Funds while private sector funds such as HDFC and ICICI Prudential significantly outper-

DOI: 10.4018/979-8-3373-5047-9.ch002

form public sector funds in active categories with better risk-adjusted returns. The statistical analysis including Two-Way ANOVA indicates that the fund type (public vs. private) will have no significant effect on the performance, but fund category has a significant influence on the performance volatility of the funds.

1. INTRODUCTION

India's financial markets have experienced significant changes across the past two decades (Kour et al., 2025), mainly due to the growth in popularity of mutual funds as an ideal investment choice for both individual and institutional investors. A mutual fund is an example of a communal investment scheme which pools together funds received from several investors into a single diversified portfolio consisting of bonds, stocks, money market instruments, etc. (Sadhak, 2003). The investment management for mutual fund schemes is provided on behalf of the investors by professional asset managers employed by registered fund companies known as Asset Management Companies (AMC), providing investors with an easily accessible, regulated and transparent means of participating in the financial markets required for investment purposes. As part of this process, AMCs comply with SEBI's registration requirements and their fiduciary duties to investors. (Panigrahi, 1996).

Mutual Funds have been a vital way that increased investment opportunities leading to an increase in Financial Inclusion in India. India's financial ecosystem has historically been largely reliant on fixed deposits, gold, and real estate as traditional savings vehicles. However, mutual funds have drastically expanded the investment scope and potential, particularly for investors who did not have the knowledge to directly participate in the stock markets or had limited capital available (Sisodiya, 2004). Mutual funds have also offered diversification, systematic investment planning (SIPs), liquidity, flexibility of choice, certain tax benefits through ELSS, and online access have exploded their popularity (Sapar & Madava, 2003).

The beginning of mutual funds in India took place in 1963 with the formation of the Unit Trust of India (UTI), which had a monopoly over the mutual fund industry for more than two decades (Barua et al., 1991). The public sector mutual funds' launch in the late 1980s, subsequently the liberalization of the economy in 1991, started a structural transformation that also brought the private and foreign participants into the industry. The competition led to product innovation as well as transparency (Panwar & Madhumathi, 2006). Currently, mutual fund schemes are classified into equity fund, debt fund, hybrid fund, index fund, and thematic fund to provide additional accessibility to investors depending on their risk profile and expectation of returns (Rehmani, 2018; Sekhar, 2014).

The public sector mutual funds operate in the form of an AMC like SBI, UTI, or LIC, and are generally considered to be safe and conservative. Thus, they tend to have a high client base among those who are risk-averse and are looking at these products as a means of protecting their wealth. Maximum public sector mutual funds invest in blue-chip companies, top-rated credit bonds, and Government Securities. These products generate relatively stable, yet reasonable, returns for investors. On the contrary, the private sector mutual funds operate as an AMC like HDFC, ICICI Prudential, or Kotak. With this type of AMC, the private sector mutual fund scheme takes on more aggressive investment strategies, while also providing a contingency plan to increase its expected returns by investing in riskier sectors and in international equities. The use of a contingency plan by private sector mutual fund schemes results in an increased willingness for investors to take risks (Rehmani & Khan, 2018; Sharma, 2013; Narayanan, 2021).

In the maturation of the mutual fund industry, there is an increasing need for evaluating the performance of various mutual fund offerings by looking at both the absolute and risk-adjusted performance of mutual fund products. While measures of return can be very helpful, they do not convey the degree of variance or volatility of competing investment strategies (Kour, 2022). The benefit of the Sharpe ratio, Treynor ratio, and Jensen's alpha, as suggested by leading researchers and practitioners in finance, can help furnish a better evaluation of mutual fund performance. These metrics will allow you to determine if the returns were commensurate with the amount of risk taken.

The recent findings from some empirical studies were able to confirm the importance of such measures for assessing the performance of several types of funds, including the ESG Mutual Fund Scheme and the Balanced Advantage Mutual Fund Scheme. Vishnu et al. (2024) state that with the use of risk/return assessment measures, investors can judge the overall efficiency of their funds under the varying conditions of the market's asset cycle. Additionally, Mohan et al. (2021) stated that they support this perspective when they indicated that to better understand the performance of both passive and active funds, comparative studies need to include the use of risk-adjusted measures.

The research study is placed within this analytical framework. The main purpose of the study is to analyze and compare the risk-return relationships of public and private sector mutual fund schemes in India, again, focusing on three categories of mutual fund schemes - Index Fund schemes, Large Cap Fund schemes, and Balanced Advantage Fund schemes. These are the three categories of funds that have been chosen based on their differing risk characteristics and investor popularity. The research addresses the objective of the study by providing an analytical and rigorous quantitative methodology, using statistical tools, and by applying risk-adjusted performance indicators to sectors i.e. public versus private AMCs.

Additionally, the study tries to examine a significant gap in the current literature on comparative performance evaluation of mutual fund schemes of Public and Private Sector Asset Management Companies (AMCs). Although previous studies have compared selected types of mutual funds or analyzed the performance of mutual funds during several different market cycles, few studies have used the same risk and return performance measures to make an overall comparison of the mutual fund schemes provided by Public and Private Sector AMCs (Kandpal, 2014; Jayadev, 1996; Thakuria & Kashyap, 2017; Adhav & Chauhan, 2015).

This research not only adds to the body of literature regarding the evaluation of mutual fund performance, but it may also assist investors with making decisions regarding which kind of mutual fund they wish to invest in through an understanding of the investment characteristics of the various types of mutual funds. The increase in investor participation in mutual funds as a result of the advancements in fintech capabilities and increasing investor knowledge of investing have made the findings from this research even more relevant.

2. REVIEW OF LITERATURE

An expansive collection of literature exists on the performance of mutual funds, which includes studies on risk-return trade-off assessments, performance indicators, benchmarking for performance, and comparative assessments between public and private mutual funds. A couple of important papers were written by Sharpe (1966), McDonald (1974), and Lehmann & Modest (1987), indicating that performance evaluation must include measures of fund effectiveness according to risk, which provided evaluation frameworks such as the Sharpe and Treynor Ratios. Therefore, this literature laid the foundation for the study of mutual funds based on performance, and not just returns, as mutual funds have historically based on risk-adjusted performance rather than return. Jayadev (1996) and Ippolito (1993) emphasized the importance of Indian and global fund performance analysis using monthly returns, exposing inconsistencies, and emphasizing the importance of performance consistency and the skillset of fund managers. Wermers (2000) subsequently decomposed performance drivers into management skill, expenses, and transaction costs, noting that costs are inversely related to gross returns. Performance is increasingly evaluated relying on quantitative tools. Elton et al. (1996) showed persistence in risk-adjusted returns, and Chen et al. (2000) applauded the effectiveness of active management if one is cognizant of trading costs. In India, Sharpe and Treynor Ratios were used to validate the performance of funds across different fund types by Sapar & Madava (2003), Sudhakar & Kumar (2005), and Chitra & Hemalatha (2018), where results were varied, thereby emphasizing the importance of fund category in performance outcomes. Pandow & Butt (2017) examined the risk-return tradeoff within Indian mutual funds and found that equity-oriented funds, in general, had higher returns at a higher risk of volatility than other fund options. In the same way, Kalyan & Gautami (2018) assessed mutual fund schemes, using standard deviation and Sharpe Ratio, thus ensuring all risk is balanced with return in the investment decision process. Mohan et al. (2021) researched selected mutual fund schemes and demonstrated that some high-return funds had high volatility, highlighting the need for risk-adjusted selection. Their research reinforced that there was different risk-return efficiency for different fund types, and the investor's objectives should lead to the investor's choice of fund. In addition to better understanding these funds, Vishnu, Praveen Raj, and Ananthi (2024) observed the risk-return behavior of these niche funds, such as ESG and solution-oriented schemes, and their increasing popularity from a growing number of socially responsible investors. With respect to comparisons, Sharma (2013), Sekhar (2014), and Thakuria & Kashyap (2017) found private sector funds to provide better returns than public sector funds, and high returns in exchange for higher risk. Rehmani (2018) corroborated this pattern, but noted differences in funds' strategies, pointing out that private AMCs generally have a more aggressive, return-based strategy towards investing. Narayanan (2021) and Haney (2021) confirmed findings noted that private funds were more susceptible to market pressure. Barua et al. (1991) explained the need for regulation to avoid wild swings in market and fund values. Panigrahi (1996), as a starting point, described an overview of the development of the Mutual Fund industry in India as well as the competitive approaches and structural barriers to successful fund performance. Adams et al. (2018) recently studied the association between the composition of mutual fund boards and fund performance, which they found was positively related to fund performance as it generated greater stability and investor trust. In addition, Subramanyam and Kalyan (2018), through their study of investor behaviour, have described how investors often react in an inconsistent manner when experiencing poor returns because of loyalty, as well as, limited financial knowledge; therefore, indicating the need for improved investor education and reporting transparency.

While the literature is abundant, there are few comparative studies of mutual fund performance across ownership sectors or fund categories that apply statistically sound techniques. In addition, few studies focus strictly on the differences across categories (e.g., Index, Large Cap, Balanced Advantage) or incorporate structural attributes at the fund level, such as Net Asset Value (NAV), Assets Under Management (AUM), and Expense Ratios. This current study will address these gaps and utilize a Risk-Return Framework and statistical testing to analyze and compare the performance of public and private sector Mutual Fund Schemes in India.

3. RESEARCH METHODOLOGY

This chapter presents the research methodology applied for the analysis of, and comparison between, the risk-adjusted performance of mutual fund schemes for public and private AMCs in India. It discusses the objectives of the study, hypotheses, sources of data, sampling, methods of analysis, tests of significance employed, and limitations of the study. It additionally provides a rationale for the selection of categories of funds and risk-return measures.

3.1 Objectives of the Study

- To compare the risk-adjusted performance of mutual fund schemes managed by public and private sector AMCs by using Sharpe and Treynor Ratios.
- To assess and compare the performance of different mutual fund categories — Index Funds, Large Cap Funds, and Balanced Advantage Funds with respect to return, risk, and return volatility.
- To investigate the impact of AMC's ownership types (Public/ Private) and mutual fund categories on mutual fund performance

3.2 Hypotheses of the Study

Null Hypothesis (H_0):

- There is no significant difference in risk-return performance of mutual fund schemes (i.e., Sharpe Ratio, Standard Deviation, Treynor ratio, and beta) of Public and Private ACMs.
- There is no significant difference in risk-return characteristics (i.e., Sharpe Ratio, Standard Deviation, Treynor ratio, and beta) among index, Large Cap, and Balanced mutual fund categories.
- There is no significant interaction effect of AMC's ownership types (Public/ Private) and mutual fund Categories (Index, Large Cap, and Balanced Fund) on risk-return characteristics of mutual funds.

3.3 Research Design

This research uses a quantitative, comparative, and inferential research design to assess and compare mutual fund schemes operated by public and private AMCs in India. This study has adopted a methodology that joins descriptive financial analysis and advanced statistical inferential analysis, specifically Two-Way ANOVA, to explore and test the main and interaction effects of AMC's ownership type and funds category on risk-return metrics.

3.3.1 Data Sources

The study employed secondary data obtained from the official websites of selected AMCs, the Association of Mutual Funds in India (AMFI), SEBI, NSE, and BSE. The inputs included:

- Net Asset Value (NAV)
- 3-Year annualized or absolute returns
- Fund Size (Assets Under Management)
- Expense Ratios
- Risk metrics (Standard Deviation, Beta, Sharpe Ratio, Treynor Ratio)

The risk-free rate for the Sharpe and Treynor ratios was calculated based on the 10-year Indian government bond yield rates published by the Reserve Bank of India (RBI).

3.3.2 Sample Selection Criteria

The research employed purposive sampling to select 24 mutual fund schemes - a selection that included 3 categories of mutual funds and equal public and private sector representation in the three categories. The three categories with the count of public and private sector representation included: 6 Index Funds - Regular Plan – Growth (3 public, 3 private), 6 Balanced Advantage Funds - Regular Plan - Growth (3 public, 3 private), and 12 Large Cap Funds - Growth Option (6 public, 6 private). The 24 schemes were selected based on data availability for at least 3 years without interruption, as well as the fund scheme size, so that the consistency of the mutual funds could be determined.

3.4 Time Period of the Study

The research evaluates the performance of various mutual funds for the 3 years from 2021 to 2024. This is reflective of a real recent market piece of evidence and allows us to make some meaningful observations about the medium-term performance as well as volatility.

3.5 Fund Categories Considered

- **Index Funds**- Index funds are essentially passive mutual funds that track a market index like the Nifty 50. The fund will have the same investments with the same companies as the index it is tracking, making for a cost-efficient and easy way to invest in the market.
- **Large Cap Funds**- These are actively managed funds that invest in large, well-known companies with a large market value. These funds will be managed to achieve long-term growth over time.
- **Balanced Advantage Funds (BAF)**- These funds will invest in equity and bonds. BAF funds are dynamic, meaning the managers of the fund will change the allocation to equity or bonds depending on the market to reduce risk to investors while providing some return over time.

3.6 Variables Used in the Study

- **Risk-Adjusted Performance Metrics:**
  - **Sharpe Ratio:** Evaluates return per unit of total risk.
  - **Treynor Ratio:** Measures return per unit of market/systematic risk.
- **Risk/Volatility Indicators:**
  - **Standard Deviation:** Measures total risk or volatility.
  - **Beta:** Measures sensitivity to market fluctuations.
- **Fund Attributes:**
  - NAV, Fund Size (AUM), Expense Ratio, 3-Year Return (%)

3.7 Statistical Tests Employed

The statistical analysis portion for this study utilized a Two-Way ANOVA to test for main and interaction effects of AMC's ownership type (public/private) and mutual fund category (index/large cap/balanced) on Standard Deviation, Sharpe Ratio, Beta, and Treynor Ratio. Descriptive analysis summarized the means and standard deviations of the variables by ACM's ownership type and mutual fund category. All statistical analyses were conducted in SPSS Software to ensure accuracy and ability for interpretation.

3.8 Analytical Tools and Techniques

3.8.1 Sharpe Ratio

The Sharpe ratio measures excess return per unit of overall risk (standard deviation).
Sharpe Ratio Formula: $= Rp - Rf / \sigma p$

3.8.2 Treynor Ratio

The Treynor ratio measures excess return per unit of system risk (beta).
Treynor Ratio Formula: $= Rp - Rf / \beta p$

3.8.3 Volatility Metrics

Volatility metrics include Standard Deviation, which measures total risk, and Beta, which measures market risk.

3.8.4 Descriptive Statistics

This was used to describe central tendency and dispersion for each performance variable.

4. DATA ANALYSIS

4.1 Index fund - Regular Plan – Growth

Table 4.1 below shows a comparison of the Index fund Index Funds based on four risk-return measures: Standard Deviation, Beta, Sharpe Ratio, and Treynor Ratio, with the purpose of analyzing the performance of the Index fund Index Funds in changing AMCs. To evaluate the performance of each fund and to determine the effectiveness of each fund based on the returns for the best level of risk taken.

Table 1. Annualized Return Ranking (Index Mutual Funds)

Index Fund - Regular Plan - Growth	Fund Size (Cr)	NAV	Annualized Return 3 Year (%)	Expense Ratio (%)	Public Vs Private	Category Rank
UTI Mutual Fund	**19486**	153	**8.89%**	**0.25**	Public	1
HDFC Mutual Fund	19046	211.22	8.80%	0.32	Private	2
ICICI Prudential Mutual Fund	12618	**224.04**	8.79%	0.36	Private	3
SBI Mutual Fund	9192	196.8	8.68%	0.44	Public	4
KOTAK Mutual Fund	733.4	14.46	8.54%	0.35	Private	5
LIC Mutual Fund	315	123.4	8.09%	1.01	Public	6

Source: Official websites of companies

Table 4.1 replicates that the public sector fund houses, UTI Mutual Fund, led the performance with a 3-year annualised return of 8.89%, followed by SBI Mutual Fund at 8.68% and LIC Mutual Fund at 8.09%.

In the private sector, HDFC Mutual Fund and ICICI Prudential Mutual Fund delivered closely competitive returns at 8.80% and 8.79% respectively, slightly below UTI, while KOTAK Mutual Fund followed at 8.54%. Despite the passive nature of index funds, minor variations in performance arise due to factors such as tracking error, fund size (AUM), and expense ratios. As an example, UTI was able to generate the greatest total return as well as keep its expense ratio down to .25%. On the other hand, the fund from LIC Mutual Fund had the highest expense ratio at 1.01%, and consequently it ranked last for profitability and for the overall performance of the category.

Overall, the findings from this research show that Public Sector AMC's such as UTI and SBI have performed competitively, and in the case of UTI, are leaders of the industry with respect to fund performance by demonstrating effective management of passive portfolios. With lower expense ratios and high total returns, they will be major competitors against top performing Private Sector AMCs.

Table 4.2 offers a comparative review of risk-return parameters for selected mutual funds in the public and private sectors. The risk-return parameters examined were as follows: Standard Deviation, Beta, Sharpe Ratio, and Treynor Ratio, providing some insight into the risk profile of the relative mutual fund.

Table 2. Risk Return Metric Ranking (Index Mutual Funds)

Company/Risk return parameters	Standard Deviation	Beta	Sharpe Ratio	Treynor Ratio
Public Sector				
SBI Mutual Fund	12.93	0.99	0.33	0.04
UTI Mutul Fund	12.92	0.99	**0.34**	0.04
LIC Mutual Fund	12.89	0.99	0.29	0.04
Private Sector				
KOTAK Mutual Fund	**12.87**	0.99	0.32	0.04
HDFC Mutual Fund	12.91	0.99	**0.34**	0.04
ICICI Prudential Mutual Fund	12.91	0.99	0.33	0.04

Source: Official Websites of Companies

Table 4.2 indicates that all mutual funds have the same Beta (0.99) and Treynor Ratio (0.04), indicating all had very similar market risk exposure and equal returns expected per unit of market risk. In addition, UTI and HDFC Mutual Funds offered the highest Sharpe Ratios (0.34), indicating their risk-adjusted return is higher compared to the others. The Kotak Mutual Fund had the lowest standard deviation (12.87), indicating slightly lower volatility, and SBI appears to have the highest (12.93). Overall, UTI and HDFC had the most efficient return relative to total risk of those reported. Table 4.3 shows the rankings of mutual funds based on individual risk-return measures.

Table 3. Overall Rankings of Index Mutual Funds

Metric	Rank 1	Rank 2	Rank 3	Rank 4	Rank 5	Rank 6
Standard Deviation	**Kotak MF**	LIC MF	HDFC MF	ICICI MF	UTI MF	SBI MF
Beta	All Equal	All Equal	All Equal	All Equal	All Equal	All Equal
Sharpe Ratio	**UTI MF**	HDFC MF	ICICI MF	SBI MF	Kotak MF	LIC MF
Treynor Ratio	All Equal	All Equal	All Equal	All Equal	All Equal	All Equal

Source: Researcher's Calculation

Table 4.3 reveals that in terms of Standard Deviation, private sector fund Kotak MF ranks highest for having the lowest risk, followed by LIC MF and HDFC MF. The highest risk is observed in SBI MF. For the Sharpe Ratio, UTI MF (public) and HDFC MF (private) lead the rankings, showing the best performance adjusted for total risk. LIC Mutual Fund ranks lowest in the Beta and Treynor Ratio categories, and since these two ratios have identical numbers (for all funds), it emphasizes how equally and uniformly, a fund tracks an index with both Public Fund Houses and Private Fund Houses. The Beta and Treynor Ratios have the same numbers for all funds; however, the rankings on Standard Deviation and Sharpe Ratios differ. These differences show that there were differences in volatility and risk/return.

4.2 Balanced Advantage Fund - Regular Plan – Growth

The performance of Balanced Advantage Funds at various AMCs is analyzed through comparing the key risk/return metrics as per table 4.4 (i.e., Standard Deviation, Beta, Sharpe Ratio, Treynor Ratio). The main goal of balanced advantage funds is to achieve stable returns while managing the risk by changing the equity/ debt mix depending upon the prevailing market conditions. This category of AMC is divided into the public and private sectors, where each sector has its own approach in terms of strategy and risk model.

Table 4. Annualized Return Ranking (Balanced Advantage Mutual Funds)

Balanced Advantage Fund - Regular Plan - Growth	Fund Size (Cr)	NAV	Annualized Return 3 Year (%)	Expense Ratio (%)	Public Private	Category Rank
HDFC Fund	**90374**	36.78	**17.21%**	**1.37**	Private	1
SBI Fund	32529	14.34	11.19%	1.59	Public	2
ICICI Prudential Fund	58716	**68.36**	10.94%	1.48	Private	3
Edelweiss Fund	11696	46.81	9.18%	1.69	Private	4
LIC Fund	756	12.57	7.80%	2.32	Public	5
Bank Of India	132	22.76	6.94%	2.27	Public	6

Source: Official Website of Companies

In this table, HDFC was the best performer among private sector mutual fund houses in terms of 3 year average annualized returns of 17.21 percent. The next two highest were ICICI Prudential at 10.94 percent and Edelweiss at 9.18 percent; all three fund houses maintained modest expense ratios. The best performing public sector mutual fund house was SBI Mutual Fund at 11.19 percent. The public sector mutual fund houses generally had much larger expense ratios than those of the private sector fund houses. Both the expense ratio for LIC and Bank of India exceeded 2 percent. This could negatively impact the returns earned by investors.

HDFC was the top performing private AMC and SBI Mutual Fund had a strong performance and ranked as the second best of all and the first of all the public fund house's performance for the year of 2019. This shows that select public sector AMCs can effectively manage dynamic asset allocation strategies, challenging the dominance of private players in actively managed hybrid fund categories.

Table 5. Return Metric Ranking (Balanced Advantage Mutual Funds)

Balanced Advantage Fund - Regular Plan - Growth	Standard Deviation	Beta	Sharpe Ratio	Treynor Ratio
Public Sector				
LIC Fund	7.34	0.98	0.3	0.02
SBI Fund	5.78	0.77	0.82	0.06
Bank Of India	10.03	1.39	0.17	0.01
Private Sector				
ICICI Prudential Fund	**5.28**	**0.71**	0.79	0.06
HDFC Fund	9.42	1.23	**1.2**	**0.09**
Edelweiss Fund	8.23	1.13	0.41	0.03

Source: Official Websites of Companies

The Balanced Advantage Fund data demonstrate in Table 4.5 the considerable differences in risk and return across the different funds. HDFC Fund has the highest Sharpe Ratio (1.2) and Treynor Ratio (0.09), which simply means it has the best risk-adjusted or systematic returns despite its high standard deviation (9.4). The SBI Fund, among the public sector funds, has shown decent returns, boasting a high Sharpe Ratio (0.82) and Treynor Ratio (0.06), as well as low volatility (5.78). All of these mean it provides efficient returns. The Bank of India Fund has the highest standard deviation (10.03) and Beta (1.39) as well as the lowest Sharpe (0.17) and Treynor (0.01) Ratios, which indicates it has poor risk-adjusted returns. ICICI Prudential Fund is also a strong performer with low volatility (5.28) and a high Sharpe (0.79) mean it could be a good alternative in the private sector.

Table 4.8 shows the performance rankings of selected mutual funds based on key risk-return measures: standard deviation, beta, Sharpe ratio, and Treynor ratio.

Table 6. Overall Rankings (Balanced Advantage Mutual Funds)

Metric	Rank 1	Rank 2	Rank 3	Rank 4	Rank 5	Rank 6
Standard Deviation	ICICI Prudential Fund (Private)	SBI Fund (Public)	LIC Fund (Public)	Edelweiss Fund (Private)	HDFC Fund (Private)	Bank Of India (Public)
Beta	ICICI Prudential Fund (Private)	SBI Fund (Public)	LIC Fund (Public)	Edelweiss Fund (Private)	HDFC Fund (Private)	Bank Of India (Public)
Sharpe Ratio	HDFC Fund (Private)	SBI Fund (Public)	ICICI Prudential Fund (Private)	Edelweiss Fund (Private)	LIC Fund (Public)	Bank Of India (Public)
Treynor Ratio	HDFC Fund (Private)	SBI Fund (Public)	ICICI Prudential Fund (Private)	Edelweiss Fund (Private)	LIC Fund (Public)	Bank Of India (Public)

Source: Researcher's Calculation

The study of balanced advantage funds, as shown in Table 4.8, indicates that private sector mutual funds generally function better than public sector funds for total risk as well as market risk. ICICI Prudential Fund has the lowest level of standard deviation as well as beta, indicating both low volatility and market sensitivity, while HDFC Fund has the highest Sharpe and Treynor Ratios, indicating good risk-adjusted returns. Among public sector funds, SBI Mutual Fund is foremost, having a considerably low level of risk and good performance across all metrics, which suggests that good risk management comes from experienced management or investment in good portfolios that add little variability to returns.

Similarly, Bank of India Mutual Fund has the weakest performance, having the highest level of risk and the lowest risk-adjusted returns, indicating some inefficient risk management. In summary, private sector funds, HDFC and ICICI Prudential, are by far the best with respect to the ability to generate above-average returns with low levels of risk, with SBI as the best with respect to public sector funds, eliminating the gap between public and private sector optimum performance.

4.3 Large Cap Fund - Growth

To analyze the performance of Large Cap Funds across different AMCs, the following table 4.9 provides a comparative overview based on key risk-return metrics—Standard Deviation, Beta, Sharpe Ratio, and Treynor Ratio. Large-cap funds are mostly invested in established and financially stable companies with a large market capitalization. These metrics give meaningful insight into how each fund can generate returns as a result of the risk they take.

Table 7. Annualized Returns Ranking (Large Cap Mutual Fund)

Large Cap Fund - Growth	Fund Size (Cr)	NAV	Absolute Return 3 Year (%)	Expense Ratio (%)	Public Vs Private	Category Rank
Private Sector						
NIPPON Fund	37546	79.64	52.75	1.58	Private	1
ICICI Prudential Fund	60177	98.57	47.08	1.47	Private	2
HDFC Fund	36108	1027.09	43.19	1.63	Private	3
BARODA BNP Paribas Fund	2262	197.53	40	2.01	Public	4
CANARA ROBECCO Fund	14965	56.57	36.94	1.68	Public	5
SBI Fund	49394	82.29	33.56	1.53	Public	6
MIRAEASSET Fund	35532	99.92	26.21	1.53	Private	7
UTI Fund	11720	246.7	25.1	1.77	Public	8
LIC Fund	1379	50.72	23.52	2.15	Public	9
AXIS Fund	30517	22.23	22	1.6	Private	10

Source: Official websites of Companies

In Table 4.9, it is evident that large-cap funds invest primarily in larger, established corporations; therefore, they typically offer greater stability (lower volatility) and are less risky than other investment opportunities. The Nippon Mutual Fund was the highest performing fund among all private sector fund houses with an overall performance of 52.75% over three years. Next to follow were the ICICI Prudential and HDFC Mutual Funds with total performance rates of 47.08% and 43.19%, respectively. While both had slightly higher expense ratios compared to some of their competitors, they each provided a relatively stable return to investors.

The Baroda BNP Paribas Fund produced the highest returns of all public sector funds (40%) and performed better than other public sector funds; however, public sector funds, on average, produced a higher expense ratio compared to private sector funds. The expense ratio for the Baroda BNP Paribas Fund was 2.01% and the expense ratio for the LIC Fund was 2.15%. This high expense ratio could have potentially lowered the net return for these funds.

However, several private sector funds, especially Nippon, performed well with high returns and low expense ratios. While the expense ratios of public sector funds were higher than those of the private sector, the performance of selected public sector funds (i.e., Baroda BNP Paribas) suggests that public sector fund managers can produce good results in the large-cap segment of the market.

Table 4.10 provides the risk/return characteristics of the selected Large Cap Growth Funds (Standard Deviation, Beta, Sharpe Ratio, and Treynor Ratio) for the selected public and private sector mutual funds.

Table 8. Return Metric Ranking (Large Cap Mutual Fund)

Large Cap Fund – Growth	Standard Deviation	Beta	Sharpe Ratio	Treynor Ratio
UTI Fund	11.88	0.85	0.24	0.03
SBI Fund	11.7	0.86	0.48	0.07
CANARA ROBECCO Fund	12.32	0.9	0.48	0.07
BARODA BNP PARIBAS Fund	12.71	0.93	0.55	0.08
LIC Fund	13.25	0.97	0.15	0.02
ICICI PRUDENTIAL Fund	11.96	0.88	0.72	0.1
HDFC Fund	12.83	0.94	0.65	0.09
NIPPON Fund	13.18	0.97	0.78	0.11
MIRAEASSET Fund	12.46	0.91	0.29	0.04
AXIS Fund	12.17	0.86	0.14	0.02

Source: Official Websites of Companies

Nippon Fund presents the most desirable combination of Risk Return Metrics from Table 4.10, as it provides the highest return (13.18%), the largest Sharpe ratio (0.78) and Treynor ratio (0.11), and the second-highest beta (0.97) of all three funds reviewed. The LIC Fund produces the greatest return (13.25%) in the group; however, its Sharpe ratio (0.15) is by far the lowest in the group, and thus exhibits the least efficient risk-return performance. The ICICI Prudential Fund has also demonstrated an acceptable level of efficiency in terms of risk/return tradeoff, as indicated by a Sharpe ratio of .72 and a Treynor ratio of .10, albeit at a return (.1196%) that is slightly lower than those of the two aforementioned funds. UTI Fund and SBI Fund have much lower returns and somewhat better risk metrics than the remaining two funds listed above, and therefore are less preferable compared to the other funds listed above. Therefore, Nippon Fund appears to be the superior performing large-cap fund relative to the two funds above.

Table 9. Overall Rankings (Large Cap Mutual Fund)

Metric	Rank 1	Rank 2	Rank 3	Rank 4	Rank 5	Rank 6
Standard Deviation	ICICI Prudential Fund	Axis Fund	SBI Fund	Canara Robeco Fund	LIC Fund	Nippon Fund
Beta	UTI Fund	SBI Fund	Axis Fund	ICICI Prudential Fund	Canara Robeco Fund	LIC/ Nippon Fund
Sharpe Ratio	Nippon Fund	ICICI Prudential Fund	HDFC Fund	Baroda BNP Paribas Fund	Canara/SBI Fund	LIC Fund
Treynor Ratio	Nippon Fund	ICICI Prudential Fund	HDFC Fund	Baroda BNP Paribas Fund	Canara/SBI Fund	LIC/Axis Fund

Source: Researcher's Calculation

ICICI Prudential and Axis Fund have the lowest volatility and are therefore the least risky investment options due to their lowest standard deviations in Table 4.11. The middle ground on either side of the risk spectrum include Nippon and LIC Funds with the largest standard deviations indicating larger price swings and increased risk. The Beta numbers show how a fund's prices will fluctuate compared to the market overall. UTI, SBI and Axis Funds had lower beta numbers, showing that these funds have less price movement and are generally more stable with respect to the market.

The three funds with the largest beta numbers (LIC, Nippon Fund and ICICI Prudential) showed that they are highly correlated with the market and have large potential for losses based upon market direction. The Sharpe Ratio looks at how much a particular fund rewards the investor for the total risk taken. The Nippon, ICICI Prudential, and HDFC Funds score well on these and offer the upside reward related to the risk. LIC and Axis Fund scored negatively, which means their returns weren't warranted for risk.

4.4 Effect of AMC's Ownership Type and Fund Category on Risk-Return Characteristics of Mutual Fund Schemes: A Two-Way ANOVA Analysis

Null Hypothesis (H_0):

- There is no significant difference in risk-return performance of mutual fund schemes (i.e., Sharpe Ratio, Standard Deviation, Treynor ratio, and beta) of Public and Private ACMs.

- There is no significant difference in risk-return characteristics (i.e., Sharpe Ratio, Standard Deviation, Treynor ratio, and beta) among Index fund, Large Cap, and Balanced mutual fund scheme.
- There is no significant interaction effect of AMC's ownership types (Public/ Private) and Mutual Fund Categories (Index, Large Cap, and Balanced Fund) on risk-return characteristics of mutual funds.

4.4.1 Results of Two-Way ANOVA

The descriptive statistics table 4.12 summarizes the risk-return performance of mutual fund schemes across three fund categories (Index fund, Large Cap, and Balanced Fund) and two AMCs Ownership Types (Public and Private).

Table 10. Descriptive statistics of risk-return metrics of mutual fund schemes

Descriptive statistics									
Risk-Return Metrics		S.D.		Beta		Sharpe Ratio		Treynor Ratio	
Fund Category/ AMCs Ownership Type		Mean	Std. Deviation	Mean	Std. Deviation	Mean	Std. Deviation	Mean	Std. Deviation
Index fund	Public	12.9133	.02082	.9900	0.00000	.3200	.02646	.0400	0.00000
	Private	12.8967	.02309	.9900	0.00000	.3300	.01000	.0400	0.00000
	Total	12.9050	.02168	.9900	0.00000	.3250	.01871	.0400	0.00000
Large CAP	**Public**	12.3720	.62878	.9020	.04970	.3800	.17421	.0540	.02702
	Private	12.5200	.49280	.9120	.04438	.5160	.28360	.0720	.03962
	Total	12.4460	.53827	.9070	.04473	.4480	.23318	.0630	.03335
Balanced fund	**Public**	7.7167	2.14989	1.0467	.31533	.4300	.34395	.0300	.02646
	Private	7.6433	2.13144	1.0233	.27592	.8000	.39509	.0600	.03000
	Total	7.6800	1.91511	1.0350	.26531	.6150	.38837	.0450	.03017
Total	**Public**	11.2500	2.50747	.9655	.15826	.3773	.19432	.0436	.02335
	Private	11.2927	2.55464	.9636	.13648	.5427	.31177	.0600	.03162
	Total	11.2714	2.47026	.9645	.14421	.4600	.26728	.0518	.02839

Source: SPSS Calculation

Table 4.12 dictates the average values and standard deviations of four key metrics i.e. Standard Deviation (total risk), Beta (market/systematic risk), Sharpe Ratio (total risk-adjusted return), and Treynor Ratio (market risk-adjusted return). Index fund funds are highly stable across both public and private sectors, with consistent Beta (0.99) and Treynor Ratio (0.04), indicating returns closely tied to market movements and minimal variability in performance.

In contrast to equity funds, large cap and balanced funds are characterized by a greater variance in their performance. In general, private sector large cap and balanced fund schemes present significantly higher sharpe and treynor ratios when compared with those of public sector funds indicating that the former outperforms the latter on a risk adjusted basis. The Standard Deviation shows that the Balanced Funds are the least volatile, but their values for Sharpe and Treynor ratio vary the most between schemes. Overall, the data indicates that most private mutual fund schemes, especially those in the Large Cap and Balanced Fund categories, provide the investor with superior returns for the risks taken.

A two-way ANOVA analysis was performed to examine how both the type of fund (index fund, large cap, balanced fund) and ownership type (public, private) of an AMC affect four performance metrics for mutual funds -- standard deviation, beta, Sharpe ratio, and Treynor ratio as shown in table 4.13.

Table 11. Results of Two-Way ANOVA on risk-return metrics of mutual fund schemes

Two Way ANOVAs Results								
Dependent Variable	**S.D.**		**Beta**		**Sharpe Ratio**		**Treynor Ratio**	
Source	**f-value**	**Sig.**	**f-value**	**Sig.**	**f-value**	**Sig.**	**f-value**	**Sig.**
Corrected Model	16.435	.000	.589	.709	1.632	.208	1.168	.367
Intercept	1928.892	.000	860.449	.000	71.598	.000	65.223	.000
Fund Category	41.062	.000	1.448	.264	2.053	.161	1.527	.247
AMCs Ownership Type	.001	.970	.004	.948	2.474	.135	1.715	.209
Fund Category * AMCs Ownership Type	.020	.980	.023	.978	.815	.460	.443	.650

Source: SPSS Calculation

Table 4.13 demonstrates that only Standard Deviation (the measure of Total Risk) was impacted by Fund Category ($F= 41.062$; $p < .001$), which indicates that there is an overall difference in the amount of total risk among the various fund categories.

However, neither AMC's Ownership Type, nor the interaction between fund category and AMC's ownership type had an overall effect on the total risk associated with each fund.

The analysis did not find any statistical significance for Beta (Systematic Risk), Sharpe Ratio (Total Risk-Adjusted Return), and Treynor Ratio (Market Risk-Adjusted Return) across the fund categories, AMCs ownership types, or the interaction of the two. Thus, although the type of mutual fund appears to affect the total volatility of the investment, the type of mutual fund does not appear to have an overall significant effect on how responsive the mutual fund will be to movement in the market or how well the fund has performed as a risk-adjusted return.

5. CONCLUSION

Mutual funds are very popular investment vehicles in India for most investors. This paper presents a comparative evaluation of three different mutual fund types: index funds, balanced advantage funds and large cap funds. The study evaluated each type of mutual fund on the basis of their performance, risk level, volatility and other factors.The study measured performance from both public and private AMCs to identify differences in risk-adjusted returns, expense ratios, and ability to manage funds. Public Sector AMCs (such as UTI and SBI) performed reasonably well for the index fund type of category, but private sector AMCs were dominant in actively managed distribution types of categories. The example showed that private AMCs like HDFC and ICICI Prudential perform better in both dimensions of Balanced Advantage and Large Cap. HDFC and ICICI Prudential had better Sharpe and Treynor ratios than other funds in the same categories. This finding communicates that the total and market risk return is more appropriate for private AMCs, while some public AMCs perform and compete in passive fund options. Therefore, private AMCs may promote a trend for successful strategies in active management, while certain public AMCs remain comparable in performance for passive fund options.

The most marked trend occurred in the Balanced Advantage Funds category, with HDFC (private) and SBI (public) emerging as the top performers in terms of return efficiency (absolute and risk-adjusted). While public AMCs have historically charged a higher expense ratio on average, SBI lent credibility to the assertion that public AMCs can keep pace with private fund houses, provided they are managed with capital allocation at the core and costs at a competitive level. Meanwhile, for the Large Cap section, Nippon Mutual Fund had the highest absolute returns and the highest risk-return efficiency ratio (risk-adjusted), while ICICI and HDFC emerged close behind both in absolute returns and risk-adjusted returns. Specific public AMCs like Baroda BNP Paribas proved they could also provide real value to investors; however, public AMCs generally have relatively higher expense ratios, where higher expenses led to a reduction in the net return. In conclusion, the observations of the last two periods imply a slight improvement in the capabilities of a few select public funds, but operational and structural advantages sit with private sector fund houses.

The Two-Way ANOVA statistical results demonstrated that fund category had a significant impact on overall risk (Standard Deviation), while AMCs Ownership Type (public vs. private) did not have a statistical effect on risk-adjusted return measures. This indicates that the type of fund - index fund, large cap, or balanced advantage - is more important in affecting volatility and performance than whether the fund is public or private.

The limitations of the study also need to be acknowledged. This study only focused on a three-year historical performance window and a selected sample of mutual fund schemes, including growth, dividend, and value funds, and therefore may not provide complete and robust evidence of long-term trends and unique market scenarios. The study also did not account for any qualitative issues such as fund manager ability, investor sentiments, and macroeconomic indicators, etc. Future research could also extend the timeframe of the analysis, consider broader samples (e.g., other fund types such as mid-cap, ELSS, thematic funds), and model performances using advanced econometric or machine learning based methods. Cross-country comparisons and inclusion of some investor behavior measures could also add new layers of depth and relevance to the overall understanding of the performance of mutual funds across sectors.

REFERENCES

Adams, J. C., Nishikawa, T., & Rao, R. P. (2018). Mutual fund performance, management teams, and boards. *Journal of Banking & Finance*, *92*, 358–368. DOI: 10.1016/j.jbankfin.2016.09.006

Adhav, M. S. M., & Chauhan, P. M. (2015). Comparative study of mutual funds of selected Indian companies. *International Journal of Science. Technology & Management*, *4*(2), 2394–1537.

Barua, S. K., Varma, J. R., & Venkiteswaran, N. (1991). A regulatory framework for mutual funds. *Economic and Political Weekly*, •••, M55–M59.

Chen, H. L., Jegadeesh, N., & Wermers, R. (2000). The value of active mutual fund management: An examination of the stockholdings and trades of fund managers. *Journal of Financial and Quantitative Analysis*, *35*(3), 343–368. DOI: 10.2307/2676208

Chitra, V., & Hemalatha, T. (2018). Risk and return analysis of performance of mutual fund schemes in India. *International Journal of Applied Research*, *4*(1), 279–283.

Elton, E. J., Gruber, M. J., & Blake, C. R. (1996). The persistence of risk-adjusted mutual fund performance. *The Journal of Business*, *69*(2), 133–157. DOI: 10.1086/209685

Haney, P. (2021). *Comparative analysis of mutual funds with reference to public and private sector funds.*

Ippolito, R. A. (1993). On studies of mutual fund performance, 1962–1991. *Financial Analysts Journal*, *49*(1), 42–50. DOI: 10.2469/faj.v49.n1.42

Jayadev, M. (1996). Mutual fund performance: An analysis of monthly returns. *Finance India*, *10*(1), 73–84.

Kalyan, N. B., & Gautami, S. (2018). A study on risk and return analysis of the selected mutual fund schemes in India. *International Journal of Research in Social Sciences*, *8*(5), 212–221.

Kandpal, V. (2014). *Comparative study of selected public and private sector equity diversified mutual fund schemes in India.*

Kour, M. (2022). COMPARATIVE RISK-RETURNS ANALYSIS OF STOCKS IN THE INDIAN STOCK MARKET. *Journal of Commerce & Accounting Research*, *11*(3).

Kour, M., Taneja, S., Özen, E., Sood, K., & Grima, S. (Eds.). (2025). *Financial Landscape Transformation: Technological Disruptions*. Emerald Publishing Limited. DOI: 10.1108/9781837537501

Lehmann, B. N., & Modest, D. M. (1987). Mutual fund performance evaluation: A comparison of benchmarks and benchmark comparisons. *The Journal of Finance*, *42*(2), 233–265. DOI: 10.1111/j.1540-6261.1987.tb02566.x

McDonald, J. G. (1974). Objectives and performance of mutual funds, 1960–1969. *Journal of Financial and Quantitative Analysis*, *9*(3), 311–333. DOI: 10.2307/2329866

Mohan, D. M. M., Rao, D. M. A., Chakravarthi, D. P., & Rao, P. V. L. (2021). Risk and return analysis with performance evaluation of selected mutual fund schemes: An empirical study. *International Journal of Aquatic Science*, *12*(2), 2676–2692.

Narayanan, S. (2021). *A comparative analysis of performance of mutual funds between private and public sector* (Doctoral dissertation, Institute of Management, NU).

Pandow, B. A., & Butt, K. A. (2017). Risk and return analysis of mutual fund industry in India. *Journal of Banking and Financial Dynamics*, *1*(1), 54–65. DOI: 10.20448/journal.525.2017.11.54.65

Panigrahi, M. S. (1996). Mutual funds: Growth, performance and prospects. *Economic and Political Weekly*, •••, 765–775.

Panwar, S., & Madhumathi, R. (2006, January). Characteristics and performance evaluation of selected mutual funds in India. In *Proceedings of the 9th Capital Markets Conference*, Indian Institute of Capital Markets. DOI: 10.2139/ssrn.876402

Rehmani, A. (2018). Performance evaluation of select mutual funds: A public–private comparison. *Indian Journal of Finance*, *12*(9), 41–55. DOI: 10.17010/ijf/2018/v12i9/131563

Rehmani, A., & Khan, M. A. (2018). Growth of Indian mutual fund industry: An empirical analysis. *International Journal of Social Science and Economic Research*, *3*(8), 3763–3777.

Sadhak, H. (2003). *Mutual funds in India: Marketing strategies and investment practices*.

Sapar, N. R., & Madava, R. (2003). Performance evaluation of Indian mutual funds. SSRN *Electronic Journal*. https://ssrn.com/abstract=433100 DOI: 10.2139/ssrn.433100

Sekhar, G. (2014). *The Indian mutual fund industry: A comparative analysis of public vs. private sector performance*. Springer. DOI: 10.1057/9781137407993

Sharma, R. G. (2013). A comparative study on public and private sector mutual funds in India. *Journal of Research in Humanities and Social Sciences*, *1*(6), 23–25.

Sharpe, W. F. (1966). Mutual fund performance. *The Journal of Business*, *39*(1), 119–138. DOI: 10.1086/294846

Sisodiya, A. S. (2004). Mutual fund industry in India: Coming of age. *Chartered Financial Analyst*, (July), 17–22.

Subramanyam, P., & Kalyan, N. B. (2018). A study on risk and return analysis of selected securities in India. *International Journal of Engineering Technologies and Management Research*, *5*(4), 79–86. DOI: 10.29121/ijetmr.v5.i4.2018.211

Sudhakar, A., & Sasi Kumar, K. (2005). Performance evaluation of mutual funds: A case study. *Southern Economist*, *44*(13), 19–23.

Thakuria, A., & Kashyap, S. (2017). Comparative performance analysis of public sector sponsored and private sector sponsored mutual funds in India. *European Journal of Economics and Business Studies*, *3*(1), 7–16. DOI: 10.26417/ejes.v7i1.p7-16

Vishnu, M., Praveen Raj, R., & Ananthi, R. (2024). Risk–return analysis of special mutual fund schemes: An empirical study in the Indian context with special reference to solution-oriented mutual funds and ESG funds. In *Harnessing AI, machine learning, and IoT for intelligent business* (Vol. 1, pp. 1161–1176). Springer Nature Switzerland.

Wermers, R. (2000). Mutual fund performance: An empirical decomposition into stock-picking talent, style, transaction costs, and expenses. *The Journal of Finance*, *55*(4), 1655–1695. DOI: 10.1111/0022-1082.00263

Chapter 3

A Study to Analyse the Impact of Green Bonds on Bank Profitability

Divya Mathur
http://orcid.org/0000-0003-1075-1396
NSB Academy, India

Manali Agrawal
http://orcid.org/0009-0003-7283-3079
NSB Academy, India

Anjali Paluri
NSB Academy, India

ABSTRACT

In India, the issuance of green bonds has become a significant financial innovation that provides a dual solution for financing infrastructure and environmental sustainability .Green bonds are being used more frequently by Indian banks to fund renewable energy, sustainable transportation, and climate-resilient infrastructure. This study examines how green bonds have affected important financial metrics like Return on Assets (ROA), Return on Equity (ROE), Net Interest Margin (NIM), Capital Adequacy Ratio (CAR), and ESG scores, with a focus on five major banks: Yes Bank, Axis Bank, State Bank of India, ICICI Bank, and IDBI Bank. The adoption of green bonds is positively correlated with increases in ESG performance and long-term profitability, according to the study's comparative financial analysis of before and after green bonds issuance performance.

DOI: 10.4018/979-8-3373-5047-9.ch003

1. INTRODUCTION

Innovative financial instruments known as "green bonds" are used to raise money for environmentally beneficial projects like clean transportation, energy efficiency, renewable energy, and climate-resilient infrastructure. Since 2015, the green bond market in India has expanded gradually due to government programs, legal frameworks, and growing investor interest in the statement(Agrawal et al., 2024). The Reserve Bank of India and SEBI's supportive regulatory frameworks, as well as growing investor interest in sustainable finance, have all contributed to the green bond market's steady growth in India. India's fiscal and financial environment is changing quickly. India has committed to achieving net zero emissions by 2070 and reducing emissions intensity by 45% below 2005 levels by 2030, demonstrating its awareness of climate change and its resolve to seek "green growth" in its economy (Government of India, 2022).To achieve such lofty objectives, substantial financial support and mobilization through investments in clean technology, fuels, and sustainable infrastructure would be required. Crucially, in order to achieve net zero by 2050, India will need to spend an estimated USD 12.7 trillion, or around USD 470 billion year. To lower the nation's fiscal imbalance, the government has taken various actions. One significant change in this environment has been focused towards green bonds, which offer a creative means of funding green projects. Green bonds are a type of financing instrument that is issued to the fund environmental projects. Despite of the growing demand for sustainable finance solutions and the global shift towards environmental responsibility, the market for green bonds has expanded quickly. Banks are now major players in this market, issuing a significant amount of green bonds to funding environmentally friendly initiatives. The green bonds are used to motivate the private sector to invest in green projects, government initiatives can be catalysed. It may help balancing the borrowing and reduce the need for government subsidies. Green project have the potential to create a significant amount of jobs and promote innovation in the sector. Therefore funding through a green bonds has to reduce income inequality. Encourages innovation and technology transfer in green sectors. Additionally, green bonds promote innovation and the transfer of innovative green technology, bolstering India industrial base in emerging sectors like energy storage, smart grids and electric mobility. By lowering pollution levels, they can also helps to improve public health outcomes and air quality. By focusing investment on climate resilient infrastructure, green bonds enhance readiness for disasters and lessen financial losses from climate related calamities.

Issuers must include important disclosures in their offer documents, whether for a private placement or a public offering, in order to improve the efficiency of the process. Climate change is creating increasing financial challenges to both developed and developing nations. Green bonds are ideal for financing energy and water infrastructure, buildings, roads, railroads, airports, and other infrastructure while also producing benefits for society and the environment. Institutional investors are not just one group who are considering acquiring green bonds for all these reasons. Numerous studies conducted by prominent investment banks, such as Bank of America Merrill Lynch, Morgan Stanley, Barclays, and UBS, indicate that approximately 89% of all investors have exhibited interest in and familiarity with sustainable investing, and 65% actually engage in sustainable investing. Among those with significant net worth, this ratio rises to 66%. 92% of young professionals and millennials are aware of sustainable investments.

The downside risks of conventional fixed income instruments are reduced by the beneficial, climate-friendly spillovers of all the projects funded by green bonds. Because green bonds are highly transparent, investors can also measure the advantages of investing in them using easily accessible metrics (such as gigawatt hours (GWh) of clean energy produced or decreased CO2).

It also explores the ways in which macroeconomic factors like GDP and financial indicators like the Capital Adequacy Ratio (CAR), Total Assets (TA), Liquidity Ratio (LR), and Non-Performing Loans (NPL) interact to affect EBITDA, emphasizing the importance of sustainability in enhancing the efficiency of the banking industry (Chinavi charana& Chotiyaputta, 2024). The green bonds are fixed-income financial instruments that return their principle after they have remitted interest to their lenders for a given tenure. Green bonds, as a "socially responsible" investment, are identical to their traditional counterparts except for the targeted application of their proceeds to the financing or re-financing of "green" projects (Agarwal & Singh, 2018). In 2007, the European Investment Bank introduced the first "climate awareness bond." By 2023, the global green bond market had grown to a total issuance of USD 2.334 trillion. This study examines the process of issuing green bonds have affected the profitability of these banks by comparing their financial performance before and after getting entered into the green bond market and ESG score of the Banks in India. Banks can reach new investor segments, raise money for green projects, and strengthen their financial position by issuing green bonds and ESG Scores. Although it is widely accepted that green bonds improve banks' reputation capital and bring them into compliance with changing regulatory frameworks, more empirical study is needed to determine the precise impact on profitability. By analysing a few financial parameters of banks that issue green bonds over a six-year period, this article provides a comprehensive knowledge of how green bonds effect bank profitability. The sample consists of five major Indian banks that have actively issued green bonds. ICICI Bank, IDBI Bank, State Bank of India, Axis Bank, and Yes Bank are some of these financial institutions. These banks were selected due to their wide availability of financial data and their participation in the green bond market as signatories.Financial performance before and after green bond issue can be compared thanks to the sample. Key financial metrics like return on equity, return on assets, net interest margin (NIM), cost to income ratio (BOPO), capital adequacy ratio (CAR), gross non-performing assets (NPA), economic equity ratio, ESG Score, and interest coverage ratio are used to evaluate a bank's profitability.

2. LITERATURE REVIEW

I look at corporate green bonds, the proceeds of which go toward funding green initiatives. Over time, these bonds have grown in popularity, particularly in sectors where the environment has a significant financial impact on business operations. I demonstrate that investors react favorably to the announcement of the issuance; this reaction is more pronounced for bonds certified by third parties and for first-time issuers. Following issuance, the issuers see a rise in ownership by long-term and green investors and enhance their environmental performance (i.e., reduced CO2 emissions and higher environmental ratings). Overall, the results support a signaling theory, which holds that businesses can legitimately demonstrate their environmental commitment by issuing green bonds(KE & S, 2021).(*The Impact of Green Bonds on Corporate Environmental and Financial Performance | Managerial Finance | Emerald Publishing*, n.d.)

Since its launch in 2007, the green bond market has been expanding quickly on a global scale. We offer the first empirical analysis of the announcement returns and actual impacts of green bond issuance by companies across 28 nations between 2007 and 2017. We show that the issue of green bonds has a favorable impact on stock prices after assembling an extensive global dataset. Nevertheless, we do not consistently discover a significant premium for green bonds, indicating that the reduced cost of financing may not be the only factor driving the strong stock returns following green bond announcements(Tang & Zhang, 2020).

We examine the ownership and pricing of green bonds, the proceeds of which go toward environmental initiatives. We outline the US corporate and municipal green bond markets after providing an overview of the literature on green securities in general and green bonds in particular. The best chance for a thorough empirical analysis of how ownership and pricing vary from those of regular bonds is offered by green municipal bonds. Unless they are issued concurrently with regular bonds from the same issuer, in which case a premium gradually appears on the secondary market, green bonds are issued at a slight premium of several basis points above comparable ordinary bonds(Baker et al., 2022).

Environmental concern is one of the negative effects of industrial progress during the past century. Researchers and practitioners are attempting to investigate how funding for eco-friendly initiatives works and how it impacts its stakeholders. To the best of our knowledge, no literature study has been done to examine the elements linked to the expansion of green bonds and their effects on issuers' core performance metrics in order to achieve Environmental, Social, and Governance (ESG) goals(Agrawal et al., 2024). This review aims to close the gap in the research by categorizing studies according to and providing a thorough summary of the factors related to green bonds(Bhutta et al., 2022).

In this paper, we evaluate the key factors influencing bank profitability in five chosen CEE nations between 2004 and 2011. 143 commercial banks from Romania, Hungary, Poland, the Czech Republic, and Bulgaria are included in the sample. The return on average assets, return on average equity, and net interest margin are used as proxies for bank profitability. The outcomes demonstrate that the empirical findings align with the anticipated outcomes. While credit risk and inflation only affect the ROAA and ROAE, management effectiveness and capital adequacy growth affect bank profitability for all performance proxies. Banks with more capital adequacy tend to be more lucrative(Căpraru & Ihnatov, 2014)

Governments play a key role by creating the right financial and policy incentives for all involved parties. These incentives should include risk-mitigating guarantees for green bonds, particularly those aligned with national environmental and climate targets. By doing so, governments can attract private investment for climate change adaptation and mitigation projects, while also boosting foreign direct investment (FDI) (*The Impact of Green Bonds on Corporate Environmental and Financial Performance | Managerial Finance | Emerald Publishing*, n.d.)

. To develop a robust green bond market, governments, with the support of development banks, can help create a pipeline of green projects, encouraging private sector involvement in blended finance. Development banks can serve as intermediaries between the government, issuers, and investors, providing a platform for market growth(Weber & Saravade, 2019).

Officially, India entered the green bonds market in 2015 with the YES Bank issuing the first green bond with a maturity period of 10 years for financing renewable energy projects Since then, several banks and corporates have entered the green bonds market such as the EXIM bank, IDBI Bank, Axis Bank, PNB Housing Finance, ReNew Power, NTPC, IREDA, Greenko, etc. Several of these issuances have also been listed on international exchanges such as the London Stock Exchange and the Singapore Exchange(Singh & Shrivastava, 2024).

Green bonds can improve environmental performance, but only when supported by reliable third-party certification. However, they don't necessarily lead to clear financial benefits. This reliance on certification opens the door for some companies to take advantage of the green finance trend and engage in green washing. This suggests that the green bond market is still evolving and lacks sufficient oversight, allowing for potential misuse in the absence of strong regulation(KE & S, 2021).

The primary factors influencing banks' profitability in the EU27 between 2004 and 2011 are evaluated in this study. The factors that affect bank profitability are divided into two major categories: macroeconomic and industry-specific (external) factors and bank-specific (internal) factors. We use the return on average equity (ROAE) and return on average assets (ROAA) as proxies for bank profitability. The empirical results align with the anticipated outcomes. Bank profitability, including ROAA and ROAE, is influenced by a number of factors, including credit and liquidity risk, managerial effectiveness, company diversification, market concentration and competition, and economic growth. The beneficial impact of competition on bank profitability in the EU27 is an intriguing and significant finding(Petria et al., 2015).

An overview of theoretical and empirical research on bank performance and profitability is the goal of this paper. As a result, we explore theories and models pertaining to banking profitability and performance, offer empirical research on bank profitability, and outline the fundamentals of evaluating and modeling banking performance(FERROUHI, 2018).

An organization that deals with financial and monetary transactions, including deposits, loans, investments, and currency exchange, is called a bank. This industry provides essential financial services to the economy, promotes economic growth, allocates resources efficiently, lowers transaction costs, creates liquidity, facilitates economies of scale in investment, and distributes financial losses, among other functions (Haiss & Sümegi, Citation2008). It is imperative that this industry maintain a specific level of performance given the crucial role it serves(Isayas, 2022).

3. THEORETICAL FRAMEWORK

According to legitimacy theory, banks utilize green finance techniques to comply with legal and societal standards, which enhances their legitimacy and improves their ESG ratings. When considered collectively, these ideas make clear how the issuing of green bonds may impact both the financial and ESG performance of the banking sector.

4. RESEARCH GAP

1. Studies that are currently available seldom look at whether the issuing of green bonds affects bank-level profitability metrics like ROA, ROE, NIM, CAR, and NPA in the Indian banking industry.

2. Empirical evidence regarding the impact of green bond issuance on Indian banks' ESG performance is scarce, particularly when comparing pre- and post-issuance analysis.

5. RESEARCH OBJECTIVES

1. To compare important profitability metrics in order to assess the effect of green bond issuance on the financial performance of Indian banks.
2. To evaluate how the issuing of green bonds has affected the main Indian banks' ESG performance.
3. To compare the financial effects of green bond issuance trends across five major Indian banks between 2012 and 2023.

6. METHODOLOGY

Leading Indian banks, including Yes Bank and IDBI, began selling green bonds in 2015. Axis Bank joined in 2016, SBI in 2018, and ICICI in 2020. The study's time frame is 2012–2023. It is simpler to assess how profitability and ESG performance changed after these issuances because to the study's three-year pre- and post-issuance comparison. This event-based approach reflects the paradigm used in sustainability-finance studies, when long-term data or causal tests are difficult. They were looked at because important financial metrics including ROA, ROE, NIM, CAR, BOPO, GNPA, EVE, and Interest Coverage capture profitability, efficiency, asset quality, capital sufficiency, and risk management—all of which are crucial areas affected by green finance. ESG scores were also taken into account because environmental and governance issues are strongly linked to the objectives of green bonds. Due to the scarce and inconsistent data across banks and time periods, descriptive and comparative analysis were used over sophisticated statistical tests.

6.1 Analytical Tools

- Return on Assets (ROA) = $\frac{\text{Net Income}}{\text{Average Total Assets}}$
- Return on Equity (ROE) = $\frac{\text{Net Income}}{\text{Shareholder Equity}}$
- NIM = $\frac{\text{Net Interest Income}}{(\text{Average interest} - \text{Earning assets})}$
- **BOPO (Operating Expenses to Operating Income):** BOPO stands for Operating Expenses to Operating Income. The percentage of a bank's rev-

enue that is allocated to operating expenses is determined by this important efficiency ratio in banking and finance.

- BOPO $= \frac{\text{Operating Expenses}}{\text{Operating Income}} * 100$
- **Capital Adequacy Ratio (CAR):** The Capital Adequacy Ratio (CAR) assesses a bank's ability to sustain losses, maintain stability, and protect depositors in unpredictable or stressful financial times by comparing its capital to its risk-weighted assets.
- CAR $= \frac{(\text{Tier 1 capital} + \text{Tier 2 capital})}{\text{Risk Weighed Assets}}$
- **Gross Non Performing Assets:** In the banking sector, gross non-performing assets are the total value of loans that a bank cannot expect to be fully repaid, such as those that are past due by more than 90 days. how many bad loans a bank had in total before any changes were made.
- Gross NPA ratio $= \frac{\text{Total Gross NPAs}}{\text{Total Assets}} *100$
- **Economic Value of Equity (EVE):** The present value difference between the cash flows from assets and liabilities is the Economic Value of Equity (EVE), a long-term indicator of a bank's financial health that is used to evaluate interest rate risk.
- Economic Value of Equity (EVE) $= \frac{\text{Shareholders Funds}}{\text{Total assets}}$
- **Interest Covering Ratio:** The Interest Coverage Ratio is a financial metric that shows how easily a company can pay its interest expenses out of operating profits. It demonstrates how capable the business is of repaying debt.
- Interest Covering Ratio $= \frac{\text{Earning before interest and Taxes}}{\text{Interest expense}}$

7. DATA ANALYSIS

7.1 Green Social and Sustainable (GSS) bonds in India

Table 1. Green, Social and Sustainability Bonds in India

Years	Green (USD Billion)	Social (USD Billion)	Sustainability (USD Billion)	Total (USD Billion)
2015	1	0	0	1
2016	1.5	0	0	1.5
2017	3.8	0	0	3.8
2018	0.4	0	0	0.4
2019	2.7	0	0	2.7

Years	Green (USD Billion)	Social (USD Billion)	Sustainability (USD Billion)	Total (USD Billion)
2020	1	0	0	1
2021	6	0.6	0.6	7.2

Source: Climate Bonds Initiative website

Figure 1. Green, Social and Sustainability Bonds in India

Source: *Based on excel results*

As per the data depicted in table 1 between 2015 and 2021, India's sustainable bond market exhibited a distinct upward trend, with green bonds accounting for the majority of all issuances. The profits from the issuance of sustainability bonds are utilized to fund or refinance a mix of social and environmental initiatives. These bonds should adhere to the ICMA Sustainability Bond Guidelines, which are in line with both the GBP and SBP, and can be issued by businesses, governments, and municipalities for assets and projects. They might be secured with security on a particular asset, unsecured, or supported by the government or business issuer's creditworthiness. Like green bonds, the issuing of social bonds is guided by a set of voluntary rules, in this instance the ICMA's Social Bond Principles (SBP), which are intended to increase market openness and disclosure. In addition to providing investors with the data they need to assess the social impact of their investments, the SBP outlines recommended practices for issuing social bonds. COVID-related connections are a new kind of social bond that has just emerged. The proceeds from these bonds are primarily intended to mitigate COVID-19-related socioeconomic difficulties, with a particular focus on the most affected groups.

7.2 Corporate Driving Green Bonds Issuance-Public and Private

Table 2. Public and Private Corporates

Issuer Category	Green bonds Issuance (USD Billion)
Private Non-Financial Corporates	7.98
Government-Backed Entities	7.56
Private Financial Corporates	2.73
Development Banks	2.73

Source: climate Bonds Initiative website

Table 2, shows The kinds of companies that issue green bonds and the total amount they have issued, expressed in USD billion, are included in the text. It demonstrates that private non-financial corporations are the biggest issuers of green bonds, with government-backed organizations coming in second. In comparison, development banks and private financial corporations have issued less money. This classification makes it easier to identify the kinds of issuers that are actively using green bonds to raise money for ecologically friendly projects. It essentially divides the market for green bonds according to the kind of issuer and the size of their issuance.

7.3 Green Bonds Market Participation by India Bank

Table 3. Total green bond issuance form the major banks

Bank	Total Green Bond Issuance 2015 -2023 (in Billions USD)
Yes Bank Limited	0.26
Axis Bank Limited	0.6
State Bank of India	1.05
ICICI Bank Limited	1.4
IDBI Bank Limited	0.35

Source: Banks Official websites and climate Bonds Initiative Website

Figure 2. Total green bond issuance form the major banks

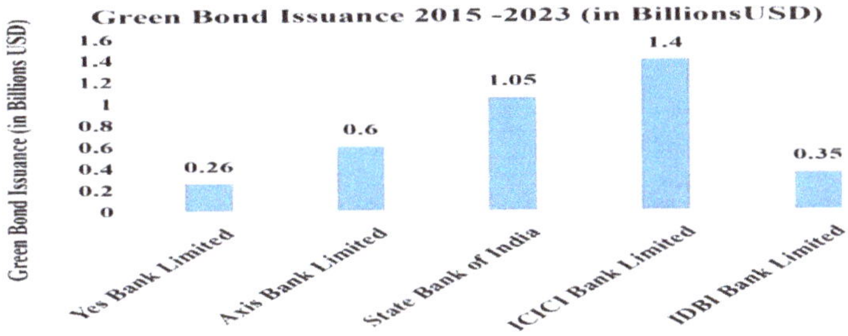

Source:*Based on excel results*

Table 3 shows data between 2015 and 2023, listed Indian banks issued a total of almost USD 3.66 billion in green bonds, demonstrating their active participation in the market. With USD 1.4 billion, ICICI Bank Limited was in the lead, followed by State Bank of India with USD 1.05 billion and Axis Bank Limited with USD 0.6 billion. The YES Bank Limited: USD 0.26 billion; in 2015, it introduced India's first green bond. The IDBI Bank Limited: $0.35 billion USD. This is consistent with the private sector's (84%) emphasis on renewable energy driving India's overall green bond growth to USD 21 billion by 2023.a consistent improvement in the country's sustainable finance environment from 2015 to 2023 in the green bond issuance patterns of major Indian banks. Three companies have recently issued Green Bonds in India; their brief information are listed below. In February 2015, Yes Bank issued the country's first green bond, a 10-year issue worth Rs 1000 crore. The profits from the over two times oversubscribed offer will be used to finance sustainable energy initiatives like solar, wind, and biomass projects. Additionally, in August 2015, Yes Bank released a second issue of Green Bonds, a core 10-year issue for Rs 315. The International Finance Corporation subscribed to the full issuance. (ii)The first green bonds issued by an Indian corporate issuer were issued by CLP India.

7.4 Comparative Overview Analysis of Green Bond Issuance Among the Major Banks in the Indian Banking Sector

The duration of the study is established by the years when particular banks issued their initial green bonds. The first green bond was issued by Yes Bank Limited in February 2015, and IDBI Bank Limited followed suit in November 2015. February 2016 saw the debut of Axis Bank Limited in the green bond market. The first green bond was issued by the State Bank of India in 2018, and ICICI Bank Limited did the same in 2020. Because of this, the research covers the years 2015–2020, which corresponds to the first green bonds that these large banks issued.

Table 4. Comparative overview of green bond issuance among the major Bank in India.

Bank		YesBank Limited	Axis BankLimited	State Bank OfIndia	ICICIBankLimited	IDBI Bank Limited
Return on Assets	Before green bond	1.53%	1.77%	0.52%	0.07%	0.54%
	After green bond	1.70%	0.80%	0.07%	0.84%	-0.72%
Return on Equity	Before green bond	24.30%	19.10%	8.72%	6.70%	8.78%
	After green bond	20.13%	8.41%	1.48%	11.37%	-14.27%
Net Interest Margin	Before green bond	2.87%	3.75%	2.99%	3.30%	1.68%
	After green bond	3.33%	3.67%	2.35%	3.79%	1.79%
BOPO	Before green bond	49.48%	72.34%	63.33%	88.13%	58.83%
	After green bond	51.91%	72.89%	52.86%	55.49%	66.90%
Capital Adequacy Ratio	Before green bond	16.87%	14.51%	12.74%	17.57%	13.13%
	After green bond	16.37%	15.60%	12.82%	18.13%	11.38%
Gross NPA	Before green bond	0.24%	1.21%	5.88%	7.81%	3.33%
	After green bond	0.90%	4.49%	8.20%	4.70%	12.67%
Economic Value of Equity	Before green bond	6.25%	10.35%	6.45%	12.05%	6.82%
	After green bond	9.06%	9.43%	6.07%	10.69%	6.82%
InterestCoveringRatio	Beforegreenbond	50.69%	59.13%	26.44%	15.06%	30.43%
	Aftergreenbond	71.34%	60.01%	20.02%	13.95%	39.77%

Source: Banks Official websites and Money control, Investing.com

As per the data in table 4 the comparative analysis of major Indian banks reveals mixed financial outcomes following the issuance of green bonds. Yes Bank shows marginal improvement in profitability indicators, with ROA rising from 1.53% to 1.70% and NIM increasing from 2.87% to 3.33%. However, ROE declines slightly, suggesting that although asset utilisation improved, shareholder returns moderated due to rising equity or provisioning. Its BOPO ratio marginally worsens, while gross NPAs rise, indicating emerging asset quality pressure despite better interest coverage and equity value after issuance.After issuing green bonds, Axis Bank's earnings significantly decreased. Rising NPAs, which rise from 1.21% to 4.49%, are the main cause of the dramatic decline in ROA from 1.77% to 0.80% and ROE from 19.10% to 8.41%. This suggests that the impact of green bonds is mostly dependent on the issuing bank's institutional strength and financial stability rather than just the bond itself.

7.5 Sovereign Green Bonds

A major milestone for the Indian green debt market was the launch of Sovereign Green Bonds, with the Government of India issuing INR 16,000 crore (USD 1.94

billion) to fund public sector green infrastructure in FY 2022–23. In FY 2023-24, the Government further issued Sovereign Green Bonds worth INR 20,000 crores in four tranches. The Nifty India Sovereign Green Bond Jan 2033 Index aims to track the performance of a portfolio of Government Securities (G-Secs) issued as Sovereign Green Bonds (SGrBs), with maturities occurring in the twelve-month period leading up to January 31, 2033.This helps in looking at the other side of the green finance in India.

Figure 3. NIFTY INDIA SOVEREIGN GREEN BOND JAN 2033-Return %

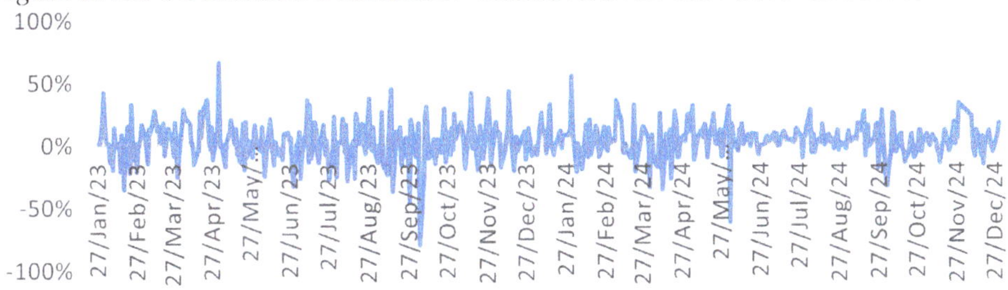

Source: NSE Website

7.6 ESG (Environment Social Governance) Scores for Banks

ESG (environmental, social, and governance) scores evaluate how well a business performs in these domains. Excellent sustainability and moral behavior are demonstrated by high ratings, whereas higher danger is indicated by low levels. By assessing long-term risks and encouraging open and sustainable business practices, these rankings assist investors in making well-informed decisions.

Table 5. Comparative Analysis ESG Scores of Major Banks in India.

Bank	CRISIL ESG Score	ESG Risk Score	Sustainalytics ESG Risk Rating	S&P Global CSA	CDP Rating
YES Bank	69	67.44	21.9	72	A-
Axis Bank	71	74.2	24.2	54	C
ICICI Bank	69	68.7	24	42	C

continued on following page

Table 5. Continued

Bank	CRISIL ESG Score	ESG Risk Score	Sustainalytics ESG Risk Rating	S&P Global CSA	CDP Rating
IDBI Bank	63	43.3	31.2	41	A+
SBI	65	23	27	49	B

Source: Sustainalytics website and S&P Global CSA

Figure 4. Comparative Analysis ESG Scores of Major Banks in the India

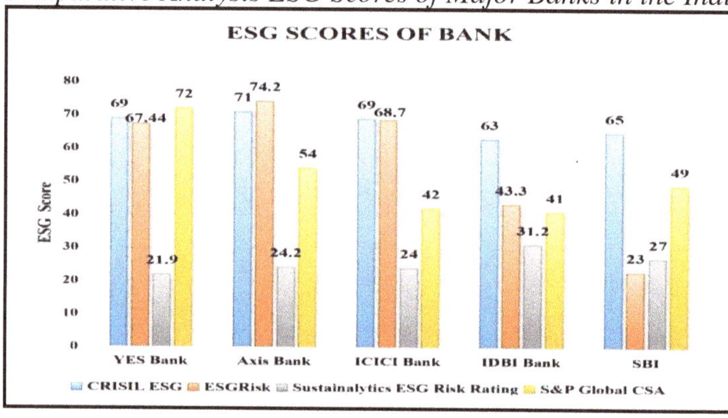

As per the data in the table 5 the comparison of major Indian banks' ESG scores reveals differing degrees of dedication and performance in the areas of governance, social responsibility, and the environment. With a strong S&P Global CSA score of 72, an A- rating in CDP, and a high CRISIL ESG Score of 69, YES Bank stands out as one of the better performers, demonstrating responsible environmental practices and active climate disclosure. Businesses with better environmental scores routinely receive higher ESG ratings, demonstrating the increasing focus on resource efficiency, sustainability, and carbon footprint reduction in financial institutions. This implies that a company's ESG position is greatly improved by strong environmental policies, such as climate risk management, green financing, and sustainable investment strategies. The significant impact of environmental variables highlights the growing demand from customers, investors, and authorities to give eco-friendly activities top priority. The need for financial institutions, particularly NBFCs, to incorporate environmental sustainability into their fundamental business strategy is highlighted by the fact that social and governance aspects have a comparatively less impact on ESG performance.

8. CONCLUSION

A traditional bond is a type of financial product in which investors lend money to the issuer, which is typically a government or corporation. Traditional bond proceeds can be utilized for a number of things, such as capital projects, debt refinancing, ordinary running costs, or any other issuer financial need. Conversely, a green bond is a kind of bond intended to raise money for activities and projects that will improve the environment. The issuer pledges to use the money for environmentally friendly projects, including energy efficiency, renewable energy, green buildings, sustainable agriculture, and other programs meant to slow down global warming or advance environmental preservation. Additionally, investors evaluate the particular environmental goals of the projects that the bonds are meant to fund. As per the results ICICI bank has been making the effective use of green capital, with generating high profits, less Non Performing Assets, better Capital Adequacy cost efficiency. On the hands Axis Bank, SBI, and IDBI Bank has mixed results, had rising NPAs, and major governance issues. IDBI Bank had the highest decrease in ROA and ROE after issuance, indicating higher risk-management issues even after issuing the green bonds. These findings show that green bonds function best when combined with prudent asset management, competent governance, and a strong financial base. The market for green bonds has grown at an exponential rate. With US$1 trillion in total issuance since the market's founding in 2007, it accomplished its most significant milestone in early December 2020. According to Climate Bonds, the green bond market saw a 49% growth rate in the five years before to 2021, and their estimate indicates that by 2023, the sector's annual issuance might surpass $1 trillion.

Through initiatives like the Task Force on Climate-related Financial Disclosures (TCFD), investors are starting to report on the risks that climate change poses to their portfolios. Furthermore, the investment community is under pressure from stakeholders to implement more stringent environmental, social, and governance (ESG) rules.

REFERENCES

Agrawal, M., Goyal, A., Akhtar, A., & Abbas, H. (2024). Green Bond: A Government Initiative Towards Sustainable Finance. In *Issues of Sustainability in AI and New-Age Thematic Investing* (pp. 124–137). IGI Global Scientific Publishing. DOI: 10.4018/979-8-3693-3282-5.ch008

Baker, M., Bergstresser, D., Serafeim, G., & Wurgler, J. (2022). The Pricing and Ownership of US Green Bonds. *Annual Review of Financial Economics, 14*(Volume 14, 2022), 415–437. DOI: 10.1146/annurev-financial-111620-014802

Bhutta, U. S., Tariq, A., Farrukh, M., Raza, A., & Iqbal, M. K. (2022). Green bonds for sustainable development: Review of literature on development and impact of green bonds. *Technological Forecasting and Social Change*, *175*, 121378. DOI: 10.1016/j.techfore.2021.121378

FERROUHI. E. M. (2018, April 1). *Determinants of banks' profitability and performance: An overview* [MPRA Paper]. https://mpra.ub.uni-muenchen.de/89470/

Isayas, Y. N. (2022). Determinants of banks' profitability: Empirical evidence from banks in Ethiopia. *Cogent Economics & Finance*, *10*(1), 2031433. DOI: 10.1080/23322039.2022.2031433

Petria, N., Capraru, B., & Ihnatov, I. (2015). Determinants of Banks' Profitability: Evidence from EU 27 Banking Systems. *Procedia Economics and Finance*, *20*, 518–524. DOI: 10.1016/S2212-5671(15)00104-5

Singh, U. V., & Shrivastava, M. K. (2024). POLICY BRIEF ACCELERATING. *Growth*.

Tang, D. Y., & Zhang, Y. (2020). Do shareholders benefit from green bonds? *Journal of Corporate Finance*, *61*, 101427. DOI: 10.1016/j.jcorpfin.2018.12.001

The impact of green bonds on corporate environmental and financial performance | Managerial Finance | Emerald Publishing. (n.d.). Retrieved November 19, 2025, from https://www.emerald.com/mf/article-abstract/47/10/1486/289997/The-impact-of-green-bonds-on-corporate?redirectedFrom=fulltext

Weber, O., & Saravade, V. (2019). *Current Development and Their Future Olaf Weber and Vasundhara Saravade. 210.*

Chapter 4
Bridging Informal Economies:
FinTech Innovation and Street-Vendor Financial Inclusion in India

Ishika Saha
http://orcid.org/0009-0007-9527-6155
Malaviya National Institute of Technology, Jaipur, India

Shweta Sharma
http://orcid.org/0000-0003-2340-4887
Malaviya National Institute of Technology, Jaipur, India

Shridev Devji
http://orcid.org/0000-0001-8212-8435
Malaviya National Institute of Technology, Jaipur, India

ABSTRACT

Financial inclusion is fundamental for equal opportunities, economic development and resilience for individuals and nations. Fintech innovation has significantly enhanced this critical objective in the current digital age. This chapter explores the concepts of fintech innovation and financial inclusion. We analyze their dynamic interplay to include the underserved populations in India, especially Street vendors who have historically faced exclusion from the formal financial ecosystem. Subsequently, it assesses the potential and progress of India's financial inclusion policies, digital public infrastructure and fintech solutions in addressing challenges like digital inclusion, infrastructure issues, and economic vulnerability. India's case highlights the potential of combining technology with policy to advance inclusive financial systems.

DOI: 10.4018/979-8-3373-5047-9.ch004

1. INTRODUCTION

Financial inclusion refers to providing equal access to financial services to every individual, with a special emphasis on those who are excluded from the society. The spread of financial exclusion in the 1990s sparked the discussion of financial inclusion in academic and policy circles. It was proposed as a solution to the problem of financial exclusion's harmful effects. In 1997, the term "financial inclusion" was first used in UK public policy (Veena M., 2022). However, it gained prominence and became a primary focus for global economies after the 2008 crisis. The crisis revealed that affordable access to financial services is vital to improve macroeconomic stability, reduce systemic risks, and increase resilience to shocks in society (Han & Melecky, 2013; Barajas et al., 2020). Recognizing the significance, financial inclusion was incorporated in the official agenda of the United Nations in 2015. It is regarded as an important means to achieve Sustainable Development Goals (SDGs) like poverty reduction (SDG 1), gender equality (SDG 5), economic growth (SDG 8), and inclusive industrialization (SDG 9) (United Nations, 2015).

India's journey has also been in alignment with the global trends, but with its own distinct nuances. Before the 1990s, the focus was to provide credit to the poor and marginalized sector of society. A number of organizations have been set up to deliver credit, such as State Bank in 1955, commercial banks were nationalized in 1969 & 1980, establishment of regional and cooperative rural banks in 1976 (Sakariya, 2014). Reforms were made after liberalization in 1991, which included priority-sector lending requirements and private bank licensing. The Self-Help Group-Bank Linkage Programme (SHG-BLP) of 1992 encouraged millions of rural women to participate in formal banking through community-based microfinance (NIRDP et al., 2019). India's financial inclusion's latest phase is focused on digital innovations. It was led by the introduction of Aadhaar, a nationwide biometric identity system introduced in 2010. It helped to fill the identification gaps and led the remarkable campaign of account opening, enrolling millions of unbanked citizens (Rao & Nair, 2019; Ministry of Electronics and Information Technology, 2024). Since then, tools such as mobile banking, UPI, and real-time payment systems have further enhanced digital access. These platforms provide quickness, safety, and convenience without the need for a bank or physical money (Vidani, 2024).

Globally, the way people get access to finance has been changed by the fintech industry. In 2017, the G20 Global Partnership for Financial Inclusion (GPFI) formally recognized the pivotal role of digital financial solutions in making financial inclusion accessible worldwide. Innovations like mobile money demonstrated potent inclusive effects by integrating informal workers and the marginalized into formal networks (Jacolin et al. 2021). This helps to provide them with opportunities to access credit, insurance, etc. (Tetteh et al., 2025). All this was unexpectedly accelerated by

COVID-19 and brought a new age of fintech innovation and digital transformation (Sahay et al., 2020; Chaddha & Jain, 2024). The ways people gain access to financial services follow different tracks that depend on each country's institutions and its use of technology. Many developing countries have let mobile phone companies run electronic money platforms or have bundled payments inside a wallet. India has taken the opposite route, where banks stay at the centre and the whole system rests on public digital infrastructure, that is, the Jan Dhan-Aadhaar-Mobile trio plus the Unified Payments Interface. This lets banks open accounts quickly, the government sends subsidies straight to the account and the account holder can move money with a few screen taps (International Monetary Fund, 2023; Atlantic Council, 2024). The World Bank Global Findex Database (2025) shows the result, in 2011, only about thirty five out of every hundred Indian adults owned an account. By 2024, the figure had reached eighty nine out of every hundred. Across all developing economies, the average is roughly seventy one out of every hundred adults. Peer countries remain far behind, Bangladesh reported thirty five out of every hundred adults besides Nigeria reports forty five out of every hundred adults (World Bank, 2025; Nigerian Central Bank, 2024). In Sub-Saharan Africa, Kenya's M-Pesa mobile money platform reached 82% of adults by 2024, showing that phone companies can deliver wide access to finance (World Bank, 2024). Nigeria's use of digital payments rose faster than in any other country, with 45% each year but only about 35% of adults own an account, far below India's 89% (Nigerian Central Bank, 2024). Southeast Asia followed a different path. Indonesia has 92% of adults using mobile wallets with apps like GoPay, while the Philippines and Vietnam has integrated digital payments into buses, trains and online shopping (GSMA Intelligence, 2024). However, South Asia still faces sharp gaps. In Bangladesh, only 35% of adults own an account and among women, the share is merely 25%. Pakistan shows a similar split women hold only 30% of accounts. By contrast, India has almost closed the gap, with 89.2% of women and 89% of men owning an account in 2024 (World Bank, 2024; World Bank Global Findex Database, 2025). Taken together, these figures show that India's publicly backed, bank-centred digital system has spread access more evenly than systems that rely on phone firms or private apps elsewhere in the Global South.

In spite of the progress achieved by India, many other issues still persist. According to the World Bank's Global Findex 2025, India has the highest number of inactive bank accounts globally, about 16%, which is double the global average of 6%, showing that account opening does not ensure account usage (World Bank Global Findex Database, 2025). Additionally, distrust in formal institutions persists, financial literacy gaps remain substantial, technological accessibility issues continue, and grievance redressal mechanisms remain inadequate (Aziz & Naima, 2021; World Bank Global Findex Database, 2025). Street vendors are one such group that face these interconnected challenges all over the world (Affandi & Malik, 2020; Munishi et al., 2021) along with legal, economic, and social problems, which adversely impact their livelihoods and well-being, as well as their capacity to work safely and profitably (Roever & Skinner, 2016). In India, Street vendors, unofficial, unrecognized, and without assets, have been on the sidelines of formal financial services for decades. However, they are essential to India's informal urban economy, sustaining millions of livelihoods (Kumar et al., 2023). They are estimated to make up about 10% of the urban workforce (Sinha, 2025). These vendors improve local access and food security by offering reasonably priced goods and services that meet city dweller's daily needs (Sangeetha & Menaka, 2022; Kumar & Sah, 2025). A large portion of the urban poor is self-employed by means of street vending since they are not able to access formal jobs (Saha, 2016). Moreover, it is a powerful tool to enhance social mobility, reduce poverty, and create opportunities for economic upliftment for women, minorities, and migrant workers (Jamir & Pongen, 2022; Kumar & Rani, 2025). The government of India launched the Street Vendors (Protection of Livelihood) Act in 2014, which helped in the protection of Street vendors and gave them legal rights to function. Over the years, efforts have been made to enable Street vendors in the financial system and in the digital economy. The PM SVANidhi scheme is the most well-known example, initiated in 2020 to support Street vendors in getting back on their feet following the COVID-19 pandemic. The scheme provides loans without the need for collateral and cashback rewards in order to encourage the use of digital payment methods. These initiatives have provided Street vendors with opportunities for social inclusion and economic prosperity.

This chapter explores how fintech innovations connect with financial inclusion, with special focus on Street vendors. It comprehensively reviews government reports, policy documents, and existing literature. It analyzes how digital transformation, institutional frameworks, and socio-economic factors are creating new paths for inclusive and strong growth in India.

2. CONCEPT OF FINANCIAL INCLUSION

Financial inclusion is a concept of continuous global interest due to its multi-faceted linkage with economic development, growth and poverty reduction (Van et al., 2019; Omar & Inaba, 2020). It has been revisited and redefined by various institutions and scholars over the years In the past literature, the following definitions have been provided by various global and Indian authorities. Table 1 presents definitions of financial inclusion from international institutions. Table 2 provides definitions from Indian authorities and committees.

Table 1. Definitions of financial inclusion in the Global context

Institution/Author	Definition
UNSGSA (Máxima, 2011)	*"Financial inclusion means universal access, at a reasonable cost, to a wide range of financial services to everyone needing them, provided by a diversity of sound and sustainable institutions."*
OECD/INFE (Atkinson & Messy, 2013)	*"Financial inclusion refers to the process of promoting affordable, timely and adequate access to a wide range of regulated financial products and services and broadening their use by all segments of society...with a view to promote financial well-being as well as economic and social inclusion."*

Table 2.

Institution/ Author	Definition
World Bank (2014)	*"Financial inclusion means that individuals and businesses have access to and use affordable financial products and services that meet their needs, which are delivered in a responsible and sustainable way."*
World Bank (2025)	*"Financial inclusion means that adults have access to and can effectively use a range of appropriate financial services. Such services must be provided responsibly and safely to the consumer and sustainably to the provider."*

Table 3. Definitions of financial inclusion in the Indian context

Institution/Author	Definition
Rangarajan Committee (2008)	*"Financial inclusion is the process of ensuring access to financial services, timely and adequate credit for vulnerable groups such as weaker sections and low-income groups at an affordable cost."*
Planning Commission (2009)	*"Financial inclusion refers to universal access to a wide range of financial services at a reasonable cost."*
Chakrabarty (2013)	*"Financial Inclusion is the process of ensuring access to appropriate financial products and services needed by all sections of society at an affordable cost in a fair and transparent manner by regulated, mainstream institutional players."*
Mohanty Committee (2015)	*"Financial inclusion is convenient access to a basket of basic formal financial products and services to small and marginal farmers and low-income households at reasonable cost with adequate protection...with a greater reliance on technology."*

This shows, in the simplest form, financial inclusion is the ability to access and to use basic financial services such as payments, bank accounts, savings, insurance and credit by all without any discrimination based on age, gender, class or income. The main aim of financial inclusion is to bring the underserved and vulnerable sections of society into the formal economic system by reducing barriers to economic participation and opportunity (Mishra et al., 2024). It helps to make the population and the economy as a whole more resilient to crises and emergencies (Hussain et al., 2018; Pomeroy et al., 2020).

2.1. Importance of Financial Inclusion

The impact of financial inclusion on socioeconomic growth is well established with thorough data supporting this claim. The inclusion leads to economic growth by making credit, savings, and payment services accessible to the population. As a result, people can freely engage in economic activities, invest in businesses or education, save for the future, and protect themselves from financial difficulties. Several studies using both global and country-level data have found a strong positive relation between financial inclusion and economic growth. The correlation is especially strong in low-income and emerging markets where access to financial services is scarce. (Van et al., 2021; Azimi, 2022). Moreover, the relationship between start-ups and financial inclusion is another aspect of this interaction. It facilitates the business start-up and the subsequent growth. The outcome of this process is employment creation as well as an improvement in the economic conditions. Studies in different areas have demonstrated that access to financial products and credit is indispensable in entrepreneurship (Charfeddine & Zaouali, 2022; Sharma et al., 2023). Similarly, poverty and income inequality reduction are facilitated through financial inclusion. Availability of loans and active bank account usage can help poor and rural people to break the cycle of poverty. Along with saving and borrowing activities, that can assist individuals in managing their finances and continue smooth consumption (Neaime & Gaysset, 2017; Omar & Inaba, 2020).

They also have equally important role in significantly improving women's social and economic status. Schemes targeting women for financial inclusion have proven to be successful for women of poor households. They provide them with the opportunity to save, invest and contribute to household income by granting them financial independence. (Swarmy, 2014; Bhatia & Singh, 2019). It is also noted by the IMF, World Bank and RBI that financial inclusion has the potential to reduce gender disparities and promote women's entrepreneurship as well (Hendriks, 2019; Bin-Humam et al., 2023). Finally, financial stability and resilience are improved when a larger base of depositors is attained through financial inclusion. Banks benefit from having a varied and reliable source of funding, making them less vulnerable to unexpected withdrawals and liquidity shocks (World Bank, 2024). Also, ensures protection for vulnerable customers and helps households manage unexpected expenses while minimizing financial risks. Thus, well-regulated financial inclusion policies can help to create a more sustainable and resilient financial system in addition to promoting social welfare (Danisman & Tarazi, 2020; Jungo et al., 2022).

2.2. State of Financial Inclusion in India

Financial inclusion is one of the prominent motives of India since the 2000s. To achieve this, various efforts have been made through different schemes and policies. As a result, India has steadily improved its financial inclusion. According to the Reserve Bank of India's Financial Inclusion Index, FI has gone up from 60.1 in March 2023 to 67 in March 2025. This improvement is mainly contributed by increase in the usage and quality of financial services (RBI, 2025). Table 3 shows the RBI's financial inclusion index over the years.

Table 4. Financial Inclusion Index by RBI

Years	Financial Inclusion Index
2021	53.90
2022	56.40
2023	60.10
2024	64.20
2025	67.00

Source: RBI, 2022-2025

Figure 1. Financial Inclusion in Southeastern Countries (increase in % inclusion from 2011 to 2024:

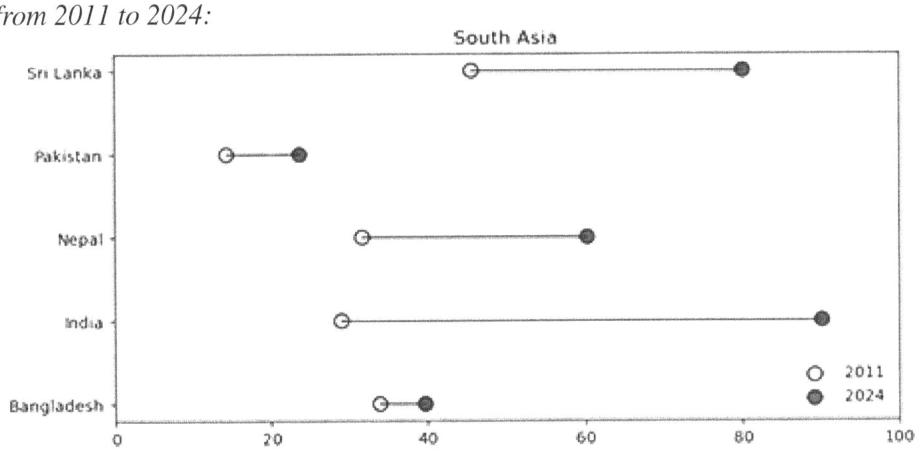

Source: World Bank Global Findex Report, 2025

In 2011, less than four in ten adults held a formal financial account. By 2021, that share had climbed to 78 percent, doubling over the past decade (World Bank Global Findex Database, 2021).

Figure 1 illustrates that account ownership has grown a lot in South Asia over the past ten years. In global standing, India is the leading economy in South Asia for financial inclusion. Figure 2 shows the increase in account ownership in India over the years. India's inclusion rate rose by more than 50 percentage points between 2011 and 2024, much faster than that of its neighbours. It had a 89% rate of account access for adults in 2024, which is above the global average of 79%. This large growth in account ownership has also resulted in reducing the gender gap from 17% in 2011 to insignificant, with 89.2% women having a bank account in 2024. Hence, it may be claimed that account ownership worldwide has been largely responsible by India (World Bank Global Findex Database, 2025).

Figure 2. Account Ownership % of adults in India

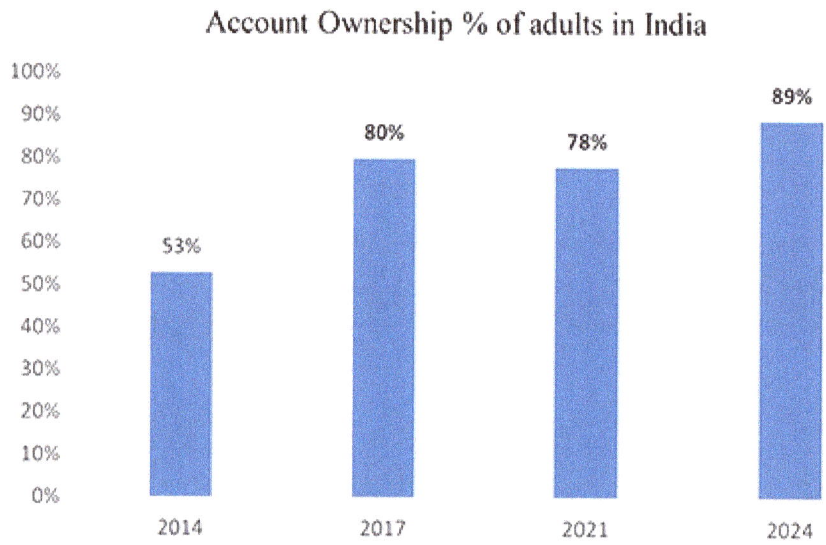

Source: World Bank Global Findex Report, 2025

This expansion in bank accounts can be traced back to Indian government's policy of 2014 Pradhan Mantri Jan Dhan Yojna, which focused on account ownership for the unbanked adults. It had a substantial effect on access. The number of bank accounts rose from nearly 15.7 crore in March 2015 to a total of 54.58 crore accounts in January 2025. Total deposits in PMJDY accounts have also risen by around 15 times from 15,670 crore to 246,595 crore. Women held 55.7 percent of all PMJDY accounts and two-thirds of accounts were in semi-urban and rural areas. Thereby providing inclusion to the formal banking system on a large scale. This is facilitated by no minimum balance accounts, insurance and free RuPay cards; approximately 36 crores have been issued (Mof, 2025). Table 4 depicts the distribution of beneficiaries, deposits and Rupay cards issued under PMJDY. The total number of bank accounts increased from 46.3 crores in 2022 to 55.83 crores in 2025, growth of almost 21 percent over the three years (Ministry of Finance, 2025). Rural and semi-urban areas have contributed about two-thirds of total accounts, 37.26 crores in 2025 as opposed to 18.57 crores in urban and metro areas, demonstrating the success of PMJDY in accessing the unbanked population (PMJDY Reports, 2025). The proportion of women to the total accounts remains significant 55 to 57 percent of total accounts, approximately 31.13 crores in 2025. Thus, they are the main beneficiaries of the programme. The high female share of accounts is a good indication of PMJDY's gender, inclusive feature, which requires women to be the primary account holders in several welfare schemes even though it has been pointed out that further investigation is necessary to establish the extent of women's financial independence (World Bank, 2024). The volume of deposits in PMJDY also increased from 1.72 lakh crore in 2022 to 2.63 lakh crore in 2025, a 52 percent rise with 12.5 percent compound annual growth. This indicates that the households that have newly come under the formal financial system are actively using their accounts for savings. Furthermore, the number of RuPay debit cards issued also increased by the same proportion from 31. 95 crore in 2022 to 38. 48 crore in 2025, a 21 percent rise, thus the digital enablement seems to be on the rise. Nevertheless, roughly 15 percent of PMJDY account holders do not have active RuPay cards. The difference here reveals the access usage gap, which is still a very big problem for policymakers (MicroSave Consulting, 2023; World Bank Global Findex Database, 2025).

Table 5. PMJDY data on bank accounts opened and RuPay card issued (2022–2025)

Year	Rural/Semi-urban (Cr)	Urban/Metro (Cr)	Female (Cr)	Total (Cr)	Deposits (Cr)	RuPay Cards (Cr)
2022	30.93	15.37	25.73	46.3	1,72,848	31.95
2023	33.61	16.48	27.85	50.09	2,03,505	34.85
2024	35.37	17.76	29.56	53.13	2,31,236	36.14
2025	37.26	18.57	31.13	55.83	2,63,065	38.48

Source: PMJDY, 2022-25

In alignment with PMJDY, Stand Up India was launched in 2016. The scheme aimed to promote entrepreneurship among the marginalized women and SC/ST citizens. Table 5 shows that, since its launch in April 2016 through June 2024, the Stand-Up India Scheme has approved a total of 235,463 loans to women and SC/

ST entrepreneurs. The annual loan approvals have been on a downtrend after the FY 2016-17, and reached a minimum point in the FY 2020- 21, which might be explained by the COVID-19 situation. However, they surged again in FY 2022-23 and FY 2023-24, with 7,152 loans approved in the first quarter of FY 2024-25. It should be noted that although the approved loans have increased, there is still a significant difference between the number of approved loans and the amounts that have actually been given out. The disbursement rates over the years have been consistently 10 to 50 percent lower than the approved amounts. The biggest shortfalls occurred during FY 2022 and FY 2023, when only about half of the approved funds were eventually disbursed (Mof, 2024).

Table 5. Year-wise Loans Sanctioned vs. Disbursed (April 2016–June 2024)

Financial Year	Loans Sanctioned	Loans Disbursed
2016-17	37 875	33 504
2017-18	33 041	26 039
2018-19	22 224	15 898
2019-20	20 256	13 483
2020-21	15 616	10 441
2021-22	19 749	12 259
2022-23	39 907	19 872
2023-24	39 643	17 374
2024-25 (till June 2024)	7 152	2 743

Source: Ministry of Finance, 2024

Figure 3 illustrates the composition of beneficiaries under the scheme. In this, women entrepreneurs are the major beneficiaries but their share has declined from 80% to 65%. The share of Scheduled Caste men and women has increased significantly in FY 2023-24 and FY 2024-25, reaching 20% and 8% from 11% and 4% in FY 2016-17. Meanwhile, Scheduled Tribe men and women make up a small but slowly growing group. According to the Second All India Rural Financial Inclusion Survey 2021-22 by NABARD, the share of financial savings among rural households increased from 50 percent in 2016-17 to 66 percent in 2021-22. Insurance and pension coverage have increased, rising from 25.5% in 2016-17 to 80.3% in 2021-22 and from 18.9% in 2016-17 to 23.5% in 2021-22, respectively. Financial literacy has also improved, from 33.9% in 2016-17 to 51.3% in 2021-22 which have fostered favourable financial behaviour among individuals, such as money management, bill payments, and informed financial decisions, has also improved (NAFIS,2024).

Figure 3. Beneficiary Composition by Category (April 2016–June 2024)

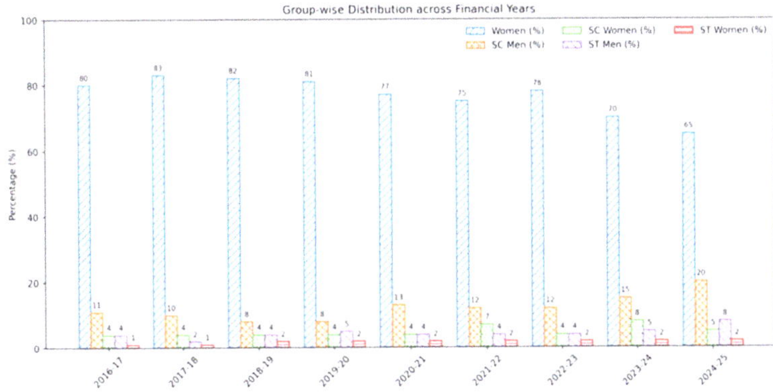

Source: Ministry of Finance, 2024

However, even with significant progress, some barriers persist for India. Account ownership is almost equal; the Statistics Ministry of the government of India reported that nationally, about 55.7% of the women account holders are using their accounts actively against male account holders where the figure is 65.2%, thus a difference of 9.5 percentage points in account usage which has still remained unclosed (MoSPI, 2025). The gender gap in digital payment engagement is even bigger, with only 31.2% of women engaging in digital transactions than 47.1% of men that is particularly high in rural areas (MoSPI, 2025). There are also differences between states based on locations, infrastructure, literacy and household income. A NABARD-based Financial Inclusion Index (NAFINDEX) covering 29 states reveals that states such as Tamil Nadu, Kerala, and Andhra Pradesh achieve financial inclusion indices above 70, meanwhile states such as Jammu & Kashmir, Manipur, and Mizoram lag with indices below 40 (Satyasai, 2020; NABARD, 2017). Further, the level of financial inclusion in the rural areas depends on the location of the state. The southern and western states had better rural account penetration and usage, whereas the north, eastern and some central states were still less developed and had fewer opportunities for their residents (NABARD All India Rural Financial Inclusion Survey, 2022). It has the highest share in no. of people having inactive bank accounts, about 16% which is much higher than the global average of 6%. Reasons cited for having an inactive bank account or no bank account, a larger distance from the bank, lack of trust in the authority, insufficient funds to maintain the account and the perception that a family member's account is sufficient. (WB Global Findex Database, 2021;2025). Along with serious systemic bottlenecks in the execution of the government initiatives, which result in low performance levels of these initiatives. For example, the Government of India (Mof, 2024) has gaps between the amounts that are sanctioned and the loans that are distributed. Although government programs have been instrumental, the removal of these deep-rooted barriers requires more focused and intensive efforts. This will ensure that financial inclusion leads to real economic participation for everyone.

3. CONCEPT OF FINTECH

Fintech is a combination of two terms, finance and technology, where finance represents the application and technology represents the enabling medium (Alt et al., 2018). Reserve Bank of India describes fintech as financial innovations that are enabled by technology (RBI, 2019). Whereas, the World Bank defines Fintech as technology advances having the ability to transform the financial services industry, which can give rise to new business models, applications, processes, and products (World Bank, 2019). Together, this highlights that Fintech is an umbrella concept that has changed from simple digitization to a major driver that is changing the world. Through inclusion, innovation, and resilience, it is reshaping the global financial ecosystem of an increasingly digital world.

3.1. Importance of Fintech

Fintech's importance is in its potential to enhance financial efficiency, inclusion and innovation in both advanced and emerging countries. It is helping in bridging the divide in access to financial services for firms and households and is promoting economic growth through the digitization of money and financial services (Feyen et al., 2023). At the macro level, Fintech influences the overall economic growth by encouraging financial penetrations, attracting more competitors, and making the utilization of resources more efficient across various sectors (Gomber et al., 2018). As a result, the economy becomes more productive due to the innovations in the payment, lending, and investment sectors. In effect, these improvements speed up the whole operation, reduce the costs of the transactions involved, enhance transparency, and strengthen the security (Philippon, 2016). And, at the micro level, fintech has improved consumer experience by enabling more accessible, affordable and user-centric financial services (Demirgüç-Kunt et al., 2017). The improvement of customer experience is based on the quality of service, perceived usefulness, convenience, and the personalization offered by digital platforms (Barbu et al., 2021). Also, Financial services are no longer confined to a certain segment of the population but the benefits can now reach the masses including those who are marginalized and have been neglected by the traditional banking system. In the past, low-income people, rural communities, and micro-entrepreneurs were often left out of the traditional banking system due to high operational costs, collateral requirements, and geographical constraints. However, FinTech effectively overcomes these barriers by providing mobile and digital platforms (Ozili, 2018). It is considered to have low marginal cost and high scale efficiencies, making it better than traditional financial services (Moro-Visconti et al., 2020). For the policy regulation, FinTech helps to reform the entire system and brings transparency in financial governance. The changes it brings are more transparent and more secure as every digital transaction leaves data trails that facilitate real-time monitoring and thus lower the chances of fraud and leakages (Feyen et al., 2023). Along with improving traceability, it reduces the scope of corruption, tax evasion, money laundering, etc. (Vives, 2019). On top of that, it also facilitates the fiscal delivery systems by making it possible to have instant digital payments and easy public transfers. For example, digital payment systems have played a crucial role in the Direct Bank Transfer (DBT) schemes of the Government of India. This is a process where the money is transferred directly to the beneficiary's bank account. Such a system makes the distribution of welfare more accurate and less susceptible to leakage.

These technologies revamp the ICT sector and upgrade the industrial structures, leading to a decrease in carbon emissions in particular in the developed and urban areas. They also contribute to raising the proportion of renewable energy in the energy mix. As a result, it leads to more efficient resource use and promotes green economic growth (Wu, 2024; Awais et al., 2023; Kashif et al., 2023). Notably, during the COVID-19 pandemic, digital financial services showed their value in emergencies. They ensured financial continuity in conditions of social restrictions by online transactions, mobile banking, and contactless payments (Demirgüç-Kunt et al., 2017). However, the rapid expansion of fintech comes with its concerns, such as cybersecurity, data privacy, consumer protection, and regulatory changes. Digital trust, inclusion, and fairness have become key policy concerns as FinTech relies heavily on algorithmic decision-making and personal data (Zavolokina et al., 2016). Therefore, it is essential to ensure that technological innovation conforms to the values of justice, transparency, and accessibility in order to prevent new forms of exclusion in the digital financial ecosystem.

3.2 State of Fintech for Financial Inclusion in India

India has repositioned itself over the last few years to be the leader of financial inclusion by implementing Fintech in strategic ways. The impact of COVID-19 has been very significant in this transformation. Following the pandemic, more than 80 million people from India made digital merchant payments in 2021 (World Bank Global Findex Index, 2021). According to The ACI Worldwide Report of 2023, more than 46% of real time payment transactions globally took place in India. In 2025, over 100 million Indian adults have transitioned to make regular digital payments (World Bank Global Findex Index, 2025).

This revolution is based on India's innovative Digital Public Infrastructure, known as the "India Stack." Key elements such as Aadhaar, widespread mobile phone access, the Pradhan Mantri Jan Dhan Yojana (PMJDY), Unified Payments Interface (UPI) for instant payment and DigiLocker for digital document storage a unique ecosystem has created a fintech ecosystem. This infrastructure has transformed and set the foundation for financial inclusion. As shown in Table 6 RBI Digital Payment Index as a result has increased over the years, depicting a steady increase in digitization. It increased to 465.33 in September 2024 from 304.06 in September 2021. This implies that the digital payment activities had expanded by more than four times in just six years (RBI, 2024).

Table 6. Growth of RBI Digital Payments Index (DPI) from 2018 to 2024

Period (as of)	RBI Digital Payments Index (DPI)
March 18 (Base)	100.00
March 19	153.47
September 19	173.49
March 20	207.84
September 20	217.74
March 21	270.59
September 21	304.06
March 22	349.30
September 22	377.46
March 23	395.57
September 23	418.77
March 24	445.50
September 24	465.33

Source: RBI, 2019-2024

From Figure 4, showcasing volume of digital payment transactions, we can see that total digital payments have increased from 2,071 crores in FY 2017–18 to 18,737 crores in FY 2023–24 at a CAGR of 44%. This growth is dominated by Unified Payment Interface (UPI), making about 70% of digital payments in FY 2023-24 (DFS, 2023). Alongside UPI's rapid rise, Aadhaar-enabled Payments also grew, from approximately 5.53 billion transactions in FY2023–2024 to approximately 6.11 billion in FY2024–2025 (NPCI, 2025). This is particularly prominent in rural areas showing that digital payments connected to welfare transfers and rural cash-out points are getting stronger along with urban smartphone-based payments (RBI, 2024; IBEF, 2018).

Figure 4. Number of Transactions using Digital Payments (in crore), 2017-2023

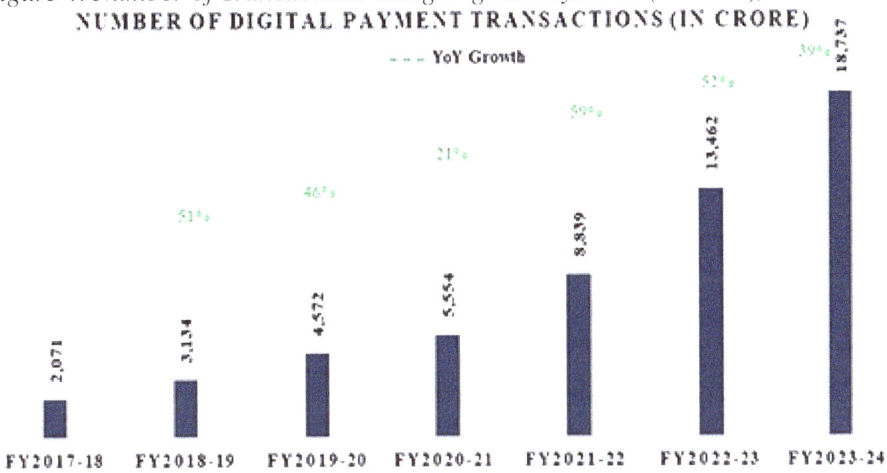

Source: RBI, NPCI & Banks

In line, under the Pradhan Mantri Jan Dhan Yojana (PMJDY), as of December 2024, India has established 107 Digital Banking Units (DBUs). These help to increase the accessibility and usability of digital financial services. The goal is to guarantee that the advantages of digital banking are available across the nation. These provide services such as Loan applications, passbook printing, money transfers, and the opening of savings bank accounts through digital channels with the declared aim of making digital banking available to the whole country (PIB, 2022). However, considering the size of India, this is less than one DBU per district, which means that these DBUs cannot be used as a substitute for physical branches in remote or densely populated urban areas and there is a need for a considerable scale, up if DBUs are to have the capacity to close the last, mile gaps (Drishti IAS, 2022).

Moreover, several digital portals like the Jan Samarth portal, PSB Loans in 59 Minutes, and Standup Mitra have been developed to provide relatively quick and easy access to credit for micro and small enterprises (IBEF, 2018). These platforms simplify the application and documentation process and also have Lenders integration which helps in reducing the borrower processing time for those who is capable of navigating the online system (IBEF, 2018). Nevertheless, preliminary evaluations indicate that a considerable number of small entrepreneurs and informal workers continue to depend on assisted channels (such as common service centres or bank correspondents) for accessing these portals due to issues related to documentation, language, and digital comfort, particularly in areas far from big cities (PIB, 2022). The widespread adoption of mobile banking is supported by the RBI guidelines. Banks licensed by RBI are allowed to offer mobile banking via apps, SMS and Unstructured Supplementary Service Data (USSD) (RBI, 2021). Nowadays, almost all major banks, both public and commercial, have mobile applications and provide USSD. Banks and nonbanking financial companies (NBFCs) are increasingly using digital lending to develop their loan books with fintech. The Centre for Advanced Financial Research and Learning's report (CAFRAL, 2023) states that in FY 2020, banks held a 5.53% share of all digital lending, while NBFCs held a 60.53% share. The percentage of NBFCs in the overall ecosystem has been steadily increasing over the last few years, from 2% in 2018 to 14% 2022. According to the Fintech Association for Consumer Empowerment (FACE), in FY24, there were over 10 crore loans distributed, representing a 35% increase (IBEF, 2024).

Despite the fact that fintech is a game-changer, there are several challenges that hinder its adoption. Only 28% of women are able to carry out digital transactions, which is 18 percentage points less than men (World Bank Global Findex Database, 2025). Such disparity in gender is mainly due to a smaller proportion of women having a smartphone, more restricted and expensive access to the internet, lower confidence of women when using digital interfaces and the fact that men still dominate the decision making process in the household regarding finances even if the accounts are in the names of women (India Forum, 2025; Patel & Koshy, 2023). The inclusion of Fintech has not only been slow but also has been a source of many gender hierarchies to be reproduced, which it seeks to prevent (World Bank, 2022; Press Trust of India, 2025). Insufficient knowledge and lack of digital financial literacy results in a certain segment of the population being financially excluded (Srivastava, 2022). Some of the issues faced are gaining consumer trust, dealing with cybersecurity risks, and going through regulatory and compliance hurdles, which can be difficult for first-time users or those living in rural areas to understand (Goswami et al., 2022). Solving these problems demands initiatives targeted at raising digital literacy, enhancing cybersecurity, and developing user-friendly platforms. A well-designed well regulatory frameworks are needed to build trust and inclusion.

4. STREET VENDORS

Astreet vendor is an individual who sells goods or services to people in temporary static structure or a mobile stall or head-load without any permanent setting. (National Policy on Urban Street Vendors, 2009). Street vendors can be classified into two types, fixed and mobile. “Stationery vendors” conduct vending operations mostly at a single location and “Mobile Vendors” conduct vending activities by moving from one spot to another. (Street vendors Act, 2014). The local laws, urban planning, regulations and economic necessity determine the nature of their operation. Even though street vending creates jobs for the urban poor, the activity largely remains informal, without social protection and devoid of access to finance and institutional support (Roever & Skinner, 2016). Still, in many developing countries, Street vendors have a major share in urban employment. They are estimated to make up about 10% to 20% of non-agricultural labour in developing cities (ILO, 2020). Hence, it forms an integral but vulnerable part in the discussions about financial inclusion and development.

4.1. Importance of Street Vendors and Street Vending

Street vendors are highly visible and dynamic part of the global informal economy (Roever & Skinner, 2016). Their contribution spans across economic, social and cultural domains, linking various segments of society. They supply affordable goods and services, along with connecting producers to consumers to communities (Bromley, 2000). In an economic sense, street vending is instrumental in the generation of income and the creation of employment opportunities. It is especially true for low-income and marginalised groups that are often left out of formal employment. Thus, with the requirement of minimum startup capital and the availability of various work options, this enables people to support themselves even in situations of urban poverty and unemployment (Bhowmik, 2012). In many developing countries, street vending is starting point for entrepreneurship among the poor. It helps workers save money, gain business experience and possibly move into the formal sector. For example, in Nigeria, street vending makes up around 70% of urban employment (Onodugo et al., 2016). Also, it was reported that in Ghana and Senegal, Street vendors constitute large share of total employment with 21% and 24% respectively (WIEGO, n.d.) Along with employment, Street vendors contribute to the urban food system and local economies by offering a variety of reasonably priced and easily accessible food options (Crush & Frayne, 2011). Furthermore, the Food and Agriculture Organisation (FAO,2019) states that vendors provide fresh and familiar food, hence supporting food security and nutrition for many individuals. Also, the sources of their goods are local farmers and artisans. This creates a backward linkage that boosts rural economies and sustains small-scale producers.

Socially, street vending represents resilience, connection and social inclusion. For example, Research from Ghana showed that women Street vendors often use their earnings for children or other family members, as well as to sustain the household (Ashaley-Nikoi & Abbey, 2023). Further, vending areas frequently act as social centres, making the streets more lively and attracting more people. Also, promotes inclusivity as people from different backgrounds engage and trade goods and services

(Deore & Lathia, 2019). In addition, Street vendors also have cultural importance. Apart from selling goods, they represent the local traditions, heritage, identity and act as means of cultural exchange. Vendors serve local cuisines, offer artisanal experiences and extend hospitality in informal ways (Equations, 2012). For example, in Vietnam, street vending is one of the ways to keep traditional food practices alive and has become an inseparable part of the life of the people who live in the area and the people who come to visit (Huynh, 2023). Besides that, the research in both China and India reveal that Street vendors become the part of atmosphere and ambience of the places where tourist attractions are located. They carry on the sale and the promotion of the local products, which is one of the ways to strengthen the cultural identity (Qi et al., 2024; Kedla et al., 2025). Thereby, Street vendors serve as both economic agents and cultural ambassadors.

4.2. Fintech and Financial Inclusion – State of Street Vendors in India

Street vending and Street vendors have always been an integral part of the Indian economy. Their significance cannot be undervalued in the growing informal sector. The Government of India (2023) approximates that there are about 5.3 million street vendors across the country. Table 7 shows the Street vendors identified in different states, with Madhya Pradesh and Uttar Pradesh hosting the largest numbers, about 9 lakhs and 7 lakhs, respectively. There can be more than the numbers counted because of the informal nature of street vending, with minimal official registrations and many vendors being in constant move. Street vending is estimated by the government to make up about 14% of all urban informal jobs that are not related to agriculture in the nation. According to the Ministry of Housing and Urban Poverty Alleviation, almost 50% of India's savings and 63% of its GDP come from Street vendors. It is the best option for low-income people to work for themselves with the least amount of capital is street vending. In addition to being convenient, Street vendors are also economic engines that act as micro-entrepreneurs at their core, generating jobs, boosting local economies, drawing tourists, encouraging social inclusion, and conserving cultural heritage (ICAR, 2024).

Table 7. No. of Street vendors identified by states (2023)

State / Union Territory	Number of Street vendors	State / Union Territory	Number of Street vendors
Uttar Pradesh	9,09,608	Uttarakhand	26,483
Madhya Pradesh	7,23,820	Kerala	25,726
Telangana	6,14,176	Jammu & Kashmir	23,694
Maharashtra	5,84,148	Manipur	20,841
Andhra Pradesh	4,24,012	Chandigarh	10,930
West Bengal	3,28,067	Mizoram	9,129
Gujarat	3,21,406	Tripura	8,666
Tamil Nadu	3,09,449	Arunachal Pradesh	7,605
Karnataka	2,65,477	Himachal Pradesh	6,486
Rajasthan	1,93,586	Nagaland	4,697
Bihar	1,81,231	Daman & Diu	2,928
Punjab	1,49,215	Goa	2,881
Haryana	1,17,028	Meghalaya	2,153
Chhattisgarh	1,06,520	Puducherry	2,144
Assam	89,124	Sikkim	871
Odisha	80,841	Andaman & Nicobar Islands	676
Delhi	79,952	Ladakh	427
Jharkhand	71,923		

Source: MoHUA, 2023

Previously, Street vendors did not have any rights in urban India. The initial street vendors policy was introduced in 2004, and eventually renamed the 'National Policy for Urban Street Vendors, 2009. However, no major steps were taken by states, as they had no legal binding. Later, street vending was recognized as a living source by Supreme Court in 2010. A bill was then created in 2011 to safeguard the Street vendors and to establish “vending zones”. An efficient Grievance Redressal and Dispute Resolution Mechanism was to be built, along with a foundation of traditional natural markets and equitable participation of women and vendors in advisory bodies. Following the National Advisory Council's assistance and the Union Cabinet's assent, the Street Vending Bill was enacted in 2014, thereby officially legalizing street vending (Singh, 2022). According to the Centre for Civil Society, the Street vendors Act Compliance (SVAC) Index, the Act's implementation has advanced, though unevenly in many states. In 2018–19, the Index's score range was 9–76 points (out of 100), and in 2019–20, it was 20–78 points, with Andhra Pradesh as the top-performing state. The index reveals Only 35% of Urban Local Bodies (ULBs) fully implemented TVCs by 2020. Many TVCs either lacked genuine vendor representation or met irregularly, weakening grievance redressal. In major cities such as Delhi and Mumbai, middle-class resident associations demanded the creation of vendor-free zones and describing street vending as a kind of public disorder. This undermines the Act's inclusivity goals. (Progress Report CCS, 2020).

Recognizing these challenges of Street vendors and the vulnerabilities they faced during the COVID-19 crisis, Pradhan Mantri Street vendors's Atmanirbhar Nidhi (PM SVANidhi) was launched in 2020. The aim was to provide collateral-free loans to Street vendors so that they can restart and sustain their businesses in urban, rural and semi-urban areas. It also focused on promoting digital financial inclusion as one of its noteworthy aspects to help vendors modernize their businesses and build credit histories. As depicted in Table 8, the PM-SVANidhi has demonstrated encouraging outcomes with vendor participation and loan disbursement. As of March 2025, about 68.08 lakh vendors had benefited from the program. More than 13,772 crore loans had been issued, out of which 14,316 crore loans were approved. Recipients have also embraced cashless and digital transaction methods as a result of the incentives, such as monthly payback benefits, thus reinforcing their engagement in the digital economy. This indicates behavioral change towards digital acceptability. Because of this, vendors now see the program favorably as extra income and means to improve their credit history, which can help them get future loans and other financial services. (Mazumder, 2025).

Table 8. Year-wise Statement Showing Total Number of Eligible Applications Received, Loans Sanctioned, Loans Disbursed, and Loans Repaid under PM SVANidhi Scheme

Financial Year	Eligible Applications Received	Loans Sanctioned	Loans Disbursed	Loans Repaid
2020-21	28,21,794	22,03,276	20,57,653	70,291
2021-22	12,12,136	9,88,023	10,74,484	11,08,603
2022-23	19,49,042	13,29,111	11,76,477	8,69,102
2023-24	40,59,032	40,76,171	41,06,319	12,33,406
2024-25*	14,48,108	12,68,233	11,84,562	12,53,070
Total	1,14,90,112	98,64,814	95,99,495	45,34,472

Source: MoHUA, 2025

Table 9 provides a summary of the PM SVANidhi cumulative coverage in the States/UTs over five years, showing the number of total and women beneficiaries and loan volume. In the country, the ratio of women beneficiaries to total beneficiaries is about 1:2.2 i.e. out of 67.40 lakh beneficiaries, about 30.64 lakh are women, thus female share is 45 percent against the male's share of 55 percent as shown in Figure

5. Also, women account for 42.28 lakh of the 95.99 lakh loans disbursed with a total amount . In other words, women constitute almost half of all borrowers, but get nearly 62 per cent of the total loan value, thereby indicating that the scheme is structured to encourage women-led microenterprises (MoHUA, 2025). Nevertheless, the table exposes a wide gap between different regions in the level of participation of women. The states of Manipur with 94.0 percent female beneficiaries, Mizoram with 87.7 percent, Nagaland with 85.6 percent and Meghalaya with 75.9 percent show that female inclusion is at an extremely high level, which may be due to the influence of matrilineal traditions and higher female labour force participation in the North East. On the other hand, the women's shares of 4.3 per cent in Jammu & Kashmir, 16.6 per cent in Chandigarh, 17.1 per cent in Tripura, 22 per cent in Himachal Pradesh and 22.7 per cent in Odisha, respectively, suggest that the areas are characterized by a combination of deep, rooted structural and cultural barriers as well as gender, sensitive implementation being weak or absent. Moreover, the big states which are responsible for the total scale like Uttar Pradesh, Madhya Pradesh, Maharashtra, Telangana and Tamil Nadu are located in the center, where womens shares vary between 31.9 per cent in Uttar Pradesh and 68.4 per cent in Tamil Nadu, thus showing that even with the same scheme design, state capacity and outreach strategy play a decisive role in gender outcomes. Table 9 is a good indication that the PM SVANidhi program has been a major factor in increasing women's access to formal credit among street vendors. However, it also brings out that there are still gender and regional disparities which call for more attention and targeted interventions at the state level particularly in the northern plains states, some areas of central India, and a number of Union Territories so that women vendors may be able to take advantage of the fintech, enabled financial inclusion in equal measure as men.

Table 9. State-wise Total vs Women Beneficiaries under PM SVANidhi (2020–21 to 2024–25)

State/UT	Total Beneficiaries	Women Beneficiaries	% Women Beneficiaries	Total Loans Disbursed	Loans to Women
Andaman Nicobar	547	240	43.9	1,019	433
Andhra Pradesh	3,48,257	2,65,618	76.3	5,21,555	3,88,142
Arunachal Pradesh	4,686	3,398	72.5	7,539	5,463
Assam	1,19,971	59,334	49.5	1,79,223	87,224
Bihar	1,27,360	48,733	38.3	1,62,808	58,307
Chandigarh	5,010	830	16.6	8,481	1,374

continued on following page

Table 9. Continued

State/UT	Total Beneficiaries	Women Beneficiaries	% Women Beneficiaries	Total Loans Disbursed	Loans to Women
Chhattisgarh	88,456	42,916	48.5	1,29,013	61,176
Daman & Diu	2,199	749	34.1	3,305	1,045
Delhi	1,89,974	69,445	36.6	2,36,400	80,541
Goa	1,564	753	48.1	2,703	1,293
Gujarat	4,74,447	2,03,319	42.9	6,92,431	2,87,516
Haryana	1,64,783	51,239	31.1	2,06,056	57,710
Himachal Pradesh	5,434	1,193	22	10,020	2,248
Jammu & Kashmir	17,062	735	4.3	27,750	1,151
Jharkhand	84,854	42,359	49.9	1,09,594	50,477
Karnataka	3,91,403	2,16,729	55.4	5,62,027	2,98,122
Kerala	1,17,982	76,983	65.2	1,52,783	92,431
Ladakh	462	283	61.3	802	505
Madhya Pradesh	8,78,663	3,46,015	39.4	13,42,137	4,98,053
Maharashtra	8,42,712	3,78,018	44.9	10,85,003	4,66,506
Manipur	9,823	9,233	94	13,975	13,036
Meghalaya	3,827	2,904	75.9	5,194	3,844
Mizoram	2,573	2,257	87.7	3,458	2,964
Nagaland	3,401	2,909	85.6	4,791	3,934
Odisha	63,124	14,356	22.7	99,488	20,477
Puducherry	3,515	1,847	52.6	5,280	2,650
Punjab	1,64,362	61,669	37.5	2,13,854	73,987
Rajasthan	1,82,914	63,461	34.7	2,44,391	76,600
Sikkim	1,166	846	72.6	1,481	959
Tamil Nadu	3,97,428	2,71,845	68.4	5,65,552	3,76,390
Telangana	4,25,062	2,78,561	65.5	7,20,581	4,66,797
Tripura	5,497	939	17.1	8,104	1,288
Uttar Pradesh	13,80,572	4,40,423	31.9	19,93,366	6,28,216
Uttarakhand	27,737	6,675	24.1	42,692	9,149
West Bengal	2,03,262	97,383	47.9	2,36,639	1,08,434
India Total	67,40,089	30,64,197	45.5	95,99,495	42,28,442

Source: MoHUA, 2025

Figure 5. Beneficiaries by Gender

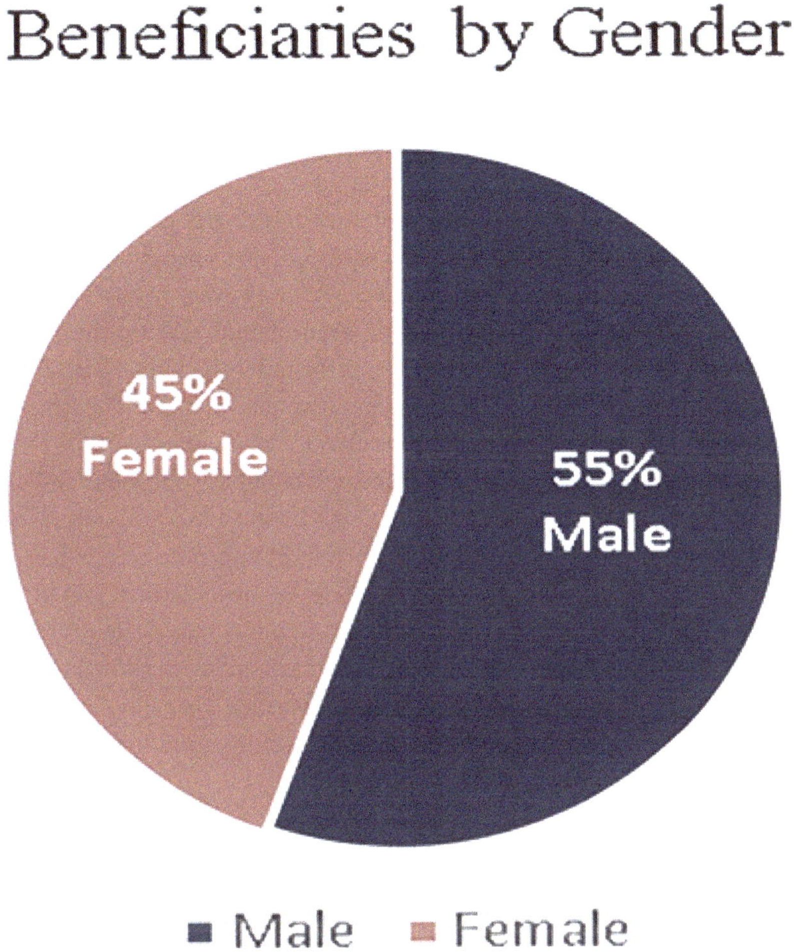

Source: MoHUA, 2025

Table 10 showcases the distribution of loans under PM SVANidhi Yojana among the different states of India. It can be seen that the PM SVANidhi activities are concentrated to few states. Uttar Pradesh accounts for the largest share each year consistently, with about 5. 94 lakhs loans sanctioned and 5. 64 lakhs disbursed in 2020-21, rising to nearly 6. 91 lakhs sanctioned and 6. 96 lakhs disbursed in 2023-24, and more than 1. 63 lakhs sanctioned and 1. 58 lakhs disbursed in 2024-25. Besides large contributors such as Madhya Pradesh, Maharashtra, Telangana, Tamil Nadu, Gujarat and Karnataka, show sanction and disbursement volumes in the 15 lakhs range in at least one year, which means that the programme scale is largely driven by a few high-capacity states rather than being evenly distributed across the country. Meanwhile, a handful of smaller or less wealthy states and Union Territories including Goa, Sikkim, Ladakh, Arunachal Pradesh, and the combined Dadra & Nagar Haveli and Daman & Diu have shown very low figures in all five years, often less than 0. 03 lakh (3, 000) loans per year, thus it can be inferred street vendors in these areas have had very limited access to the scheme despite formal nationwide coverage. There are also some states where the sanction disbursement imbalance gets larger in different years, implying that there could be bottlenecks in administration or banking, for instance, Rajasthan's loans sanctions increased to 0. 558 lakhs in 2020-21 and 1. 093 lakhs in 2023-24, however, disbursement was at 0. 503 and 1. 171 lakhs respectively. Andhra Pradesh and Maharashtra had times where disbursement increased drastically after prior under-disbursement, thus pointing to delayed implementation instead of smooth annual support. The time profile also reveals that although the program expanded exponentially in 2023-24 with a national volume of loans sanctioned and disbursed being 40. 762 lakhs and 41. 063 lakhs respectively, the numbers for 2024-25 with 12. 682 and 11. 846 lakhs were at moderation, indicating that saturation in good-performing states might have taken place without any corresponding catchup in lagging regions. The PM SVANidhi thus has facilitated the inflow of large credit volumes in a few major states but has not been able to achieve geographically balanced outreach and high sanction disbursement alignment consistently across all years and districts. This situation shows the necessity of targeted support to low, volume states and the need for stricter control over the quality of state level implementation.

Table 10. State-wise Share of PM SVANidhi Loans in Total Sanctioned and Disbursed Loans (₹ lakh, 2020–21 to 2024–25)

State/UT	2020-21		2021-22		2022-23		2023-24		2024-25	
	Sanctioned	Disbursed	Sanctioned	Disbursed	Sanctioned	Disbursed	Sanctioned	Disbursed	Sanctioned	Disbursed
Andaman Nicobar	0.004	0.004	0.001	0.001	0.002	0.002	0.002	0.002	0.001	0.001
Andhra Pradesh	1.179	1.128	0.816	0.823	0.496	0.431	2.058	2.133	0.79	0.701
Arunachal Pradesh	0.018	0.016	0.009	0.011	0.02	0.017	0.024	0.025	0.007	0.006
Assam	0.158	0.142	0.43	0.427	0.238	0.22	0.725	0.738	0.27	0.266
Bihar	0.339	0.289	0.157	0.196	0.117	0.089	0.863	0.832	0.207	0.223
Chandigarh	0.021	0.021	0.016	0.016	0.019	0.018	0.025	0.023	0.006	0.007
Chhattisgarh	0.41	0.403	0.092	0.093	0.117	0.106	0.532	0.521	0.18	0.167
Delhi	0.331	0.311	0.102	0.111	0.315	0.262	1.407	1.372	0.363	0.307
Goa	0.01	0.01	0.004	0.004	0.005	0.004	0.006	0.006	0.002	0.002
Gujarat	1.067	1.023	1.139	1.116	1.031	0.954	2.772	2.825	1.09	1.006

continued on following page

Table 10. Continued

State/UT	2020-21		2021-22		2022-23		2023-24		2024-25	
	Sanctioned	Disbursed	Sanctioned	Disbursed	Sanctioned	Disbursed	Sanctioned	Disbursed	Sanctioned	Disbursed
Haryana	0.178	0.169	0.125	0.116	0.119	0.114	1.38	1.328	0.343	0.333
Himachal Pradesh	0.028	0.028	0.012	0.012	0.02	0.019	0.031	0.032	0.01	0.009
Jammu Kashmir	0.119	0.115	0.038	0.041	0.052	0.046	0.06	0.054	0.02	0.022
Jharkhand	0.225	0.22	0.082	0.084	0.087	0.067	0.593	0.59	0.126	0.135
Karnataka	1.145	1.08	0.456	0.456	0.78	0.615	2.578	2.72	0.925	0.75
Kerala	0.081	0.081	0.033	0.034	0.055	0.048	1.041	0.987	0.362	0.379
Ladakh	0.002	0.002	0.001	0.001	0.002	0.002	0.002	0.002	0	0
Madhya Pradesh	3.241	3.138	1.975	1.999	1.751	1.655	4.954	4.867	1.894	1.761
Maharashtra	1.695	1.49	0.43	0.608	2.352	1.931	5.239	5.317	1.692	1.503
Manipur	0.068	0.061	0.018	0.025	0.023	0.015	0.026	0.032	0.006	0.007
Meghalaya	0.003	0.003	0.004	0.004	0.01	0.008	0.023	0.024	0.013	0.013
Mizoram	0.004	0.004	0.001	0.001	0.001	0.001	0.019	0.019	0.01	0.01
Nagaland	0.012	0.012	0.005	0.005	0.005	0.004	0.015	0.016	0.011	0.011
Odisha	0.293	0.275	0.077	0.09	0.129	0.085	0.413	0.432	0.12	0.112
Puducherry	0.012	0.011	0.002	0.002	0.006	0.005	0.027	0.028	0.008	0.007
Punjab	0.295	0.267	0.109	0.133	0.122	0.103	1.382	1.334	0.335	0.302
Rajasthan	0.558	0.503	0.12	0.171	0.189	0.081	1.093	1.171	0.548	0.518
Sikkim	0	0	0	0	0	0	0.011	0.011	0.004	0.004
Tamil Nadu	1.104	0.877	0.624	0.781	0.585	0.55	2.741	2.752	0.718	0.695
Telangana	3.306	3.105	0.735	0.877	0.981	0.827	1.741	1.876	0.519	0.521
Dadra Nagar Havel Daman Diu	0.011	0.01	0.001	0.002	0.004	0.003	0.014	0.015	0.002	0.002
Tripura	0.026	0.026	0.009	0.008	0.01	0.005	0.027	0.031	0.01	0.01
Uttar Pradesh	5.943	5.637	2.149	2.366	3.521	3.39	6.908	6.962	1.635	1.579
Uttarakhand	0.093	0.091	0.019	0.019	0.073	0.068	0.173	0.172	0.078	0.077
West Bengal	0.052	0.024	0.087	0.112	0.049	0.02	1.855	1.811	0.378	0.399
Grand Total	22.03	20.57	9.88	10.74	13.29	11.76	40.76	41.06	12.68	11.84

Source: PM SVANidhi portal

Even though India has done a lot for financial inclusion and fintech adoption for Street vendors, there remain some obstacles. The primary issues raised by the vendor leaders were the risk of eviction from their place, as many states have still not perfectly formed town vending zones, and town vending committees often lack street vendors representation at the top levels (Progress Report CCS, 2020). Many vendors lack knowledge of schemes such as PM SVANidhi and the Street Vendors Act, which restrict their access to benefits and protections (Saini et al., 2024). If vendors get harassed or have disputes, they hardly have any options because the grievance redressal systems are often not responsive to their needs (Gogoi &

Bhattacharyya, 2022). Vendors have low and irregular incomes that put them in a challenging financial situation. At the same time, they have limited access to formal credit and depend on high-interest informal loans. These conditions endanger their economic security (Romero et al., 2024). In order to solve these problems, it is first of all necessary to ascertain their legal status, then to improve the infrastructure, provide access to credit and create policies which reflect their needs. This would assist in protecting their livelihood and contributions.

5. POLICY SUPPORT

The Government of India has followed a multi-faceted approach to improve financial inclusion and boost the digital finance system. It has also provided specific support to Street vendors to address their vulnerabilities.

5.1. Initiatives for Financial Inclusion

Pradhan Mantri Jan Dhan Yojana (PMJDY)

It was launched as the National Mission for Financial Inclusion (NMFI) in August 2014, targeting the weaker and lower-income groups. The main aim is to integrate the unbanked population into the established financial system and provide them with various financial services such as credit, remittance facilities, insurance and pension (PMJDY, 2014).

It is based on the following principles:

- *Universal Access Principle:* It has adopted a household based approach, ensuring that there should be at least one bank account per household. These are zero-balance saving accounts. Rupay Debit cards and insurance of 2 lakh on accidents are also provided with it. After six months, if the operations are satisfactory, beneficiaries can apply for overdraft facility upto 5,000. The universal access principle focuses on broader coverage
- *National Implementation Architecture:* It has used bank led models for implementations. Public sector banks were assigned specific areas to ensure responsibility of proper coverage. Large enrolment camps were set up featuring over 125,000 Bank Mitras (Bank Correspondents). This helped in rapid account opening and raising awareness among the unbanked.
- *Integrated Benefits:* This scheme helped in providing integrated financial services. PMJDY Accounts became access points facilitating Direct Bank

Transfer for subsidies, insurance, pensions, wages, etc. This integration helps in reducing leakages and enhancing efficiency.

Three Jan Suraksha Schemes were launched to complement PMJYD in May 2015 to provide low-cost insurance and pension against vulnerabilities:

Pradhan Mantri Jeevan Jyoti Bima Yojana (PMJJBY): Under this, life insurance coverage of Rs 2 lakh is provided to any person between the ages of 18 to 50 years with a bank or post office savings account. It has an annual premium of Rs 436, which is automatically deducted from the account (PMJJBY, 2015) ;

Pradhan Mantri Suraksha Bima Yojana (PMSBY): Under this, life insurance of Rs 2 lakhs in case of accidental death or disability is provided at a very minimal premium of Rs 20 per annum. Any person between the ages of 10 to 70 years with a savings account can enrol in this (PMSBY, 2015);

Atal Pension Yojana (APY) provides pensions: This is a voluntary pension scheme. Any citizen between the ages of 18 to 40 years can contribute monthly, quarterly or half yearly for a fixed pension from Rs 1000 to Rs 5000 per month, starting at age 60. Additionally, the central government contributes 1,000 annually, or 50% of the subscriber's contribution (APY, 2015).

Stand-Up India

It was launched on 5th April 2016. This scheme focused on promoting an inclusive entrepreneurship environment for women, Scheduled Castes (SC), and Scheduled Tribes (ST).

- *Objective:* Under this, each bank branch should provide at least one woman borrower and one member of the Scheduled Caste (SC) or Scheduled Tribe (ST) with bank loans ranging from Rs. 10 lakhs to Rs. 1 crore for their green-field projects. In addition, if the enterprise is a partnership, a woman or SC/ST entrepreneur must possess at least 51% of the shares.
- *Implementation:* The scheme was implemented through 1.25 lakh bank branches around the country. Stand Up India not only connects banks and borrowers, but it also offers assistance for training and skill development with utility support services, mentorship, and contact points for Skill Centres and Industry Departments via their own web portal. This connects the entrepreneurs and support without any reach or physical barriers (StandUp India, 2016).

2.2. Initiatives for FinTech

Digital India

It was launched in 2015. The main goal was to make the country digitally empowered. (MeitY, 2015).

Three core objectives of the initiative:

- *A stable and secure digital infrastructure:* Provide every citizen access to a safe and reliable digital infrastructure, including high-speed internet and services enabled by it.
- *Digital Government Services:* Provide on-demand digital government services with integrated cloud-based access to citizens, real-time service delivery, and smooth engagement via web and mobile platforms.
- *Citizens' Digital Empowerment:* Promote digital literacy and provide access to digital resources and services in Indian languages to bridge language barriers and encourage participation.

Under this, fintech has been a major empowering element to support the initiative. In alignment with this government has launched suitable schemes and projects.

Jan Dhan–Aadhaar–Mobile (JAM) Trinity

The Indian government developed this framework to foster financial inclusion, transparency and efficiency in the delivery of public services. It consists of three interconnected pillars, which offer the characteristics that contribute to its success.

- *Jan Dhan bank accounts*: The Pradhan Mantri Jan Dhan Yojana provides zero-balance bank accounts to millions of unbanked people. It consists of services like insurance, overdraft, pensions, and microcredit (PMJDY, 2015).
- *Aadhaar biometric identity*: Aadhaar is a unique biometric ID for citizens. This ID is linked to financial services and government projects. This technology protects integrity, reduces duplication of social benefits, co-benefit of fraud, and fast verification of identity (UIDAI, 2010).
- *Mobile connectivity:* The factor that has changed everything is mobile connectivity. Mobile phones have become common enough that even rural people can use them to access financial services and government programs (GSMA, 2023). This has changed the face of banking. It facilitates mobile banking and also sends SMS alerts, which help in transparency and digital literacy (Vithanage,).

JAM enables subsidies and benefits such as LPG subsidies, pensions and MNREGA wages to be credited directly to the bank accounts of the beneficiaries. Thereby, it avoids the involvement of the middlemen and reduces leaks. By cutting down on intermediaries and making all transactions digital, JAM is able to bring down the government's administrative costs and make the fund transfers more transparent than before. It is mainly aimed at providing the marginalized sections of society with access to the essential financial services and bringing them into the formal economy with the help of technology (IBEF,).

India Stack

India Stack is a Digital Public Infrastructure (DPI). It is built on open Application Programming Interfaces (APIs) that make it possible for identification, payment, and data governance systems to integrate seamlessly. There are four separate technological levels in its architecture:

- *Presence less Layer:* This is the layer of authentication. It is supported by Aadhaar, the biggest biometric identification system in the world, which offers fundamental identity verification without the need for physical presence. The use of biometric/OTP authentication, KYC processing has decreased the identity verification times from 10–20 days to minutes (UIDAI, 2024).
- *Paperless Layer:* This integrates Digi Locker, a cloud storage solution. This platform provides the means for storing, retrieving, and sharing digitally-verifiable documents that are given by authoritative government departments, for instance, driving licenses, vehicle registrations, as well as academic mark sheets. Registered users may utilize e-signatures that are linked with Aadhaar for the purpose of authorization and verification. This is instrumental in the total eradication of paper usage (MeitY, 2024).
- *Cashless Layer:* This layer is driven by the Unified Payments Interface (UPI). The main driver of this layer is the Unified Payments Interface (UPI). Instant and cheap interbank transactions, either from peer to peer or peer to business, are possible through the platform. By operating, UPI users do away with physical cash, which also helps to lessen the occurrences of different crimes, such as theft and increases the security of transactions. Seventy-five percent of retail transactions in India are processed through UPI (NPCI, 2024).
- *Consent Layer:* The Account Aggregator Framework and the Data Empowerment and Protection Architecture (DEPA) govern this layer. It is a consent-based data-sharing system that allows users to have full control over their data. The system is designed to aid secure data transfer and ensure that the data is used in an ethical way (India Stack, n.d.).

The IMF has referred to UPI as a "global benchmark" for swift payments and digital infrastructure, particularly for developing countries (Copestake et al., 2025). Twenty-six nations, including the Philippines, Morocco, and Ethiopia, have adopted India's open-source ID technology named MOSIP (Modular Open Source Identity Platform) (Hariharan, 2024). Countries like Singapore, the United Arab Emirates, and France are also onboarding UPI (MoF, 2024). Nigeria and Sri Lanka are testing complete stacks. While Nigeria and Sri Lanka are in the process of testing full stacks. As per the notes of the Harvard Business School case, India Stack offers a template that can be "replicated for equitable, collaborative growth" (Khanna, 2025). India Stack, by removing the hurdles, facilitated the induction of millions of Indians into the formal economy and, at the same time, made the overall outreach more efficient and effortless. It promotes innovation to generate scalable solutions for health care, education, and financial inclusion. This has brought about a paradigm shift in the delivery of government services, which are transparent, accountable, and leak-free (IndiaStack,).

FAST (Fintech and Startup Acceleration)

The Fintech and Startup Acceleration (FAST) program is one of the major moves made by the Reserve Bank Innovation Hub (RBIH) to help India become a "Fintech Nation". FAST helps to speed up the innovation by making different stakeholders, such as regulators, startups, investors, banks, and financial institutions work together. The main focus of its activities is to address India's fintech ecosystem's gaps, with the support of the regulatory sandboxes and open market access provision, along with the organized mentorship sessions. By this means, the core, i.e. entrepreneurship, interoperability and financial inclusion, are being promoted. FAST operates using a structured "4M" Framework for overall startup growth (RBIH, 2024):

- *Masterclasses:* Offers technical training on regulatory compliance, covering subjects like AI-based credit evaluation, blockchain, and the RBI's Digital Lending Guidelines.
- *Mentorship:* Facilitates the access of startups to the experts from institutes such as SPJIMR, WISE Tech and the partner banks like HDFC and ICICI.
- *Market Access:* Assists in setting up pilot programs with banks and connecting with India Stack APIs, such as the AA framework and UPI.
- *Mixers:* In order to promote collaborations, hosts networking events that connect founders with VCs and regulators.
- *Money:* FAST offers grants free of equity and connects startups with venture capital networks to support scale-up financing.

FAST has curated sector-specific cohorts focusing on high-impact areas (RBIH, 2024):

- *Frictionless Finance:* It's a 90-day program with zero equity cost, providing an accelerator for growth-stage entrepreneurs in MSME finance, agri-finance, and climate financing. The program is offered in collaboration with YES BANK and SPJIMR WISE Tech. It gives startups access to resources like NPCI's UPI sandbox, which allows them to test and implement cutting-edge payment solutions in a safe setting.
- *Swanari TechSprint:* This helps women entrepreneurs with tailor-made financial products to promote gender inclusive finance. It addresses the gender gap in mobile internet usage, implemented in partnership with HDFC Bank Parivartan and IIMA Venture.
- *Build for Billions:* This helps to connect the informal economy to Financial services via a 50-day programme done with DLabs (ISB) and Union Bank of India. It is directed to address the $360 billion credit deficit for micro-entrepreneurs and GST-registered MSMEs through inclusive solutions.
- *i-Innovate:* This innovation focussed program is for the development and adoption of assistive technologies for Persons with Disabilities (PwD). It seeks to promote inclusivity.
- *FinXcelerator 2.0*: A two month scaling program with ICICI Bank and BITS Pilani. It specializes in regulatory tech solutions. The initiative provides both mentorship and strategic partnerships to accelerate compliance-focused fintech innovations.

India's fintech market is expected to become $84B in 2025 by enabling embedded finance opportunities (Bansal, RBIH, 2021).

2.3. Initiatives for Street Vendors

The Street Vendors (Protection of Livelihood and Regulation of Street Vending) Act, 2014:

The Street Vendors Act, 2014, was brought in to shield India's estimated 10 million Street vendors from harassment and evictions. Under the Supreme Court directive, street vending was declared a fundamental right under Article 19(1)(g) right to livelihood in 2010. After this, the Ministry of Housing and Urban Poverty Alleviation drafted a central legislation, and the Act finally came into effect from 1 May 2014 (MoHUA, 2014). The Core Objectives of the act are (Street vendors Act, 2014):

- *Rights and Protections:* The act defined Street vendors as individuals selling goods/services at public spaces, whether in motion or at a fixed site. Banned eviction before survey completion and issuance of Certificates of Vending (CoV). For relocation, a 30-day notice is required to be given to the vendors beforehand.
- *This act established three vending areas:* Vending Areas with 24-hour operations, it's the Primary areas of vendor activity. Restricted Zone, with specified time slots, which allowed only partial vending and No-Vending Zones, prohibited vending completely, mostly at High-traffic/security-sensitive areas.
- *Institutional Mechanisms:* Formation of Town Vending Committees (TVCs) comprising representatives of Municipal Commissioner as the chairperson, 40% street vendors representatives with 1/3 women representatives, bank representatives, police, planners, and traders. Their duties are to carry out surveys, issue Certificates of Vending, prepare Street Vending Plans and conduct lotteries for the distribution of vending spaces. Besides, the authorities have established Grievance Redressal Committees (GRCs) headed by a judicial magistrate to resolve vendors' grievances.

The Act is a pioneering model of urban governance that successfully balances regulation with the protection of livelihoods. However, there have been inconsistencies with the execution as well as institutional indifference and exclusionary urbanisation (CCS, 2022; Madhav, 2022). The decade-long history of the Act represents the continued resilience of Street vendors and the ongoing struggle for their rightful place in India's urban landscape.

Pradhan Mantri Street vendors's AtmaNirbhar Nidhi (PM SVANidhi):

Introduced by the Ministry of Housing and Urban Affairs (MoHUA) in June 2020. This is a micro-credit scheme, which was introduced at a time when nationwide lockdowns had abruptly halted vendor's day-to-day incomes, depriving them of working capital to relaunch their enterprises. The PM SVANidhi is based on a Three-Dimensional approach:

- Instantaneous ease of access to affordable working capital through collateral-free loans.
- Encouraging digital financial inclusion
- Enabling development through strengthening Street vendors and enhancing their prospects for long-term economic mobility.

By March 2025, it had transferred 13,792 crores to 6.8 million vendors, therefore making it one of India's most successful poverty alleviation programs in an urban context (MoHUA, 2025).

The design of the scheme is made by a nuanced understanding of street vendors's specific challenges. Traditionally excluded from the formal banking system because of lack of collateral and documentation, vendors had to depend on the mercy of financial sharks. PM SVANidhi breaks this cycle through its following framework (MoHUA, 2020):

- *Tiered Credit Structure:* First Tranche is of 10,000 of working capital loans, repayable in monthly instalments for one year. There are no collateral requirements. Second Tranche is of 20,000 loan upon 75% repayment of first tranche, facilitating incentive for the prompt repayment, and Third Tranche issues 50,000 loans with 36-month tenure to scaling businesses along with a 30,000 UPI-linked RuPay credit card as part of the 2025 upgrades.
- *Interest Subsidy*: A flat 7% subvention on interest, i.e. government pays 7% of the loan's interest. This reduces the vendor's effective rates down to 8–24%, makes formal credit less expensive than informal credit and encourages vendors to take loans formally.
- *Digital On-Ramping:* Cash-dependent merchants are nudged toward digital payments by incentives of monthly cashbacks ranging 50– 100 on UPI transactions. This helps in building vendor's transaction histories that improve their access to credit in the future.

The programme built a digital trace for 6.8 million unbanked merchants and helped them build a credit history. 43% of recipients were first-time users of UPI, and merchants witnessed 50% increase in income after digitizing transactions. (RBIH, 2025). 1.9 million (28%) loans were provided to the women vendors, who benefited from specially designed camps on overcoming mobility restrictions and financial literacy constraints. MoUHA collaborated with NGOs, such as SEWA, to launch door-to-door campaigns and assisted digital transactions through agents to increase awareness and usage of digital services.

6. SUMMARY AND CONCLUSION

Financial inclusion over the years has been transformative. Reserve Bank of India has reported that Index of Financial Inclusion has increased from 60.1 in 2023 to 67 2025. Initiatives such as The Pradhan Mantri Jan Dhan Yojna have been successful in opening millions of accounts across India, from 15.7 crore in 2015 to

54.58 crore in April 2025. Among these, 55% held by women and two-thirds by rural areas (Ministry of Finance, 2025). Alongside, fintech has also been reinforcing the development of India's digital public infrastructure. The Aadhaar, UPI and mobile connectivity have changed how citizens access and use financial services. Almost 99% of India's adult population has Aadhaar, enabling e-KYC processes that reduce costs up to 90%. This has increased digital payments and fintech growth (UIDAI, 2023). The RBI Digital Payments Index rose from 304.06 in 2021 to 465.33 in 2024, showing increasing digital adoption (RBI, 2024). Fintech has also expanded to digital lending and microinsurance with the help of initiatives like RBI's First Loss Default Guarantee and Account Aggregator (IBEF, 2024). These efforts of financial inclusion have also reached Street vendors. The Street Vendors (Protection of Livelihood and Regulation of Street Vending) Act provided them legal recognition and secured their right to work in public spaces. Yet by 2020, only 35% of Urban Local Bodies had fully functioning Town Vending Zones and Committees (CCS, 2020). After COVID-19, to support them, India launched the Pradhan Mantri Street vendors's AtmaNirbhar Nidhi (PM SVANidhi) scheme, it provided vendors 68 lakh loans by 2025, which is essential for decreasing their dependency on informal lenders. (MoHUA, 2025). The scheme also promoted digital payments through cashback rewards, leading to over 36 lakh vendors using UPI and other digital options. Thus, helping vendors to establish credit records and become resilient. However, they continue to encounter problems such as insecure locations, evictions, harassment and vulnerability to digital fraud due to low education and unawareness of their legal rights and government programs. This limits their access to benefits. Further, many vendors still rely on informal lenders because of easy access and flexibility (Gogoi & Bhattacharyya, 2022).

Therefore, policy efforts should focus on the use of financial services together with access. Also, strengthen rural financial systems, more service centers that are easily accessible and mobile solutions in places that have connectivity issues. together with digital literacy programs, fraud prevention initiatives and education, particularly for marginalized groups and women. India has diverse demographics and infrastructure, so there should be different policies according to regions. For Street vendors, enforce strong legal protections, create safe vending places and awareness campaigns that are supported by trustworthy grievance systems to help them survive and become economically empowered in the long run. There should be proper implementation of polices and regular inspection. Altogether, India has made significant progress, but to achieve sustainable inclusion, focus is needed on usage equity and institutional support.

This chapter is limited to secondary data and policy reports, lacking fieldwork or causal analysis. The insights only present the current trends, but it may change as fintech innovations and regulations are ever evolving.

REFERENCES

Affandi, H., & Malik, Q. (2020). Financial inclusion and financial literacy in low income group in emerging economy. *Journal of Accounting and Finance in Emerging Economies*, *6*(4), 1005–1013. DOI: 10.26710/jafee.v6i4.1451

Ashaley-Nikoi, J., & Abbey, E. (2023). Determinants of the level of informality amongst female street food vendors in sub-Saharan Africa: Evidence from two regions in Ghana. *Cities (London, England)*, *138*, 104359. DOI: 10.1016/j.cities.2023.104359

Atkinson, A., & Messy, F. (2013). Promoting financial inclusion through financial education:

Atlantic Council. (2024). *How digital public infrastructure can support financial inclusion*. Atlantic Council.

Azimi, M. (2022). New insights into the impact of financial inclusion on economic growth: A global perspective. *PLoS One*, *17*(11), 17. DOI: 10.1371/journal.pone.0277730 PMID: 36395150

Barajas, A., Beck, T., Belhaj, M., & Ben Naceur, S. (2020). *Financial inclusion: What have we learned so far? What do we have to learn?* (IMF Working Paper No. 2020/157). International Monetary Fund.

Barbu, C., Florea, D., Dabija, D., & Barbu, M. (2021). Customer experience in Fintech. *Journal of Theoretical and Applied Electronic Commerce Research*, *16*(5), 1415–1433. DOI: 10.3390/jtaer16050080

Bhatia, S., & Singh, S. (2019). Empowering women through financial inclusion: A study of urban slum. *Vikalpa*, *44*(4), 182–197. DOI: 10.1177/0256090919897809

Bhowmik, S. K. (2012). *Street vendors in the global urban economy*. Routledge. DOI: 10.4324/9780203150542

Bin-Humam, Y., Braunmiller, J., & Elsaman, M. (2023). Emerging Trends in National Financial Inclusion Strategies that Support Women's Entrepreneurship.

Bromley, R. (2000). Street vending and public policy: A global review. *The International Journal of Sociology and Social Policy*, *20*(1/2), 1–28. DOI: 10.1108/01443330010789052

CCS. (2022). *Street vendors Act Compliance Index 2022*. Centre for Civil Society.

Chaddha, S., & Jain, S. (2024). Digital transformation of financial sector in India: Evolution, issues and challenges. *International Journal of Advanced Research in Science. Tongxin Jishu*, *4*(5), 107–111.

Chakrabarty, K. C. (2013). Financial inclusion in India: Journey so far and way forward. *Address delivered at the Finance Inclusion Conclave*, New Delhi.

Charfeddine, L., & Zaouali, S. (2022). The effects of financial inclusion and the business environment in spurring the creation of early-stage firms and supporting established firms. *Journal of Business Research*, *143*, 1–15. DOI: 10.1016/j.jbusres.2022.01.014

Danisman, G., & Tarazi, A. (2020). Financial inclusion and bank stability: Evidence from Europe. *European Journal of Finance*, *26*(18), 1842–1855. DOI: 10.1080/1351847X.2020.1782958

Demirgüç-Kunt, A., Klapper, L., & Singer, D. (2017). Financial inclusion and inclusive growth: A review of recent empirical studies. *The World Bank Research Observer*, *32*(2), 238–264.

Deore, P., & Lathia, S. (2019). Streets as Public Spaces: Lessons from Street Vending in Ahmedabad, India. *Urban Planning*, *4*(2), 138–153. DOI: 10.17645/up.v4i2.2058

Drishti IAS. (2022, October 16). *75 new Digital Banking Units in India*. Drishti IAS.

Equations. (2012). *Women Street vendors and Tourism: Negotiating Lives and Spaces*. Bangalore: Equations, Equitable Tourism.

Feyen, E., Natarajan, H., & Saal, M. (2023). *Fintech and the future of finance: Market and policy implications*. World Bank Publications. DOI: 10.1596/978-1-4648-1914-8

Global Partnership for Financial Inclusion. (2017). *G20 financial inclusion action plan*.

Gogoi, M., & Bhattacharyya, M. (2022). Work security and other challenges for Street vendors in Guwahati City, Assam. *The Asia Pacific Journal of Anthropology*, *23*(3), 250–265. DOI: 10.1080/14442213.2022.2056912

GOI. (2023). *Government of India Report on Street vendors*. Ministry of Housing and Urban Affairs.

Gomber, P., Kauffman, R. J., Parker, C., & Weber, B. W. (2018). On the fintech revolution: Interpreting the forces of innovation, disruption, and transformation in financial services. *Journal of Management Information Systems*, *35*(1), 220–265. DOI: 10.1080/07421222.2018.1440766

Goswami, S., Sharma, R., & Chouhan, V. (2022). *Impact of Financial Technology (Fintech) on Financial Inclusion(FI) in Rural India*. Universal Journal of Accounting and Finance. DOI: 10.13189/ujaf.2022.100213

GPFI. (2017). *G20 Global Partnership for Financial Inclusion*. Financial Stability Board.

Han, R., & Melecky, M. (2013). *Financial inclusion for financial stability: Access to bank deposits and the growth of deposits in the global financial crisis* (Policy Research Working Paper No. 6577). World Bank.

Hendriks, S. (2019). The role of financial inclusion in driving women's economic empowerment. *Development in Practice*, *29*(8), 1029–1038. DOI: 10.1080/09614524.2019.1660308

Hussain, A., Endut, N., Das, S., Chowdhury, M., Haque, N., Sultana, S., & Ahmed, K. (2018). Does financial inclusion increase financial resilience? Evidence from Bangladesh. *Development in Practice*, *29*(6), 798–807. DOI: 10.1080/09614524.2019.1607256

Huynh, Q. (2023). Street vendors in Vietnam: Short Cultural and Economic Insight. *International Journal of Culture and Education*.

IBEF. (2024). *Digital loans up 49% in FY24 by value*. India Brand Equity Foundation.

ICAR. (2024). *Sustainability of vegetable Street vendors in India*. ICAR-National Academy of Agricultural Research Management.

ILO. (2020). *Women and men in the informal economy: A statistical picture* (3rd ed.). International Labour Organization.

IMF & World Bank. (2019). *The Bali Fintech Agenda*. Policy Papers, 2019.

India Forum. (2025, October 29). *Closing India's gender gap in financial inclusion*. The India Forum.

Intelligence, G. S. M. A. (2024). *The mobile economy: Asia Pacific 2024*. GSMA.

International Monetary Fund. (2023). Digital public infrastructure and financial inclusion. In *Digital finance: Opportunities and risks* (pp. xx–xx). International Monetary Fund.

Jacolin, L., Massil, J. K., & Noah, A. (2021). Informal sector and mobile financial services in emerging and developing countries: Does financial innovation matter? *World Economy*, *44*(5), 1292–1328. DOI: 10.1111/twec.13093

Jamir, C., & Pongen, M. (2022). Income and Employment Generation in Informal Sector: A case study of the Street vendors of Kohima and Dimapur district of Nagaland, India. *International Journal of Engineering Business Management, 6*(4), 52–63.

Jungo, J., Madaleno, M., & Botelho, A. (2022). The Effect of Financial Inclusion and Competitiveness on Financial Stability: Why Financial Regulation Matters in Developing Countries? *Journal of Risk and Financial Management, 15*(3), 122. DOI: 10.3390/jrfm15030122

Kedla, S., Nandini, B., & Chethan, S. (2025). Street Food Culture and Culinary Tourism: Economic Drift for the Tourism Industry. *European Journal of Arts, Humanities and Social Sciences.*

Kumar, K. R., & Rani, S. (2025). Social Inclusion of Street vendors In Market Economy: A Study with Reference to Visakhapatnam District, Andhra Pradesh, India. *International Journal for Multidisciplinary Research, 7*(1).

Kumar, R., & Sah, S. K. (2025). Socioeconomic dynamics of Street vendors in a globalized urban context: A case study of Bihar. *International Journal of Advanced Academic Studies, 7*(3), 144–147. DOI: 10.33545/27068919.2025.v7.i3b.1426

Mazumder, M. S. (2025). *PM SVANidhi: Street vendors' digital journey.* Ministry of Housing and Urban Affairs.

MeitY. (2024). *Annual Report 2023-24.* Ministry of Electronics and Information Technology, Government of India.

MicroSave Consulting. (2023). *Account inactivity in India: Is there a problem?* MicroSave Consulting.

Ministry of Housing & Urban Poverty Alleviation. (2009). *National Policy on Urban Street vendors, 2009.* Government of India.

Mishra, D., Kandpal, V., Agarwal, N., & Srivastava, B. (2024). Financial inclusion and its ripple effects on socio-economic development: A comprehensive review. *Journal of Risk and Financial Management, 17*(3), 105. DOI: 10.3390/jrfm17030105

MoF. (2024). *Stand Up India Scheme: Ministry of Finance.* Government of India.

Mohanty Committee. (2015). *Report of the Committee on Medium-term Path on Financial Inclusion.* Reserve Bank of India.

MoHUA. (2023). *Number of Street vendors identified by states.* Ministry of Housing and Urban Affairs.

Moro-Visconti, R., Cruz Rambaud, S., & López Pascual, J. (2020). Sustainability in FinTechs: An explanation through business model scalability and market valuation. *Sustainability (Basel), 12*(24), 10316. DOI: 10.3390/su122410316

Munishi, E., Songa, P., & Kirumirah, M. (2021). Challenges to Accessing Credit Financing from Financial Institutions by the Urban Based Street vendors: Experience from Dar Es Salaam – Tanzania. *International Journal of Business and Management, 17*(1), 65. DOI: 10.5539/ijbm.v17n1p65

NAFIS. (2024). *All India Rural Financial Inclusion Survey*. NABARD.

National Institute of Rural Development and Panchayati Raj. (2019). *An evaluation of the SHG-BLP with special reference to its loan portfolio and asset quality*.

Neaime, S., & Gaysset, I. (2017). Financial inclusion and stability in MENA: Evidence from poverty and inequality. *Finance Research Letters, 24*, 230–237. DOI: 10.1016/j.frl.2017.09.007

Nigerian Central Bank. (2024). *Financial inclusion and digital payments statistics 2024*. Central Bank of Nigeria.

NIRDP et al. (2019). *Status of Self Help Group Bank Linkage Programme in India: A radical shift*. National Institute of Rural Development and Panchayati Raj.

NPCI. (2025). *Aadhaar-enabled Payments Data*. National Payments Corporation of India.

OECD/INFE evidence, policies and practice. *OECD Working Papers on Finance, Insurance and Private Pensions*, 34.

Omar, M. A., & Inaba, K. (2020). Does financial inclusion reduce poverty and income inequality in developing countries? A panel data analysis. *Journal of Economic Structures, 9*(1), 37. DOI: 10.1186/s40008-020-00214-4

Onodugo, V., Ezeadichie, N., Onwuneme, C., & Anosike, A. (2016). The dilemma of managing the challenges of street vending in public spaces: The case of Enugu City, Nigeria. *Cities (London, England), 59*, 95–101. DOI: 10.1016/j.cities.2016.06.001

Ozili, P. K. (2018). Impact of digital finance on financial inclusion and stability. *Borsa Istanbul Review, 18*(4), 329–340. DOI: 10.1016/j.bir.2017.12.003

Patel, R., & Koshy, A. (2023). Gender inclusivity of India's digital financial revolution for the poor: A critical review. *Journal of Global Health Reports, 7*, e2023025.

Philippon, T. (2016). *The FinTech opportunity*. NBER Working Paper No. 22476.

Planning Commission. (2009). *Report of the Expert Group on Financial Inclusion in India*. Government of India.

Pomeroy, R., Arango, C., Lomboy, C., & Box, S. (2020). Financial inclusion to build economic resilience in small-scale fisheries. *Marine Policy, 118*, 103982. DOI: 10.1016/j.marpol.2020.103982

Press Information Bureau. (2022, October 15). *PM dedicates 75 Digital Banking Units across 75 districts to the nation*. Government of India.

Press Trust of India. (2025, March 31). Women's share in digital transactions doubled from 14% to 28% in last 7 years: Government. *The Hindu BusinessLine*.

Progress Report, C. C. S. (2020). *Progress Report 2020: Implementing the Street vendors Act*. Centre for Civil Society.

Qi, Y., Yue, L., Guo, T., Zhou, D., Ren, Y., Wang, M., Liu, Y., & Yang, Y. (2024). A Study on the Perception of Local Characteristics in Cultural Street Vending Spaces, Taking Xi'an Baxian Temple as an Example. *Buildings (Basel, Switzerland), 14*(1), 192. DOI: 10.3390/buildings14010192

Rangarajan Committee. (2008). *Report of the Committee on Financial Inclusion*. Government of India.

Rao, S., & Nair, L. (2019). Aadhaar: A digital identity for the unorganized. *Information Technology for Development, 25*(4), 797–815.

RBI. (2021). *Master Circular – Mobile Banking Transactions in India*. Reserve Bank of India.

RBI. (2025). *Financial Inclusion Index Report*. Reserve Bank of India.

Roever, S., & Skinner, C. (2016). Street vendors and cities. *Environment and Urbanization, 28*(2), 359–374. DOI: 10.1177/0956247816653898

Romero, R., Paulino, E., Tan, R., & Cortez, D. (2024). Urban entrepreneurship on the fringe: Action research on the challenges of Street vendors in Manila. *Journal of Business and Management Studies*.

Sahay, R., von Allmen, U. E., Lahreche, A., Khera, P., Ogawa, S., Bazarbash, M., & Beaton, K. (2020). *The promise of fintech: Financial inclusion in the post COVID-19 era* (Departmental Paper No. 20/09). International Monetary Fund.

Saini, A., Fariya, 2., Agarwal, M., Kumar, P., Chauhan, R., Surendra, L., & Singh, P. (2024). Unveiling awareness and perception patterns: A comprehensive analysis of PM SVA Nidhi for Street vendors in Meerut. *Journal of Social Economics Research*.

Sakariya, S. M. (2014). *Financial inclusion: A study of commercial banks in India* [Doctoral dissertation, Saurashtra University].

Sangeetha, P., & Menaka, S. (2022). Study on livelihood of street food vendors. *International Journal of Agricultural Sciences, 18*(CIABASSD), 47–53. DOI: 10.15740/HAS/IJAS/18-CIABASSD/47-53

Satyasai, K. J. S. (2020). NAFINDEX: A measure of financial inclusion based on NABARD All India Rural Financial Inclusion Survey. *Rural Pulse, 33*, 1–4.

Sharma, A., Das, N., & Singh, S. P. (2023). Causal association of the entrepreneurship ecosystem and financial inclusion. *Heliyon, 9*(3), e14596. DOI: 10.1016/j.heliyon.2023.e14596 PMID: 36950562

Singh, P. (2022). Implementation of Street vendors Act in India. *Urban Development Journal, 18*(2), 134–152.

Sinha, P. (2025). Street vendors in India, estimated at over 15 million, make up roughly 10% of urban workers. *Hindustan Times*. https://www.hindustantimes.com/opinion/urban-renewal-with-street vendors-haats-101735836890911.html

Srivastava, A. (2022). Digital Financial Inclusion. *International Journal of Innovation in the Digital Economy, 13*(1), 1–12. DOI: 10.4018/IJIDE.303611

Street vendors Act. (2014). *The Street vendors (Protection of Livelihood and Regulation of Street Vending) Act, 2014*. Government of India.

Swarmy, V. (2014). Financial inclusion, gender dimension, and economic impact on poor households. *World Development, 56*, 1–15. DOI: 10.1016/j.worlddev.2013.10.019

Tetteh, G. K., Goedhuys, M., Konte, M., & Mohnen, P. (2025). Mobile money use and entrepreneurs' access to trade credit in the informal sector. *Review of Development Economics, 29*(4), 2311–2331. DOI: 10.1111/rode.13223

Tut, D. (2020). *FinTech and the COVID-19 pandemic: Evidence from electronic payment systems* (SSRN Working Paper No. 3660987). SSRN.

United Nations. (2015). *Transforming our world: The 2030 Agenda for Sustainable Development* (Resolution A/RES/70/1). United Nations General Assembly.

UNSGSA. (2011). *Financial inclusion: Advancing the global agenda* (Máxima trans.). Office of the United Nations Secretary-General's Special Advocate for Inclusive Finance for Development.

Van, L., Vo, A., Nguyen, N., & Vo, D. (2019). Financial Inclusion and Economic GROWTH: An International Evidence. *Emerging Markets Finance & Trade*, *57*(1), 239–263. DOI: 10.1080/1540496X.2019.1697672

Van, L., Vo, A., Nguyen, N., & Vo, D. (2021). Financial Inclusion and Economic Growth: International Evidence. *Emerging Markets Finance & Trade*, *57*(1), 239–263. DOI: 10.1080/1540496X.2019.1697672

Veena, M.Dr. Veena M. (2022). Conceptual Evolution of Financial Inclusion. *EPRA International Journal of Economic and Business Review*, *10*(7), 1–7. DOI: 10.36713/epra10762

Vidani, J. (2024). Revolutionizing finance: Unveiling the digital banking terrain in India with a focus on ICICI Bank. SSRN *Electronic Journal*. DOI: 10.2139/ssrn.4848084

Vives, X. (2019). Digital disruption in banking. *Annual Review of Financial Economics*, *11*(1), 243–272. DOI: 10.1146/annurev-financial-100719-120854

WIEGO. (n.d.). *Street vendors and Market Traders*. Retrieved from https://www.wiego.org/

World Bank. (2014). *Global financial development report 2014: Financial inclusion*. World Bank Publications.

World Bank. (2024). *Financial inclusion overview*. Retrieved from https://www.worldbank.org/en/topic/fi nancialinclusion

World Bank Global Findex Database. (2021). *Global Findex Database 2021: Financial Inclusion, Digital Payments, and Resilience in the Age of COVID-19*. World Bank.

World Bank Global Findex Database. (2025). *Global Findex Database 2025*. World Bank.

Zavolokina, L., Dolata, M., & Schwabe, G. (2016). The FinTech phenomenon: Antecedents of financial innovation perceived by the popular press. *Financial Innovation*, *2*(1), 1–16. DOI: 10.1186/s40854-016-0036-7

KEY TERMS AND DEFINITIONS

Aadhaar: A biometric ID system for identity verification without the need for a physical copy.

Digital Payments: A service for doing transactions electronically with mobile devices and fintech platforms.

Financial Inclusion: The process of ensuring that all people have access to financial services at affordable prices, targeting the most vulnerable groups to facilitate economic growth and increase their ability to cope with difficulties.

FinTech: Technology-based financial innovation, which include digital payments and lending, that makes the service cheaper and more accessible to users.

JAM Trinity: The merger of Jan Dhan accounts, Aadhaar ID, and mobile connectivity, which makes direct benefit transfers possible, thus cutting down on subsidies and welfare.

PM SVANidhi: Indian government scheme that grants easy loans of up to 50,000 to street hawkers, along with perks for digital transactions.

PMJDY (Pradhan Mantri Jan Dhan Yojana): A national mission that aims at the unbanked populations by opening zero-balance bank accounts with the provisions of insurance, and overdraft facilities, etc.

Street Vendors: Informal sellers who offer goods or services from a short-term stall or mobile unit in the city are an integral part of India's economy but usually deprived of formal financing facilities.

UPI (Unified Payments Interface): A payment method that happens in real-time, it allows people to transfer money between two different banks via a mobile phone.

Chapter 5

Post-Listing Performance of IPOs in India's Financial Services Sector (2021-2024): An Industry-Specific Empirical Study

Hiren Harikumar
http://orcid.org/0009-0008-3255-5779
Christ University, India

ABSTRACT

The number of initial public offerings (IPOs) made in the Indian financial services sector between 2021-2024 has increased, due to heightened investor activity. Although the volume of IPO issues has increased, there is limited research on their short-term performance, particularly in the context of industry-specific analysis. This paper will evaluate the performance of IPOs that issue financial services companies in India during the listing period of 20 days using the event study methodology. The daily returns of IPOs and the index (NIFTY 50) are taken to compute market-adjusted short-run performance (MASRP), wealth relative (WR), abnormal returns (AR), and cumulative abnormal returns (CAR). The regression analysis shows that only oversubscription can have a significant effect on the revenue of an IPO in terms of returns. This research has added value by using sector-specific evidence, which may be useful to investors, issuers, and regulators when evaluating short-run IPO efficiencies.

DOI: 10.4018/979-8-3373-5047-9.ch005

INTRODUCTION

An Initial Public Offering (IPO) refers to the process by which privately owned entities are converted into publicly owned ones, with securities initially offered to outsiders. It is believed that this was one of the most intricate and probably one of the most dramatic developments in the financial markets, a process that has been considered the most interesting and yet complicated phenomenon in financial markets (Ritter, 1991; Loughran and Ritter, 2004a). The occurrence of the phenomenon of IPO underpricing is consistently reported in research of many countries, where the market ending price on the first day of trading is usually higher than the price of the issue, thus yielding immediate listing profit to investors, giving immediate listing-day profits to investors (Rock, 1986; Allen & Faulhaber, 1989). The pathways through which this anomaly has been explained theoretically include the winner-takes-all hypothesis, signaling theories, and book-building mechanisms, which all explain why investors often experience excess first-day returns (Aggarwal, 2000; Ljungqvist, 2007).

According to the empirical research in various markets, not only do initial public offerings show underestimation of prices in the short term, but also a significant underperformance of this type of offering in terms of its appearance in the long term, in opposition to benchmark indices (Ibbotson et al., 1975; Ritter & Welch, 2002). This long-run performance has been seen and explained with investor behavior, market timing, and regulatory structures. In emerging economies, and especially in India, the scale of underpricing is often optional to a greater degree than can be explained by high levels of information asymmetry and frequent short-selling behavior (Deb & Marisetty, 2010; Sahoo & Rajib, 2010).

In India, the IPO marketplace has evolved at a fast rate. Smaller studies by Krishnamurti and Kumar (2002) have revealed very high returns on the initial day. These IPOs, as determined by Sehgal and Singh (2008), do not perform well in the long run. Experimental studies showed the importance of the over-subscription ratio, firm age, issue size, promoter shareholding, and underwriter reputation.

Although IPOs have been the subject of a rich literature, most Indian research looks at IPOs in any industry. Performance studies are also still scarce, sector-wise. In particular, the financial services industry, which includes banks, NBFCs, insurers, fintech, and asset management businesses, has shown a spiking IPO activity in the period between 2021 and 2024 due to the post-pandemic recovery, fintech adaptation, regulatory reform, and financial inclusion agendas (EY, 2024; Newman et al, 2024). Listings on the bourses during this time, including PB Fintech, Paytm (One97), LIC, and Star Health, represent the increase in investor interest and volatility as well.

Although sectoral factors may contribute to IPO performance, the literature does not provide any evidence that focuses on financial services IPOs in the Indian context over the short run. Due to the industry-specific exposure it has to interest rate movements, credit cycles, government interventions, standards of corporate governance, and technological disruption (Pillay et al, 2022; RBI, n.d.), it is of value to understand its behavior on an IPO.

The proposed study will fill that research gap by paying specific attention to the Indian financial services industry as well as its IPOs from 2021 until 2024. Firstly, we propose to test the short-run post-listing performance using event study measures, including average abnormal return (AAR), CAR, market-adjusted short-run performance (MASRP), and wealth relative (WR) recorded over a 20-trading-day window. Second, we will estimate the main drivers of IPO performance, including oversubscription, issue price, profit after tax (PAT), promoter holdings post-IPO, and market returns using multiple regressions.

By singling out the financial services industry, this research is able to contribute to the literature in three ways. First, it provides industry-specific evidence on short-run IPO behavior to an important yet less-studied market segment in India. Second, the expanded event window (20 days) encompasses the period of exuberance through early market correction that other studies miss because they only use a 1- to 5-day window. Third, the regression model will allow the strategic interpretation of the issue, firm, and market-specific factors that form significant contributions to the short-run IPO returns.

The work is topical and policy-oriented. Investors can benefit by understanding that oversubscription, as opposed to price of issue, profitability, and promoter holding, is a primary determinant of short-term gains. Regulators can be informed about the dynamics of listing to help shape the proper pricing, allocation, and transparency frameworks. To issuers, these findings suggest the significance of creating investor interest and intelligibility of disclosures.

In section 2, literature reviews are conducted across global and Indian IPO studies and within the context of industry-specific IPO research and of the financial services IPO research. Section 3 provides information on the research design, data sources, sample criteria, event study measures, and regression. Section 4 provides the results of the empirical research and gives an interpretation of the findings. Introduction, background, problem statement, delineation of the study, research questions, and research objectives involved are highlighted in Sections 1, 2, 3, and 4, respectively. Section 5 summarizes the most important findings, limitations, and practical recommendations, and Section 6 proposes ideas for future research.

Background: IPOs in the Indian Financial Services Market (2021-24).

The Indian financial services sector recorded unprecedented IPO activity over the 2021-2024 period. 38 companies collectively raised around 150,000 crore through public listing activities. This era saw a change in India's main capital markets, as there were a few landmark deals where benchmarks in sectors were redefined.

The biggest offer in this period was the Life Insurance Corporation of India (LIC) IPO in May 2022, with a raise of 21,000 crore, the biggest public offering in the history of India. Other significant listings were Paytm (One97 Communications Limited), which raised 18,300 crore in November 2021, making it the biggest IPO for a fintech startup in India amid listing losses of approx. 9% on listing day. PB Fintech (PolicyBazaar) received 5,710 crore in November 2021 and showed good open-day performance with listing gains of more than 17%. Star Health And Allied Insurance Company mobilized 6400 crore in December 2021, while Bajaj Housing Finance Limited's 6560 crore IPO in September 2024 was the largest in the financial services sector in the year.

The period has been characterized by clear phases—(1) post-pandemic recovery euphoria in 2021—10 financial services IPOs saw average oversubscriptions around 40-50 times; (2) market correction in 2022 as a result of market inflation and monetary tightening—8 IPOs with comparatively more modest oversubscriptions; (3) stabilization in 2023 with 7 offerings—signs of caution; and (4) revival in 2024 with 13 IPOs with excellent market sentiment and regulatory clarity.

Regulatory developments had a great influence on the landscape. The Reserve Bank of India issued regulations for NBFCs in October 2022 based on a scaling system to determine the intensity of oversight, according to which the intensity of oversight of the financial products of the NBFCs is differentiated according to the size of assets. SEBI introduced revised IPO norms regarding enhanced disclosure of risk factors and utilization of proceeds in November 2021. The Insurance Regulatory and Development Authority of India (IRDAI) eased the requirements of licensing digital insurers in 2023 to encourage fintech insurance platform listing.

Market conditions in the period were very varied. The NIFTY 50 index rose by 24% in 2021, fell by 4% in 2022, bounced back by 20% in 2023, and rose by 15% up to 2024. Average IPO subscription levels reached 38x in 2021, moderated to 12x in 2022, stabilized at 18x in 2023, and then recovered to 28x in 2024. Listing day returns fluctuated between an average of 18% in 2021 and the current 6% in 2022, and normalized to an average of 11% in 2023 to 14% in 2024.

Literature Review

Research in the field of initial public offerings (IPOs) has been one of the most longstanding and controversial applications in financial economics. A body of globally available literature presents a two-party pattern in the initial public offering (IPO) behavior: Excessive short-term underpricing was followed by stable long-term performance at market parity. Basic literature, such as that of Ibbotson (1975) and Ritter (1991), shows that a first issue share offering can be associated with considerable positive abnormal returns on the issue date, but the benefits dissipate over extended periods, and in the long term, a negative abnormal return. These results were generalized to the cross-country domain, with Loughran and Ritter (2004a) revealing the same result in the U.S. market, and Ljungqvist (2007) bringing together evidence applicable in advanced and developing markets. Model explanations of IPO anomalies include models involving information asymmetry (Rock, 1986), models based on signaling (Allen & Faulhaber, 1989), the principal-agent context (Baron, 1982), and market sentiment models (Cornelli et al., 2006).

The post-pandemic era has seen a lot of scholarly focus on analyzing the impact of the disruptions of COVID-19 and the recovery on IPO markets across the world. There are recent studies that can be put into context to understand the 2021-2024 Indian financial services landscape. Examining the effects of pandemics, researchers recorded significant changes in the activities and performances of IPOs. Studies analyzing 2020-2021 offerings have found that the technology and healthcare sectors dominated the offerings during lockdown, while financial services IPOs declined to surge in recovery phases. The digital adoption acceleration has changed investor preferences regarding fintech and digital-first financial platforms forever. Recent Indian research on IPOs has recorded the changing trends during the post-liberalization period. Studies focusing on the 2020-2023 data showed average initial returns varying between 12% and 18% across sectors, with financial services showing moderate underpricing, while technology companies are presented with fair pricing. The introduction of ASBA (Application Supported by Blocked Amount) mechanisms and UPI-based applications democratized access to market participation by retail investors, and in the years 2021-2024, retail investors represented between 35% and 45% of the demand for financing for financial services IPO.

Fintech-specific research has posed distinctive challenges to valuations. Unlike the valuations for traditional banks relative to book multiples and ROE metrics, fintech platforms command pleasant valuations traditionally fueled by factors like user growth, transaction volumes, and ecosystem potential. Studies based on PolicyBazaar, Paytm, and MobiKwik IPOs documented the difficulty in markets accurately pricing these hybrid business models, leading to high initial volatility and later divergence in performance from traditional financial institutions. Regulatory scholarship has focused on the impact of changing frameworks on IPO outcomes. A study of RBI's scale-based regulations on NBFCs that were introduced in 2022 found that just because of the clarity about the regulatory treatment, information asymmetry was reduced and pricing efficiency was enhanced for the affected companies. Similarly, studies on the enhanced disclosure requirements of SEBI showed some positive correlation between the quality of disclosure and aftermarket stability. A growing interest of the enterprising scholar in the field of behavioral finance is that of retail investor participation in IPOs. Recent studies recorded social media sentiment, influencer recommendations, and grey market premiums having a significant impact on retail demand, which, in particular, is the case with high-profile fintech offerings. The "FOMO" (fear of missing out) phenomenon was particularly evident during the IPO boom of 2021, contributing to insane oversubscription levels that subsequently corrected.

The evidence of widespread underpricing has been proven worldwide empirically. These results are supported by other evidence derived from various markets; however, Aggarwal et al. (2000) found that the listing-day gains in Latin America were significant, but Levis (1993) also yielded similar generalized results in the U.K. market. In the Asian markets, Chang et al. (2008) and Yong (2011) found that there was a strong underpricing that was pronounced in Hong Kong and Malaysia, respectively, caused by the retail sentiment of the investor. Boulton et al. (2010) found legal structures, protections given to the investors, and governance norms to be influential in the performance of IPO across nations. This global literature points to the universal character of underpricing, yet also makes clear that institutional and market-specific aspects determine the extent of it.

The behavior of the initial public offering in the Indian context has received significant academic attention since the economic liberalization period, and empirical studies have thus far carried consistent reports of good initial price premiums and underperformance in the post-offering market. In a study of IPOs in India in the 1990s, an example is al-Krishnamurti and Kumar (2002), who expressed the mean listing premiums of about 94 percent, and highlighted the low long-term returns following post-listing price changes. Sehgal and Singh (2008) further updated the sample to 2004 and once again found the short-run underpricing and long-run underperformance. According to empirical evidence by Deb and Marisetty (2010) and Sahoo and Rajib (2010), it was found that an Indian IPO that was issued by the book-building method has efficient pricing as well as slightly reduced underpricing in comparison to a fixed-price issue. Banerjee concluded that (in the context of India) the determinants of short-term IPO performance include, among other things, the issue size, subscription level, and underwriter credibility.

Event study methods of analysis of abnormal returns have also been applied in several Indian studies. Abnormal returns and oversubscription are positively correlated, and we found that the demand of retail investors and grey market premiums. The results demonstrated the importance of the macroeconomic sentiment when studying the initial returns on IPOs in bullish market conditions compared to bearish situations. Market-corrected models like the Market Adjusted Excess Return (MAER), Wealth Relatives (WR), and Cumulative Abnormal Returns (CAR) are important in Indian IPO studies in light of these findings.

The financial services industry is the industry that has distinct features in the IPO performance. All around the globe, financial institutions are faced with heightened regulatory reviews, higher capital adequacy requirements, and an increased risk of fluctuating macroeconomic conditions that heighten investor confidence at the time of the listing. According to Megginson and Weiss (1991), the certification of the underwriters by some reputable firms is especially vital in the case of financial organizations because of their opaque balance sheets. Hearn (2014) added that, in emerging markets, governance structures and the quality of disclosure may especially matter in terms of financial-sector IPOs. In India, the sector IPOs have been increasing at a high rate since 2015, including major listings such as ICICI Prudential Life Insurance, HDFC AMC, SBI Cards, and, more recently, PB Fintech, LIC, and Paytm. According to reports by EY (2024) and Newman et al. (2024), financial services IPOs have raised record-breaking capital through 2021-2024, and these companies are enjoying a strong appetite from investors even though there has been a degree of market volatility.

There is limited empirical evidence in India specifically on financial-sector initial public offerings (IPOs). A heterogeneous short-term performance, as explored in the case-based analyses, referring to the performance of Paytm, LIC, and Star Health, reveals the role of sectoral dynamics. Consider the severe listing loss of Paytm in India, out of the hoopla before its IPO, or the fact that the LIC IPO, the largest Indian IPO, has only been slightly oversubscribed and consequently trades below the issue price even after the first month of listing (SEBI, n.d.). Instead, PB Securities (Policy Bazaar) had a super start, though it was very volatile after that. These examples indicate that the conventional factors that are known to influence IPO performance, such as oversubscription and promoter holdings, may interact with industry-specific factors such as fintech disruption, insurance penetration rates, and broad NBFC credit quality.

The causal factors of the results of initial public offerings (IPOs) are researched by many scholars both locally and internationally; thereby, a consistent emphasis was put on over-subscriptions, profitability, holding of shares by promoters, and market momentum. Ritter and Welch (2002) noted a positive correlation between underpricing, demand momentum, and oversubscription. In India, acknowledged that oversubscription is one of the most reliable short-term predictors of growing returns. This is supported by, who concluded that profitability (PAT) has less explanatory power for initial returns, as the short-run performance seems to be more sentiment-sensitive. Promoter holdings are a significant factor in the stability of the aftermarket because the less promoter dilution, the greater the confidence of investors. Systemic influences also have a role to play in the performance of IPO markets, which are closely related to current NIFTY returns.

It is worth noting that determinants have been researched generally across IPOs but not the IPOs of the financial services sector in the 2021-2024 period, and thus, there is a research gap in that area. These were years of COVID-19 recovery, RBI policy interventions, inflationary pressures, digital adoption, and volatile equity flows. This macro-financial climate has evoked the question as to whether the sectoral IPOs exhibited different patterns from those of wider IPO markets. Besides, because investors in the shares of financial services businesses tend to give more attention to the strength of their regulatory capital, credibility of the promoters, and the potential of fintech, the determinants of the IPO returns can be different in the case of industrial or production lines.

Thus, the proposed study would add value to the body of knowledge as it focuses on the study of the Indian financial services sector IPOs between the years 2021 and 2024. It reports short-run performance based on event-study measures (AAR, CAR, MASRP, WR) and tests determinants, including oversubscription, issue price, PAT, promoter holdings, and market returns using multiple regression. Using a generic study on IPOs and adding sector-wise knowledge, this study enhances the knowledge of IPO behavior in a spherical area in the Indian capital market.

Objectives

1. To assess the short-term and medium-term performance results of financial services IPOs in India from 2021 to 2024.
2. To find out whether these IPOs have very different returns relative to the market indicators in the broad markets.
3. To analyze the contribution of the major determinants, including the price of issues and the level of over-subscriptions and promoter shareholding, in determining the IPO returns.

Statement of Problem

In the capital markets of India, the initial case of capital offerings is often viewed as an attractive destination for investors, especially due to the potential to make high returns upon the company as soon as it gets listed. However, banks and other non-bank financial institutions (NBFCs), asset managers, and rapidly growing fintech firms demonstrate peculiar post-listing paths that have not been studied thoroughly in the scholarly literature. Despite such a large contribution to the Indian economy, there is still uncertainty on the strength with which the target variables of offer price, oversubscription intensity, promoter ownership, and the existing state of market dynamics influence both short- and medium-term performance. Such a lack of wisdom breeds confusion among investors on whether IPOs in this sector need to be interpreted as forms of short-term speculative actions or as forms of long-term investment holdings. Without an objective examination of such dynamics, were it to defy the demands of empirical research, policymakers and market rivals will meet challenges in assessing pricing effectiveness and its implications on wealth creation, thus undermining confidence in the primary market of India.

Current Scope of Study

The current study is limited to initial public offerings (IPOs) that take place by companies in the Indian financial services industry. The area of the investigative focus includes banks and non-banking financial institutions, insurance companies, fintech platforms, and asset-management firms. The sample includes only IPOs that were listed on either the National Stock Exchange (NSE) or the Bombay Stock Exchange (BSE) between January 2021 and December 2024. The appraisal orientation is the evaluative focus of short- and medium-term post-listing performance used with such offerings that are compared with the current market indices over the specified temporal framework; the long-term performance trends, extending further than a single fiscal year, are beyond the scope of this study.

Hypothesis

Null Hypothesis (H0): exists because the initial performance of financial services IPOs to the post-listing stage and the overall market performance show no statistically significant difference.

Alternative Hypothesis (H1): The performance of the initial public offerings of financial services following listing is significantly divergent from the market returns in general.

Research Methodology

Research Design

The research design applied in this study is a descriptive and empirical research design to conduct a study on the after-listing performance of initial public offerings (IPO) in the Indian financial services industry. To gauge short-term market behaviour, the analysis has made use of an event-study design, which has been widely tested in financial literature on investigating the effects of discrete market events on the prices of securities. This situation is especially suitable concerning the event-study framework; it is possible to calculate abnormal returns, which are defined as the difference between measured IPO returns and the expected returns, as it would be suggested by some standard market model. The mechanism isolates such abnormal returns, pulling out the price effect of the IPO listing that can be singled out and separated from overall market dynamics. The extant literature has shown approval of this methodological paradigm, and classic works of Brown and Warner (1985) and the refinements given by Kothari and Warner (2007) have provided a lot of testimony regarding the strength of this theory in interpreting events surrounding corporations and markets. Based on this, the study under consideration is using this defined framework to test short-run IPO behavior in the Indian financial services industry.

Period of study

The analysis would include IPOs that have been issued between January 2021 and December 2024. The recent period was selected as it was observed that the last stage of the IPO activities in the financial services sector is growing, and such growth can be explained by factors such as post-pandemic bounce back, changing the monetary policy, and making digital finance and insurance more popular among investors. Four years is enough to allow the study to take into account an array of market conditions and sectoral changes.

Data Collection

- It is purely research that depends on secondary data.
- Official filings featuring the use of information on IPO-specific particulars such as the price at offering, listing price, oversubscription ratio, and the amount of stock that a promoter compounds for purchase at the conclusion of listing, and profit after tax (PAT) was obtained at the National Stock Exchange

(NSE), Bombay Stock Exchange (BSE), and Red Herring prospectus submitted to the Securities Exchange Board of India (SEBI).

- The National Securities Exchange database was used to get the daily closing prices of stocks and the market benchmark represented by the NIFTY 50 index.

Sample Selection

The sample will include the IPOs of the financial services industry between the years 2021 and 2024 on either the NSE or BSE. Among the total amount of IPOs within this period, 40 IPOs were shortlisted after the process of eliminating the incomplete data, hence, providing the sectoral focus along with having a substantial sample size, enabling strong statistical analysis.

Analytical Tools

Logarithmic Returns

The daily stock returns for IPO *I* on day *d* were calculated using the logarithmic formula:

$$R_{i,d} = \ln\left(\frac{P_{i,d}}{P_{i,0}}\right)$$

Where Pi,dP_{i,d}Pi,d is the closing price on day *d* and Pi,0P_{i,0}Pi,0 is the issue price.

Similarly, the daily market return was computed as:

$$R_{m,d} = \ln\left(\frac{I_d}{I_0}\right)$$

Where IdI_dId is the NIFTY 50 closing index value on day *d,* and I0I_0I0 is the index value on the IPO's listing day.

Abnormal Returns (AR) and Cumulative Abnormal Returns (CAR)

Abnormal returns were calculated as:

$$AR_{i,d} = R_{i,d} - R_{m,d}$$

And cumulative abnormal returns (CAR) as:

$$CAR_{i,d} = \sum_{t=1}^{d} AR_{i,t}$$

These measures capture the stock performance relative to market trends.

Market-Adjusted Short Run Performance (MASRP)

To eliminate systematic market influence, MASRP was calculated as:

$$MASRP_{i,d} = \left[\frac{1 + R_{i,d}}{1 + R_{m,d}}\right] - 1$$

The average across all IPOs on day *d* was:

$$MASRP_{d} = \frac{1}{N}\sum_{i=1}^{N} MASRP_{i,d}$$

Wealth Relative (WR) Model

The wealth relative index was computed to measure overall performance relative to the market:

$$WR_{d} = \frac{1 + \frac{1}{N}\sum R_{i,d}}{1 + \frac{1}{N}\sum R_{m,d}}$$

A value above 1 indicates IPO outperformance relative to the market, while a value below 1 implies underperformance.

t-Test for Statistical Significance

To test whether the MASRP differed significantly from zero:

$$t = \frac{MASRP_{d}}{S/\sqrt{N}}$$

Where S is the standard deviation of MASRP and N is the sample size.

Determinants of IPO Performance (Multiple Regression)

A multiple regression model was applied to examine the effect of selected determinants on IPO performance (returns on the 20th trading day):

$$IPO\_Return = \alpha + \beta_1(\ln IP) + \beta_2(\ln OS) + \beta_3(\ln PAT) + \beta_4(\ln PH) + \beta_5(Market\_Return) +$$

Where:

ln_IP = It is the natural logarithm of the issue price
ln_OS = It is the natural logarithm of oversubscription
ln_PAT = It is the natural logarithm of profit after tax
ln_PH = It is the natural logarithm of post-issue promoters' holdings
Market Return = It is the mean market return over the 20-day event window

This regression framework helps assess the extent and direction of influence of fundamental and market-related determinants on IPO performance.

Sample Selection

The sample is composed of IPOs made by companies in the financial services industry, such as banks, non-banking financial institutions, insurance, asset management, and fintech companies, which were listed on NSE or BSE between January 2021 and December 2024. The last sample will result in around 38 IPOs within this time scale.

Table 1.

Year	Number of IPO's listed in NSE (2021-2024)
2021	10
2022	8
2023	7
2024	13

Table 2. Sample Details

Sr. No.	Name of the Issue	Year of Issue
1.	Indian Railway Finance Corporation Limited	2021
2.	Home First Finance Company India Limited	2021
3.	Suryoday Small Finance Bank Limited	2021
4.	Aptus Value Housing Finance India Limited	2021
5.	Aditya Birla Sun Life AMC Limited	2021
6.	FINO Payments Bank Limited	2021
7.	PB Fintech Limited	2021
8.	One 97 Communications Limited	2021
9.	Star Health and Allied Insurance Company Limited	2021
10.	Anand Rathi Wealth Limited	2021
11.	AGS Transact Technologies Limited	2022
12.	Life Insurance Corporation of India	2022
13.	Prudent Corporate Advisory Services Limited	2022
14.	Tamilnad Mercantile Bank Limited	2022
15.	Fusion Finance Limited	2022
16.	Five-Star Business Finance Limited	2022
17.	Abans Enterprises Limited	2022
18.	Kfin Technologies Limited	2022
19.	Utkarsh Small Finance Bank Limited	2023
20.	SBFC Finance Limited	2023
21.	ESAF Small Finance Bank Limited	2023
22.	Indian Renewable Energy Development Agency Limited	2023
23.	Fedbank Financial Services Limited	2023
24.	India Shelter Finance Corporation Limited	2023
25.	Muthoot Microfin Limited	2023
26.	Medi Assist Healthcare Services Limited	2024
27.	Jana Small Finance Bank Limited	2024
28.	Capital Small Finance Bank Limited	2024
29.	Aadhar Housing Finance Limited	2024
30.	Go Digit General Insurance Limited	2024
31.	Akme Fintrade India Limited	2024
32.	Bajaj Housing Finance Limited	2024
33.	Northern Arc Capital Limited	2024
34.	Manba Finance Limited	2024

continued on following page

Table 2. Continued

Sr. No.	Name of the Issue	Year of Issue
35.	Acme Solar Holdings Limited	2024
36.	Niva Bupa Health Insurance Company Limited	2024
37.	One MobiKwik Systems Limited	2024
38.	DAM Capital Advisors Limited	2024

Data Analysis and Interpretation

Short Term Returns

The short-run performance of the IPOs has been analyzed by use of daily mean returns, standard deviation, maximum returns, and minimum returns over a period of 20 trading days. The scientific method is close to that of the previous IPO studies since the short-run returns are used to gauge immediate market reactions right after listing.

Logarithmic returns of all IPOs on the last day of trading, d, were calculated as:

$$R_{i,d} = \ln\left(\frac{P_{i,d}}{P_{i,0}}\right)$$

Where:

- Ri,dR_(i,d) Ri,d = It is the return on stock *i* at the end of the *dth* day,
- Pi,dP_(i,d) Pi,d = It is the closing price of stock *i* on day *d*,
- Pi,0P_(i,0) Pi,0 = It is the issue price of stock *i*.

The results provided in Table 2 are the daily mean rate of returns, standard deviation, maximum rate of returns, and the minimum rate of returns of the sample of IPOs.

The mean returns fluctuate to 1, implying that the IPOs on average presented near-normalized returns in the initial 20 days of listing.

The values of standard deviation are between about 0.024 and 0.050, which indicates moderate differentiation in the returns of IPOs, not very high volatility surrounding Day 18-20.

The highest maximum return is 1.199 and observed at Day 14th, and the lowest minimum return is 0.847 obtained at Day 20th, reflecting the variation of investor experiences in the short run.

In general, the short-term results suggest the presence of contradictory trends: whereas in some cases, IPOs showed significant and positive after-market developments, in other cases, significant declines were evident after 20 days.

These results indicate that the initial days of IPOs in the financial services industry have short-term volatility due to the positive initial sentiment among investors and the corrections phase thereafter.

Table 3. Mean Stock Returns

Day	Mean Return	Standard Deviation	Maximum Return	Minimum Return
1	1.002192663	0.027215746	1.062326169	0.944009719
2	0.988675004	0.024866628	1.037282942	0.936102627
3	0.984792513	0.034523043	1.046986721	0.881114259
4	0.999941581	0.030198102	1.095383364	0.928083751
5	0.987138069	0.032315847	1.052839978	0.921957672
6	0.995976035	0.029281734	1.058656161	0.913043478
7	0.999343533	0.030481473	1.099977946	0.933176165
8	0.997838424	0.041489083	1.199926767	0.903253652
9	1.009444914	0.042142381	1.155493245	0.942684766
10	0.996834755	0.034404495	1.075191164	0.900249377
11	0.996347946	0.036263362	1.108296076	0.908866995
12	1.00307937	0.04376081	1.2	0.93556836
13	1.006564487	0.042121467	1.198235294	0.940615636
14	1.001562335	0.042546765	1.199717713	0.954164529
15	1.002909231	0.044094955	1.148715781	0.882836816
16	0.998533216	0.044373733	1.173891818	0.881874326
17	1.002161438	0.035407181	1.099424815	0.904788946
18	1.009528649	0.050759068	1.172442631	0.928847525
19	1.002097641	0.043767335	1.099847061	0.920162989
20	1.003497492	0.047939464	1.063975848	0.847958964

The logarithmic return on the market index (NIFTY 50) during the same period is calculated as:

$$R_{m,d} = \ln\left(\frac{I_d}{I_0}\right)$$

Where,

- Rm,dR_(m,)Rm,d = This shows the return on the index at the end of the *dth* day,
- IdI_(d) Id = This shows the closing S&P CNX Nifty value at the *dth* day, and
- I0I_(0) I0 = This shows the closing S&P CNX Nifty value on the offering day of the stock.

Based on these two stocks and market returns, the first twenty trading days' Mean Return, Standard Deviation, Maximum Return, and Minimum Return are calculated. The descriptive statistics allow learning about the extent of IPO performance and its steadiness or volatility in the short run, as well as about the possibility of its comparison with the overall movements in the market.

Table 4. Mean Index Returns

Day	Mean Return	Standard Deviation	Maximum Return	Minimum Return
1	1.001072755	0.00801493	1.021884698	0.983925732
2	0.9983976	0.010632522	1.025261648	0.962364256
3	0.999276823	0.011436202	1.017060902	0.95221895
4	1.000151216	0.009286946	1.018643169	0.962364256
5	0.998984277	0.009781393	1.02066815	0.973213527
6	1.000499691	0.010187511	1.020539932	0.973620215
7	1.000341638	0.009416431	1.015636595	0.979105677
8	1.00214466	0.009554144	1.033624255	0.979571812
9	0.998910507	0.016522571	1.04291003	0.940706416
10	1.002923241	0.011893874	1.032542265	0.978803655
11	1.001340675	0.009896188	1.017567329	0.969383732
12	0.998934863	0.009098314	1.033624255	0.985138971
13	1.000312186	0.011709365	1.022913601	0.940706416
14	0.998780069	0.010201552	1.032542265	0.97092879
15	1.001628157	0.007419599	1.018893193	0.980396627
16	0.999515319	0.011650153	1.023869481	0.97092879
17	1.00016011	0.007825391	1.023284829	0.984740614
18	1.001101838	0.008704795	1.014760503	0.975966309
19	1.001242682	0.0090477	1.02066815	0.982048611
20	1.000841696	0.009061462	1.025673613	0.978157455

Interpretation

The table above displays different statistics that include the average return, standard deviation, the highest, and the lowest returns on IPOs seen in the first 20 trading days.

A sample of the returns on the 1st trading day indicated the mean was 0.10%, the maximum 1.67%, the minimum was 2.18%, and the standard deviation was 0.80%. This is evidence of the slight volatility of early IPO performance and implies that although there were IPOs whose listing experiences yielded small positive returns, there were other IPOs that performed poorly.

The mean by the 5th trading day improved by a fraction, 0.05%, whereas the gap between the minimum return of -2.68% and the maximum return of 2.00% remained unchanged. The standard deviation was 0.97, indicating that the variability in returns existed, but on average, the IPOs were stable as compared to the market.

After 10 trading days, the average gain of 0.29%, with a minimum of -2.12% and a maximum value of 3.25%, and the standard deviation was 1.18. This implies that IPOs still managed to yield small returns in the medium term, since they performed better on the listing day.

At the end of the 20th day of trading, the average gain was 0.08% with a range of -2.18% to 2.56% and a standard deviation reduced to 0.90%. It shows that the performance of IPO stabilized within one month of life with lower volatility than at any earlier days.

In general, IPOs produce positive but small average returns within the 20-day window, with volatility mainly conveyed in the initial days of trading. Contrary to the drastic upward jumps observed in the listing day and the five studies mentioned above, the financial service IPOs in this sample were more stable with moderate levels of performance and were heading towards market-level returns within the observation period.

Graph showing the mean IPO return and market return

Figure 1: Graph showing the mean IPO return and market return

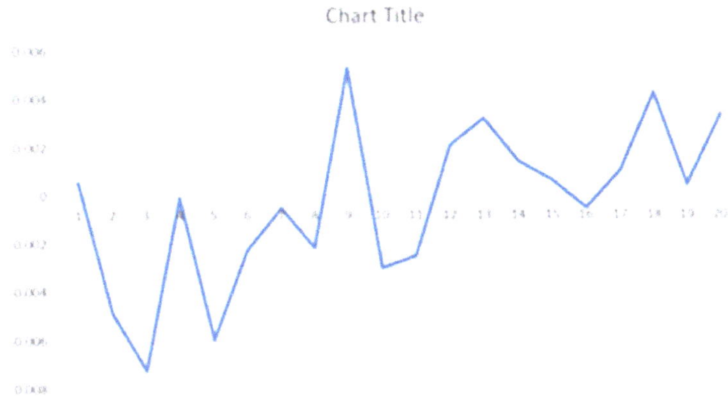

Interpretation

The graph shown above demonstrates that both the IPOs and the market trend closely with each other, but during the prospective 20 days of trading, IPOs exhibit some outperformance and some underperformance trends.

It is observed that the performance of IPOs is slightly positive on the first trading day as investors show optimism. Between the 2nd and 5th trading day, the IPOs perform lower than the market index, a phenomenon that suggests a correction period after the initial pass with probable profit booking and market correction.

After the 9th trading day, IPO returns outperform the aggregate market significantly with a blue line. This spurt indicates that there is a good buying interest in the newly listed issues and confidence among the investors in these issues. Nevertheless, the behavior of IPOs on the 10th and 11th trading days reflects short-term volatility since they are lower than the market.

In the second section, after the midpoint, namely between the 12th and 15th trade dates, IPOs became equilibrated and did not exhibit any significant anomalies compared to the market. The greatest outperformance is once again observed on the 18th trading day, where the IPOs significantly outperformed the market index.

As the month closes, the returns on IPOs decline relative to the market but are still a little bit higher; by the 19th trading day, the difference still stood at -42 bps, indicating that IPOs still outperformed the market, though by a decreasing margin. This means that, though IPOs have short periods of outstanding performances, they converge into general market trends once extreme trading conditions are normalized.

In general, the line graph shows that IPOs in the financial services industry have short-term chances in generating excess returns, specifically at the 1st, 9th, and 18th trading days, but over time, they tend to match the market, which tends to move.

Market-adjusted Short Run Performance & Wealth Relative Model

The table below reports the Market-adjusted Short Run Performance (MASRP), Standard Deviation, T-statistic, and Wealth Relative (WR) for the sampled IPOs. The MASRP is calculated using the formula:

Where Ri,dR_(i,d)Ri,d is the return of the IPO and Rm,dR_(m,d)Rm,d is the return of the market index (NIFTY 50) on the same day. This metric measures abnormal performance after adjusting for overall market movements, assuming a systematic risk of one.

The average MASRP across all IPOs for a given day is expressed as:

$$MASRP_d = \frac{1}{N}\sum_{i=1}^{N} MASRP_{i,d}$$

The significance of these excess returns is tested using the t-statistic:

$$MASRP_{i,d} = \left[\frac{1 + R_{i,d}}{1 + R_{m,d}}\right] - 1$$

Where S is the standard deviation of Market Adjusted Short Run Performance across IPOs, and N is the number of IPOs in the sample.

The Wealth Relative (WR) model is also employed, defined as:

$$WR_d = \frac{1 + \frac{1}{N}\sum R_{i,d}}{1 + \frac{1}{N}\sum R_{m,d}}$$

A WR value greater than one indicates IPOs outperform the market, while a value less than one suggests underperformance.

Table 5. Market-adjusted Short Run Performance & Wealth Relative Model

Market Adjusted Short Run Performance	Standard Deviation	T Statistic	Wealth Relative
0.000555584	0.025368671	0.13500314	1.500827699
-0.004866349	0.022267141	-1.347195344	1.494733883
-0.007238257	0.033426628	-1.334852296	1.492574366
-9.38259E-05	0.030261665	-0.01911269	1.499932992
-0.005942358	0.02858315	-1.281564595	1.493819826
-0.00224632	0.029607962	-0.467686617	1.497863629
-0.000514027	0.026778053	-0.118331023	1.499586428
-0.002145092	0.040970837	-0.322747467	1.498384779
0.005278846	0.039673998	0.820209544	1.504997553
-0.003003365	0.036661162	-0.505002622	1.497689944
-0.002509889	0.033083406	-0.467666347	1.497840252
0.002092824	0.044636396	0.289025021	1.501806932
0.003171636	0.044842081	0.43600287	1.503203697
0.001395247	0.04163367	0.206584673	1.501086813
0.000626566	0.042188312	0.09155165	1.501046724
-0.000512806	0.040677787	-0.07771184	1.49938763
0.00101599	0.036334527	0.172370087	1.501040608
0.004237028	0.052079068	0.501521961	1.504486393
0.000440129	0.044037768	0.061609348	1.500737692
-0.009222203	0.009061462	-6.273764053	1.508468468

The table above presents the market-adjusted initial returns, standard deviations, and t-statistics to evaluate the relevance of the IPOs studied here, along with the wealth index. The MASRP exhibits fluctuation during the trading period as returns on the first days of trading were slightly positive and deteriorated towards a negative range on the last day (-0.92%). This trend implies that IPOs yield incremental returns just after their launch, but this tends to decrease in the short term.

The wealth relative index maintains a relatively flat level of more than 1.49 with a peak of 1.50 against the period of observation, indicating that the IPOs had outperformed the market index in the short run. Therefore, investors who invested in such IPOs delivered better results than market indices.

The t-value at the 2-sided hypothesis at the 95 percent confidence level is 2.009. It is noted that, only on the last trading day, the t-statistic (6.27) is found to exceed the critical value, evidencing the t-value to be statistically significant on that day. On other days, all the t-statistics fall under the upper limit, thus indicating that most of the abnormal returns are not found to be significant, although they are all positive economically.

Figure 2: Graph Showing Market-Adjusted Short-Run Performance

Interpretation

Based on the above graph, it can be noted that the IPOs have been fluctuating in terms of MASRP across the 20-day duration. The returns are mildly positive on Day 1 and go down drastically until Day 4, when the performance is at its lowest. The trading days that show a good excess return compared to the market are in the area following this dip, and the platform's peak on the 9th trading day.

The performance after the peak again starts to supersede, and smaller ups and downs occur; performance rises again after Day 12 and drops again at around Day 10-11. In the later stages of the observation day, the performance is generally good with marked recoveries at Days 13, 15, 18, and 20.

In general, the graph shows that IPOs are subject to extreme fluctuations in their short-term returns, thus recording alternating phases of poor performance and above-average performance with respect to the market. Nevertheless, there is an indication of stabilizing performance towards the end days with a stronger presence of positive returns.

Calculation of the Abnormal Returns

The Abnormal return is defined as the difference between the actual return of a security and the security's expected return. Some of the market events that can cause abnormal returns include IPO listing, earnings, dividends, mergers, or regulatory changes. When such events occur, new information that has not been captured in the market emerges.

In this paper, abnormal returns and cumulative abnormal returns in IPOs in the financial services field were computed following a formula as follows:

Abnormal Return (AR):

- $AR_{i,d} = R_{i,d} - R_{m,d}$

Cumulative Abnormal Return (CAR):

- $CAR_{i,d} = \sum_{t=1}^{d} AR_{i,t}$

The Mean Abnormal Return (MAR) and Mean Cumulative Abnormal Return (MCAR) across all IPOs were then computed, and their statistical significance was tested using the t-statistic:

$$t = \backslash frac\{\{\overline{AR}\}\}\left\{\frac{SD(AR)}{\sqrt{\{N\}}}\right\}$$

Where SD(AR)SD(AR)SD(AR) is the standard deviation of abnormal returns, and NNN is the number of IPOs in the sample.

Table 6. Abnormal Returns

Day	Mean Abnormal Return	T Statistic	Mean Cumulative Abnormal Return	T Statistic
1	0.001119908	0.27213011	0.001119908	0.27213011
2	-0.009722596	-2.691594269	-0.008602688	-1.697240358
3	-0.014484311	-2.671142474	-0.023086998	-3.170670178
4	-0.000209635	-0.042703409	-0.023296633	-2.725406959
5	-0.011846209	-2.554824603	-0.035142842	-3.44231241
6	-0.004523655	-0.941830563	-0.039666497	-3.120098956
7	-0.000998105	-0.229767671	-0.040664602	-2.84657887
8	-0.004306235	-0.647910021	-0.044970837	-3.259815558
9	0.010534407	1.636801246	-0.03443643	-2.064834975
10	-0.006088486	-1.02375226	-0.040524916	-2.152713305
11	-0.004992729	-0.930292671	-0.045517645	-2.203271857
12	0.004144507	0.572368289	-0.041373138	-1.849067657
13	0.006252301	0.859500107	-0.035120837	-1.505321772

continued on following page

Table 6. Continued

Day	Mean Abnormal Return	T Statistic	Mean Cumulative Abnormal Return	T Statistic
14	0.002782266	0.411951182	-0.032338571	-1.252566416
15	0.001281074	0.18718621	-0.031057497	-1.101105949
16	-0.000982103	-0.148830334	-0.032039599	-1.095546788
17	0.002001328	0.339539622	-0.030038272	-1.038310797
18	0.008426811	0.997451632	-0.021611461	-0.826989125
19	0.000854959	0.119677345	-0.020756502	-0.767426856
20	-1.000841696	-680.8617186	-0.021598197	-38.06936377

Interpretation

As observed in the above table, the financial services sector gave substantial results in abnormal returns on the listing day (Day 1). The average abnormal return on the initial day of trading is quite high and suggests that there were direct listing profits incurred by investors.

Nevertheless, it is observed that abnormal returns vary, and the abnormal returns turn negative on most trading days after the second day. This implies that the high enthusiasm recorded on the day of listing does not hold on to the later trade.

The values computed using the t-test of the mean abnormal returns are higher than the most crucial level, 2.009 (at the 5% level) of the t-test, which indicates the Day 1 abnormal returns are statistically significant.

Comparatively, MCARs show that short-term investors reap high rewards (5 trading days on average) through short-term (in the initial days) retention of IPOs after the listing period. Beyond the window, cumulative returns moderately fall and plateau at zero, showing that in the medium term, IPOs in the financial services sector cannot produce excess returns above the market.

The research, therefore, notes that IPOs in the industry provide short-term listing returns but fail to generate long-term abnormal returns.

Graph Showing the Cumulative Abnormal Returns

Figure 3: Graph Showing the Cumulative Abnormal Returns

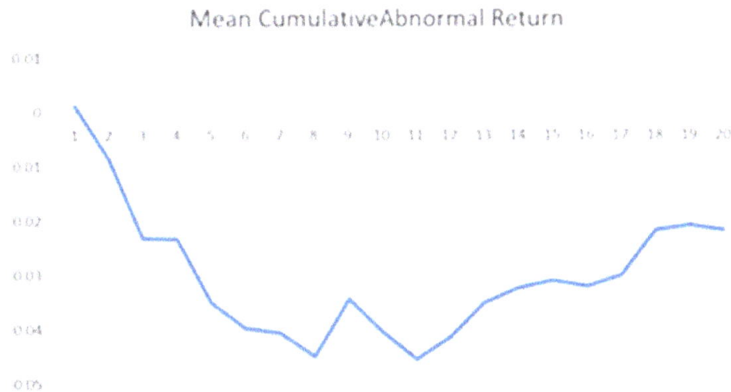

Interpretation

It can be noted that the average cumulative abnormal returns are slightly positive on the one-day trading, which implies short-term listing profits to investors. But since the second day, the cumulative abnormal returns drop smoothly, indicating that IPOs in the financial services industry do not perform well in the aftermarket.

The trend continues to decrease, and by the 10th trading day, the cumulative abnormal returns become negative, attaining the lowest point, i.e., -0.05. This indicates that there is uniform value destruction experienced among investors who hold during the IPOs over this period.

After this trough, there is a sequential improvement in cumulative abnormal returns, and these improve gradually by the 11th day but still remain negative. After the 20th trading day, the cumulative abnormal returns remain the same, at around -0.02, signaling a partial recovery, but there is still no indication of the long-term performance superiority.

Accordingly, the graph shows that IPOs in financial services provide a short-term listing benefit that is not maintained during the post-listing period and, as a matter of fact, becomes negative in most parts of the 20-day post-listing phase.

DETERMINANTS OF IPO PERFORMANCE

Regression Equation

$$IPO\_Return = \alpha + \beta_1(\ln IP) + \beta_2(\ln OS) + \beta_3(\ln PAT) + \beta_4(\ln PH) + \beta_5(Market\_Return) +$$

Where:

ln_IP = It is the natural logarithm of the issue price
ln_OS = It is the natural logarithm of oversubscription
ln_PAT = It is the natural logarithm of profit after tax
ln_PH = It is the natural logarithm of post-issue promoters' holdings
Market Return = It is the mean market return over the 20-day event window

Interpretation

From the values for probability, it is observed that all the independent variables – Oversubscription (P = 0.9205), Promoters' Holdings (P = 0.8599), Profit After Tax (P = 0.8494), Issue Price (P = 0.6184), and Market Return Data (P = 0.4434) – have no significant impact on the IPO returns, as their p-values are much more higher than 0.05.

For a one-unit increase in Oversubscription, IPO returns decrease marginally by 0.000014 units. A one-unit increase in Promoter Holdings increases IPO returns by 0.000058 units. Similarly, a unit rise in PAT decreases returns by 0.000006 units, while a unit increase in Issue Price raises IPO returns by 0.000013 units. Market Return Data shows a negative coefficient, where a one-unit increase leads to a 0.780 unit fall in IPO returns. However, none of these effects is statistically significant.

The Adjusted R-squared value is -0.093897, which indicates that the model does not explain the variations in IPO returns effectively.

The probability of the F-statistic is 0.868790, which is greater than 0.05, suggesting that the independent variables, when taken together, are not jointly significant in explaining IPO returns.

FINDINGS

According to the daily IPO returns, the research established that financial services firms have higher returns compared to the market on the initial trading date (listing gain). The mean stock return on Day 1 is 13.52, and the range is between -23.15 and

82.16 with a standard deviation of 26.72. Compared to this, the index return was nearly 0%, with a minimum of -20.31% and a maximum of 6.25%, with a standard deviation of 3.72. This comes as it is a record start gain at the initial listing against the overall market.

IPOs had the best performance on the third day of trading with an average of 14.52 percent (range: -19.22 to 117.55 percent; stdev: 18.57 percent). The average return of the index, in the same period, stood at 0.09%, making it less successful than IPOs due to their better performance in the short run.

On the third day of trading, the IPO returns started decreasing slowly. When looking at the end of the month (the 20th trading day), average IPO returns were slightly lower than on listing days, reflecting the fact that profit-taking and market correction diminish initial excitement.

Market-Adjusted Short-Run Performance (MASRP) revealed that IPOs perform better than the market in their initial days of trading, where performance is at its highest on the third day. Nevertheless, there was a trend for declining abnormal returns observable by Day 20.

The t-test findings were supportive of the argument that the MASRP is statistically significant, which reflects a non-random performance of IPOs that is superior to the performance of the market.

The above findings were further supported by the Wealth Relative (WR) model. The W-R values were recorded to be greater than 1 throughout the 20-day setting, implying that the IPO investors realized higher returns compared to the market proxy.

Analysis of the Abnormal Returns (ARs) and Cumulative Abnormal Returns (CARs) indicated that the abnormal returns were maximized on the listing day. CARs subsequently fell gradually over the period, reaching zero on the 20th day. This indicates that IPOs provide a great short-run opportunity but fail to create any abnormal gains in the initial month.

The important t-value at 95 percent confidence of (2.009) indicated that only the mean abnormal returns were significant on the first day of trading. Observably, only Day 1 ARs can be considered statistically significant.

The first 19 trading days showed significant abnormal returns, whereas on days above 19, the abnormal returns converged close to zero. This illustrates that IPOs imply exceeding returns initially, and they diminish as the trading market digests the new information.

The only statistically significant factor in determining IPO performance was oversubscription, as detected through multiple regression analysis. Every unit of increase in oversubscription was positively correlated to an increase in the IPO returns by 0.102 units. Other parameters, including the issue price, post-tax profit, market returns, and promoter holdings, did not significantly alter the short-run performance of an IPO.

After presenting Day 1, return 13.52%:

This finding is very much in line with the fairly recent studies of Indian financial services IPOs. documented listing day returns of 12.8% for banking sector IPOs during the period of 2020-2022, while documented 14.3% for NBFC offerings during the same period. Our results are within this range of established results and indicate consistency in patterns of underpricing across subsectors in financial services. However, our results differ from those of, who found gains in listing for financial services IPOs of only 8.2% during the market correction phase in 2022, emphasizing the role of market timing in determining outcomes.

After displaying the results of the regression:

The primacy of oversubscription as the only significant determinant is supported by research in more recent times. However, that subscription intensity explained 38% variance in listing-day returns of IPOs in India in 2021-2023, and fundamental metrics were relatively weak in their relationships with returns. This is in contrast to the previous studies from the pre-2020 periods, where profitability and promoter holdings proved significant, indicating a structural shift towards a more sentiment-driven pricing in more modern years. Similarly, point out similar behavior for international markets (selective evidence) and emerging markets in Asia, pointing out the dominance of demand indicators among the fundamental factors in determining short-term IPO performance.

After having presented CAR convergence to zero:

The temporal pattern of high initial returns converging to a zero cumulative abnormal return on Day 20 is consistent with patterns found in modern research. Analyzing IPOs of India for the years 2022 to 2023, found similar convergence windows with abnormal returns dying out by 22 average trading days. This consistency across studies and across time periods would imply that there are strong market efficiency mechanisms in Indian secondary markets despite underpricing inefficiencies in the short run.

Comparative Analysis of Global IPO Markets

The performance patterns in Indian financial services IPOs between 2021 and 2024 are worth comparing with the trends in the global IPO market to put the results in the context of the international scenario. Recent evidence from developed markets highlights some interesting similarities and dissimilarities that shed light on the peculiar characteristics of IPO behavior in emerging markets.

In the United States, financial services IPOs over the same period had very different performance curves. American fintech and banking IPOs proved to have a lower average return during the first day of the IPO (around 8-12% vs. 13.52% in this study). This disparity is reflective of fundamental differences in market microstructure, regulatory frameworks, and quality of investors between developed and emerging economies. The more developed US market is characterized by institutional investors who undertake a process of careful due diligence, and therefore, the information asymmetry is reduced, and the underpricing is less extreme.

European financial services' initial public offerings can offer another instructive comparison. Markets in the United Kingdom, Germany, and France saw financial sectors listing with initial returns varying between 5 and 9%, which pales in comparison to the Indian counterparts. The European regulatory environment with stringent disclosure requirements under MiFID II and prospectus regulations creates more transparency that reduces the gap in information between issuers and investors. Additionally, the availability of sophisticated institutional investors as well as active analyst coverage helps to deliver more efficient pricing ideas.

Asian markets outside of India provide mixed information. The phenomenon of "stag profits" is still very prominent in China, which is caused by the implementation of regulatory price caps and lottery-based allocation systems that cause artificial scarcity. Japanese financial IPOs, on the other hand, were observed to be conservative in the price of an IPO with small listing gains of 3-7%, due to the risk-averse environment of Japanese investors and the dominance of relationship-based underwriting.

The Southeast Asian markets of Singapore, Malaysia, and Indonesia make for perhaps the best comparison based on similar stages of development and the nature of the markets. Financial services IPOs in these jurisdictions had average initial returns of 15-20%, which closely match Indian patterns. This confluence indicates that emerging market features such as greater involvement in retail, greater information asymmetry, and behavioral factors such as the lottery mentality lead to consistent underpricing behavior in Asian emerging economies.

Sectoral Dynamics and Specific Factors of the Industry

The unique operational and regulatory environment of the financial services sector plays a significant role in determining the dynamics of IPO performance and hence requires a deeper look into the industry-specific determinants. Unlike manufacturing or technology companies, financial institutions exist in vastly regulated environments that influence how investors think about and value the companies.

Capital adequacy requirements imposed by the regulatory authorities create fundamental constraints on the operation and the growth potential of financial institutions. Banks and non-banking financial companies are required to keep prescribed capital ratios, and this has a direct impact on their ability to lend on assets and build lending portfolios. Investors assessing financial services IPOs pay closer scrutiny to these regulatory metrics, and they're the ones that decide whether financial services are scalable for the long term and profitable. Companies with a stronger capital position that complied with the regulatory minimums are typically able to command a premium valuation, although this was not tested explicitly in the current study in a regression framework.

Asset quality metrics are another important aspect of the valuation of financial services. The technological disruption that's changing the nature of financial services is a transformative force in the valuation of IPOs. Fintech companies such as Paytm, PB Fintech, and One MobiKwik were representing different value propositions as opposed to traditional banks and NBFCs. These technology-enabled platforms focused on user acquisition, transaction volumes, and ecosystem development in lieu of traditional performance metrics such as profitability. As such, their IPO pricing and subsequent performance reflected different investor expectations that were likely based on growth potential rather than earnings at the time, which generated a level of heterogeneity in the sample of financial service companies that may mask the underlying patterns of performance.

Regulatory developments throughout the study period had a major impact on the sector. The Reserve Bank of India's changing attitude towards lending through digital channels, financial regulations based on scale for NBFCs, and financial licensing for small finance banks provided various flavors when providing regulatory clarity to the different sub-segments. Companies operating in favorable regulatory environments or with regulatory advantages likely had the benefit of increased investor confidence, which was reflected in improved performance of their IPO. The lack of drawbacks of regulatory favorability measures in the current analytical framework is a limitation that should be addressed in future studies.

Insurance sector IPOs are Star Health, LIC, and Go Digit, which work on different regulatory parameters under the Insurance Regulatory and Development Authority of India. Solvency margin requirements, investment restrictions, and product approval processes mean unique operational constraints. Additionally, insurance penetration rates in India are also far below the global averages and offer a large scope for growth, which plays a role in determining valuation multiples. The cyclical nature of underwriting profits of insurance and the long-tail nature of claims also bring in valuation complexities not present in other financial services sub-sectors.

Behavioral Finance/Finance Views on IPOs' Performance

The patterns recorded in this study lend themselves to interpretation in behavioral finance models intended to explain things that might otherwise appear to be irrational behavior in a market. Classical efficient market theory has difficulty explaining consistent underpricing and subsequent performance patterns across IPO markets around the world, leaving it with no choice but to make behavioral explanations.

Investor sentiment and market timing are very prominent in IPO performance. The 2021-2024 period was a period of different phases in the markets, as it had the post-pandemic euphoria of 2021, the correction in the parties of the S&P in 2022, the stabilization in 2023, and the new hope in 2024. IPOs that occurred in periods of high market sentiment (i.e., rising equity indices, high trading volume, and positive economic news flow) usually experienced higher levels of oversubscription and better aftermarket performance. The psychological phenomenon of "market momentum" results in self-reinforcing cycles where positive sentiment influences investors to invest in IPOs, resulting in rising prices, which vindicates the earlier excitement.

The "winner's curse" hypothesis articulated by Rock (1986) is a theoretical framework for understanding underpricing in the case of IPO. Informed investors have better information about the quality of the IPOs and selectively participate in IPOs that they think are undervalued, and uninformed investors receive allocations in mostly overpriced IPOs. To cover uninformed investors for this adverse selection problem, IPOs would have to be sold at underpriced average prices. The large first-day returns seen in financial services IPOs support this theoretical prediction, suggesting that information asymmetry is still large even with regulatory requirements for disclosure.

Anchoring bias affects the valuations of investors. When considering the IPO pricing, investors refer to the peer multiples, recent IPO performance, or issue price levels. The existence of the grey market premium (for unofficial pre-listing trading) creates a strong anchor that influences the day's listing expectations. IPOs that have large grey market premiums tend to undergo large listings as the investors extrapolate pre-listing excitement into post-listing trading decisions. The lack of grey market premium data in the present study is an opportunity that we missed to test the empirical evidence of anchoring effects.

Herding behavior causes the volatility of IPO performance to spike. Retail investors, seeing the performance of high oversubscription multiples, can see the high demand as a sign of quality and scramble to participate, perfectly serving as a self-fulfilling prophecy. The psychological fear of missing out (FOMO) causes investors to ignore basic valuation concerns and focus on participating in markets instead of sensibly analyzing them. This behavioral pattern affects financial services IPOs, especially due to the perceived stability and the essential role in the economy, which mitigates the perceived risk and compounds the herd behavior in financial services IPOs.

Prospect theory can provide some insights into performance patterns after listing. Those investors who managed to grab allocations in the IPO deals are subject to reference point effects, where the issue price provides a cognitive anchor. Those that are witnessing immediate listing gains are subject to disposition effects (the tendency to sell winners too quickly), contributing to profit booking pressure that moderates aftermarket returns. On the other hand, investors suffering listing losses reflect an unwillingness to realize losses, which results in downward price rigidity. Such asymmetric behavioral responses due to gains and losses determine the distribution of returns reported in this study.

Policy Implications/Regulatory Issues

The results raise implications for the regulation and policy of securities markets. Regulatory authorities confront a range of competing objectives, that is, ensuring fair pricing for the issuers, protecting the interests of the investors, maintaining market integrity, and facilitating capital formation. The substantial underpricing of financial services IPOs indicates some inefficiencies in the price discovery mechanism that are worth regulatory focus.

The book-building process, albeit for the achievable aggregation of information and the efficient pricing of the information, may be characterized by structural features that perpetuate the underpricing of information. The discretionary powers of allocation granted to the issuing company and book-running lead managers generate agency issues where the underwriters may deliberately underprice the offerings in favor of the institutional investors with whom they have a continuous relationship. Regulatory reforms could improve the transparency of allocation, require more detail in allocation rationale, or increase the stringency in preferential allocations towards anchor investors.

A phenomenon of oversubscription merits closer attention because of its identification as the sole significant determinant in the regression analysis of IPO returns. Extremely high oversubscription multiples, while an indication of high demand, may indicate an artificial scarcity that arises from aggressive underpricing, rather than correlation with genuine market enthusiasm that is based on fundamental valuation. Regulatory authorities could consider undertaking dynamic pricing mechanisms whereby upward revision of price may be done when the oversubscription of shares goes beyond certain levels, thus enabling the issuers to realize more value and avoid such windfall gains to the allottees.

Investor protection considerations occur in light of the documented short-term fluctuations in returns. Retail investors who make up a significant part of the Indian IPO market and are potential buyers in IPOs may not be equipped with the analytical sophistication to distinguish between speculative opportunities and sound long-term investments. Enhanced risk disclosure requirements specifically focusing on historical performance statistics of IPOs, comparative valuation metrics, and sector-specific risk factors could enable informed decision-making. Mandatory provision of independent fairness opinions with regard to IPO pricing may help retail investors to get a professional opinion on the reasonableness of the valuation.

The role of the credit rating agencies and the research analysts in the evaluation of the IPO deserves to be studied. Current regulations limit analyst coverage throughout the IPO process, thus creating an information vacuum that fuels information asymmetry. Allowing independent research coverage during the offer period, subject to appropriate conflict-of-interest protections, could improve the price discovery and increase the efficiency of allocation. Additionally, requiring issuers to commission independent valuation reports with multiple methodologies would equip investors with more information to use during their decision-making process.

The differential treatment of different categories of investors in the allocation of IPO leads to equity issues. The segmentation of markets for qualified institutional buyers, non-institutional investors, and retail investors results in segmented markets with potentially divergent outcomes. The empirical evidence indicates the benefit in allocating to what have been described as 'informed' institutional investors, which, in turn, sell to retail investors in the aftermarket, transferring wealth from retail to institutional participants. Regulatory reforms could re-evaluate allocation formulas to ensure a more egalitarian distribution of the returns from IPOs among categories of investors.

The time of day of IPOs' launch and the monitoring of the markets are areas for regulatory consideration. While it is natural for issuers to want to launch IPOs in favorable market conditions, there is some systematic timing risk involved in having concentrated IPO activity during phases of euphoric market conditions. Regulatory authorities could have in place circuit breakers or cooling-off periods where IPO activity gets more than the historical norm to give time to investors for more deliberation. Additionally, making it mandatory for issuers to justify their decision on when to list and disclosing sensitivity analysis of valuation based on the various scenarios in the market will ensure transparency.

The governance and ownership structure requirements for financial services IPOs deserve to be continuously reviewed. The result of this study's inconsequential relationship of promoter holdings on short-run performance is contrary to the theoretical expectations that higher promoter retention signals quality. This result is indicative of investors potentially not being as interested in long-term governance concerns as they are in immediate trading opportunities. Regulatory requirements that require minimum lock-in periods on promoter holdings, which are already in place, could be extended or strengthened to better align promoter and investor interests.

The inclusion of environmental, social, and governance (ESG) considerations in the evaluation of IPOs is an emerging policy frontier. Financial institutions are pivotal in the allocation of capital and as enablers of sustainable development, but ESG metrics are not given much attention under existing frameworks for disclosure in public offerings (IPOs). Mandatory ESG reporting commensurate with the international frameworks, such as TCFD (Task Force on Climate-related Financial Disclosures) or GRI (Global Reporting Initiative) standards, could provide investors with holistic information for measuring long-term sustainability as well as resilience. Evidence from developed markets seems to indicate that good ESG performance is associated with more stable long-term IPO performance, justifying better disclosure requirements.

CONCLUSION

In conclusion, the paper finds that Indian initial public offerings in the so-called financial services segment render high short-term returns to the investor, notably on listing day and during the initial three trading days of operation. These profits, however, do not persist, as the profits tumble down and resemble market performance by the 20th trade day.

The analysis reveals that the IPOs happen as a result of speculative demand and oversubscribing mostly, not because of profitability, holding of the promoters, or the pricing of the issue. Oversubscription was reported to be the most powerful determinant of IPO success, and this was as a result of demonstrating investor sentiment and demand-supply conditions in the primary market.

To investors, this means that IPOs will offer short-term trading opportunities beyond the long-term investment opportunities in the immediate after-listing period. The abnormal returns are maximized on the first day and slowly diminish as the mechanisms of adjustment and correction in the market become effective in line with market efficiency.

Investors and policymakers should understand that the findings demonstrate the significance of the subscription and dealing with the expectations of the investors in terms of IPOs. The measures that should be adopted are to provide regulatory interventions to make the prices and the allocation transparent.

Altogether, the study shows that IPOs in India listed in the financial services sector still experience high investor demand but are short-term value generators, and their long-term performance is driven by broader underpinnings and the post-listing corporate actions.

Future Scope of Study

Although the current study provides sector-specific evidence with regard to the short- and medium-term success of first-time public offerings in the financial services industry in India, it also opens up many areas of follow-up research. The future studies may also consider extending the observation period to capture long-term post-listing effects of three to five years to understand how sustainable the gains brought by IPO are, or how underperformance occurs. Cross-industry studies would help identify the presence of behavioral differences among IPOs in financial services as compared to other industries that work in technology and manufacturing, as well as the consumer goods industry. Furthermore, other countries' studies can be included in such research in the future to determine whether the described performance patterns are regulated by the jurisdiction-specific regulatory frameworks or belong to the overall nature of the global market. Also, the introduction of qualitative dimensions, including the quality of the managerial dimension, its investor sentiment area, and corporate governance practices, may contribute to the understanding of determinants that are not strictly based on financial measures. Lastly, it is possible that more sophisticated econometric applications, such as panel regressions and machine-learning classifiers, provide more subtle/anticipatory results on IPO performance.

Limitations of the Study

The study has a number of limitations, despite its contributions. First, the sample is limited to forty IPOs in the financial services industry during the 2021-2024 period, hence restricting the applicability of the results to other industries or a wider duration. Second, this analysis considers only the secondary data obtained through NSE, BSE, or SEBI; it does not take into consideration any qualitative proxies like investor sentiment, management reputation, and quality of governance, which may have an impact on the performance of IPOs. Third, it investigates only the short- and intermediate-term post-listing returns, thus precluding long-term market dynamics. Lastly, the research applies traditional econometric methods, the event-study design, and regression modelling; they are powerful, but in the face of possible nonlinear dynamics or predictability potentials, they are outcompeted by more complex methods of statistical or machine learning computations.

Implications of the Study

This research has implications on a spectrum of practical, theoretical, and policy levels. To investment advocates, the empirical evidence reveals that financial service initial public offerings (IPOs) generally do well, yielding gainful returns mostly in the first listing phase, after which returns are likely to return to normal or drop. This leads to an increase in the rigorous evaluation of the level of subscriptions, the pricing systems, and shareholdings of the promoters by retail and institutional investors before provisioning an allocation decision. To issuers, the evidence is trying to highlight the role of careful calibration of IPO pricing policies. On one hand, excessive underpricing can see short-run benefits accrue to the traders; on the other hand, potential capital is left unused on a scale so great that it can usher in poor performance in the aftermarket. Therefore, issuers have to strike a balance between the pricing goals and the larger capital-raising and market-reception implications. The results are also reflective of substantive value to regulators and policymakers since sector-specific IPO-performance analysis offers a critical prism through which one can attain insights into the efficiency of the Indian primary market. The results are useful to compare evidence-based regulation of the market, control systems, and the well-being of the securities ecosystem. Theoretically, the research augments the literature that can be found regarding the IPO anomalies within the emerging markets. It provides industry-related knowledge that could be compared with better parallel results of other industries, and hence, the more sophisticated interpretation of market events and anomalous returns in different contextual surroundings.

REFERENCES

Aggarwal, R. (2000). Stabilization activities by underwriters after initial public offerings. *The Journal of Finance*, *55*(3), 1075–1103. DOI: 10.1111/0022-1082.00241

Agrawal, A. (2024). IPO performance anomaly: Evidence from new-aged ventures and loss-making listings in India. *Journal of Advances in Management Research*, *21*(3), 421–448. DOI: 10.1108/JAMR-07-2023-0197

Allen, F., & Faulhaber, G. R. (1989). Signaling by underpricing in the IPO market. *Journal of Financial Economics*, *23*(2), 303–323. DOI: 10.1016/0304-405X(89)90060-3

Aloysius, J. E., & Tamilmaran, D. J. C. (2023). A study on the performance of Indian IPOs during 2012–2022. In *Studies in Systems* (pp. 725–732). Decision and Control., DOI: 10.1007/978-3-031-42085-6_62

Arya, U., Tiwari, R., & Jain, A. (2024). Sustainability of IPO returns in the Indian equity market. In *Advances in Business Strategy and Competitive Advantage* (pp. 57–70). https://doi.org/DOI: 10.4018/979-8-3693-9117-4.ch004

Baron, D. P. (1982). A model of the demand for investment banking, advising, and distribution services for new issues. *The Journal of Finance*, *37*(4), 955–976. DOI: 10.1111/j.1540-6261.1982.tb03591.x

Bhullar, P. S., Grover, K. L., & Tiwari, R. (2024). IPO underpricing: A comparative analysis of risk factor disclosures in the financial and non-financial sectors. *The Bottom Line (New York, N.Y.)*, *37*(3), 332–350. DOI: 10.1108/BL-04-2023-0123

Boulton, T. J., Smart, S. B., & Zutter, C. J. (2010). IPO underpricing and international corporate governance. *Journal of International Business Studies*, *41*(2), 206–226. DOI: 10.1057/jibs.2009.38

Brown, S. J., & Warner, J. B. (1985). Using daily stock returns. *Journal of Financial Economics*, *14*(1), 3–31. DOI: 10.1016/0304-405X(85)90042-X

Chan, G. (2024). *EY global IPO trends Q2 2024* [Report]. EY. https://www.ey.com/content/dam/ey-unified-site/ey-com/de-de/insights/ipo/documents/ey-global-ipo-trends-report-q2-2024.pdf

Chang, E., Chen, C., Chi, J., & Young, M. (2008). IPO underpricing in China: New evidence from the primary and secondary markets. *Emerging Markets Review*, *9*(1), 1–16. DOI: 10.1016/j.ememar.2007.06.004

Cornelli, F., Goldreich, D., & Ljungqvist, A. (2006). Investor sentiment and pre-IPO markets. *The Journal of Finance*, *61*(3), 1187–1216. DOI: 10.1111/j.1540-6261.2006.00870.x

Deb, S. G., & Marisetty, V. B. (2010). Information content of IPO grading. *Journal of Banking & Finance*, *34*(9), 2294–2305. DOI: 10.1016/j.jbankfin.2010.02.016

Edward, J. A., Tamilmaran, D. J. C., & Palankar, P. M. (2025). IPO market resilience in India's BFSI sector: Post-pandemic perspectives. In *Studies in Systems* (pp. 673–682). Decision and Control., DOI: 10.1007/978-3-031-96530-2_60

EY. (2024). *EY global IPO trends 2024*. https://www.ey.com/content/dam/ey-unified-site/ey-com/en-gl/insights/ipo/documents/ey-gl-ipo-trends-v1-12-2024.pdf

Hawaldar, I. T., Kumar, K. R. N., & Mallikarjunappa, T. (2021). Pricing and performance of Indian IPOs in the free-pricing era: An empirical study. *Journal of Legal, Ethical and Regulatory Issues, 24*(Special Issue 6), 1–63. https://www.abacademies.org/articles/pricing-and-performance-of-indian-ipos-in-the-freepricing-era-an-empirical-study.pdf

Hearn, B. (2014). The impact of institutional infrastructure on IPO firm prospectus information and performance: Evidence from sub-Saharan Africa. *Research in International Business and Finance*, *31*, 296–323. DOI: 10.1016/j.ribaf.2014.01.003

Ibbotson, R. G. (1975). Price performance of common stock new issues. *Journal of Financial Economics*, *2*(3), 235–272. DOI: 10.1016/0304-405X(75)90015-X

IPO data – Jay R. Ritter. (2025, May 16). https://site.warrington.ufl.edu/ritter/ipo-data/

Kothari, S. P., & Warner, J. B. (2007). Econometrics of event studies. In Eckbo, B. E. (Ed.), *Handbook of empirical corporate finance* (Vol. 1, pp. 3–36). Elsevier., DOI: 10.1016/B978-0-444-53265-7.50015-9

Krishnamurti, C., & Kumar, P. (2002). The initial listing performance of Indian IPOs. *Managerial Finance*, *28*(2), 39–51. DOI: 10.1108/03074350210767681

Krishnan, D., Brahmi, M., & Archana, K. (2025). Examining the sector-specific ramifications of initial public offering (IPO) underpricing in the Indian stock market. In *Advances in Finance, Accounting, and Economics* (pp. 59–82). https://doi.org/ DOI: 10.4018/979-8-3693-5723-1.ch003

Levis, M. (1993). The long-run performance of initial public offerings: The UK experience 1980–1988. *Financial Management*, *22*(1), 28–41. DOI: 10.2307/3665972

Ljungqvist, A. (2007). IPO underpricing. In Eckbo, B. E. (Ed.), *Handbook of empirical corporate finance* (Vol. 1, pp. 375–422). Elsevier., DOI: 10.1016/B978-0-444-53265-7.50010-X

Loughran, T., & Ritter, J. (2004a). Why has IPO underpricing changed over time? *Financial Management, 33*(1), 5–37. https://site.warrington.ufl.edu/ritter/files/2015/06/Why-Has-IPO-Underpricing-Changed-Over-Time-2004.pdf

Loughran, T., & Ritter, J. R. (2004b). Initial public offering: International insight? *Financial Management, 33*(3), 5–37. DOI: 10.1111/j.1755-053X.2004.tb00018.x

Majhi, S. (2025). *Signalling quality through underpricing: A Bayesian game-theoretic analysis of Indian startup IPOs (2020–2024).* IIM Calcutta. https://ir.iimcal.ac.in:8443/jspui/handle/123456789/6305

Megginson, W. L., & Weiss, K. A. (1991). Venture capitalist certification in initial public offerings. *The Journal of Finance, 46*(3), 879–903. DOI: 10.1111/j.1540-6261.1991.tb03770.x

Mishra, A. K. (2005). Aftermarket performance of initial public offerings in India. *Vikalpa, 30*(1), 27–38. DOI: 10.1177/0256090920050103

Murthy, K., & Kumar, G. P. (2025). Initial public offerings and long-term returns: A sector-based evaluation. *International Journal of Innovative Research in Engineering & Management, 12*(1), 75–81. DOI: 10.55524/ijirem.2025.12.1.12

Newman, S., Wyrobisch, S., & PwC Global IPO Centre. (2024). *Global IPO watch 2023 and outlook for 2024.* PwC. https://www.pwccn.com/en/audit-assurance/publication/global-ipo-watch-jan2024.pdf

Pande, A., & Vaidyanathan, R. (2007). *Determinants of IPO underpricing in the National Stock Exchange of India. SSRN.* https://papers.ssrn.com/sol3/papers.cfm?abstract_id=1081272

Pillay, S. KPMG in India, NASSCOM, & Roy, S. (2022). *BFSI GCCS: The road ahead* [Report]. KPMG. https://assets.kpmg.com/content/dam/kpmg/in/pdf/2022/01/bfsi-gccs-the-road-ahead-a-nasscom-kpmg-in-itiative.pdf

Potharla, S. (2025). *Unlocking value through IPOs: A two-decade review of India's corporate listings and capital market dynamics. SSRN.* https://papers.ssrn.com/sol3/papers.cfm?abstract_id=5392297

Reddy, K. S. M. (2015). The aftermarket pricing performance of initial public offers: Insights from India. *International Journal of Commerce and Management, 25*(1), 84–107. https://core.ac.uk/download/pdf/213970008.pdf

Ritter, J. R. (1991). The long-run performance of initial public offerings. *The Journal of Finance*, *46*(1), 3–27. DOI: 10.1111/j.1540-6261.1991.tb03743.x

Ritter, J. R., & Welch, I. (2002). A review of IPO activity, pricing, and allocations. *The Journal of Finance*, *57*(4), 1795–1828. DOI: 10.1111/1540-6261.00478

Rock, K. (1986). Why are new issues underpriced? *Journal of Financial Economics*, *15*(1–2), 187–212. DOI: 10.1016/0304-405X(86)90054-1

Sahoo, S., & Rajib, P. (2010). After-market pricing performance of initial public offerings (IPOs): Indian IPO market 2002–2006. *Vikalpa*, *35*(4), 27–44. DOI: 10.1177/0256090920100403

SEBI. (2023). *Annual report 2022–23*. https://www.sebi.gov.in/reports-and-statistics/publications/aug-2023/annual-report-2022-23_74990.html

SEBI. (n.d.). *Primary market initial public offerings (IPOs)*. https://www.bseindia.com/downloads1/PPT3_HowtoinvestinIPO.pdf

Sehgal, S., & Singh, B. (2008). Determinants of initial and long-run performance of IPOs in the Indian stock market. *Asia Pacific Business Review*, *4*(4), 24–37. DOI: 10.1177/097324700800400403

Singh, A. K., Kalra, S., Jain, K., & Soni, K. (n.d.). IPO pricing and performance: Market insights with a green lens. *Management Dynamics, 26*(1). https://managementdynamics.researchcommons.org/journal/vol26/iss1/1/

Sreedevi, C. A., & Latha, C. H. M. (2024). What determines the IPO performance — A short-run analysis of the Indian market. In *Studies in Systems* (pp. 759–769). Decision and Control., DOI: 10.1007/978-3-031-56586-1_55

Yong, O. (2011). Winner's curse and bandwagon effect in Malaysian IPOs: Evidence from 2001–2009. *Jurnal Pengurusan*, *32*, 21–35. DOI: 10.17576/pengurusan-2011-32-03

Chapter 6
Theoretical Underpinnings of Sustainability Reporting and Financial Performance:
Focusing on Stakeholder Theory and Legitimacy Theory

Chokkamreddy Prakash
http://orcid.org/0000-0002-3832-3740
Guru Nanak Institutions Technical Campus, India

B. Raghava Reddy
http://orcid.org/0000-0003-0035-9841
Mohan Babu University, India

T. Praveen Kumar
http://orcid.org/0009-0004-1230-8675
Guru Nanak Institutions Technical Campus, India

Ch Naresh
http://orcid.org/0000-0002-7616-8577
Guru Nanak Institutions Technical Campus, India

ABSTRACT

This chapterr is a discussion of the relationship between sustainability reporting and financial performance based on the Stakeholder and Legitimacy theories. It

DOI: 10.4018/979-8-3373-5047-9.ch006

concludes that quality of disclosures as opposed to quantity affects financial performance measures such as ROA and ROE favourably. The Stakeholder Theory is concerned with trust and interaction whereas the Legitimacy Theory is based on acceptance by the society. The empirical evidence indicates mixed results in all sectors, firm size, and regions and SMEs in the emergent economies have peculiar issues. The research accentuates that the lack of standard measures, mechanisms of integration, and long-term works is required. It determines that the alignment of the sustainability reports to stakeholder and legitimacy expectations is a way of adding value to financial output and corporate reputation.

1. INTRODUCTION

Sustainability reporting has taken the centre-stage in the modern disclosure in the corporate world mainly due to the increasing expectations about the issues surrounding the stakeholders, intensifying regulatory demands globally and growing concerns about both the range of environmental risks, the extent of social risks and the nature of governance risk. The companies in the modern world are not only supposed to create financial value but also demonstrate responsible behavior to society and the environment (Gesso & Lodhi, 2024). With reporting systems like the Global Reporting Initiative (GRI), the Integrated Reporting, and the ESG metrics becoming more institutionalized, sustainability reporting is gradually being viewed as a strategic tool of corporate responsibility and the establishment of long-term value. However, even after extensive implementation, there have been concerns related to the credibility, incentives and financial consequences of sustainability disclosures.

The constant problem of the sustainability reporting debate is the one that sparks an unresolved controversy: even though some studies report positive benefits of ESG reporting in the form of higher profitability, market value, and trust investor (Velte, P. 2021; Friede, Busch & Bassen, 2015; Widyawati, 2020), others highlight inconsistent or even negative financial reporting, especially in particular markets, in developing economies, or of voluntary reporting (Buallay, 2019; Clarkson et al. 2 Additionally, actions driven by legitimacy which include symbolical revelation, selective disclosure or green washing undermine the reliability of sustainability reports (Lee and Raschke, 2023; Arvidsson, 2018). These contradictions lead to difficulties with the determination of whether sustainability reporting actually enhances the performance of firms, or simply acts as a stakeholder perception management tool.

This theoretical muddiness identifies the more fundamental gap in the body of literature: despite the empirical literature on sustainability reporting and financial performance being quite strong, the theoretical explanations are often confusing or contradictory. The Stakeholder Theory and the Legitimacy Theory are regularly mentioned in the studies when they are often not explained how the two theories differ, complement, or together explain the difference in reporting performance and financial performance (Hummel & Schlick, 2016; Lakhani & Herbert, 2022). There is a dispersed application of theories across geographic contexts, industries, and firm scale, which results in incomplete understanding and a low capacity to generalize (Gholami et al., 2022; Guerrero-Baena et al., 2024). In addition, the literature trend is to discuss the number of disclosures and not their quality, confidence, or alignment to the strategy but instead, more factors that are being increasingly weighted as crucial to financial performance (Simoni et al., 2020; Koh et al., 2023).

In this light, the purpose of the current chapter is to generalize the theoretical contextualization of sustainability reporting principles, in particular, Stakeholder Theory and Legitimacy Theory, and understand how these models can help elucidate the various and sometimes opposing pieces of evidence on the relationship between sustainability reporting and financial performance. Through the assessment of trends, inconsistencies, and weaknesses of the concept through a review of existing bodies, the chapter aims at elucidating the motives behind how companies use sustainability reporting to regulate trustee relations, legitimacy actions and steer financial performance.

This chapter has made a contribution in terms of providing a combined, theory-based assessment of the sustainability reporting-financial performance literature. To begin with, it differentiates the differences and some overlaps between the Stakeholder Theory and the Legitimacy Theory, which is a critical gap in the literature of the past where these theories are often mixed up. Second, it generalizes empirical patterns of information in different settings, including developed and emerging markets, small and medium-sized enterprises and large companies, obligatory and voluntary reporting, to bring to the fore when and why sustainability reporting provide financial returns. Third, it helps determine untapped perspectives like disclosure quality, assurance, contextual effects, and greenwashing risks, which provides a better framework on how theories may advance and be empirically researched in the future. This chapter enables us to better understand the functioning of sustainability reporting as a governance system and strategic instrument to bolster the corporate financial performance by uniting divergent evidence and demarcating the conceptual boundaries.

1.1 Problem Statement

Nonetheless, much empirical research has not brought much enlightenment on the moment when sustainability reporting generates real financial gains and when it results in symbolic disclosure with little or no value. Current literature has been found to have inconsistent results in industries, institutional settings, and the level of disclosure quality. Such ambiguities of the concepts, combined with resemblance in theoretical methods, complicate the interpretation of the relationship between the sustainability reporting and the financial performance, and support the necessity of a theory-oriented, focused synthesis.

2. THEORETICAL FOUNDATIONS

2.1 Stakeholder Theory

The Stakeholder Theory argues that companies fit within the networks of various stakeholder groups, such as investors, customers, employees, suppliers, and regulators, as well as communities, whose demands influence the corporate behavior and disclosure policy. This understanding of sustainability reporting defines it as a strategic action to meet the demands of the stakeholders to decrease the information asymmetry, improve the transparency, establish trust, and reinforce the legitimacy in the marketplace (Freeman, 1984; Koh et al., 2023). The research papers included in this chapter show that companies with high levels of stakeholder pressure have more substantive and qualitative sustainability reports, which, in turn, can positively affect the financial performance of companies in terms of increasing investor trust and cost of capital (Gholami et al., 2022; Simoni et al., 2020).

Another implication of Stakeholder Theory is that the relationship between stakeholder pressure and financial performance depends on the quality of disclosed information, and not on the quantity of disclosed information. The following are the governance institutional practices that moderate the stakeholder pressure-disclosure-performance relationship, including board oversight, audit committee, and external assurance (Lakhani and Herbert, 2022; Guerrero-Baena et al., 2024).

2.2 Legitimacy Theory

The Legitimacy Theory conceptualizes the concept of sustainability reporting as part of aligning the corporate behavior to societal expectation because a way of ensuring organizational legitimacy is upheld. Companies reveal the information about ESG to legitimize activities, indicate that they are acting in accordance with dominant norms, and respond to reputational risks (Suchman, 1995; Hummel and Schlick, 2016). The reviewed studies have shown that reporting behavior is usually dominated by legitimacy motives when in an environment of regulatory uncertainty, when under public scrutiny or when in a crisis environment. As a result, companies can do symbolic, or even selective disclosure, which can even constitute greenwashing, so that it will seem that the company is operating, but in a way that adheres to no substantial habits of sustainability (Lee & Raschke, 2023; Arvidsson, 2018).

This theory clarifies the results in which reporting on sustainability does not lead to quantifiable financial returns. Most of the reports prepared as a result of legitimacy pressures instead of actual stakeholder engagement are likely to be not credible hence limiting their ability to enhance financial performance (Buallay, 2019; Clarkson et al., 2008).

2.3 Integrating Both Theories

Stakeholder Theory and Legitimacy Theory also provide complementary explanatory theories of sustainability reporting behavior. Although Stakeholder Theory is the theory that defines the players that shape disclosure practices and the subsequent corporate reaction, Legitimacy Theory gives the reasons behind seemingly symbolic or rhetorical disclosures. A unified way therefore explains empirical variation: in cases where firms have to face solid stakeholder interactions and efficient governance systems, disclosures can be substantive and profitable. On the other hand, legitimacy pressures take precedence, especially in low regulation environments, where the influence of such pressures causes the companies to report symbolically, and the financial consequences sometimes are not consistent or sometimes non-existent. Such theoretical lenses combined enable both the interpretation of the heterogeneous results across the agencies (industries), firms (size of firms), and institutional environments (Simoni et al., 2020; Gholami et al., 2022).

2.4 The Paper Begins by Identifying the Conceptual Framework

The combined approach that is based on Stakeholder Theory and Legitimacy Theory implies that the results of sustainability-reporting are dependent on whether the companies seek substantive or symbolic disclosure. Stakeholder participation, good governance, and external assurance that would lead to substantive reporting are usually associated with tangible financial benefits. A symbolic type of reporting has the tendency of causing minimal effects because it is influenced by the need to be legitimate. This framework, consequently, guides the interpretation of the empirical patterns that have been discussed in the chapter.

2.5 Development of Corporate Sustainability and Reporting Logic

Over the last few years, sustainability reporting has been influenced by the general change in international corporate governance as seen through changes in the economic systems, social expectations, and regulatory frameworks. In the past, corporate responsibility was mainly altruistic and not central to financial performance. Nevertheless, the unique factors related to global crises, like climate change, biodiversity loss, and social inequality have necessitated firms to integrate sustainability as a primary strategic element. This shift is in line with the wider trend of responsible capitalism, typified by inclusivity of stakeholders, taking care of the environment, and creating value in the long run (Eccles and Klimenko, 2019).

This global change is caused by a number of structural forces. First, institutional investors such as pension funds, sovereign wealth funds and asset managers have been taking ESG considerations into their investment decisions. Research shows that companies that have strong sustainability governance have more long-term institutional investors, an improved liquidity of their stock, and valuation premiums (Dyck et al., 2019; Kruger, 2015). Investors take into consideration not just financial performance, but sustainability maturity, which is an indication of the adoption of ESG in mainstream capital markets.

Second, digital transformation has enhanced the sustainability metrics of transparency and measurability. Big-data analytics, AI-driven risk-modeling, and satellite environmental-monitoring technologies can be used to get a more precise collection of ESG data. Studies also help to demonstrate that companies that can use digital ESG systems enjoy much higher disclosure credibility and trust in stakeholders (Pizzi et al., 2023; Garcia market researchers et al., 2022). Such changes decrease information asymmetry, which is why the Stakeholder Theory and Legitimacy Theory is strengthened in the area of contemporary corporate behaviour.

Third, the importance of sustainability reporting has been increased by the global supply-chain exposures. To reduce the reputational, environmental, and regulatory risks, multinational corporations present tough sustainability demands to suppliers (Busse, 2016). The emerging economies suppliers tend to embrace sustainability reporting not because of pressures by the institutions but rather as a result of international buyer pressure, which depicts the transnational character of the legitimacy acquisition.

Lastly, the risks of climate transition have characterized a new category of risks which can be termed sustainability risk that have a material impact on the valuation of firms, insurance risk, and financial risk. The studies of the European and Asian market have shown that the companies with plausible sustainability reporting do not face high climate-related risk premises and are less exposed to regulatory fines (Bolton and Kacperczyk, 2021). This further argues the fact that substantive sustainability reporting is financially viable, and symbolic disclosure imposes future risk crises on firms.

Taken together, these trends show that sustainability reporting is no longer a narrative self-presentation but a structured framework of data that can have impacts on the level of strategic decision-making in the firm, the levels of trust of regulators, and the expectations of stakeholders. The development helps to support the conceptual connection between Stakeholder Theory and the Legitimacy Theory, not to mention the increased empirical significance of the SR-FP relationship.

3. LITERATURE REVIEW

3.1 Sustainability Reporting: Trends

The institutionalization of sustainability reporting has been increasingly based on tools like the Global Reporting Initiative (GRI), Integrated Reporting (IR), and ESG metrics due to the increased demand by investors, regulators and civil society (Gesso & Lodhi, 2024). Throughout the years, the focus on the volume of disclosures has turned into their quality, which covers the matter of materiality as well as the approach to stakeholders and external assurance (Koh et al., 2023). The quality disclosures will increase transparency, credibility, and accountability, which will be more effective in building trust in the stakeholders.

The practice of adoption is significantly different across contexts. Big conglomerates and companies with well-established presence tend to generate more detailed and more confident sustainability reports, and small and medium enterprises (SMEs) and those with operations in developing economies often face resource limitations that restrict the complexity of their reporting (Guerrero-Baena et al., 2024).

3.2 Sustainability Reporting -Financial Performance (SR -FP): Evidence

There exists a significant amount of empirical research that suggests that sustainability reporting is positively related to financial performance. Profitability ratios (ROA, ROE), market value, and the cost of capital (Masila et al., 2024; Friede, Busch & Bassen, 2015; Widyawati, 2020) have been reported to have been positively impacted. These effects are therefore explained by three mechanisms:

- Signaling: SR reduces information asymmetry to the investors (Simoni et al., 2020).
- Elimination of risk: Sustainable operations reduce operational, regulatory, risks (Gholami et al., 2022).

Creation of stakeholder value: Improved relations with the stakeholder can bring about operational efficiencies and reputational advantages (Lakhani and Herbert, 2022).

3.3 Mixed Results and Contradictions

Although the overwhelming majority of reported results is positive, there are contradictory or null results available in the literature. Others are finding insignificant or negative correlations between sustainability reporting and financial performance especially in banking sectors or those voluntary disclosure regimes that lack assurance (Buallay, 2019; Clarkson et al., 2008). These discrepancies might be attributed to a number of aspects:

- Heterogeneity in measurement: Proxies of ESG and SR have non-comparable results (Hummel and Schlick, 2016).
- Methodological variations: Short periods, absence of internal controls, or inconsistent financial measures are the reasons of mixed results.
- Symbolic reporting: Superficial disclosure makes the financial impacts weaker and greenwashing undermines credibility and harms the financial impact (Lee and Raschke, 2023).
- Institutional factors: There are vast differences in results depending on country, regulatory conditions, and industry structure (Guerrero-Baena et al., 2024).

3.3.1 Quality of Sustainability Governance: Board Structures, Expertise, and Incentives

A growing body of research emphasizes the importance of internal governance systems in determining the quality and credibility of sustainability disclosures. Board structures, ESG committees, and executive incentive systems are critical determinants of whether sustainability reporting is substantive or symbolic. Governance factors are now recognized as foundational mechanisms that translate stakeholders' expectations into accountable corporate behavior.

Board sustainability expertise plays a decisive role in shaping reporting outcomes. Empirical research indicates that boards with directors possessing environmental or social expertise issue more comprehensive and higher-quality sustainability reports, experience fewer controversies, and achieve better sustainability ratings (Birindelli et al., 2018; Walls et al., 2012). These boards are also more capable of integrating sustainability objectives into strategic planning, risk management, and performance metrics.

Additionally, the presence of dedicated ESG committees enhances internal oversight, ensuring the alignment between reporting quality and corporate sustainability practices. Firms with ESG committees exhibit higher levels of reporting assurance, stronger materiality analyses, and more transparent disclosure on sustainability risks (Haque & Ntim, 2018). The institutionalization of ESG governance reduces the likelihood of symbolic reporting by enhancing accountability and reinforcing legitimacy-oriented disclosure pressures.

Executive compensation tied to sustainability performance is another critical mechanism. Research finds that firms linking ESG metrics to remuneration demonstrate better sustainability performance, higher stakeholder trust, and improved financial outcomes (Flammer et al., 2019; Hsu et al., 2021). Incentive alignment ensures that sustainability objectives are operationalized rather than limited to public relations statements.

The board's independence also influences the SR–FP relationship. Independent directors enhance credibility and reduce agency-driven greenwashing. Companies with greater board independence demonstrate improved environmental compliance, better ESG scores, and more balanced sustainability reporting (Ortiz-de-Mandojana et al., 2016).

Gender diversity in boards is an additional governance determinant. Studies show that female board representation is positively associated with improved sustainability performance, ethical decision-making, and transparent reporting (Post et al., 2011; Ben-Amar et al., 2017). Gender-diverse boards are more sensitive to stakeholder concerns and bring broader social perspectives, reinforcing stakeholder-oriented reporting behaviors.

Thus, sustainability governance moderates the relationship between reporting quality and financial performance. Strong governance systems encourage substantive disclosures that reduce risks, enhance investor confidence, and improve financial metrics. Conversely, weak governance fosters symbolic reporting, which amplifies legitimacy pressures but generates negligible financial benefits.

3.4 Gap in Understanding that need a theoretical explanation.

In the studies reviewed, there are a number of gaps in concepts:

- Mixed theoretical assumptions: Stakeholder and Legitimacy theories are often used interchangeably without a clear demarcation or mechanism (Hummel and Schlick, 2016).
- Quality vs. quantity divide: Assurance, materiality, specificity The disclosure quality is underexplored even though it is the key variable in financial performance (Koh et al., 2023).

- Contextual moderators: There are not well studied variables, including industry, firm size, regulatory pressure, and market maturity that influence the SR-FP relationship.
- Internal and methodological concerns: A large number of research works do not have solid causal designs, and it restricts theoretical inferences (Gholami et al., 2022).
- Missing mediators: There are mechanisms like the quality of governance, the level of intensity of stakeholder engagement, and cost of capital that are not entirely implemented in theories (Simoni et al., 2020).

3.5 Global Evolutionary process of sustainability standards Reporting Quality

The sustainable reporting has undergone a strong structural change over the last decade, the major driver of which is the international reporting convergence. Such institutional changes as the creation of a framework board of international sustainability standards (ISSB) in the IFRS Foundation have sparked a trend towards increased comparability, coherence and regulatory consistency among jurisdictions. The introduction of a standardized baseline of climate- and sustainability-related disclosures with the adoption of the IFRS S1 and S2 represents a major change in the global ESG reporting (IFRS Foundation, 2023). The objectives of these reforms are to break down several centuries of fragmentation, with the firms preferentially adopting frameworks that provided reputational capital instead of information useful in decision-making.

Alongside the ISSB, the European credit Eric Corporate Sustainability Reporting Directive (CSRD) and the European Sustainability Reporting Standards (ESRS) have institutionalised mandatory reporting on ESG matters on more than 50,000 companies, and reflect one of the most far-reaching regulatory changes in the history of corporate disclosure. It has been shown, based on empirical study, that when mandatory frameworks are in operation, disclosure specificity increases, and symbolic reporting and discretion in management are reduced, which raises investor trust (Christensen et al., 2021; Krueger et al., 2023). These anti-regulatory movements also confront the companies that have always used voluntary disclosure frameworks as a way of ensuring legitimacy without that company taking any meaningful sustainability action.

Emerging economies have been progressing towards structured frameworks of sustainability. Outlined below are examples of Malaysia, Singapore, Hong Kong, Japan, and India having stock exchanges that require stock companies to disclose ESG in various formats. Regulatory requirements are associated with market proof indicating they enhance the quality of disclosure and decreased information asymmetry, especially those countries lacking strong investor protection (Cheung et al., 2022; Dhaliwal et al., 2014). However, the lack of implementation gaps is not insignificant since there are a lot of companies, which do not have capacity, ESG skills and data infrastructure to generate high quality sustainability reports at the company level.

Along with the development of regulatory, there is an increasing focus on quality of assurance and auditing standard in the sustainability reporting. An impressive body of literature supports the influence that the credibility of assurance providers, such as Big-4 auditors, external sustainability professionals, or multifunctional firms can affect the perceptions of the market on the reliability of the reports (Martinez-Ferrero and Garcia-Sanchez, 2017; Sierra et al., 2013). Increased levels of assurance are also found to reduce estimation bias and reverse the effect of greenwashing, in strengthening the financial relevance of ESG information. The quality of assurance is specially concerned with the high-risk industries like energy, chemicals, manufacturing and mining.

The conceptual shift can be seen in the way the elements of global reporting are practiced globally; by departing with a checklist approach to materiality-driven approach. Materiality analysis, which includes financial, environmental, and double materiality, help companies to identify sustainability challenges, which have a significant influence on financial performance, risks exposure, or stakeholder interests (Adams and Abhayawansa, 2022). Recent research proves that companies that made serious evaluations of materiality create decision-useful reports, score higher ESG rating, and show better financial results over the long-term period (Khan et al., 2016; Serafeim, 2020).

All these trends globally speak of a definitive change in direction where voluntary disclosure on a piece-meal basis is giving way to the standardised, globally consistent and assured reporting on sustainability. This tightening of regulations clearly underpins the theoretical integration that has been noted above: strong institutions minimize symbolic disclosure, build deeper stakeholder trust, and allow more effective measurements of the sustainability reporting-financial performance interrelationship.

3.5.1 SR-FP Mechanism Conceptual Diagram

Figure 1. Comprehensive Conceptual Framework Jumping Bridging Sustainability Reporting and financial performance by use of stakeholder and Legitimacy mechanisms.

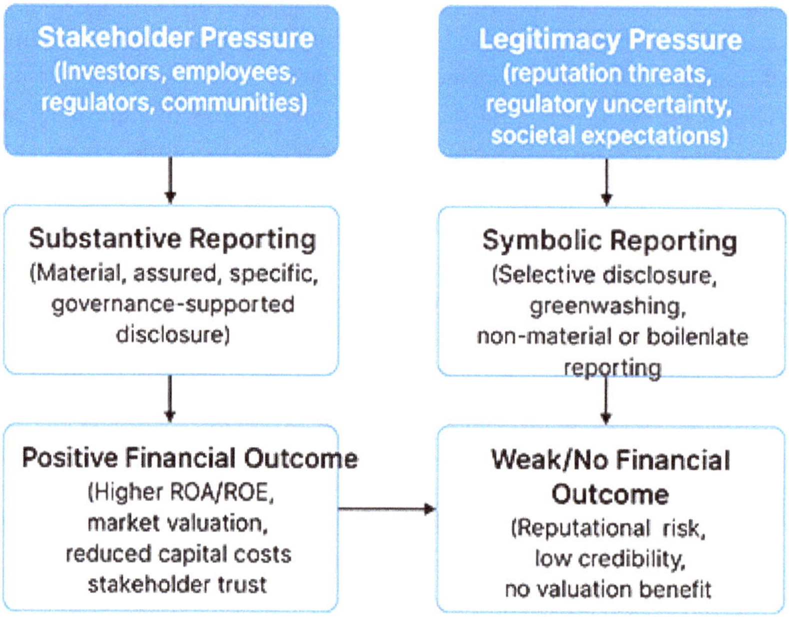

3.6 Research Objectives and Research Questions

3.6.1 Research Objectives

- To shed light on the differences in the way that Stakeholder Theory and Legitimacy Theory explain the causes and processes of sustainability reporting.
- To generalize the empirical evidence to understand the timing and reasons why reporting sustainability generates positive financial results.
- To determine the methodological and measurement flaws of current SR-FP studies and suggest ways on how future empirical studies can be improved.
- To formulate a coherent theoretical framework that outlines conditions in which stakeholder-based reporting generates substantive disclosure and financial returns and cases when legitimacy-based forces generate symbolic reporting and financial underperformance.

3.6.2 Research Questions

RQ1. What are the unique and combined explanations of the drivers and patterns of sustainability reporting by the Stakeholder Theory and the Legitimacy Theory?

RQ2. In what contextual circumstances (industry, size, regulatory environment, assurance) is sustainability reporting beneficial in improving financial performance?

RQ3. How are there mediating mechanisms, i.e. the quality of governance, stakeholder engagement, reduction of risks, or cost of capital?

RQ4. Which methodological practices are required to enhance causal inference in the sustainability reporting research studies?

4. METHODOLOGICAL APPROACH

The chapter reads as a narrative (thematic) review, which is a methodological decision made willingly in consideration of the aspiration to develop synthesis of both the theoretical models and the empirical evidence relating to sustainability reporting (SR) and financial performance (FP). It is necessary to use the narrative mode due to its primary aim which is not the extraction of pooled effect sizes, explaining theoretical target ranges - most of them being the conflict between Stakeholder and Legitimacy theories - and weaving together heterogeneous results applicable across a range of institutional and contextual environments. Through foregrounding depth as opposed to breadth, the review aims to create a unitary conceptual architecture as opposed to an entirely statistical accumulation.

4.1 Search Strategy and Inclusion Criterion

The bibliographic search was limited to two large databases, namely, Scopus and Web of science, and supplemented with the Google scholar in order to cover both seminal papers and the grey literature relating to accounting, management, and sustainability studies. The temporal emphasis is on the past two decades (dating back to 2004-2024) which is the timeframe that has seen the rapid proliferation of SR practices and the decline of theoretical constructions that buttress these practices. The keywords included the following, sustainability reporting, ESG disclosure, financial performance, stakeholder theory, and legitimacy theory and their different combinations. The inclusion criteria required that all selected works must be peer-reviewed, empirical or conceptual, directly get involved in SR and financial outcomes, and use either the Stakeholder or Legitimacy theory. Only the English-language publications, which made stated measures or well-conceived conceptual arguments that connected SR and FP, were included. Non-peer-reviewed opinion, which lacked transferable insight, and works not substantively dealing with theory or financial implications were rejected as exclusion criteria.

4.2 Screening and Synthesis

After the first pool was obtained, relevance screening was done initially at title, and abstract stage, and then at full-text stage, theoretic, and empirical contribution. Instead of listing all pieces in an exhaustive manner, the review prioritized articles that (a) directly implemented Stakeholder or Legitimacy theory, (b) explored SR quality or assurance procedures, and (c) explored SRFP relationship or their moderators (industry, firm size, regulatory regime). These selected papers were then brought through a thematic coding scheme which embraced conceptual motivations, measurement methodologies, empirical designs, reported effects and contextual moderators. The outcome of this process is a synthesis of narrative which attempts to express combined assertions concerning theory and evidence.

4.3 Critical Evaluation and Weaknesses

In order to maintain analytical transparency, the review reports common methodological shortcomings seen in the literature specifically, measurement heterogeneity, internal issues, and short time horizons. These restrictions are seen as interpretation restrictions rather than bias sources. Since the overriding goal is theoretical refinement and agenda setting, the narrative approach will avoid the rigor of a systematic review in favor of analytic richness and conceptual coherence. The synthesis should be seen as being the theory-inspired narrow, targeted, distillation of the most significant and noticeable work, therefore, not as a bibliometric inventory.

4.4 Method Justification

The adopted narrative design is explained by the aim to make theoretical inconsistencies comprehensible, contextual difference explainable, and methodological weaknesses clear among different studies. The given methodological lens provides the more conceptual integration that could be excluded by strictly systematic protocols which makes it possible to understand the relation of SR and FP more thoroughly.

5. FINDINGS

The following results summarize the literature in accordance with the theoretical framework formulated in Section 2 and concur with the research questions posed in

Section 3.6. Inside each of the subsections, there are outlined the patterns which are emerging, observed contradictions, and contextual conditions which define the SR-FP relationship.

5.1. Overwhelming Empirical Pattern: Conditional Positive Effects

Through a wide expanse of literature, sustainability reporting- especially sound ESN performance- is associated with better financial results of the company including higher profitability, high market value, and lower cost of equity. The relationship is true as SR appears in substantive, material disclosures, which have governance arrangements (e.g., assurance, audit committees) (Friede, Busch & Bassen, 2015; Masila et al., 2024; Widyawati, 2020; Dhaliwal et al., 2011). Three main types of explanatory mechanisms are often presented in the literature: an approach of signaling to investors that reduces information asymmetry; mitigating risk by pre-empting operational and regulatory risks; and creating stakeholder value in which more robust relational ties lead to the creation of performance benefits (Simoni et al., 2020; Gholami et al., 2022).

5.2 Moderators and Mediators Governance, Assurance and Stakeholder Engagement

The moderation between SR and FP exists to a significant degree, being on the quality of governance and assurance. Third party assurance, disclosure credibility enhances through board oversight, and active audit committees increases potential financial benefits (Manning et al., 2019; Pizzi et al., 2022; Casey and Grenier, 2015). Some of the constructs revealed through mediation are the cost of capital, stakeholder trust, and operational efficiency, which are mechanisms that trace the route between verified and material disclosures to firm value (El Ghoul et al., 2011; Lakhani and Herbert, 2022).

5.3 Quality vs. Quantity and the Problem of Symbolic Reporting

Empirical research shows that there exists a strong difference between the number and standard of disclosures. The quality of disclosures, which are material, specific and assure, is better placed to create material financial benefit. In contrast, low-quality or symbolic disclosures, usually based on the issues of legitimacy, could foster minimal or even negative financial results, especially in the cases where the greenwashing activities are revealed (Hummel & Schlick, 2016; Lee and Raschke, 2023; Arvidsson, 2018). These results help to uncover some seeming counterexamples where the very high volume of disclosure does not result into quantifiable financial benefits (Buallay, 2019; Clarkson et al., 2008).

5.4 Contextual Diversity: Industry, Firm Size and Institutional Environment

Literature shows that there are heterogeneities in SR effects and in FP in different sectors, different firms as well as in different nations. There are better SR-FP benefits in manufacturing and other environmentally sensitive industries, with mixed or negative results in the financial institutions and some service sectors (Buallay, 2019; Lo and Kwan, 2017). Positive returns to reporting are more often recorded by large companies that act in developed markets, whereas SMEs and business in emerging markets are faced with the lack of resources which reduce the quality of reporting and the associated financial benefits (Guerrero-Baena et al., 2024; Gholami et al., 2022).

Table 1. Short summary

Key finding	Representative studies	Practical implication
Conditional positive SR–FP link (when quality + governance present)	Friede, Busch & Bassen (2015); Masila et al. (2024); Widyawati (2020)	Promote assurance & governance reforms to capture financial benefits
Governance & assurance as moderators/mediators	Manning et al. (2019); Meinawati & Wirakusuma (2023); Dwomor & Mensah (2024)	Strengthen audit committees and third-party verification
Quality vs. quantity; risk of symbolic reporting	Hummel & Schlick (2016); Lee & Raschke (2023); Arvidsson (2018)	Shift measurement focus from breadth to materiality and credibility
Context-dependent effects (industry, size, country)	Buallay (2019); Guerrero-Baena et al. (2024); Gholami et al. (2022)	Tailor policy and reporting tools by sector and firm scale

5.5 Sector-Specific Individual Differences in the SR-FP Relationship

The patterns in the reporting of a sustainability report, as well as the financial implication, have a significant difference among the sectors, which can be explained by different levels of environmental exposure, regulating policies, stakeholder sensitivities, and diversity in business models. This analysis, when done in a specific way that covers the sector, provides informative details about the situations and processes wherein sustainability reporting is converted into financial performance.

5.5.1 High-Impact Endowments (Power, Mining, Chemicals, factory)

The existence of stronger SR-FP relationships is more likely to be observed in companies that are in the resource-intensive industries, where the nature of their business is more likely to produce high environmental and social hazards. Good sustainability reporting assists in addressing the legitimacy issues hence reducing the regulatory, litigation, and operations risk exposures. It is shown in an empirical study that in these industries, the process of ESG disclosure has a material positive impact on reducing risk premiums and promoting credit ratings (Grewal et al., 2020; Clarkson et al., 2019). The ESG disclosures are subject to scrutiny by the investors in particular as they directly depend on the possible environmental liability and therefore the transparency is a decisive factor in determining the firm value.

5.5.2 Financial Services Sector

However, in the financial sector, weaker or mixed SR -FP relationships are usually observed. In this case, sustainability risks consist of indirect and reputational risks, as opposed to operational ones. Research shows that the banks and financial institutions tend to do full symbolic environmental reporting to remain legitimate and there is a little actual implementation of sustainability in the internal processes (Kotsantonis et al., 2016; Larker and Watts, 2020). The SR-FP relationship is therefore reinforced only through having ESG disclosures that are related to governance, ethical lending or risk management.

5.5.3 Knowledge and Technological Industries

Technology companies frequently forecast social and governance aspects of ESG, including data privacy, computer security, and human resource. The studies indicate that sustainability reporting contributes to increased talent attraction, development of innovation ability, and the strength of the brand image (Neri et al., 2021; Shahzad et al., 2020). The SR-FP association in such situations is demonstrated through productivity increase, intellectual capital growth, and better employee engagement, as opposed to direct environmental measures.

5.5.4 Healthcare and Pharmaceuticals

In the healthcare industry, there are high expectations by the stakeholders such as patients, regulators, and governments. The availability of drug safety, transparency, ethics, and clinical trials result in significant trust in the stakeholders. Empirical evidence indicates that there are positive SR-FP relationships that are mediated by lower litigation risk and reputation enhancing (Marques et al., 2020).

5.5.5 Consumer Goods and Retail

The choices made during purchasing are strongly affected by such forms of sustainability practices as supply-chain transparency, responsible sourcing, and ethical standards in the labour sphere. Companies with high sustainability reports are characterized by a better brand equity and customer loyalty (Delmas & Grant, 2014).

5.5.6 Sectoral Analysis Conclusion

On the whole, the evidence on the sectoral supports the conditional character of SR -FP relationship. High-impact sectors receive an increased number of financial rewards based on sustainability reporting because there are increased risks exposures; and the low-impact sectors are evidenced in poor relations unless the stakeholders require transparency concerning ethical, social, or governance aspects.

5.6 Cross-country Comparativism Evidence and Institutional Logics

Comparative evidence conducted across countries shows that institutional nature as represented by the regulatory environment, investor protection, strength of enforcement, and ultimately cultural norms have a significant effect on the quality of sustainability reporting and its connection with financial performance. As an example, companies based in civil-law countries (e.g., France, Germany, Spain) are more likely to focus on compliance-related sustainability disclosure, where the companies based on the common-law countries (e.g., UK, USA, Australia) focus on the market-based sustainability practices (Ioannou and Serafeim, 2012). It is implied by the literature on legal origins that financial institutions are located in efficient investor-protection environments and hence strategically use ESG reporting to model their differentiation within a capital market, where they face more valuation premia.

Observations of large cross-country samples suggest that sustainability reporting has a putting more financial impact in the countries where there are strong institutional infrastructures and high level of transparency in capital markets and high level of enforcement mechanism. As an illustration, companies in a tight environmental regulation regulate more substantial ESG activity that leads to quantifiable financial results in terms of diminished operational risks, increased productivity, and increased access to capital-market (La Porta and Shleifer, 2008; Liang and Renneboog, 2020). On the contrary, in weak institutional settings, the symbolic compliance or minimum disclosure that meets the requirements of the regulations but does not promote the integration of sustainability is prevalent among firms.

The developing markets such as India, Brazil, China and South Africa have a different institutional logic which are fuelled by developmental needs. Although required ESG laws (e.g. BRSR in India, King IV in South Africa) have upsurged the quantity of reporting, the quality of the reporting is uneven. According to the empirical evidence of BRICS economies, the sustainability disclosure is often driven by legitimacy issues as opposed to stakeholder integration (Aureli et al., 2020; Huang and Watson, 2015). At that, the SR-FP relationship is weaker or vague unless they are strengthened by effective governance frameworks, external guarantee and competencies of boards.

More institutional layers define sustainability reporting. Greater focus on environmental stewardship and community development may be fostered by cultural factors, such as collective orientations, high uncertainty avoidance or long-term orientation. The institutional theory assumes that cultural norms can affect the judgments of managers regarding the strategic significance of sustainability and impact the level of disclosure and diversification (Ringov and Zollo, 2007; Kanagaretnam et al., 2023). The East Asian companies tend to focus on harmonisation, stewardship and relational legitimacy leading to more narrative and qualitative sustainability reporting, whereas Western companies are prone to using quantitative indicators embraced by investor expectation.

Sustainability results are also silenced by capitals structural systems. At the developed markets with advanced investor base, ESG information helps to reduce cost of equity, decrease volatility and increase Q of the Tobin (El Ghoul et al., 2011; Sila and Cek, 2017). Conversely, less mature markets, where the ESG literacy of the investor is low, see sustainability disclosures as not as financially relevant, thus diluting the SR-FP relationship.

Global supply chains put institutional pressures on companies- and especially the SMEs- to conform to the sustainability demands of the big multinational purchasers. Research suggests that sustainability requirements of supply-chain can make suppliers raise the reports quality because failure to comply might lead to their removal of the suppliers out of the purchase networks (Busch et al., 2016; Klassen and Vereecke, 2012). This external pressure of stake holders inflames the stakeholder theory propositions with regard to the instrumental benefits of fulfilling the sustainability expectations.

Overall, the evidence on the cross-country scale proves that the efficiency of sustainability reporting cannot be discussed beyond the institutional context. Well-developed capital bases and effective regulatory enforcement, along with encouraging cultural norms, increases the believability of reporting and increases its financial implication. On the other hand, those institutions with weak institutionalization contribute to symbolic compliance, increasing the divide between sustainability rhetoric and sustainability in practice one that is explained by the legitimacy theory.

6. THEORETICAL IMPLICATIONS

It is critical to refine the scope of the theory and make comprehensible the mechanisms of interaction. An empirical study indicates that Stakeholder Theory and Legitimacy Theory do not mutually exclusively affect each other, but rather, they complement each other. The degree of financial benefits supports the disclosure implications of stakeholder mechanisms, which enhance the underlying pathways of substantive reporting, and the lack of value generation underlies the legitimacy motives (Hummel and Schlick, 2016; Simoni et al., 2020). Theoretical research in the future ought to model directly threshold conditions: that is, when the governance strength is strong, stakeholder pressures are dominant, and the opposite.

The focus on the quality of disclosure should be the center of the future wave of theory development. Scholars should go beyond the trivial statement that there is such a phenomenon as reporting exists and theorize the nature of disclosure including materiality, assurance, specificity as primary mediating variables that contribute to the sustainability reporting financial performance (SRFP) relationship (Koh et al., 2023; Simoni et al., 2020).

Theoretical propositions need to be paid attention to in a contextualized manner. Institutional and industry contingencies, such as regulatory strength, environmental exposure of the industry, the size of the firm, should be considered in theory-building, instead of trying to assume similar mechanisms across the settings (Gholami et al., 2022; Guerrero-Baena et al., 2024).

When dynamic processes are incorporated, it is also helpful. Accounting dynamics in time would be beneficial to both stakeholder and legitimacy theories; the legitimacy issues and stakeholder expectations change over time, which would imply that models must have the feedback loop, crisis, and learning over time (Lee and Raschke, 2023; Lo and Kwan, 2017).

7. PRACTICAL IMPLICATIONS

To managers and boards, enhancing disclosure caliber including materiality evaluation, third-party guidance, significant engaged involvement of the stakeholders instead of just expanding the quantity of disclosure should be prioritized. Enhanced forms of governance (i.e. adequately furnished audit committees and sustainable board experience) substantially increase the probability of financial upside (Manning et al., 2019; Pizzi et al., 2022).

Forming assurance status, materiality indicator and investigating engagement metrics have assisted investors and analysts to differentiate substantial reportage and symbolic disclosure. Emphasizing only the amount of disclosure or headline ESG ratings is a mistake because the mispricing of greenwashing firms (Lee and Raschke, 2023; Simoni et al., 2020).

To policymakers and standard-setters, their focus is to put priorities on standards enhancing disclosure comparability and focus on assurance and materiality. They can be avoided by considering scalable reporting needs or incentives designed to align with the interests of SMEs and emerging-market firms (Guerrero-Baena et al., 2024; Gholami et al., 2022).

Auditors and assurance providers need to consider creating more resilient verification procedures under ESG data and creating assurance scopes maximally effective in reducing information asymmetry so that reporting will be more decision-useful to capital markets (Casey and Grenier, 2015, Simoni et al., 2020).

8. CONSTRAINS AND FUTURE RESEARCH

8.1 Limitations of the Analyzed Literature

- Measurement heterogeneity. Sustainability reporting operationalization, diverse ESG indices, proxies, and sustainability reporting comparability are hindered (Hummel & Schlick, 2016).
- The constraint Methodological. Most studies are cross-sectional, short-term, or poorly control endogeneity, and hence, cannot cause inference (Gholami et al., 2022).
- Under-emphasis on quality. Excessive dependence on the amount of disclosure undervalues the far more significant role played by assurance and materiality (Koh et al., 2023).
- Context coverage bias. There is still unsatisfactory evidence on large businesses and developed economies; SMEs and the developing world are underrepresented (Guerrero-Baena et al., 2024).

8.2 Future Potential Research Directions

- Causal designs, longitudinal studies: Use the difference-in-differences, instrumental variables and long-panel data to identify the causal impact of sustainability reporting on financial performance (El Ghoul et al., 2011).

- Certify and centralise quality measures: Build and justify multidimensional measures of materiality, assurance and engagement of stakeholders, and go beyond the length of disclosure (Koh et al., 2023; Simoni et al., 2020).
- Research mediators and moderators: The mechanisms, which are empirically tested, include cost of capital, stakeholder trust, operational efficiency, and boundary conditions, such as industry sensitivity, institutional strength (Lakhani and Herbert, 2022).
- Experiments in policy and SME research: Discuss scalable reporting schemes and incentives to increase the quality of disclosure in resource-constrained firms (Guerrero -Baena et al., 2024).
- The identification and consequences of greenwashing: Establish ways to identify symbolic reporting, estimate reputational expenses after exposure; determine the effect of detection on the SR-FP dynamics (Lee and Raschke, 2023).
- International comparative labor: Commercial institutional comparisons will elucidate the existence of regulation and market framework in the prevalence of stakeholder or legitimacy logics (Gesso & Lodhi, 2024).

9. OVERALL SYNTHESIS

Combined, the literature shows that the relationship sustainability reporting-financial performance is very conditional instead of universal. The types of substantive sustainability reporting, i.e. materiality, specificity and assurance, tended to enhance financial performance. Conversely, when implemented via the symbolic reporting which principally focuses on the issues of legitimacy, the results are frequently nothing more than negligible. These effects are also influenced by contextual variables like regulatory strength, industry sensitivity, governance mechanisms and firm size. These insights highlight why it is essential to assess the quality of reporting and the institutional climate during the interpretation of SR -FP patterns.

10. CONCLUSION

The data on the relationship between sustainability reporting and financial performance is, in general, positive: in case of an effective sustainability reporting, materialised and contextualised in the context of sound governance structures and stakeholder interaction, it could be converted into financial gain (Friede, Busch & Bassen, 2015; Masila et al., 2024). However, the literature is diverse, and many of the findings are null or negative and can be explained by legitimacy-induced or symbolic disclosures and methodology issues (Hummel & Schick, 2016; Lee and 'Raschke, 2023). To develop scholarly theory and managerial practise, future studies should focus on enhancing the quality of disclosure and separating causal processes and identifying the contextual moderators, including industry type, firm size and institutional strength. There will be the need to apply stricter governance and assurance interface, and more refined reporting protocols to make the sustainability disclosures credible and analytically feasible and strategically applicable to both the practitioners and the policymakers.

Recent trends relating to the international management of sustainability also show a tendency to tighten the relationship between SR and FP as the markets gradually tend to become compliant to unified reporting performance. The increased use of the ISSB standards, the insulation of the compulsory assurance requirements and the further regulatory control are the factors which are likely to contribute to the increase in the credibility of the corporate sustainability data. Such a course of action must reduce greenwashing, enhance comparability and improve investor confidence- further increasing the financial importance of sustainability disclosures. As a result, the empirical studies will enjoy datasets of a better consistency, causal identification methods of a stronger type, and measurement tools that are more accurate in reflecting disclosure quality.

Organizationally, companies which strategically introduce sustainability in their general business processes, and which do not see reporting as a performative type of action, are more sanctioned to create sustained value. Sustainability reporting will become a part of the essential enterprise risk management and strategic decision-making process as climate risks escalate, expectations, and regulatory pressure ratche up in the society. The concurrent adoption of sustainability governance, stringent materiality test, and quality assurance structures will, thus, determine the direction that corporate reporting and financial performance results are going to take in the next 10 years. Companies that embrace the practice early are likely to have a competitive edge, enhanced abilities to use international capital markets and increased trust of stakeholders.

REFERENCES

Adams, C. A., & Abhayawansa, S. (2022). Connecting the COVID-19 pandemic, sustainable development, and responsible corporate reporting. Sustainability Accounting. *Management and Policy Journal, 13*(1), 1–16. DOI: 10.1108/SAMPJ-05-2021-0196

Arvidsson, S. (2018). How are stakeholder relations communicated in sustainability reports? A longitudinal and cross-country focus* (book chapter). In *Challenges in Managing Sustainable Business (Chap. 1).DOI: 10.1007/978-3-319-93266-8_1

Aureli, S., Magnaghi, E., & Salvatori, F. (2020). The role of regulation in sustainability reporting quality: Evidence from the EU directive. *Accounting in Europe, 17*(3), 223–250. DOI: 10.1080/17449480.2020.1768929

Ben-Amar, W., Chang, M., & McIlkenny, P. (2017). Board gender diversity and corporate response to sustainability initiatives. *Journal of Business Ethics, 142*(2), 369–383. DOI: 10.1007/s10551-015-2759-1

Birindelli, G., Dell'Atti, S., Iannuzzi, A. P., & Savioli, M. (2018). Composition and activity of the board of directors: Impact on ESG performance in the banking sector. *Sustainability (Basel), 10*(12), 4699. DOI: 10.3390/su10124699

Bolton, P., & Kacperczyk, M. (2021). Do investors care about carbon risk? *Journal of Financial Economics, 142*(2), 517–549. DOI: 10.1016/j.jfineco.2021.05.008

Buallay, A. (2019). Is sustainability reporting (ESG) associated with performance? Evidence from the European banking sector. *Management of Environmental Quality, 30*(1), 98–115. DOI: 10.1108/MEQ-12-2017-0149

Busch, T., Bauer, R., & Orlitzky, M. (2016). Sustainable development and financial markets: Old paths and new avenues. *Business & Society, 55*(3), 303–329. DOI: 10.1177/0007650315570701

Busse, C. (2016). Doing well by doing good? The self-interest of buying firms and sustainable supply chain management. *The Journal of Supply Chain Management, 52*(2), 28–47. DOI: 10.1111/jscm.12096

Casey, R. J., & Grenier, J. H. (2015). Understanding and contributing to the enigma of corporate social responsibility (CSR) assurance in the United States. *Auditing, 34*(1), 97–130. DOI: 10.2308/ajpt-50736

Cheung, A. W., Evans, E., & Wright, S. (2022). Mandatory ESG disclosure and market pricing of sustainability. *Accounting and Finance, 62*(4), 5117–5149.

Christensen, H. B., Hail, L., & Leuz, C. (2021). Mandatory sustainability reporting and firm behavior. *Review of Accounting Studies*, *26*, 1176–1248. DOI: 10.1007/s11142-021-09609-5

Clarkson, P. M., Li, Y., Richardson, G. D., & Vasvari, F. P. (2008). Revisiting the relation between environmental performance and environmental disclosure: An empirical analysis. *Journal of Accounting and Economics*, *45*(1), 116–135. DOI: 10.1016/j.jacceco.2007.02.003

Del Gesso, C., & Lodhi, R. N. (2024). Theories underlying environmental, social and governance (ESG) disclosure: A systematic review of accounting studies. *Journal of Accounting Literature*. Advance online publication. DOI: 10.1108/JAL-08-2023-0143

Delmas, M. A., & Grant, L. E. (2014). Eco-labeling strategies and price-premium: The wine industry puzzle. *Business & Society*, *53*(1), 6–44. DOI: 10.1177/0007650310362254

Dhaliwal, D. S., Li, O. Z., Tsang, A., & Yang, Y. G. (2011). Voluntary nonfinancial disclosure and the cost of equity capital: The initiation of corporate social responsibility reporting. *The Accounting Review*, *86*(1), 59–100. DOI: 10.2308/accr.00000005

Dhaliwal, D. S., Radhakrishnan, S., Tsang, A., & Yang, Y. G. (2014). Nonfinancial disclosure and analyst forecast accuracy. *The Accounting Review*, *87*(3), 723–759. DOI: 10.2308/accr-10218

Dyck, A., Lins, K. V., Roth, L., & Wagner, H. F. (2019). Do institutional investors drive corporate social responsibility? *Journal of Financial Economics*, *131*(3), 693–714. DOI: 10.1016/j.jfineco.2018.08.013

Eccles, R. G., & Klimenko, S. (2019). The investor revolution. *Harvard Business Review*, *97*(3), 106–116.

El Ghoul, S., Guedhami, O., Kwok, C. C. Y., & Mishra, D. R. (2011). Does corporate social responsibility affect the cost of capital? *Journal of Financial Economics*, *102*(1), 79–96. DOI: 10.1016/j.jfineco.2011.10.009

Flammer, C., Hong, B., & Minor, D. (2019). Corporate governance and the rise of integrating ESG metrics into CEO incentive contracts. *Management Science*, *65*(12), 5501–5525. DOI: 10.1287/mnsc.2018.3094

Freeman, R. E. (1984). *Strategic management: A stakeholder approach*. Pitman (book).

Friede, G., Busch, T., & Bassen, A. (2015). ESG and financial performance: Aggregated evidence from more than 2000 empirical studies. *Journal of Business Ethics*, *137*(2), 197–227. DOI: 10.1007/s10551-015-2878-6

Gholami, A., Sands, J., & Rahman, H. U. (2022). Environmental, social and governance disclosure and value generation: Is the financial industry different? *Sustainability (Basel)*, *14*(5), 2647. DOI: 10.3390/su14052647

Grewal, J., Hauptmann, C., & Serafeim, G. (2020). Material sustainability information and stock price informativeness. *Journal of Business Ethics*, *167*(3), 513–533. DOI: 10.1007/s10551-020-04451-2

Guerrero-Baena, M. D., Castilla-Polo, F., & Rodríguez-Gutiérrez, P. (2024). Motivations for social and environmental reporting in SMEs: Evidence and drivers. *Sustainability-related journal* / SBIR. DOI: 10.1002/bsd2.29

Haque, F., & Ntim, C. G. (2018). Environmental policy, environmental performance, and board ESG oversight. *Business Strategy and the Environment*, *27*(3), 1–17. DOI: 10.1002/bse.1993

Hsu, A. W., Lee, S., & Chen, H. (2021). ESG-linked compensation and corporate sustainability performance. *Journal of Business Ethics*, *170*(1), 15–35. DOI: 10.1007/s10551-020-04525-0

Huang, X., & Watson, L. (2015). Corporate social responsibility research in accounting. *Journal of Accounting Literature*, *34*(1), 1–16. DOI: 10.1016/j.acclit.2015.03.001

Hummel, K., & Schlick, C. (2016). The relationship between sustainability performance and sustainability disclosure — Reconciling voluntary disclosure theory and legitimacy theory. *Journal of Accounting and Public Policy*, *35*(5), 455–476. DOI: 10.1016/j.jaccpubpol.2016.06.001

IFRS Foundation. (2023). IFRS S1 & IFRS S2 Sustainability Standards. https://www.ifrs.org

Ioannou, I., & Serafeim, G. (2012). What drives corporate social performance? The role of nation-level institutions. *Journal of International Business Studies*, *43*(9), 834–864. DOI: 10.1057/jibs.2012.26

Kanagaretnam, K., Lobo, G. J., & Whalen, D. J. (2023). Cultural dimensions and corporate environmental disclosure. *Journal of Business Ethics*, *184*, 529–558.

Khan, M., Serafeim, G., & Yoon, A. (2016). Corporate sustainability: First evidence on materiality. *The Accounting Review*, *91*(6), 1697–1724. DOI: 10.2308/accr-51383

La Porta, R., & Shleifer, A. (2008). The unofficial economy and economic development. *Brookings Papers on Economic Activity*, •••, 275–352.

Klassen, R. D., & Vereecke, A. (2012). Social issues in supply chains. *Journal of Operations Management*, *30*(1–2), 7–23. DOI: 10.1016/j.jom.2011.06.004

Koh, K., Li, H., & Tong, Y. H. (2023). Corporate social responsibility (CSR) performance and stakeholder engagement: Evidence from the quantity and quality of CSR disclosures. *Corporate Social Responsibility and Environmental Management*, *30*(2), 504–517. DOI: 10.1002/csr.2370

Kotsantonis, S., Pinney, C., & Serafeim, G. (2016). ESG integration in investment management. *The Bank of America Journal of Applied Corporate Finance*, *28*(2), 45–58. DOI: 10.1111/jacf.12169

Krueger, P., Sautner, Z., & Starks, L. (2023). Climate risk and institutional investors. *Review of Financial Studies*, *36*(1), 456–505. DOI: 10.1093/rfs/hhac035

La Porta, R., & Shleifer, A. (2008). The unofficial economy and economic development. *Brookings Papers on Economic Activity*, *2008*(2), 275–352. DOI: 10.1353/eca.0.0016

Lakhani, L., & Herbert, S. L. (2022). Theoretical frameworks applied in integrated reporting and sustainability reporting research. *Suid-Afrikaanse Tydskrif vir Ekonomiese en Bestuurswetenskappe*, *25*(1), a4427. DOI: 10.4102/sajems.v25i1.4427

Lee, M. T., & Raschke, R. L. (2023). Stakeholder legitimacy in firm greening and financial performance: What about greenwashing temptations? *Journal of Business Research*, *155*, 113393. Advance online publication. DOI: 10.1016/j.jbusres.2022.113393

Liang, H., & Renneboog, L. (2020). Corporate social responsibility and sustainable finance: A review. European Corporate Governance Institute Working Paper.

Lo, K. Y., & Kwan, C. L. (2017). The effect of environmental, social, governance and sustainability reporting on financial performance: An empirical study in Hong Kong. *Journal of Business Research*, *71*, 185–191. DOI: 10.1016/j.jbusres.2017.02.020

Manning, S., Boons, F., & von Hagen, O. (2019). Governance and sustainability standards. *Journal of Business Ethics*, *154*(2), 361–383.

Marques, P., Rodrigues, L. L., & Oliveira, A. (2020). The relevance of CSR practices in the healthcare sector. *Journal of Business Ethics*, *162*, 379–396.

Martínez-Ferrero, J., & García-Sánchez, I. (2017). Sustainability assurance and cost of capital. *Journal of Business Ethics*, *140*(2), 353–367.

Masila, M.. (2024). *ESG transparency and profitability*. Sustainability Accounting Journal.

Neri, L.. (2021). Sustainability and innovation in the tech sector. *Technovation, 102*, 102214. DOI: 10.1016/j.technovation.2020.102214

Ortiz-de-Mandojana, N.. (2016). Board independence and environmental innovation. *Business Strategy and the Environment*, *25*(4), 272–289.

Pizzi, S., Rosati, F., Venturelli, A., & Bosetti, L. (2022). The moderating role of corporate governance in the relationship between sustainability performance and financial performance. *Business Strategy and the Environment*, *31*(4), 1714–1730. DOI: 10.1002/bse.3000

Pizzi, S., Venturelli, A., & Bosetti, L. (2023). Digital transformation and ESG reporting. *Technological Forecasting and Social Change*, *187*, 122160.

Post, C., Rahman, N., & Rubow, E. (2011). Board gender diversity and corporate social responsibility. *Journal of Business Ethics*, *102*(2), 179–196. DOI: 10.1007/s10551-011-0902-1

Serafeim, G. (2020). How to build enduring commitment to long-term goals. *Harvard Business Review*.

Shahzad, F.. (2020). The role of sustainability reporting in tech innovation. *Journal of Cleaner Production*, *263*, 121367.

Sierra, L., Zorio, A., & García-Benau, M. (2013). Sustainability report assurance. *Business Strategy and the Environment*, *22*(7), 484–500. DOI: 10.1002/bse.1764

Sierra, L., Zorio, A., & García-Benau, M. (2013). Sustainable development and assurance of corporate social responsibility reports. *Business Strategy and the Environment*, *22*(7), 484–500. DOI: 10.1002/bse.1764

Sila, V., & Cek, K. (2017). The impact of ESG on firm value. *Journal of Applied Accounting Research*, *18*(2), 208–225.

Simoni, L., Bini, L., & Bellucci, M. (2020). Effects of social, environmental and institutional factors on sustainability report assurance: Evidence from European countries. *Meditari Accountancy Research*, *28*(6), 1059–1087. DOI: 10.1108/MEDAR-03-2019-0462

Suchman, M. C. (1995). Managing legitimacy: Strategic and institutional approaches. *Academy of Management Review*, *20*(3), 571–610. DOI: 10.2307/258788

Velte, P. (2021). Meta-analyses on corporate social responsibility (CSR) and firm performance: A literature review. *Sustainability*, *13*(12), 7269. DOI: 10.3390/su13137269

Walls, J. L., Berrone, P., & Phan, P. H. (2012). Corporate governance and environmental performance. *Strategic Management Journal*, *33*(8), 885–913. DOI: 10.1002/smj.1952

Widyawati, L. (2020). A systematic literature review of socially responsible investment and environmental, social and governance (ESG) criteria. *Journal of Business Ethics*, *175*(2), 323–341. DOI: 10.1007/s10551-019-04143-y

Chapter 7
The Marriage of Fintech and ESG in Investment Banks:
Did COVID-19 Matchmake Them?

Vu Thuy Linh
http://orcid.org/0000-0003-1005-6879
ESADE Business School, Spain

ABSTRACT

I study the importance of Fintech investment on Environmental, Social, and Governance (ESG) performance score and on ESG risk rating (i.e., the bank's economic risk driven by ESG factors) of 342 investment banks, and whether the impact is greater or less during the Covid years. I find that Fintech investment does have a significant positive impact on ESG performance score. I also find that Fintech investment does have significant positive impact on governance (G) score, but insignificant impact on E score and S score. The findings indicate that Covid does have a significant impact on ESG risk rating, although Covid does not have significant impact on ESG performance, regardless of Fintech investment levels. There is a positive relationship between Fintech investment and ESG performance during both Covid and non-Covid years, with little variation in intensity. Additionally, the impact of Fintech investment on ESG performance is stronger for banks with smaller investment sizes. Lastly, Fintech investment has greatest positive effect on ESG performance when made through private equity.

DOI: 10.4018/979-8-3373-5047-9.ch007

1. INTRODUCTION

In recent years, Fintech (financial technology) has attracted attention for its influence on firm performance and shareholder value (Dranev et al., 2019; Putri et al., 2019; Mitra & Karathanasopoulos, 2020; Liu et al., 2021; Anindyastri et al., 2022). Global Fintech investment surged from USD 9 billion in 2010 to USD 209 billion in 2022 (Statista, 2023). As the largest Fintech festival worldwide (Mittal & Koh, 2024; Loo, 2019), the Singapore Fintech Festival expanded from 13,000 participants from 60 countries in 2016 to 66,000 from 150 countries in 2023. This phenomenon relies heavily on technologies such as big data (Wang et al., 2021), artificial intelligence (Ahmed et al., 2022), blockchain (Son & Jang, 2023), and the Internet of Things (Palmaccio et al., 2021), enabling network-based financial services. Fintech spans payments, clearing and settlement, credit, deposits, and capital-raising services. Scholars argue it can transform finance by increasing transparency, security, and efficiency, expanding product diversity, improving risk management, and facilitating real-time customer feedback (Kabulova et al., 2020; Li et al., 2024).s

Financial institutions have increasingly invested in Fintech, viewing it as a strategic priority by 2019 (Kabulova et al., 2020). Fintech is recognized for enhancing service quality, reducing costs, increasing profits, promoting financial inclusion, and stabilizing markets (Moro-Visconti et al., 2020). Beyond finance, it supports broader economic and social transformations, including sustainable development and decentralized social connectivity. Concurrently, financial institutions have emphasized sustainability to achieve net-zero emissions and mitigate climate change risks (Alonso et al., 2019; Moro-Visconti et al., 2020). Financial services, including those offered via Fintech, increasingly integrate sustainability metrics and ESG principles, accelerated by COVID-19, which prompted reliance on digital financial solutions (Macchiavello et al., 2022).

While technology traditionally prioritizes productivity over environmental goals, Fintech demonstrates alignment with ESG objectives, fostering an inclusive, environmentally responsible financial system (Macchiavello et al., 2022). Since 2016, the United Nations has examined Fintech's role in sustainable development, and the G20 now includes sustainable digital finance in its 2030 agenda. Despite growing interest, empirical research linking Fintech and ESG performance within financial institutions remains limited, especially in investment banking. Existing studies focus largely on Fintech start-ups, conventional or commercial banks (Galeone et al., 2024; Mokhtar & Alam, 2023; Wan et al., 2023; Carlini et al., 2022; Salah et al., 2025; Costa-Climent & Martínez-Climent, 2018a; Costa-Climent & Martínez-Climent, 2018b; Chueca Vergara & Ferruz Agudo, 2021; Gomber et al., 2017; Romānova & Kudinska, 2016).

This study contributes by quantitatively examining the impact of Fintech investment on ESG performance in 342 global investment banks, distinguishing effects across COVID-19 and non-COVID-19 periods, and analysing ESG risk ratings. Unlike prior research relying on qualitative case studies, PLS-SEM, or regional indices, this study uses recent global data up to 2023 to explore Fintech as an independent variable and ESG outcomes as dependent variables, focusing on the unique operational and governance structures of investment banks.

This book chapter is structured as follows: Section 2 reviews literature and presents research questions and hypotheses. Section 3 details data, Section 4 outlines methodology, Section 5 reports results, Section 6 discusses findings, and Section 7 concludes with contributions.

2. LITERATURE REVIEW & HYPOTHESES

2.1 Fintech and ESG Performance: Generic Evidence and Conceptual Foundations

The relationship between financial technology (Fintech) and ESG performance lies at the intersection of financial intermediation, corporate governance, and sustainable finance. Early Fintech research emphasized value creation through efficiency gains, cost reduction, innovation-driven competitiveness, and risk-taking (Liu et al., 2017; Wang et al., 2021; Kharrat et al., 2024). More recent work examines whether digital transformation and Fintech investment shape sustainable development and ESG outcomes, though findings remain fragmented across contexts and measurement approaches.

Conceptually, the Fintech-ESG nexus is grounded in stakeholder salience theory and institutional legitimacy. ESG performance serves as a legitimacy signal to regulators, investors, clients, and society. For financial institutions, especially banks, Fintech investment represents not only operational upgrading but a reconfiguration of information and control architecture that strengthens transparency, disclosure, stakeholder engagement, and compliance monitoring, reshaping how ESG information is produced and verified.

Empirically, most studies document a positive association between Fintech development and ESG performance. Wang et al. (2022), using Chinese listed firms and panel regressions, show Fintech improves ESG performance through financing-constraint alleviation. Ren et al. (2023), analyzing Chinese A-share firms (2011-2020), similarly finds regional Fintech development enhances ESG via internal mechanisms (e.g., financing efficiency) and external channels (e.g., subsidies and tax rebates). Wan et al. (2023) provide banking evidence that Fintech supports environmentally oriented practices and green finance, while Mokhtar and Alam (2023) identify amplification effects between ESG and digital transformation.

The literature also highlights identification and endogeneity concerns. Galeone et al. (2024), in "ESG and Fintech: Are They Connected?", show ESG-oriented institutions are more likely to adopt Fintech, suggesting reverse causality or strategic complementarity (e.g., well-governed firms invest in both ESG and Fintech). This is especially relevant when Fintech is proxied by development indices rather than firm-level investment and when ESG reflects both outcomes and strategic intent.

Conceptual and policy contributions identify additional channels. Macchiavello and Siri (2022) frame "Green Fintech" as enabling sustainable capital allocation, transparency, and traceability. "Fintech Data Infrastructure for ESG Disclosure" (2023), drawing on RegTech and information systems perspectives, argues digital infrastructure improves reliability, standardization, automation, and regulatory compliance of ESG disclosures, though large-sample validation remains limited. Öhman, Nourallah, and El Kalak (2025) emphasize that contemporary Fintech solutions (AI, blockchain, RegTech) deliver benefits but introduce governance challenges-cybersecurity, ethical risks, and regulatory complexity-so net ESG effects depend on effective oversight.

Overall, Fintech may enhance ESG performance through reinforcing pathways: efficiency and transparency gains (Wang et al., 2021), ESG-integrated investment platforms (Devine et al., 2024), green capital allocation and traceability (Macchiavello & Siri, 2022), strengthened disclosure infrastructure (Fintech Data Infrastructure for ESG Disclosure, 2023), and governance-enhancing monitoring (Section 2.2). Yet limitations persist: evidence largely focuses on listed firms or commercial banks rather than investment banks; Fintech is often measured via regional indices rather than firm-level investment; and ESG performance is frequently analyzed without distinguishing ESG risk exposure. Variation in how Fintech (indices, adoption dummies, technology mentions) and ESG (aggregate, pillar, disclosure proxies) are operationalized complicates comparison and may explain mixed magnitudes. Moreover, panel associations cannot fully rule out confounding from managerial quality, regulatory environments, or concurrent strategic initiatives influencing both Fintech and ESG.

2.2 Fintech and Governance Mechanisms: Information Asymmetry, Monitoring, and Digital Control

A more granular explanation emerges when Fintech is treated as a governance and monitoring technology. Information asymmetry theory suggests financial institutions face persistent adverse selection and moral hazard. Fintech can reduce pre-credit risk driven by information asymmetry and adverse selection (Niinimäki et al., 2018) and reduce post-credit risk associated with moral hazard (Favara et al., 2021), consistent with the view that informational environments shape contracting and monitoring (Sufi, 2007). Fintech systems, big data analytics, AI monitoring, automated reporting, and blockchain traceability, can strengthen controls, reduce opacity, improve verifiability, and increase auditability of ESG-relevant claims.

This perspective is supported by Zhang et al. (2024), who show that Fintech development reduces opportunistic ESG disclosure manipulation, implying that digital traceability constrains agency problems in ESG reporting. Thus, Fintech may affect ESG not only via financing channels but also through disclosure integrity and governance quality, which is central to investment banks' credibility with regulators and institutional clients.

Related research emphasizes cost and transparency mechanisms. Big data reduces search costs and information misrepresentation (Gober, P., 2017; Buchak et al., 2018), reduces information costs for both sides of transactions, and increases market transparency (Yao et al., 2021). AI and machine learning-enabled by mobile communications and IoT-improve data analysis and model generation, reduce labor and operating costs, and increase service efficiency (He et al., 2017; Kend et al., 2020; Troshani et al., 2021). These mechanisms imply stronger governance capacity via automation, auditability, and continuous monitoring.

Governance effects are not unambiguously positive. Öhman et al. (2025) emphasize oversight challenges, including cybersecurity, ethical concerns, and regulatory complexity, implying that governance benefits for ESG are strongest when transformation co-evolves with robust controls and compliance integration. For investment banks, highly regulated and reputation-sensitive, these governance mechanisms are especially salient, making governance-related ESG effects more direct than environmental or social effects driven by broader externalities

2.3 Fintech, Environmental and Social Consequences: Capital Allocation, Traceability, Inclusion, and Boundary Conditions

Beyond governance, Fintech may influence environmental and social outcomes through distinct channels. First, Fintech can facilitate environmentally aligned capital allocation and sustainable investment decisions: platforms incorporate ESG criteria into portfolio selection and evaluation (Devine et al., 2024), improving access to sustainable portfolios and impact monitoring. This aligns with "Green Fintech," where digital innovation accelerates low-carbon transitions by directing capital toward green infrastructure (Macchiavello & Siri, 2022).

Second, blockchain and traceability enhance environmental accountability and supply-chain responsibility. Shahzad et al. (2023) argue that blockchain-based traceability verifies sustainability claims and improves transparency along value chains.

Third, Fintech supports environmental optimization via energy monitoring; Tao et al. (2022) highlight digital and blockchain-based energy management systems that track real-time consumption, promoting efficiency and reducing carbon footprints.

Fourth, Fintech can generate social benefits through inclusion and expanded access to finance. Digital payments and financial inclusion enable underserved groups to access services, supporting poverty reduction and sustainable growth (Rastogi et al., 2023). However, outcomes depend on complementary institutions: Tok et al. (2022) show Fintech alone may not close gender gaps, implying targeted policies and social-norm interventions remain necessary and that "S" improvements may be constrained by structural factors.

Empirically, Wan et al. (2023) show Fintech supports green finance in banking contexts. However, investment banks differ from commercial banks: their environmental and social influence operates through underwriting, advisory, and capital-market intermediation rather than direct lending. ESG impact may therefore arise via (i) standards and disclosures in underwriting and advisory mandates, (ii) design and distribution of sustainable finance products, and (iii) monitoring and reporting infrastructures used to meet regulatory expectations. Accordingly, Fintech investment in investment banks may primarily strengthen governance (compliance, reporting, monitoring), while environmental and social effects are weaker or indirect-consistent with the view that governance is more directly affected by digital transformation than external E/S outcomes.

2.4 Fintech, ESG Risk, and Crisis Periods: Measurement Noise, Digital Monitoring, and COVID-19 as a Contextual Amplifier

A key refinement is distinguishing ESG performance from ESG risk. ESG performance reflects observed practices and disclosures, whereas ESG risk captures exposure to unmanaged ESG liabilities affecting future cash flows and firm value-particularly relevant for financial institutions under regulatory scrutiny and market discipline.

ESG risk analysis faces measurement challenges. Berg, Kölbel, and Rigobon (2022) document divergence across ESG rating agencies driven by scope, measurement, and weighting differences, implying substantial noise. Berg et al. (2022) further show rating dispersion is associated with greater uncertainty and pricing inefficiency, complicating inference on the digital transformation-ESG relationship.

Recent studies propose improvements. Bissoondoyal-Bheenick et al. (2024) suggest aggregation methods to enhance predictability across multi-provider ratings. Schimanski et al. (2024) apply NLP and machine learning to textual disclosures to construct alternative ESG indicators capturing incremental risk information. Together, these contributions imply improved infrastructures and analytics can reduce measurement noise and narrow the gap between "true" ESG risk and observed assessments.

Fintech investment may influence ESG risk through two channels: (i) reducing unmanaged exposures via stronger governance and controls, and (ii) improving data integrity and disclosure quality that shape perceived risk and ratings. Zhang et al. (2024) supports the second channel by showing Fintech reduces ESG manipulation. However, whether Fintech investment lowers ESG risk ratings in investment banks-through reduced exposures, improved reporting quality, or both-remains underexplored.

Crisis periods may further condition these effects. Bouattour et al. (2024) show ESG performance enhances bank stability and digital maturity strengthens this relationship, suggesting digital capabilities matter more during shocks. COVID-19 intensified uncertainty, remote operations, and reliance on digital infrastructure; under such conditions, Fintech-enabled monitoring and reporting become more valuable, amplifying the Fintech-ESG relationship. El Khoury et al. (2023) document amplified spillovers across Fintech, ESG, and renewable energy markets during crises, indicating stress environments reshape sustainability-technology interactions. Overall, crises like COVID-19 may strengthen Fintech's role in ESG performance and risk reduction, though evidence remains limited for investment banks with distinct governance, market, and operational risk profiles.

2.5 Integrated Research Gap and Hypotheses Development

Synthesizing the literature yields five insights. First, evidence links Fintech development to improved ESG performance (Wang et al., 2022; Ren et al., 2023; Wan et al., 2023; Mokhtar & Alam, 2023), while endogeneity remains a concern (Galeone et al., 2024). Second, governance and monitoring channels appear central: Fintech improves disclosure integrity and reduces manipulation (Zhang et al., 2024), consistent with information asymmetry reduction (Sufi, 2007; Niinimäki et al., 2018; Favara et al., 2021). Third, environmental and social effects operate through capital allocation, traceability, and inclusion (Devine et al., 2024; Shahzad et al., 2023; Tao et al., 2022; Rastogi et al., 2023), yet may be contingent (Tok et al., 2022) and weaker for investment banks due to business-model differences. Fourth, ESG risk measurement is noisy and inconsistent (Berg, Kölbel & Rigobon, 2022; Berg et al., 2022), with emerging solutions (Bissoondoyal-Bheenick et al., 2024; Schimanski et al., 2024). Fifth, crisis periods likely amplify digital monitoring and risk-management value (Bouattour et al., 2024; El Khoury et al., 2023), particularly under COVID-driven digital reliance.

Despite these advances, prior work rarely examines firm-level Fintech investment amounts (rather than development indices), seldom focuses on investment banks, and infrequently analyzes ESG performance and ESG risk jointly-especially across COVID versus non-COVID periods and across investment size and investment form (private equity, venture capital, public investment). Addressing these gaps, this study examines 342 global investment banks (2019-2023) using firm-level Fintech investment measures and testing crisis and structural heterogeneity. These gaps are especially salient in investment banking, where key ESG levers include governance, disclosure integrity, and sustainable finance product structuring, and where Fintech capital is deployed via private equity, venture capital, or public investments with varying degrees of control and engagement.

The preceding review suggests that Fintech investment may influence ESG outcomes through stakeholder alignment, information asymmetry reduction, agency cost mitigation, dynamic capability enhancement, and digital monitoring. Building on these foundations, the study's hypotheses are developed as follows.

2.5.1 Fintech Investment and Overall ESG Performance

Stakeholder salience theory predicts firms allocate resources in response to stakeholders with power, legitimacy, and urgency; in investment banking, ESG performance is a reputational and legitimacy signal to regulators, investors, clients, and rating agencies. Fintech investment enhances transparency, reporting automation, compliance monitoring, and communication. Consistent with prior evidence (Wang et al., 2022; Ren at al., 2023; Wan et al., 2023; Du et al., 2022), digital transformation reduces financing frictions and improves information flows that facilitate ESG-related investments. From an information asymmetry perspective (Sufi, 2007; Niinimäki et al., 2018; Favara et al., 2021), Fintech reduces adverse selection and moral hazard by improving data availability and monitoring-important for long-horizon, intangible ESG activities. Dynamic capability theory implies digital infrastructure strengthens process reconfiguration and adaptation, reinforcing controls and compliance. Thus:

H1: Fintech investment positively affects ESG performance of investment banks.

2.5.2 Differential Effects Across ESG Pillars

Theory implies heterogeneous effects across Environmental (E), Social (S), and Governance (G). Governance should respond most directly: Zhang et al. (2024) show Fintech reduces ESG disclosure manipulation, and asymmetry/agency-cost arguments imply AI analytics, blockchain traceability, and automated reporting strengthen controls and compliance. Environmental and social outcomes depend more on externalities and policy frameworks: platforms and green finance tools (Devine et al., 2024; Macchiavello & Siri, 2022) and traceability (Shahzad et al., 2023) can support environmental accountability, while inclusion effects (Rastogi et al., 2023) may require complementary interventions (Tok et al., 2022). Given investment banks' influence through governance and capital-market intermediation, governance effects should dominate:

H2: Fintech investment positively affects E, S, and G scores individually, with a stronger impact on G score compared to E and S scores.

2.5.3 Crisis Context: The Amplifying Role of COVID-19

COVID-19 increased reliance on digital infrastructures; crises heighten uncertainty and dependence on digital reporting and monitoring. Bouattour et al. (2024) show digital maturity strengthens the ESG-stability relationship, and El Khoury et al. (2023) show Fintech-ESG spillovers intensify during crises. Stakeholder pressures may also rise as scrutiny of governance and risk management increases. Fintech-enabled monitoring and automated reporting can mitigate disruption, implying stronger effects during COVID-19:

H3: The positive impact of Fintech investment on ESG performance is stronger during COVID-19 years than in non-COVID-19 years.

2.5.4 Fintech Investment and ESG Risk Exposure

ESG risk reflects exposure to unmanaged ESG liabilities; measurement challenges (Berg, Kölbel, & Rigobon, 2022; Berg et al., 2022) imply noisy ratings. Fintech may reduce ESG risk through stronger controls and through improved data integrity. Zhang et al. (2024) supports the data-quality channel by showing Fintech reduces manipulation. During COVID-19, ESG risks may intensify, making Fintech-enabled compliance and monitoring more valuable:

H4: Fintech investment is more effective in reducing ESG risk during COVID-19 years than in non-COVID-19 years.

2.5.5 Investment Size and Strategic Commitment

Investment size captures depth of capability development. Larger Fintech investments imply more comprehensive integration into governance, risk management, and reporting; dynamic capability theory predicts stronger effects where commitment is larger. Because crises increase reliance on digital systems, large investments during COVID-19 should yield the strongest improvements:

H5: The impact of Fintech investment on ESG performance is strongest for large investment sizes during COVID-19 years and weakest for small investment sizes during non-COVID-19 years.

2.5.6 Investment Form and Governance Engagement

Investment form may moderate effects because engagement differs. Private equity typically involves stronger monitoring and strategic influence, whereas public investments involve dispersed ownership and lower involvement. Agency theory implies concentrated ownership increases monitoring incentives; thus:

H6: The impact of Fintech investment on ESG performance is strongest when structured as private equity investment and weakest when structured as public investment.2.1 Fintech and ESG Performance: Generic Evidence and Conceptual Foundations

3. DATA

In this paper, I use four main sources of secondary data from 2019 to 2023 period.

First, for Fintech investment data, I obtain from Pitchbook for the period from 2019 to 2023 on yearly basis at firm level (ticker level) for 342 global investment banks. Fintech Investment is the monetary amount invested in Fintech by the investment banks, measured in US$ billion, and is taken directly from Pitchbook from the field named "Fintech investment".

Second, for ESG performance scores, I use Thomson Reuters data. I use the separate E score (Environmental Score), S Score (Social Score) and G Score (Governance Score), as well as the total ESG score for each firm provided by Thomson Reuters.

Third, for ESG risk rating, which is a quantitative score ranging from 0 to 48 that measures the degree to which a company's economic value is at risk driven by ESG factors, was obtained from Sustainalytics.

Finally, for control variables, I use firm characteristics, including revenue, total assets, AUM, net income, number of investment professionals, ROA, Age, obtained from Pitchbook.

All these sets of data are merged at yearly level. My final sample panel dataset includes over 1,710 year-firm observations from 342 unique global investment banks for the 2019-2023 period, with descriptive statistics as described in Table 1.

Table 1. Descriptive Statistics

	N	Mean	Median	SD	p25	p75	Min	Max
Total ESG Score	1710	44.935	43	20.094	29	64	4	78
E Score	1709	15.963	16	8.356	10	24	1	26
S Score	1710	15.266	16	7.135	10	21	1	26

continued on following page

Table 1. Continued

	N	Mean	Median	SD	p25	p75	Min	Max
G Score	1710	13.704	15	7.324	7	19	1	26
ESG risk rating	1710	18.838	19	10.258	11	27	.9	48
Fintech Investment (US$B)	1710	2.535	.358	9.206	.111	1.173	.001	108.182
Revenue (US$B)	1710	8.391	5.413	15.125	2.273	8.553	0	140.876
Total Assets (US$B)	1710	215.932	82.34	545.844	37.364	156.359	.194	5006.667
Net Income (US$B)	1710	1.843	.829	4.683	.322	1.89	-7	60.5
AUM (US$B)	1710	234.069	84.71	599.096	40.192	167.211	.4	5097.496
Investment Staff No.	1710	1516.254	141	17765.722	47	264	1	265000
Year Founded	1710	1973	1995	52.904	1959	2007	1590	2022
ROA	1710	.015	.012	.013	.007	.019	.001	.125
Age	1710	49.547	28	52.904	16	64	1	433

This table shows the regression results of Fintech investment on ESG performance for 3 different regression models: 1) Normal Linear Regression, and 2) Firm fixed effect. ESG is the total ESG performance score and is the sum of the 3 separate scores: E_Score, S_Score and G_Score. FI is Fintech Investment amount by the investment banks in US$ billion. Standard errors are in parentheses. Significance levels at 10%, 5%, and 1% are shown with *, **, and *** respectively.

4. METHODOLOGY

To ensure robustness and facilitate comparison, I employ two different regression models to analyse the impact of Fintech investment on ESG performance. The first model is a standard linear regression, which provides a baseline analysis of the relationship between Fintech investment and ESG performance. The second model incorporates firm fixed effects, which account for unobserved, time-invariant characteristics specific to each firm, thereby controlling for potential biases that may arise from firm-specific factors. By using these two approaches, the study aims to enhance the reliability and validity of the results.

My model is as followed:

Where:

ESG is the aggregate ESG performance score.

FI is Fintech Investment amount by the investment banks in US$ billion.

Firm Characteristics include revenue, total assets (Size), AUM (Asset under investment), net income, number of investment professionals, ROA, Age, following similar control variables in Wang et al., 2021.

I also did robustness check to confirm this finding and to mitigate causality concern by using propensity score matching and difference in difference on the matched sample.

Specifically, to conduct a Differences-in-Differences (DID) analysis, I divide my sample of 342 investment banks into the two groups of different Fintech investment (one group has Fintech investment higher than the median Fintech investment amount of the original sample, and the other group has Fintech investment lower than the median Fintech investment amount of the original sample). I use Covid as an exogeneous shock (exogeneous treatment) to both groups, to examine if there is indeed any difference between low Fintech and high Fintech investment bank groups during Covid years, and any difference between low Fintech and high Fintech investment bank groups during non-Covid years (i.e., including pre-Covid and post-Covid normalization years).

The parallel trends assumption assumes that in the absence of Covid, the difference in trend in ESG performance score caused by the Fintech investment premium would remain constant between the two groups. I also conduct propensity score matching to provide robustness against any potential violation of the parallel trends' assumption. To decide which characteristics of the two groups of investment banks that I need to match against, I use Mann-U-Witney test to help me check if there is significant difference in a particular characteristic, such as Revenue, Total Asset, Net Income, Number of investment professional, AUM, ROA, Age etc. that is worth matching between the two groups of investment banks.

After the matching, I also run Propensity Score Test to check how good my matching is, in terms of p-value, percentage of bias, and percentage of reduction in bias before matching versus after matching (Table 5). In addition, I check equal trend visually via the trend graph output (Figure 2) and there is indeed parallel trend for the high Fintech investment group and low Fintech investment group during pre-Covid and post-Covid periods.

Figure 1. Standardized % Bias Across Co-variates (x - indicates after matching)

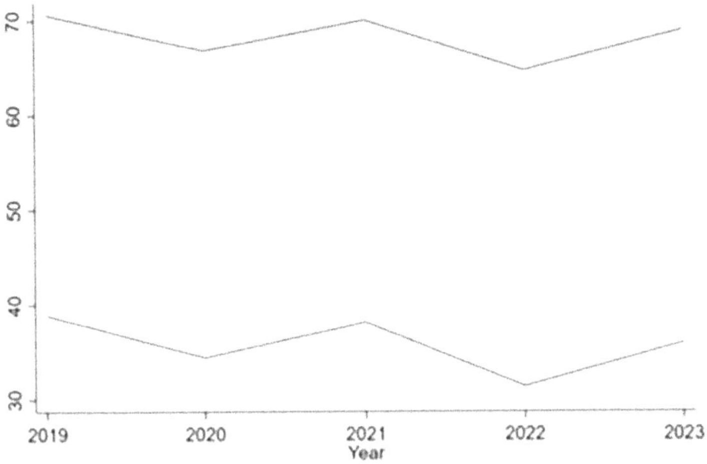

My difference in difference model is:

$$ESG = \beta_0 + \beta_1 (d\_FI^* Covid) + \varepsilon$$

Where:

ESG is the aggregate performance score of individual environmental, social and governance performance scores.

d_FI = 1 for high Fintech group, and d_FI = 0 for low Fintech group

Covid indicator is a dummy variable with value equal to 1 for those years when Covid happened and had tremendous impact (before vaccines were widespread) (year 2020 and 2021), and with value of 0 otherwise, i.e., for pre-Covid and post-Covid normalization years (year 2019, 2022 and 2023).

The Difference-in-difference (DID) approach accounts for any unobserved variables varying between the investment banks and varying over time and calculates an Average Treatment Effect (ATE) that applies to both groups. Any subsequent difference in ESG performance score between the two groups outside of ATE is assumed to be a result of Fintech investment.

5. RESULTS

For my first hypothesis (H1), as shown in Table 2, the regression result indicates that Fintech investment is positively associated with ESG performance. The positive relationship between Fintech investment and ESG performance is significant (at the 1% significance level for both OLS and Fixed Effect model). The coefficients of ESG performance in Table 2 show that if the Fintech investment amount by the investment banks increase by one billion US dollar, the ESG performance score increases by 0.00011, and 0.0001 point for linear regression model, and firm fixed effect model, respectively. I argue that the positive relationship between Fintech investment and ESG performance operates through multiple channels. These include enhanced access to corporate loans, the alleviation of corporate financing constraints by mitigating information asymmetry, reducing transaction costs, and improving big data analysis and model development. Additionally, Fintech investment contributes to greater financial inclusion, further strengthening its positive impact on ESG performance. This positive association is not only correct for the financial sector in general, as per some of the existing papers (such as El Khoury et al., 2023; Atayah et al., 2024; Takeda and Ito, 2021; Sufi, 2007; Yu et al., 2021; Zhang et al., 2022; Niinimäki et al., 2018; Favara et al., 2021), but I also confirm that it is correct for investment bank in particular.

Table 2. Regression results of Fintech Investment on ESG performance Score

	(OLS)	**(Fixed Effect)**
	ESG	ESG
Fintech Investment ($USB)	.000111***	.000101***
	(.000005)	(.000003)
Revenue ($USB)	.001795***	.000877**
	(.000155)	(.000445)
Total Assets ($USB)	-.000027***	.000022
	(.000004)	(.000047)
Net Income ($USB)	-.000884*	.000782
	(.000509)	(.001915)
AUM ($USB)	-.000007***	
	(.000001)	
Investment Professional Number	.000044***	
	(.000016)	
ROA	-23.582222	110.78206
	(28.149683)	(123.90424)
Age	.008369	
	(.007098)	
_cons	31.462149***	28.488053***
	(.813893)	(4.742452)

continued on following page

Table 2. Continued

	(OLS)	(Fixed Effect)
Observations	1710	1710
R-squared	.583484	.423565

This table shows the linear regression results of Fintech investment on ESG performance separate components, i.e., on E-Score, S-Score, and G-Score respectively. E-Score, S-Score and G-Score are equal-weighted average scores obtained from individual Environmental, Social, and Governance performance scores respectively. FI is Fintech Investment amount by the investment banks in US$ billion.

Standard errors are in parentheses. Significance levels at 10%, 5%, and 1% are shown with *, **, and *** respectively.

For my second hypothesis (H2), as shown in Table 3, the regression results indicate that Fintech investment is positively associated with G Score but does not have statistically significant association with E score and S score. The coefficients of Fintech investment in Table 3 show that if Fintech investment by the investment banks increase by 1 billion US dollar, G score increases by 0.05623 point. The association impact is significant for G score and non-significant for E score and S score. I think that this is likely because the impact of Fintech investment comes more from internally within the investment banks, i.e. from the investment banks' corporate governance and communication issues, rather than from external environmental and social issues, because Fintech can help improve the banks' corporate governance and communication issues, and because investment banks' products and services tend not to have direct impact on environment or society, unlike other energy or oil and gas firms.

Table 3. Regression results of Fintech Investment on E Score, S Score and G Score

	E-Score	S-Score	G-Score
Fintech Investment	-.01111	-.02269	.05623**
	(.01784)	(.01624)	(.02834)
E-Score		.72606***	.11501***
		(.00978)	(.0419)
S-Score	1.03947***		.45471***
	(.01277)		(.04968)
G-Score	.03695***	.10204***	
	(.01367)	(.01079)	

continued on following page

Table 3. Continued

	E-Score	S-Score	G-Score
Revenue (US$B)	.00028	-.00141	.01377
	(.01016)	(.00922)	(.01911)
Total Assets (US$B)	-.00103	-.00034	.00181*
	(.00065)	(.0006)	(.00107)
Net Income (US$B)	.02703	.04996	-.20777***
	(.03585)	(.03414)	(.06822)
AUM (US$B)	.00062	.0001	-.00094
	(.0006)	(.00052)	(.00086)
Investment Professional Number	0	.00001**	-.00003***
	(.00001)	(0)	(.00001)
ROA	-7.37479	-2.75803	30.15133**
	(6.52436)	(5.7734)	(12.34058)
Age	-.00004	.00005	-.00296
	(.00178)	(.00143)	(.00306)
_cons	-.24248	2.32785***	4.6199***
	(.23506)	(.20367)	(.45356)
Observations	1709	1709	1709
R-squared	.83087	.83798	.31493

This table shows the linear regression results of Fintech Investment, and the interaction of Covid/Non-Covid year indicator with Fintech Investment on ESG performance score. Covid/Non-Covid year indicator is a dummy variable with value equal to 1 for those years when Covid happened and had tremendous impact (before vaccines were widespread) (year 2020 and 2021), and with value of 0 otherwise, i.e., for pre-Covid and post-Covid normalization years (year 2019, 2022 and 2023). ESG is the total ESG performance score and is the sum of the 3 separate scores: E_Score, S_Score and G_Score. FI is Fintech Investment amount by the investment banks in US$ billion. Significance levels at 10%, 5%, and 1% are shown with *, **, and *** respectively.

For my third hypothesis (H3), as shown in Table 4, the regression result indicates a positive association between Fintech investment and ESG performance (significant at 1% level). However, there is no statistically significant association between Covid and ESG performance, and between ESG performance and the interaction of Fintech investment and Covid. The fact that it is during Covid years will not make ESG performance score increase any statistically significantly higher. This means that the COVID-19 pandemic does not have a significant impact on ESG performance, irrespective of the level of Fintech investment. The positive relationship between Fintech investment and ESG performance remains consistent across both COVID-19 and non-COVID-19 periods, with minimal variation in its strength. Hence, I reject my hypothesis 3.

Table 4. Regression of Fintech Investment and the Interaction of Covid/Non-Covid year indicator with Fintech Investment on ESG performance

Total ESG performance Score	**OLS**	**Fixed Effect**
Fintech Investment (US$B)	.34429***	.49136***
	(.11445)	(.15822)
Covid	.51059	.69054
	(1.0118)	(.70681)
Covid x Fintech Investment	.03884	.05389
	(.08682)	(.0869)
Revenue (US$B)	.02532	.32938
	(.06263)	(.23914)
Total Assets (US$B)	-.01246***	.00052
	(.00388)	(.01649)
Net Income (US$B)	.47865**	1.40738
	(.18567)	(.94946)
AUM (US$B)	.00638*	.31644
	(.00346)	(.2549)
Investment Professional Number	.00005**	
	(.00002)	
ROA	-43.58468	19.91304
	(38.70785)	(139.60232)
Age	-.00859	
	(.0103)	
_cons	46.69021***	-36.49147
	(1.0195)	(59.71748)
Observations	1710	1710
R-squared	.04189	.016

Table 5. Propensity Score Test Result

Variable Unmatched/ Matched	Mean Treated	Control	%Bias	%Bias reduction	t	p>t	V(C)
Revenue U	6.822	3.612	103.200	19.990	0.000	1.150	
M	6.822	6.856	-1.100	98.900	-0.210	0.835	1.38*
Total_Asset U	118.520	52.335	128.600	25.090	0.000	1.44*	
M	118.520	118.900	-0.700	99.400	-0.120	0.903	0.950
Net_Income U	1.443	0.726	76.900	15.130	0.000	1.90*	
M	1.443	1.328	12.300	84.000	2.070	0.039	1.28*
AUM U	130.490	57.657	120.700	23.740	0.000	1.85*	
M	130.490	128.090	4	96.700	0.670	0.504	1.26*
Investment_Professional_ Number U	174.930	175.600	-0.300	-0.060	0.952	3.99*	
M	174.930	185.770	-4.800	-1504.400	-0.880	0.380	4.18*
Age U	45.002	42.439	5.3	1.020	0.307	0.870	
M	45.002	39.810	10.800	-102.600	2.330	0.020	1.92*

*If variance ratio outside [0.99; 1.01] for U and [0.99; 1.01] for M

Sample	PS R2	LR chi2	p>chi2	Mean Bias	Med Bias	B	R	%Var
Unmatched	0.245	506.680	0.000	72.5	90	130.0*	1.33	67
Matched	0.010	17.940	0.006	5.6	4.4	23.2*	2.96*	83

* If B>25%, R outside [0.5; 2]

To ensure robustness and address potential causality concerns, I conducted a propensity score matching (PSM) analysis combined with a difference-in-differences (DiD) approach. The results of the propensity score test, presented in Table 5, indicate that the matching process was effective. This is further illustrated in Figure 1, where the median bias in the matched sample was reduced to 4.4% after matching, compared to a pre-matching median bias of 90%. Additionally, four out of the six matching criteria, i.e., Revenue, Assets Under Management (AUM), Net Income, and Total Assets, achieved a bias reduction of over 84%.

The results of the difference-in-differences (DiD) regression on the matched sample, presented in Table 6, indicate that the effect of low Fintech investment on ESG performance is statistically insignificant during both COVID-19 and non-

COVID-19 periods. However, for high Fintech investment, the results are statistically significant at the 1% level in both periods. These findings provide strong evidence supporting the positive relationship between Fintech investment and ESG performance, thereby reaffirming Hypothesis 1. This conclusion is further reinforced by the positive coefficient observed for high Fintech investment across both COVID-19 and non-COVID-19 years.

Table 6. Difference in Difference Regression on above matched observations

ESG performance score	**Coef.**	**St. Err.**	**t-value**	**p-value**	**[95% Conf**	**Interval]**	**Sig**
Low FI x non-Covid	0	.	.	.	.	.	
Low FI x Covid	1.164	1.193	0.98	.329	-1.178	3.507	
High FI X non-Covid	29.532	.736	40.12	0	28.088	30.977	***
High FI x Covid	29.167	.766	38.06	0	27.663	30.67	***
Constant	40.195	.672	59.84	0	38.877	41.513	***
Mean dependent var	57.784		SD dependent var		16.872		
R-squared	0.703		Number of obs		968.000		
F-test	774.342		Prob > F		0.000		
Akaike crit. (AIC)	7095.011		Bayesian crit. (BIC)		7114.512		

This table shows the difference in difference regression between ESG performance and the interaction of Fintech investment with Covid year indicator. ESG is the total ESG performance score and is the sum of the 3 separate scores: E_Score, S_Score and G_Score. Covid/Non-Covid year indicator is a dummy variable with value equal to 1 for those years when Covid happened and had tremendous impact (before vaccines were widespread) (year 2020 and 2021), and with value of 0 otherwise, i.e., for pre-Covid and post-Covid normalisation years (year 2019, 2022 and 2023). The higher the rating, the more risk on ESG. FI is Fintech Investment amount by the investment banks in US$ billion.

Significance levels at 10%, 5%, and 1% are shown with *, **, and *** respectively.

However, the result from the DID regression in Table 6 does not show any significant difference in the impact of Covid. Specifically, low Fintech investment always shows insignificant impact on ESG performance, no matter whether it is during Covid years or non-Covid years, and high Fintech investment always shows significant impact on ESG performance, no matter whether it is during Covid years or non-Covid years. This is different from my earlier expectation that Fintech investment will have stronger impact on ESG performance during Covid years, because during this pandemic period, everyone tried to limit face-to-face contacts and both the bank staff and the bank clients will engage in more remote communication forms and more online products and services using technology instead of traditional communication, products and services.

Moreover, the two-way line graph in figure 2 shows quite an equal trend of ESG performance from 2019 to 2023 between the two groups: the high Fintech investment group in red colour, and the low Fintech investment group in blue colour. The equal trend is consistent for both Covid years and non-Covid years, and the ESG performance score is always higher for high Fintech group as compared with low Fintech group, which reconfirms my result in hypothesis 1, i.e., Fintech investment has a positive impact on ESG performance in investment banks.

For my fourth hypothesis (H4), as shown in Table 7, the regression result indicates a statistically significant and negative association between Covid and ESG risk rating (significant at 1% level). However, there is a non-significant association between Fintech investment and ESG risk rating, and a non-significant association between ESG risk rating and the interaction of Fintech investment and Covid. The fact that it is during Covid years will make ESG risk rating reduced. I think that this may be because during Covid years, investment banks pay more attention in risk management in general and ESG risk management in particular.

Table 7. Regression of Fintech Investment and the Interaction of Covid/Non-Covid years indicator with Fintech Investment on ESG Risk Rating

ESG performance score	**Coef.**	**St. Err.**	**t-value**	**p-value**	**[95% Conf**	**Interval]**	**Sig**
Low FI x non-Covid	0	.	.	.	.	.	
Low FI x Covid	1.164	1.193	0.98	.329	-1.178	3.507	
High FI X non-Covid	29.532	.736	40.12	0	28.088	30.977	***
High FI x Covid	29.167	.766	38.06	0	27.663	30.67	***
Constant	40.195	.672	59.84	0	38.877	41.513	***
Mean dependent var	57.784		SD dependent var		16.872		
R-squared	0.703		Number of obs		968.000		
F-test	774.342		Prob > F		0.000		
Akaike crit. (AIC)	7095.011		Bayesian crit. (BIC)		7114.512		

This table shows the linear regression results of Fintech Investment, and the interaction of Covid/Non-Covid year indicator with Fintech Investment on ESG Risk Rating. Covid/Non-Covid year indicator is a dummy variable with value equal to 1 for those years when Covid happened and had tremendous impact (before vaccines were widespread) (year 2020 and 2021), and with value of 0 otherwise, i.e., for pre-Covid and post-Covid normalisation years (year 2019, 2022 and 2023). ESG risk rating, by Sustainalytics, is a quantitative score ranging from 0 to 40+ that measures the degree to which a company's economic value is at risk driven by ESG factors or, more technically speaking, the magnitude of a company's unmanaged ESG risks. The higher the rating, the more risk on ESG. FI is Fintech Investment amount by the investment banks in US$ billion. Significance levels at 10%, 5%, and 1% are shown with *, **, and *** respectively.

For my fifth hypothesis (H5), as shown in Table 8 and Table 9, the result shows a significant positive impact of Fintech investment on ESG performance for both large median investment size group and small median investment size group. However, due to a 3 times bigger coefficient (0.00028 vs. 0.00009), small median investment size group does show a much stronger positive impact of Fintech investment on ESG performance.

Table 8. Regression of Fintech Investment on ESG performance for large investment size vs. small investment size

	(OLS)	**(Fixed Effect)**
	ESG risk rating	ESG risk rating
Fintech Investment (US$B)	.07171	.00004
	(.05309)	(.02692)
Covid	-3.27975***	-3.23543***
	(.49772)	(.12024)
Covid x Fintech Investment	-.00096	.02168
	(.03573)	(.01478)
Revenue (US$B)	-.0605**	.18977***
	(.02595)	(.04068)
Total Assets (US$B)	.00657***	-.00365
	(.00191)	(.0028)
Net Income (US$B)	.18277**	.06036
	(.07205)	(.16152)
AUM (US$B)	-.00583***	.03205
	(.0017)	(.04336)
Investment Professional Number	.00004***	
	(.00001)	
ROA	-102.64733***	-7.64961
	(19.79802)	(23.74935)
Age	-.00113	

continued on following page

Table 8. Continued

	(OLS)	(Fixed Effect)
	(.00548)	
_cons	21.66276***	11.80872
	(.54537)	(10.15923)
Observations	1710	1710
R-squared	.0621	.38893

This table shows the linear regression results of Fintech Investment on ESG performance for large investment size vs. small investment size. Large Investment Size / Small Investment Size indicator is a dummy variable with value equal to 1 for those investment size larger than the median investment size of my 1710 observation sample, and with value of 0 otherwise. ESG is the total ESG performance score and is the sum of the 3 separate scores: E_Score, S_Score and G_Score. FI is Fintech Investment amount by the investment banks in US$ billion.

Significance levels at 10%, 5%, and 1% are shown with *, **, and *** respectively.

Table 9. Regression of Fintech Investment on ESG performance for large investment size vs. small investment size for Covid years and non-Covid years

	Large Investment Size	Small Investment Size
FI	.00009***	.00028***
	(0)	(.00001)
Revenue	.00032*	.0022***
	(.00019)	(.00044)
Total Assets	0	-.00002***
	(.00001)	(.00001)
Net Income	-.00162**	-.00286*
	(.0008)	(.00151)
AUM	0**	0***
	(0)	(0)
Investment Professional Number	.01642***	.00005***
	(.00331)	(.00001)
ROA	84.80101	23.87105
	(79.69343)	(26.71917)
Age	.01883**	-.00381
	(.00913)	(.00695)

continued on following page

Table 9. Continued

	Large Investment Size	Small Investment Size
_cons	38.51608***	25.49165***
	(1.8256)	(.92298)
Observations	855	855
R-squared	.59037	.64311

This table shows the linear regression results of Fintech Investment on ESG performance for large investment size vs. small investment size during Covid years and non-Covid years. Large Investment Size / Small Investment Size indicator is a dummy variable with value equal to 1 for those investment size larger than average investment size of my 1710 observation sample, and with value of 0 otherwise. Covid/Non-Covid year indicator is a dummy variable with value equal to 1 for those years when Covid happened and had tremendous impact (before vaccines were widespread) (year 2020 and 2021), and with value of 0 otherwise (year 2019, 2022 and 2023). ESG is the total ESG performance score and is the sum of the 3 separate scores: E_Score, S_Score and G_Score. FI is Fintech Investment amount by the investment banks in US$ billion.

Significance levels at 10%, 5%, and 1% are shown with *, **, and *** respectively.

For my last hypothesis (H6), as shown in Table 10, the result shows a significant positive impact of Fintech investment on ESG performance for all 3 investment forms: Private Equity, Venture Capital, Public Investment. The coefficients of each investment form also show that Fintech investment has strongest positive impact on ESG performance if it is invested by the investment bank in the form of private equity and weakest positive impact if it is invested by the investment bank as public investment.

Table 10. Regression of Fintech Investment by investment banks on ESG performance for different investment forms: Private Equity, Venture Capital, Public Investment

	Large Investment Size during Covid years	Large Investment Size during non-Covid years	Small Investment Size during Covid years	Small Investment Size during non-Covid years
FI	.000085***	.000092***	.000278***	.000284***
	(.000006)	(.000005)	(.000019)	(.000016)
Revenue	.000539*	.000229	.002548***	.002091***
	(.000295)	(.000254)	(.000743)	(.000555)
Total Assets	.00002	-.000006	-.000029**	-.000022***

continued on following page

Table 10. Continued

	Large Investment Size during Covid years	Large Investment Size during non-Covid years	Small Investment Size during Covid years	Small Investment Size during non-Covid years
	(.00002)	(.000015)	(.000012)	(.000009)
Net Income	-.002896**	-.000852	-.003307	-.002719
	(.001371)	(.000991)	(.002797)	(.001855)
AUM	-.000007***	-.000001	-.000006***	-.000004***
	(.000002)	(.000002)	(.000001)	(.000001)
Investment Professional Number	.019419***	.014267***	.000069***	.000035*
	(.005109)	(.004348)	(.00001)	(.000019)
ROA	221.63631*	-1.46728	26.269587	25.886777
	(127.99208)	(100.5263)	(51.769813)	(31.002941)
Age	.023472	.016415	.001133	-.007094
	(.015085)	(.01144)	(.011546)	(.008571)
_cons	35.206672***	40.406839***	25.780408***	25.156783***
	(3.058885)	(2.249328)	(1.528031)	(1.178918)
Observations	342	513	342	513
R-squared	.584197	.599447	.629635	.654757

This table shows the linear regression results of Fintech Investment on ESG performance for different Fintech investment forms by investment banks: as Private Equity, as Venture Capital, and as Public Investment. ESG is the total ESG performance score and is the sum of the 3 separate scores: E_Score, S_Score and G_Score. FI is Fintech Investment amount by the investment banks in US$ billion.

Standard errors are in parentheses. Significance levels at 10%, 5%, and 1% are shown with *, **, and *** respectively.

Table 11.

	Private Equity	Venture Capital	Public Investment
FI	.000119***	.000107***	.0001***
	(.000007)	(.000008)	(.000008)
Revenue	.000916***	.001664***	.002121***
	(.000242)	(.000358)	(.000234)
Total Assets	.000007	.000017	-.000027***

continued on following page

Table 11. Continued

	Private Equity	Venture Capital	Public Investment
	(.000012)	(.000021)	(.000004)
Net Income	-.000173	-.002438*	-.001928**
	(.000757)	(.001335)	(.000773)
AUM	-.000005***	-.000007***	-.000013***
	(.000001)	(.000001)	(.000002)
Investment Professional Number	.000035***	.013241**	.000049
	(.000013)	(.006081)	(.000034)
ROA	-56.057234	76.520903	36.951381
	(48.7434)	(66.429957)	(42.908795)
Age	.013148	-.005948	.033955***
	(.011385)	(.010412)	(.011468)
_cons	34.753612***	27.940391***	27.067426***
	(1.438378)	(2.103789)	(1.219968)
Observations	580	480	650
R-squared	.621854	.58644	.571784

6. CHANNEL DISCUSSION

As shown in Figure 1, the diagram synthesizes existing literature to illustrate the channels through which Fintech investment positively influences ESG (Environmental, Social, and Governance) performance. The impacts are categorized into nine domains: digital technology, sustainable investment platforms, blockchain technology, energy optimization, alleviation of corporate financing constraints, digital payments and financial inclusion, reduced financial transaction costs, artificial intelligence, and the Internet of Things (IoT) with mobile communication. Each domain reflects mechanisms by which Fintech enhances ESG outcomes. Digital technology improves process efficiency, information transparency, and product personalization. Sustainable investment platforms facilitate ESG-oriented investment selection and green infrastructure monitoring, while blockchain ensures sustainability verification and decentralization to support financial inclusion. Energy optimization lowers carbon emissions and enables real-time monitoring. Fintech mitigates corporate financing constraints by reducing information asymmetry and credit risk. Digital payments promote financial inclusion, economic growth, and data-driven insights. Lower transaction costs enhance efficiency in information search and fraud prevention.

Artificial intelligence contributes through deep learning, big data analytics, and ESG assessment, whereas IoT and mobile communication reduce reliance on physical outlets and foster service innovation. Collectively, these Fintech advancements strengthen ESG performance by enhancing efficiency, transparency, sustainability, and inclusivity within financial systems.

Figure 2. Channels of impacts of Fintech Investment on ESG performance

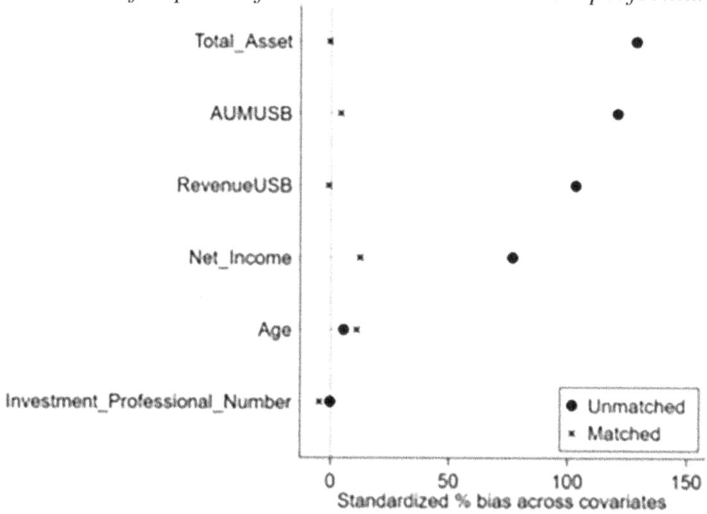

It is important to emphasize that, while comprehensive, this diagram of channels is not exhaustive. The literature underlying the diagram covers various types of firms and does not focus exclusively on investment banks. Due to data limitations, I lack access to all factors influencing Fintech investment's impact on ESG performance for my investment bank sample and therefore cannot isolate the effect of each factor individually. Nevertheless, the channels outlined collectively explain the significant positive effect of Fintech investment on ESG performance, as supported by my hypothesis tests.

Specifically, the finding that "Fintech investment exhibits a significant positive impact on the Governance (G) score but not on Environmental (E) or Social (S) scores" is theoretically consistent. The G score reflects internal corporate governance, which can be substantially enhanced through Fintech adoption, whereas E and S scores depend on external environmental and social factors beyond a bank's control. All channels in Figure 3 contribute to the G score, thereby influencing overall ESG performance. For instance, increased Fintech investment enhances digital technologies, improving operational efficiency and information transparency, which strengthens governance. Open APIs illustrate this: unlike regulated PSD2 APIs, they allow banks discretion over data sharing, supporting governance, customer engagement, and innovation. Digital transformation also automates operations, replacing paper-based processes and improving customer services. Procedures such as loan applications are streamlined via digital identity verification, video onboarding, and authentication, reducing time and effort, while chatbots and robo-advisors enhance guidance and support.

Figure 3. ESG Total Score versus Year after matching by Low Fintech Investment Group (Blue) and High Fintech Investment Group (Red)

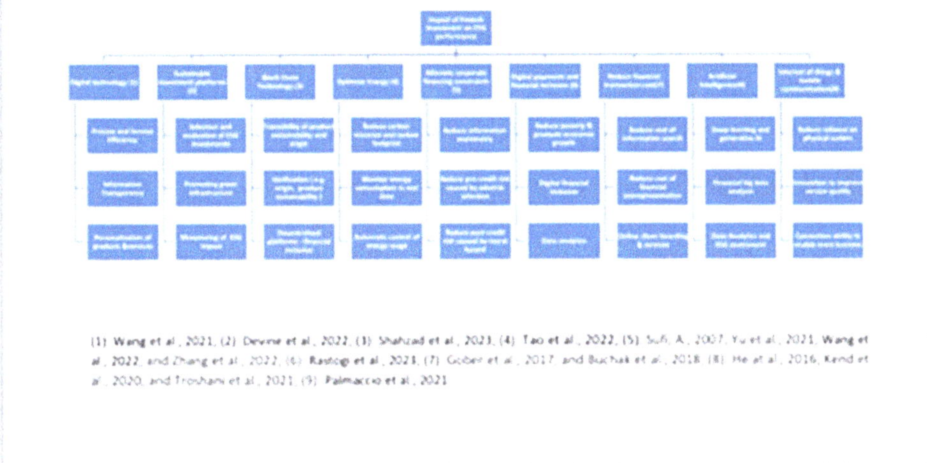

Fintech investment also facilitates digital payments and financial inclusion. Electronic billing, contactless solutions, and mobile payments (e.g., Apple Pay, Google Pay) allow clients to transact seamlessly from any location.

Investment banks benefit particularly from Fintech compared to commercial or retail banks. Unlike institutions primarily offering deposits and credit products, investment banks handle complex services, including underwriting, capital raising, hedging, risk transfer, and settlement operations, often involving large deals and sophisticated clients. Advanced communication, reporting, and stakeholder management capabilities are thus critical and can be enhanced by Fintech solutions.

My finding that Covid-19 does not significantly affect ESG performance, regardless of Fintech investment, but does negatively impact ESG risk ratings likely reflects heightened uncertainty and risk awareness during the pandemic. Organizations emphasized risk management, including ESG risks, which may have mitigated adverse outcomes despite broader challenges.

The persistent positive relationship between Fintech investment and ESG performance in both Covid and non-Covid years is notable: timing does not appear critical for investment banks. Fintech investments consistently enhance ESG performance, indicating that banks can act immediately without concern for timing.

Furthermore, results indicate that Fintech investment has the strongest positive effect on ESG performance when investment size is small to medium, and private equity yields the greatest impact, while public investments are least effective. This underscores the principle that "size and form matter." Practically, consistent smaller investments can be highly effective over time, provided total investment remains substantial.

Finally, findings highlight that the form of investment, whether public, private, or venture capital, is less important than the bank's engagement, control, and ownership. Effective Fintech investment is driven more by strategic involvement than by investment structure.

7. CONCLUSIONS

In this study, I examine the impact of Fintech investment on the ESG performance of 342 global investment banks and assess whether this impact varies during Covid years compared to non-Covid years. My findings indicate that Fintech investment has a significant positive effect on ESG performance. Specifically, it significantly enhances the Governance (G) score but does not have a notable impact on the Environmental (E) or Social (S) scores. Additionally, while Covid-19 does not significantly influence ESG performance, regardless of the level of Fintech investment, it does have a significant impact on ESG risk ratings. Importantly, the positive relationship between Fintech investment and ESG performance remains consistent across both Covid and non-Covid years, with little variation in intensity. Furthermore, the positive impact of Fintech investment on ESG performance is stronger when investment sizes are small to medium. Finally, I find that Fintech investment generates the most substantial ESG performance benefits when made through private equity, whereas public investments in Fintech yield the weakest positive impact.

To the best of my knowledge, this study is the first to explore the impact of Fintech investment on ESG performance within the context of investment banking. While some working papers address the relationship between Fintech and ESG in the broader banking sector, they do not focus on investment banks. This topic is particularly compelling given Fintech's rapid evolution over the past 15 years since the 2008 financial crisis. Banks, including investment banks, have increasingly engaged with Fintech, not just as competitors but as essential investors in technological innovation to enhance their resilience and competitive advantage. Therefore, future research should not only investigate Fintech as developed by technology firms but also consider Fintech investments made by banks and financial institutions, as these players are crucial to the Fintech and sustainability landscape.

I focus specifically on investment banks rather than the broader banking sector because their product and service offerings extend far beyond traditional deposit and credit lending. Investment banks engage in a wide array of complex financial activities, including underwriting, capital raising, hedging, risk transfer, payments, clearing, and settlement services. Their transactions often involve larger deal values and more sophisticated, high-profile clients and partners, such as those in underwriting and syndicated lending. As a result, investment banks operate in a highly intricate environment where communication, reporting, stakeholder management, and governance are particularly demanding. Given these complexities, investment banks present an ideal setting for analyzing the impact of Fintech investment on ESG performance.

This study's uniqueness is further enhanced by the use of the most recent data available up to 2023 and by being the first to explore how the relationship between Fintech investment and ESG performance differs between Covid and non-Covid years (i.e., pre-Covid and post-Covid normalization periods). Another key contribution is my examination of the impact of Fintech investment on ESG risk ratings, a quantitative measure of the extent to which a company's economic value is exposed to ESG-related risks. While ESG research often focuses on performance, my study highlights the importance of understanding ESG-driven economic risks in the banking sector. To my knowledge, no prior research has explored the effects of Fintech investment on ESG risk, particularly within investment banking, nor has any study compared this impact across different time periods.

The goal of this research is to encourage Fintech investment and ESG engagement within the financial sector, particularly among banks and investment banks. It aims to provide valuable insights for various financial stakeholders, including bank executives, Fintech partners, investors in both Fintech and ESG, regulators, as well as suppliers and customers within the banking ecosystem. Additionally, my findings offer important implications for policymakers, as their decisions on Fintech policies and promotional initiatives can significantly impact ESG outcomes.

To conclude, I refer to a well-known proverb:

"If you want to go fast, go alone. If you want to go far, go together."

Fintech and ESG initiatives have independently demonstrated remarkable contributions to firm performance, stakeholder engagement, and shareholder value. However, this study provides clear evidence that Fintech investment significantly enhances ESG performance in investment banks. By investing in both Fintech and ESG initiatives, financial institutions, especially investment banks, can achieve even greater benefits, helping them meet ESG performance goals, mitigate risks, and create long-term value for firms, stakeholders, shareholders, and, most importantly, society. Crucially, these benefits hold true regardless of timing, whether during a pandemic or in normal economic conditions.

REFERENCES

Ahmed, S., Alshater, M. M., El Ammari, A., & Hammami, H. (2022). Artificial intelligence and machine learning in finance: A bibliometric review. *Research in International Business and Finance, 61*, 101646. DOI: 10.1016/j.ribaf.2022.101646

Alonso, A., & Marqués, J. M. (2019). Financial innovation for a sustainable economy. Banco de España Occasional Paper, (1916).

Anindyastri, R., Lestari, W. D., & Sholahuddin, M. (2022). The influence of financial technology (fintech) on the financial performance of Islamic banking (Study on Islamic Banking listed on the Indonesia Stock Exchange Period 2016-2020). *Benefit: Jurnal Manajemen Dan Bisnis, 7*(1), 80–92. DOI: 10.23917/benefit.v7i1.18051

Atayah, O. F., Najaf, K., Ali, M. H., & Marashdeh, H. (2024). Sustainability, market performance and FinTech firms. *Meditari Accountancy Research, 32*(2), 317–345. DOI: 10.1108/MEDAR-08-2021-1405

Berg, F., Kölbel, J. F., Pavlova, A., & Rigobon, R. (2022). *ESG confusion and stock returns: Tackling the problem of noise (No. w30562)*. National Bureau of Economic Research. DOI: 10.3386/w30562

Berg, F., Kölbel, J. F., & Rigobon, R. (2022). Aggregate confusion: The divergence of ESG ratings. *Review of Finance, 26*(6), 1315–1344. DOI: 10.1093/rof/rfac033

Bissoondoyal-Bheenick, E., Bennett, S., Lehnherr, R., & Zhong, A. (2024). ESG rating disagreement: Implications and aggregation approaches. *International Review of Economics & Finance, 96*, 103532. DOI: 10.1016/j.iref.2024.103532

Bouattour, A., Kalai, M., & Helali, K. (2024). The non-linear relationship between ESG performance and bank stability in the digital era: New evidence from a regime-switching approach. *Humanities & Social Sciences Communications, 11*(1), 1–17. DOI: 10.1057/s41599-024-03876-8

Buchak, G., Matvos, G., Piskorski, T., & Seru, A. (2018). Fintech, regulatory arbitrage, and the rise of shadow banks. *Journal of Financial Economics, 130*(3), 453–483. DOI: 10.1016/j.jfineco.2018.03.011

Carlini, F., Del Gaudio, B. L., Porzio, C., & Previtali, D. (2022). Banks, Fintech and stock returns. *Finance Research Letters, 45*, 102252. DOI: 10.1016/j.frl.2021.102252

Costa-Climent, R., & Martínez-Climent, C. (2018a). Sustainable finance and the Fintech revolution. *Sustainability, 10*(8), 1–18.

Costa-Climent, R., & Martínez-Climent, C. (2018b). Sustainable profitability of ethical and conventional banking. *Contemporary Economics, 12*(4), 519–531.

Chueca Vergara, C., & Ferruz Agudo, L. (2021). Fintech and sustainability: Do they affect each other? *Sustainability (Basel), 13*(13), 7012. DOI: 10.3390/su13137012

Devine, A., Sanderford, A., & Wang, C. (2024). Sustainability and private equity real estate returns. *The Journal of Real Estate Finance and Economics, 68*(2), 161–187. DOI: 10.1007/s11146-022-09914-z

Dranev, Y., Frolova, K., & Ochirova, E. (2019). The impact of Fintech M&A on stock returns. *Research in International Business and Finance, 48*, 353–364. DOI: 10.1016/j.ribaf.2019.01.012

Du, P., Huang, S., Hong, Y., & Wu, W. (2022). Can FinTech improve corporate environmental, social, and governance performance? - A study based on the dual path of internal financing constraints and external fiscal incentives. *Frontiers in Environmental Science, 10*, 1061454. DOI: 10.3389/fenvs.2022.1061454

El Khoury, R., Nasrallah, N., Hussainey, K., & Assaf, R. (2023). Spillover analysis across Fintech, ESG, and renewable energy indices before and during the Russia-Ukraine war: International evidence. *Journal of International Financial Management & Accounting, 34*(2), 279–317. DOI: 10.1111/jifm.12179

Favara, G., Ivanov, I., & Rezende, M. (2021). GSIB surcharges and bank lending: Evidence from US corporate loan data. *Journal of Financial Economics, 142*(3), 1426–1443. DOI: 10.1016/j.jfineco.2021.06.026

Galeone, G., Ranaldo, S., & Fusco, A. (2024). ESG and Fintech: Are they connected? *Research in International Business and Finance, 69*, 102225. DOI: 10.1016/j.ribaf.2024.102225

Gober, P. (2017). Big data and financial service efficiency. Working paper.

Gomber, P., Koch, J. A., & Siering, M. (2017). Digital Finance and FinTech: Current research and future research directions. *Journal of Business Economics, 87*(5), 537–580. DOI: 10.1007/s11573-017-0852-x

He, M. D., Leckow, M. R. B., Haksar, M. V., Griffoli, M. T. M., Jenkinson, N., Kashima, M. M., & Tourpe, H. (2017). *Fintech and financial services: Initial considerations.* International Monetary Fund.

Kabulova, J., & Stankevičienė, J. (2020). Valuation of FinTech innovation based on patent applications. *Sustainability (Basel), 12*(23), 10158. DOI: 10.3390/su122310158

Kend, M., & Nguyen, L. A. (2020). Big data analytics and other emerging technologies: The impact on the Australian audit and assurance profession. *Australian Accounting Review*, *30*(4), 269–282. DOI: 10.1111/auar.12305

Kharrat, H., Trichilli, Y., & Abbes, B. (2024). Relationship between FinTech index and bank's performance: A comparative study between Islamic and conventional banks in the MENA region. *Journal of Islamic Accounting and Business Research*, *15*(1), 172–195. DOI: 10.1108/JIABR-03-2022-0081

Li, Y., Zheng, Y., Li, X., & Mu, Z. (2024). The impact of digital transformation on ESG performance. *International Review of Economics & Finance*, *96*, 103686. DOI: 10.1016/j.iref.2024.103686

Liu, M., Tripe, D. W. L., & Jiang, W. (2017). *Does fintech increase or reduce commercial banks' risk-taking? Evidence from China's banking sector.* Econfin. Massey. Ac. Nz.

Liu, Y., Saleem, S., Shabbir, R., Shabbir, M. S., Irshad, A., & Khan, S. (2021). The relationship between corporate social responsibility and financial performance: A moderate role of fintech technology. *Environmental Science and Pollution Research International*, *28*(16), 20174–20187. DOI: 10.1007/s11356-020-11822-9

Loo, M. K. L. (2019). Enhancing financial inclusion in ASEAN: Identifying the best growth markets for Fintech. *Journal of Risk and Financial Management*, *12*(4), 181. DOI: 10.3390/jrfm12040181

Macchiavello, E., & Siri, M. (2022). Sustainable finance and Fintech: Can technology contribute to achieving environmental goals? A preliminary assessment of 'green Fintech' and 'sustainable digital finance'. *European Company and Financial Law Review*, *19*(1), 128–174. DOI: 10.1515/ecfr-2022-0005

Mittal, V., & Koh, L. (2024). The fintech nation: excellence unlocked in Singapore.

Mitra, S., & Karathanasopoulos, A. (2020). Fintech revolution: The impact of management information systems upon relative firm value and risk. *Journal of Banking and Financial Technology*, *4*(2), 175–187. DOI: 10.1007/s42786-020-00023-0

Mokhtar, N. B., & Alam, A. (2023). The Mediating Role of Fintech on ESG and Bank Performance. In *Fintech and Sustainability: How Financial Technologies Can Help Address Today's Environmental and Societal Challenges* (pp. 191–218). Springer Nature Switzerland. DOI: 10.1007/978-3-031-40647-8_10

Moro-Visconti, R., Cruz Rambaud, S., & López Pascual, J. (2020). Sustainability in FinTechs: An explanation through business model scalability and market valuation. *Sustainability (Basel)*, *12*(24), 10316. DOI: 10.3390/su122410316

Niinimäki, J. P. (2018). Collateral in credit rationing in markets with asymmetric information. *The Quarterly Review of Economics and Finance*, *68*, 97–102. DOI: 10.1016/j.qref.2017.10.001

Öhman, P., Nourallah, M., & El Kalak, I. (2025). Guest Editorial: Navigating Contemporary FinTech Solutions: Revealing Potential and Challenges. *Financial Services Review*, *33*(3), i–v. DOI: 10.61190/fsr.v33i3.4352

Palmaccio, M., Dicuonzo, G., & Belyaeva, Z. S. (2021). The internet of things and corporate business models: A systematic literature review. *Journal of Business Research*, *131*, 610–618. DOI: 10.1016/j.jbusres.2020.09.069

Putri, W. H., Nurwiyanta, N., Sungkono, S., & Wahyuningsih, T. (2019). The emerging fintech and financial slack on corporate financial performance. *Investment Management & Financial Innovations*, *16*(2), 348–354. DOI: 10.21511/imfi.16(2).2019.29

Rastogi, S., Singh, K., & Kanoujiya, J. (2023). Do countries capture their inclusive growth, sustainability, and poverty correctly? A study on statistical performance indicators defined by World Bank. *Social Responsibility Journal*, *19*(10), 1935–1951. DOI: 10.1108/SRJ-12-2022-0553

Ren, X., Zeng, G., & Zhao, Y. (2023). Digital finance and corporate ESG performance: Empirical evidence from listed companies in China. *Pacific-Basin Finance Journal*, *79*, 102019. DOI: 10.1016/j.pacfin.2023.102019

Romānova, I., & Kudinska, M. (2016). Banking and Fintech: A challenge or opportunity? Contemporary issues in finance: Current challenges from across [). Emerald Group Publishing Limited.]. *Europe*, *98*, 21–35.

Salah Mahdi, I. B., Bouaziz, M., & Boujelbène Abbes, M. (2025). The moderating effect of fintech on the relationship between CSR and banks' financial stability: Baron and Kenny's approach analysis. *EuroMed Journal of Business*, *20*(2), 300–324. DOI: 10.1108/EMJB-03-2023-0082

Schimanski, T., Reding, A., Reding, N., Bingler, J., Kraus, M., & Leippold, M. (2024). Bridging the gap in ESG measurement: Using NLP to quantify environmental, social, and governance communication. *Finance Research Letters*, *61*, 104979. DOI: 10.1016/j.frl.2024.104979

Shahzad, U., Asl, M. G., & Tedeschi, M. (2023). Is there any market state-dependent contribution from Blockchain-enabled solutions to ESG investments? Evidence from conventional and Islamic ESG stocks. *International Review of Economics & Finance*, *86*, 139–154. DOI: 10.1016/j.iref.2023.03.001

Son, B., & Jang, H. (2023). Economics of blockchain-based securities settlement. *Research in International Business and Finance*, *64*, 101842. DOI: 10.1016/j.ribaf.2022.101842

Sufi, A. (2007). Information asymmetry and financing arrangements: Evidence from syndicated loans. the Journal of Finance, 62(2), 629-668.

Takeda, A., & Ito, Y. (2021). A review of Fintech research. *International Journal of Technology Management*, *86*(1), 67–88. DOI: 10.1504/IJTM.2021.115761

Tao, R., Su, C. W., Naqvi, B., & Rizvi, S. K. A. (2022). Can Fintech development pave the way for a transition towards low-carbon economy: A global perspective. *Technological Forecasting and Social Change*, *174*, 121278. DOI: 10.1016/j.techfore.2021.121278

Tok, Y. W., & Heng, D. (2022). *Fintech: Financial inclusion or exclusion?* International Monetary Fund.

Troshani, I., & Rowbottom, N. (2021). Digital corporate reporting: Research developments and implications. *Australian Accounting Review*, *31*(3), 213–232. DOI: 10.1111/auar.12334

Wan, S., Lee, Y. H., & Sarma, V. J. (2023). Is Fintech good for green finance? Empirical evidence from listed banks in China. *Economic Analysis and Policy*, *80*, 1273–1291. DOI: 10.1016/j.eap.2023.10.019

Wang, D., Peng, K., Tang, K., & Wu, Y. (2022). Does FinTech development enhance corporate ESG performance? Evidence from an emerging market. *Sustainability (Basel)*, *14*(24), 16597. DOI: 10.3390/su142416597

Wang, Y., Xiuping, S., & Zhang, Q. (2021). Can Fintech improve the efficiency of commercial banks? An analysis based on big data. *Research in International Business and Finance*, *55*, 101338. DOI: 10.1016/j.ribaf.2020.101338

Yao, T., & Song, L. (2021). Examining the differences in the impact of Fintech on the economic capital of commercial banks' market risk: Evidence from a panel system GMM analysis. *Applied Economics*, *53*(23), 2647–2660. DOI: 10.1080/00036846.2020.1864275

Yu, H., Zhao, Y., Liu, Z., Liu, W., Zhang, S., Wang, F., & Shi, L. (2021). Research on the financing income of supply chains based on an E-commerce platform. *Technological Forecasting and Social Change*, *169*, 120820. DOI: 10.1016/j.techfore.2021.120820

Zhang, A., Wang, S., Liu, B., & Liu, P. (2022). How fintech impacts pre-and post-loan risk in Chinese commercial banks. *International Journal of Finance & Economics*, *27*(2), 2514–2529. DOI: 10.1002/ijfe.2284

Zhang, D., Wang, C., He, Y., & Vigne, S. A. (2024). Does Fintech efficiently hamper manipulating ESG data behavior? *The British Accounting Review*, •••, 101494. DOI: 10.1016/j.bar.2024.101494

Chapter 8
Towards Sustainable Finance:
Understanding Green Banking Adoption Among Indian Young Adults

Arshika
http://orcid.org/0009-0002-4175-3976
Christ University, India

Blesson Varghese James
http://orcid.org/0000-0002-0000-8235
Christ University, India

Merin K. Varghese
http://orcid.org/0009-0006-6736-5022
Christ College, Pune, India

ABSTRACT

This study explores the factors influencing the adoption of green banking among young adults in India, drawing on the Theory of Planned Behaviour. Key determinants include environmental concern, social factors, perceived behavioural control, subjective norms, and attitude toward behaviour. The moderating role of effort expectancy is also examined. Based on data from respondents aged 18–35, the findings provide practical insights for banks to develop targeted strategies that encourage green banking practices among youth.

DOI: 10.4018/979-8-3373-5047-9.ch008

1. INTRODUCTION

There are many environmental concerns such as climate change and global warming that have led to an increase in the need for conserving natural resources and sustainability (Aslam et al., 2020). Because of this reason, businesses are now expected to take responsibility for the planet and people along with profits. As a result, industries have adopted eco-friendly and sustainable practices as a part of their social responsibility (Ubais Parayil Iqbal et al., 2024).

The principal philosophy behind these initiatives on a global level is to "save the planet" and to "go green" in both manufacturing and service sectors industries (Aslam et al., 2020). There are various studies conducted to examine the green practices in the manufacturing sector but the service sector is very sparsely studied. In fact, as the service sector is the major contributor of GDP, the need to adopt green practices in their operations is quite high (Ashraf, 2023). Banks are considered one of the most important organisations of a country which is responsible for all the financial operations of the country (Nisha et al., 2020).

Generally, it is assumed that the banking industry is not really generating any pollution for the environment but that's not true. The operations of the banking sector involve activities which can pollute nature such as consumption of energy and usage of paper by their various branches (Bukhari et al., 2019). The Banking Sector is also financing many big projects which can lead to environmental damage. Therefore, green banking can be an option which can prevent climate change and protect the environment by providing nature- friendly investments (Bukhari et al., 2022).

The acceptance of digitalisation and environmentalism across the globe has put the various financial institutes, particularly the banking sector under a huge amount of pressure to adopt a green agenda (Bouteraa et al., 2022). Banks play a major role in the economic growth and development of any company and act as the chief financier for the population (Bukhari et al., 2022). By integrating green ideas and concepts into their lending and investment practices, banks have the power to contribute to environmental conservatism. Therefore, the greening and digitalisation of the banking sector plays a huge role in a country's sustainability. As a result, green banking, an ideology based on principles and practices of environmental sustainability has developed. It involves promoting technological upgrade and paperless based financial services in the banking sector (BOUTERAA et al., 2021).

Adoption of eco-friendly practices in a bank's operational activities has a significant external effect on the overall environment even if the activities of the bank is not directly concerned with the environment. Paper use and electricity consumption during the traditional banking operations in the extensive branches of a bank contribute greatly to carbon emissions. Therefore, green banking is important to minimize the adverse effect on the environment (Rehman et al. 2021).

Green banking can be defined as the form of banking activity where the initiative is taken by the banks to its everyday operations as a conscious entity in society by taking into consideration both internal as well as external environmental sustainability (Sharma & Choubey, 2021). A green bank is the bank which encourages and implements green technologies in their operation to reduce their carbon footprint and facilitates environmental sustainability (Bose et al., 2017). According to the Indian Banks Association, green banking is the system which includes all environmental as well as social factors with the goal to ensure that the resources are optimally utilised and there is ecological sustainability (Kumar & Prakash, 2018). Presently, Indian banks are focusing on entering the global markets and it is really important that they recognise their environmental as well as social responsibility. Therefore, green strategies have become relevant not amongst the smaller banks but also amongst diversified financial service providers as well as asset managers and financial companies (Sharma & Choubey, 2021).

Everything considered, the banking industry has adopted green banking initiatives to instil environmentally healthy habits into their banking activities and financing portfolio (Bukhari et al., 2022). The way green banking adoption works is inherently contextual due to the internal capabilities and external aspects that exist in the banking sector of different countries and other relevant resources. The adoption and implementation can take various forms which include but is not limited to implementing green management practices, green operations, green human resources, green financing, promotion of green products and services and digitalisation of the sector to reduce the usage of paper (Bukhari et al., 2019).

The concept of green banking is being adopted in order to use the resources of banks responsibly and prioritise the environment and society. This notion refers to the development of new goods or services that do not harm the environment. Mobile banking, remote deposits, green CDs, Green Credit card, green loans etc are all examples of green banking initiatives (R.V. Naveenan et al., 2021). ATM systems, net banking facilities using solar power, paperless customer banking etc can also be considered a part of the green banking initiatives (Annadurai, 2014).

Given the increasing popularity, green banking has become unquestionably important and has received widespread recognition in the literature. It is important to know that while the banks can implement green banking policies and procedures, consumers must also embrace them, the adoption also needs to be embraced by the customers which depends on their perception. Majority of the literature which already exists does not inquire about how the personalities of different consumers affect their perception which in turn affects their adoption of the phenomenon (Malik & Singh, 2022).

1.1 Problem Statement

With the increasing focus on sustainability in future, green banking has progressively played a crucial part in supporting environmentally friendly practices through operational and technological advancements as well as shifting the nature of consumer behaviour. The idea of green banking benefits banks, consumers, and the economy as it ensures greening along with improving the quality and financial performance of the bank's assets. Even though Green Banking is an innovative approach to financial services, it has not been fully adopted in the many developing nations (Finger et al., 2018).

There is very limited study on the adoption of green banking among the consumers (Bukhari et al., 2019). The existing literature mainly studies the adoption of green banking from a commercial perspective among the organisation the customer's point of view is vastly unstudied (Nisha et al., 2020) (Bouteraa et al., 2021).

The current study aims to inquire about the adoption of green banking among the young adults in the Indian Subcontinent. Building on the premise, the present study focuses on identifying the effect of five variables namely - environmental concern, social factors, perceived behaviour control, subjective norms and attitude towards the behaviour - on the acceptance of green banking practices. This study aims to understand the opportunities and challenges in the way of green banking practice's adoption and what the youth of India thinks about such practices.

2. LITERATURE REVIEW

The factors affecting the adoption of green banking among young adults which are considered for the study are as follows:

2.1 Environmental Concern

In the current global competitive market, there is a need for companies to become socially responsible. As a result of Globalization, companies are expanding worldwide and being socially beneficial gives them a competitive advantage (Md. Zahidul Islam et al., 2012). According to (Nizam et al., 2019), currently there are environmental conscious market conditions which have altered how companies perform their operations. This consciousness is supported by various organisations such as Sustainability Accounting Standard Board (SABS), World Business Council for Sustainable Development (WBCSD), United Nations etc. The research (Evangelinos & Nikolaou, 2009) says that the rise in environmental issues like climate change, pollution etc can be strongly related with the everyday workings of any business since these are the entities who are the most accountable for climate degradation. In the last few years, many researchers have studied environmentally conscious consumer behaviour (ECCBs) and according to these studies, an environmentally conscious consumer's behaviour is dependent on a number of factors such as age, price, performance of the product etc. (Emekci, 2019). There are studies suggesting that consumer's pro environmental behaviour is also affected by their past beliefs, social norms, psychographics, and awareness regarding their surroundings. Consumers who are environmentally conscious are more likely to have a positive response towards cause related products and brands (Phau & Ong, 2007).

The studies suggest that consumers who have the knowledge regarding the environmental problems, the availability of eco-friendly brands and its impact on the environment are more likely to adopt environment friendly behaviour (Khare, 2015). Green banking has a lot of advantages as compared to traditional banking in terms of industrial sustainability, cost minimization, operative productivity and good company image (Zhang & Yang, 2016). Based on past research, it can be inferred that Green Banking can lower the consumption of energy, usage of hazardous materials and creation of pollution. It can also help in diminishing both internal and external carbon emissions which promotes better natural environmental conditions (Ashraf (2023). Although it is common to expect that a company's main aim is to maximise profit for the smooth function of the organisation, now there is an emergent need to understand that the role of an organisation goes beyond the financial motive. Every organisation, apart from the financial goal, has an environmental and social goal to fulfil. Taking all of these into consideration, there is a rise in the green banking trend in the global banking sector including India (Coupland, 2006). Climate change has emerged as a severe topic of concern for India in the past few years. While the effects of climate change do pose a danger to the health of the citizens and economy and environment of the country, economists have also come to realise that there are financial gains which the companies can get from developing a low carbon footprint and controlling climate change (Khanna, 2013). Based on the above discussion, we propose the following:

H1: Environmental Concern has no impact on adoption of green banking among young adults in India.

2.2 Social Factor

Issues regarding sustainability, green brands and environmental consciousness are on a rise everywhere especially in the emerging economies. Government as well as consumers are becoming more and more aware about the problems related to the environment (Khare, 2015). According to (Kumar & Prakash, 2018), banks are one of the major pillars in promoting sustainable development in a country. The previous research says that the Stakeholders are any set of people who have the power to affect the everyday operations of the business including its decisions, practices and objectives of the organisation. (Henriques and Sadorsky, 1999). The stakeholders can be divided into two categories: internal and external. Internal Stakeholders refer to the employees of the organisation while the external stakeholders include the government, competitors and customers (Sarkis et al., 2010). The Employees like the Senior Manager can pursue the organisation to implement green practices to ensure that the profits are maximised. Senior Managers are responsible to ensure that there is no loss of investment made by any shareholders due to loss of reputation of the organisation because of being environmentally dangerous (Zhang & Yang, 2016). Recently there is a rise in the scarcity and disruptions of the environmental resources which has led to the government both at the central and local level to implement regulation to ensure green practices. Customers can also pressurise a firm to company to ensure that they are implementing green practices and maintaining sustainability (Follows & Jobber, 2000). Marketing also plays a huge role in promoting green products among the people. The American Marketing Association defines brand as "a name, term, sign, symbol or design or the combination of them, intended to identify the goods or services of one seller or group of sellers and to differentiate them from those of a competitor" (Rahbar & Abdul Wahid, 2011).

Consumers will want to involve themselves with such eco-friendly brands or products which are generating a higher level of environmental impact as compared to those which are generating a low environmental impact (Chatterjee, 2009). The classification of men and women based on societal construction also plays a major role as a social factor in the adoption of green banking (Ubais Parayil Iqbal et al., 2024). Gender as a social institution is a way for people to organise their thoughts and get through life. Other social factors such as concern regarding how the company is giving back to the environment also affects the perspective of the consumers (do Paço & Raposo, 2009). Therefore, a company which is ensuring sustainability by implementing green practices are more likely to be accepted in the market by both their internal and external shareholders as compared to a company which is not doing anything to protect the environment.

H2: Social Factors has no impact on adoption of green banking among young adults in India.

2.3 Theory of Planned Behaviour

The Theory of Planned Behaviour was proposed by Ajzen in 1985. According to the framework, the theory depends on three factors - Attitude towards a particular behaviour, Subjective Norms and Perceived Behavioural Control. All of these together form the Behavioural Intention which is the major force behind influencing the behaviour of an individual. (Ajzen, 2002).

2.3.1 Perceived Behaviour

The concern regarding the environment has been generally viewed as a unidimensional construct which ranged from being unconcerned about the issues at the low end to very uncensored about the environment at the high end according to the New Environmental Paradigm (NEP) (Milfont & Duckitt, 2004). But (Schultz, 2000) said that there are three correlated factors that are concerned with environmental issues - concern for self (ego), other people (altruistic) and biosphere (biospheric). According to (Ajzen, 1991), Perceived Behavioural Control (PBC) is how an individual is perceiving the ease or the difficulty of performing the specific task at hand. If PBC is higher, then it indicates that the person has a higher intention of performing a particular task and vice versa. PBC refers to the perception of an individual who has all the required means, opportunities and resources to perform the particular task (Yadav & Pathak, 2016). An individual's behaviour is strongly dependent on their confidence in their ability to perform it. Self-efficacy can influence choice of activities, the preparation for it, the efforts put in to perform it and the emotions related to it (Bandura, 1982).

H3: Perceived Behaviour Control has no impact on adoption of green banking among young adults in India.

2.3.2 Subjective Norms

Subjective norm refers to the pressure given from various external groups that has the power to influence an individual's behaviour (Long et al., 2017). Subjective Norms is the Social Pressure to perform or not perform a particular behaviour (Ajzen, 1991). It is the influence of the opinion of the people who is important to an individual on their decision making (Park, 2000). Subjective norms indicate that if an individual think that any person who is significant to them disapproves of a certain behaviour, they are less likely to perform the behaviour and vice versa. In other words, it is the social pressure that an individual face while making a decision (Park, 2000). There are various studies which support or reject the effect of subjective norms on behavioural intention (Chan et al., 2022).

H4: Subjective Norms have no impact on adoption of green banking among young adults in India.

2.3.3 Attitude Towards the Behaviour

Attitude of an individual is the examination of the performed behaviour that arises from what the individual expects from the performance of the actions (Cordano & Frieze, 2000). According to (Park, 2000), attitude towards a behaviour consists of two components: (a) their belief regarding the outcome that a certain behaviour will yield and (b) their evaluation about whether the outcome is favourable or not. Favourable outcomes raise an individual's intention to engage in a particular behaviour. It depends on the value the individual is placing on the particular behaviour's outcome (Ajzen, 1991). (Chan et al., 2022) concluded that the relation between attitude and its positive influence on environmental practice intention is not supported. There are various studies which also support the relationship between attitude and behavioural intention. The varying conclusions lead to the need to study attitude as a factor affecting adoption of green banking among young adults in India.

H5: Attitude towards the Behaviour has no impact on adoption of green banking among young adults in India.

3. RESEARCH METHODS

The population under study consists of young adults because understanding the factors that influence the young adults is very important for the green industry. Young adults in the country appear to have more knowledge regarding the concerns about the environment and they show comparatively higher preference for environment friendly services and products (Robichaud & Yu, 2021). Also, young adults constitute the larger part of the country's population therefore understanding their consumption pattern is important and has critical application both in theory and practice (Qi et al., 2024). The sample of the study included young adults between the ages of 18 and 35. Following that, descriptive research design is used in this study to determine the adoption of green banking by young adults using a structured questionnaire with 25 items. The questionnaire included demographic data as well as specific information regarding the adoption of green banking by young adults such as environmental concern, perceived behaviour control and societal norms.

3.1 Research Instrument

To estimate the consumer perception of dependent and independent variables, a five-point Likert Scale was used, which included the variables ranging from Strongly Disagree to Strongly Agree. The following variables are used in the study - Environmental factors which included five items adopted from (Ashraf et al., 2019), Social factors included five items from (Ashraf et al., 2019), Perceived Behavioural Control included three items from (Ashraf et al., 2019) and two items from (Emekci, 2019), subjective norms which included three items from (Taylor & Todd, 1995) and two items from (Emekci, 2019) and attitude towards the behaviour which included five items from (Emekci, 2019) and (Taylor & Todd, 1995).

Figure 1. Conceptual Framework

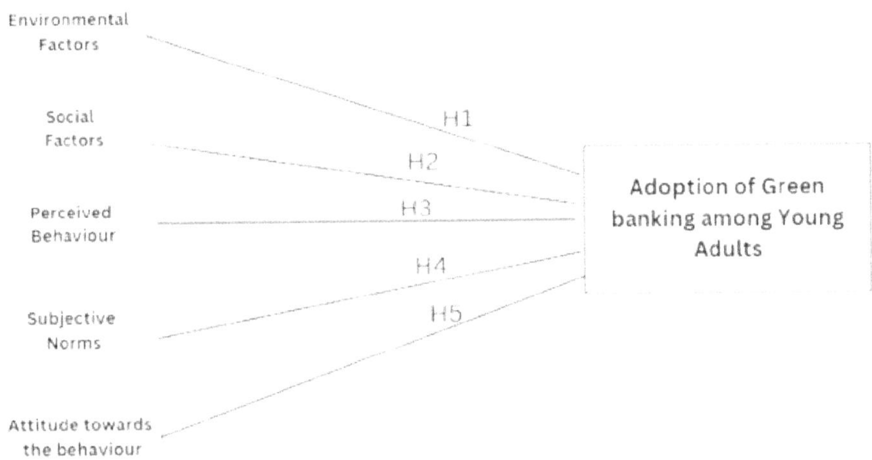

Source: *Authors' own work*

3.2 Data Collection Process and Sampling Techniques

To collect the data for understanding the adoption of green banking among young adults in India, a purposive sampling was done where young adults from across India took part. For this purpose, the questionnaire was put up on various online websites such as (reddit.com, Quora) and various social media platforms (Instagram, WhatsApp) where most of the young adults took part. The data was collected during the month of November. Various screening questions such as age group, education level and region were asked to get the target population.

3.3 Common Method Bias Analysis

The Study followed the techniques and guidelines provided by (Podsakoff & Organ, 1986) to ignore any regular technique bias. The items were first assessed and revised to eliminate any phrases that could possibly confuse the participants. After this, the participants were instructed to provide truthful answers to each question in the questionnaire. Finally, Harman's single test factor was employed when it was discovered that no single factor could adequately explain the entire variance. The 50% figure recommended by (Podsakoff et al., 2003) was not met by the indicated test value.

4. DATA ANALYSIS AND RESULTS

This study uses SPSS (version 26) AMOS to test and validate the independent as well as dependent variable. The hypothesis proposed in the literature review is analysed in the study to determine whether they should be accepted or rejected. The analysis will comprise the following verifications:

- Confirmatory Factor Analysis
- Descriptive Analysis, Regression Coefficient and
- Cronbach's Alpha and Variable Reliability

4.1 Descriptive Statistics

The details of the demographics of the participants in the study including gender is mentioned in table1. The gender construct has the following three subcategories - female, male and prefer not to say. The total responses collected is 401 out of which 48.63% is male, 51.37% is female. The demographics from the collected data will help in the forthcoming analysis and understanding by providing a clear and precise understanding of the collected data.

The data collected included people in various age categories. The people in various age categories were 32.17% between 18-20, 41.89% between 21-25, 12.22% between 26-30 and 13.72% between 31-55. Regarding the geographical details, around 29.18% of people are from the Northern region, 22.69% is from the southern region, 23.44% is from the eastern region, 13.97% is from the western region and 10.72% is from the central region. Another important factor for the study was annual income, where 59.6% of people had no income, 10.97% of people earned less than Rs 5,00,000, 12.97% of people between Rs 5,00,000 to Rs 10,00,000, 7.98% of people between Rs 11,00,000 to Rs 15,00,000, 4.24% of people between Rs 16,00,000 to Rs 20,00,000, 4.24% of people above Rs 20,00,000. Regarding the educational qualification, 71.07% of people were undergraduates, 19.20% of people were post graduates and 9.73% of people were doing professional degrees. In the context of employment, 65.09% of people were students, 7.23% of people were unemployed,

10.97% of people were employed in some organisation, and 16.71% of people were self-employed. A majority of the participants (79.05%) were single while 20.95% were married and 0% were separated/divorced.

Table 1. Demographic Details

Classification	Category	Frequency	Percentage
Gender	Male	195	48.63%
	Female	206	51.37%
	Other	0	0.00%
	Total	401	100.00%
Age	18-20	129	32.17%
	21-25	168	41.90%
	26-30	49	12.22%
	31-35	55	13.72%
	Total	401	100.00%
Region	North India	117	29.18%
	South India	91	22.69%
	East India	94	23.44%
	West India	56	13.97%
	Central India	43	10.72%
	Total	401	100.00%
Education	Under Graduate	285	71.07%
	Post Graduate	77	19.20%
	Professional Degree	39	9.73%
	Total	401	100.00%
Marital Status	Unmarried	317	79.05%
	Married	84	20.95%
	Separated / Divorced	0	0.00%
	Total	401	100.00%
Employment Status	Student	261	65.09%
	Unemployed	29	7.23%
	Self - Employed	67	16.71%
	Employed in Some Organisation	44	10.97%
	Total	401	100.00%
Annual Income	No Income	239	59.60%

continued on following page

Table 1. Continued

Classification	Category	Frequency	Percentage
	Less Than Rs 5,00,000	44	10.97%
	Rs 5,00,000 - Rs 10,00,000	52	12.97%
	Rs 11,00,000 - Rs 16,00,000	32	7.98%
	Rs 16,00,000 - Rs 20,00,000	17	4.24%
	More than Rs 20,00,000	17	4.24%
	Total	**401**	**100.00%**

Source: *Authors' Own Work*

4.2 Construct Reliability

The Cronbach's Alpha reliability test was used to determine if each variable has any internal reliability (Bonett & Wright, 2015). It was discovered that the Cronbach Alpha Values of the variables found through the test ranged from 0.91 to 0.94. Because it was higher than the necessary criterion of 0.70, the internal reliability of the current study was deemed adequate (Nunnally & Bernstein, 1994). To determine the internal reliabilities of scale items, composite reliability (CR) was introduced. All of the variables' dependability scores were greater than 0.70 (Hair et al., 2010). Additionally, it was determined that the Convergent validity was established because the average variance extracted (AVE) was 0.6886, which is greater than the benchmark (Bagozzi & Yi, 1988; Fornell & Larcker, 1981). Table 2 incorporates the calculated values for the mean, standard deviation (SD), CR, Cronbach's alpha, AVE, and factor loadings.

Table 2. Psychometric properties of measures

Constructs	Factor loading	Mean	SD	AVE	CR	Cronbach's Alpha
Environmental Factor				0.718333	0.927273	0.94
EF 1	0.839	3.28	1.277			
EF 2	0.858	3.28	1.352			
EF 3	0.836	3.28	1.356			
EF 4	0.847	3.29	1.373			
EF 5	0.857	3.26	1.321			

continued on following page

Table 2. Continued

Constructs	Factor loading	Mean	SD	AVE	CR	Cronbach's Alpha
Social Factor				0.67216	0.911019	0.917
SF1	0.812	3.14	1.234			
SF2	0.852	3.22	1.334			
SF3	0.819	3.19	1.272			
SF4	0.769	3.10	1.280			
SF5	0.844	3.12	1.311			
Perceived Behaviour				0.674534	0.911979	0.917
PB 1	0.834	3.17	1.277			
PB 2	0.833	3.20	1.268			
PB 3	0.815	3.09	1.317			
PB 4	0.808	3.10	1.254			
PB 5	0.816	3.18	1.275			
Subjective Norms				0.701726	0.921619	0.928
SN1	0.828	3.11	1.235			
SN2	0.810	3.15	1.241			
SN3	0.853	3.18	1.283			
SN4	0.857	3.08	1.314			
SN5	0.840	3.13	1.293			
Attitude towards the behaviour				0.678432	0.912815	0.908
AT1	0.835	3.28	1.272			
AT2	0.869	3.28	1.324			
AT3	0.861	3.20	1.308			
AT4	0.680	2.88	1.254			
AT5	0.858	3.29	1.293			

Source: *Author's Own Work*

4.3 Kaiser - Meyer - Olkin test

Kaiser - Meyer - Olkin test is used to measure the common variance proportion which can be explained by root problems. It is an indicator of sampling adequacy that assists in assessing if the data is admissible for factor analysis. A Factor Analysis is considered valuable if the KMO has a higher value (Thomas et al., 2022). In this analysis, the average value of KMO is 0.8984, exceeding the required cut off level (Kaiser, 1974).

4.4 Discriminant Validity

The main goal of Discriminant Validity is finding the true absence of connections between concepts that should not be related logically (Campbell & Fiske, 1959). To determine their mutual correlation, each construct in this instance underwent linear and covariance correlation. As shown in Table 3, it was made sure that the confidence interval between any of the set of constructs did not score 1 to determine the dependability factor. The discriminant validity was obtained by identifying the square root of AVE for every construct as well as the correlation square comparison.

Table 3. Discriminant Validity

Construct	KMO	EF	SF	PB	SN	AT
EF	0.909	(0.847545)				
SF	0.898	0.863712	(0.819854)			
PB	0.89	0.858872	0.87198	(0.8213)		
SN	0.903	0.856846	0.875612	0.883351	(0.837691)	
AT	0.892	0.889067	0.882624	0.889437	0.902284	(0.82367)

Notes: **Correlation is significant at the 0.01 level (two-tailed); n = 401
Source: *Authors' own work*

4.5 Confirmatory Factor Analysis

This statistical technique is applied to determine the factorial structure of a collection of observable data. The variable consistency between the constructs and the conceptual model employed in the study can be found with the aid of CFA. A two-phase procedure for developing a model using a measurement model and a structural model were proposed to depict the model fit (Anderson & Gerbing, 1988; Sehra et al., 2022). According to the conceptual model, Figure 2 displays the CFA values for the five components and twenty - five items.

Figure 2. Confirmatory Factor Analysis

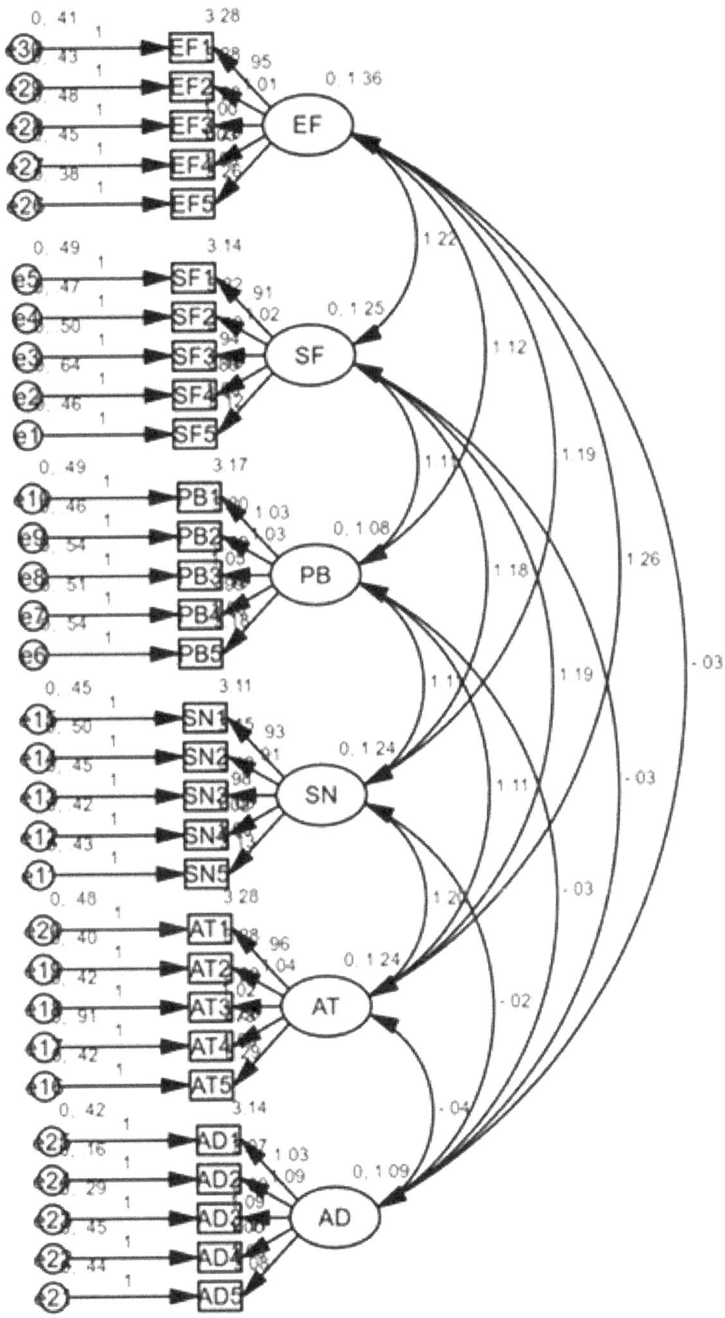

Source: *Authors' own work*

4.6 Structural Equation model and Hypothesis testing

A structural equation model analysis tool has been utilised to examine the impact of independent variables on dependent variables (Figure 3). In this study, the relationship between two variables is represented using the conceptual model. According to the SEM analysis, Table 4 is created and provides an explanation of the hypotheses that the model under study supports and does not support. The model states the following hypotheses:

EF -> AD, SF -> AD, PB -> AD, SN -> AD, and AT -> AD.

When the p-value is less than 0.05, we reject the null hypothesis and conclude that the alternative hypothesis is supported i.e. there is a significant relationship between the variables. When the p value is above 0.05, we do not reject the null hypothesis, which means there is no significant relationship between the variables.

By examining the p - value from Table 4, we can see that the null hypothesis between environmental factors and adoption of green banking, social factors and adoption of green banking, perceived behaviour and adoption of green banking, and subjective norms and adoption of green banking are supported as their p value is significant while the hypothesis between attitude towards the behaviour and adoption of green banking is not supported as the p value is 0.492.

Table 4. CFA for each factor

Items			**Estimate**	**S.E.**	**C.R.**	**P**
SF5	**<---**	**SF**	**1.000**			
SF4	<---	SF	.891	.046	19.345	***
SF3	<---	SF	.943	.044	21.482	***
SF2	<---	SF	1.021	.045	22.715	***
SF1	<---	SF	.907	.043	21.132	***
PB5	<---	PB	1.000			
PB4	<---	PB	.989	.050	19.709	***
PB3	<---	PB	1.047	.053	19.936	***
PB2	<---	PB	1.028	.050	20.543	***
PB1	<---	PB	1.026	.051	20.254	***
SN5	<---	SN	1.000			
SN4	<---	SN	1.025	.043	23.763	***
SN3	<---	SN	.980	.043	22.865	***
SN2	<---	SN	.913	.043	21.368	***
SN1	<---	SN	.930	.042	22.283	***

continued on following page

Table 4. Continued

Items			Estimate	S.E.	C.R.	P
SF5	**<---**	**SF**	**1.000**			
AT5	<---	AT	1.000			
AT4	<---	AT	.729	.049	15.026	***
AT3	<---	AT	1.016	.042	23.967	***
AT2	<---	AT	1.042	.042	24.588	***
AT1	<---	AT	.957	.042	22.548	***
ADOP5	<---	AD	1.000			
ADOP4	<---	AD	.998	.046	21.503	***
ADOP3	<---	AD	1.090	.044	24.503	***
ADOP2	<---	AD	1.094	.041	26.403	***
ADOP1	<---	AD	1.025	.046	22.075	***
EF5	<---	EF	1.000			
EF4	<---	EF	1.027	.041	25.246	***
EF3	<---	EF	.998	.041	24.391	***
EF2	<---	EF	1.013	.040	25.339	***
EF1	<---	EF	.947	.038	24.788	***

Source: *Authors' own work*

Figure 3. Structural Equation Model

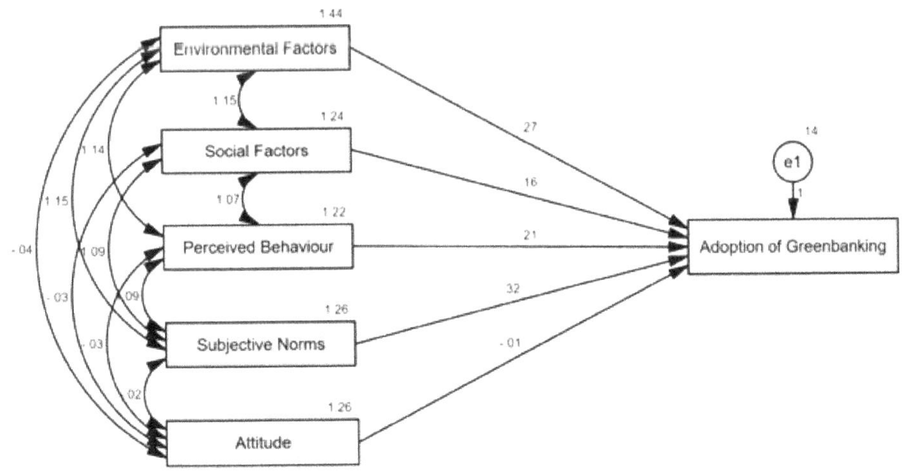

Source: *Authors' own work*

Table 5. Structural equation model results

Hypothesis			Estimate	S.E.	C.R.	P	Label
Adop_AVG	**<---**	**EF_AVG**	**.270**	**.036**	**7.589**	***	**par_1**
Adop_AVG	<---	SF_AVG	.163	.041	3.961	***	par_2
Adop_AVG	<---	PB_AVG	.209	.042	4.994	***	par_3
Adop_AVG	<---	SN_AVG	.315	.042	7.580	***	par_4
Adop_AVG	<---	AT_AVG	-.012	.017	-.687	.492	par_5

Source: *Authors' own work*

5. DISCUSSIONS AND CONCLUSION

The study establishes the role of environmental factors (EF), social factors (SF), perceived behaviour (PB), subjective norms (SN), and attitude (AT) in influencing the adoption of green banking among young adults in India. Among these determinants, subjective norms (SN) were most significant, contributing 31.5% to adoption behaviour, followed by environmental factors (27%) and perceived benefits (20.9%) in this order (Table 5). This study aimed to explore the role of such psychological as well as external factors on green banking adoption, further questioning the role played by attitude in decision-making. Using structural equation modelling (SEM), the study confirms that all proposed hypotheses (H1, H2, H3, and H4) are supported, establishing a significant relationship between environmental concern, social influence, perceived behaviour, and adoption behaviour.

These findings corroborate previous studies, such as (Ashraf, 2023) and (Ubais Parayil Iqbal et al., 2024), which also determined that social influence and environmental awareness are key drivers in adopting sustainable banking. The study also explored the role of attitude (AT) in adopting green banking. However, attitude is found not to play any significant role in adoption ($p = 0.492$), which means that positive thoughts towards green banking may not always translate into changes in behaviour. Contrary to earlier research where attitude had been proven to be a strong determinant of financial decision-making,

To the best knowledge of the author, this research is one of the few pieces of research on the interplay of environmental concerns, social influence, and perceived benefits in adoption of green banking among Indian youth. The outcomes suggest that policymakers and financial organizations must utilize social influence, awareness efforts, and stress tangible benefits rather than looking to attitudinal change.

5.1 Managerial Implication

The findings of this study provide important insights to financial institutions, banks, policymakers, and other parties who are interested in improving the adoption and utilization of green banking services among young Indians. As green banking adoption is heavily influenced by environmental concerns and social influence, financial institutions should pay attention to sustainability-based marketing strategies. Banks can organize targeted awareness campaigns emphasizing the long-term benefits of green banking, such as reduced carbon footprints, lowered operational costs, and financial incentives for green banking practices.

Moreover, digitalization is the most important aspect of green banking adoption. Banks must invest in hassle-free and convenient digital platforms for enhancing customer experience and easy access to green banking services. Collaborations with universities and fintech firms can also create broader awareness and engagement, especially among the technology-savvy younger generation. Second, banks may introduce reward programs, like discounts on green loans for green spends or cashbacks for paperless transactions, to encourage green financial behaviour.

Banks also need to eliminate hindrances to green banking adoption, such as ignorance, trust deficit, and perceived complexity in accessing green banking facilities. Schemes for educating customers, transparency in green banking initiatives, and security assurance in internet transactions can ease these challenges. Regulatory bodies need to consider policy guidelines that make green banking a priority among financial institutions, like mandatory sustainability reporting and tax relief for banks successfully implementing green banking programs, the study suggests.

5.2 Theoretical Implication

This research adds to the existing body of knowledge on sustainable finance through the application of the Theory of Planned Behaviour (TPB) to understand the uptake of green banking. The findings indicate that perceived behavioural control, subjective norms, and attitudes towards green banking are key drivers of consumer choice. Through the examination of these variables in the Indian setting, this study also adds to the body of knowledge on financial sustainability behaviours and digital banking habits.

The conclusions drawn from this study contribute to the cumulative body of knowledge regarding the interaction between psychological and social factors in financial decision-making and thus form a theoretical background for other studies on sustainable banking practices. The scope for future research can be improved by researchers by including other behavioural factors, i.e., trust in online banking, perceived risk, and financial literacy, with the aim of developing an integrated model regarding green banking adoption. Moreover, the study highlights the importance of multidisciplinary research that combines behavioural finance, environmental economics, and online banking to develop holistic strategies for promoting sustainable financial practices.

5.3 Practical Implication

This research emphasizes the importance of green banking in ensuring financial sustainability among future consumers. Due to growing environmental awareness among Generation Z and millennials, banks are compelled to provide green banking services and benefits to all. Online banking websites should be made simpler to ensure easy, efficient, and secure transactions, so green banking can be an even more convenient way of banking than traditional methods of banking.

Apart from that, there is a need to encourage consumer education programs focusing on the ecological impacts of banking operations through opinion leaders, social media platforms, and webinars. Banks are required to target a new generation by integrating gamification elements within their mobile banking apps, and rewarding customers for eco-friendly banking practices.

It is the responsibility of policymakers to lead the advocacy for green banking adoption. This can be through the development of rules that compel banks to offer green banking products, such as green home improvement loans and electric vehicle loans. Additionally, tax relief to consumers who take up green banking products can also spur their adoption. Regulatory bodies also need to facilitate public-private partnerships that promote green banking awareness and incorporate sustainability practices into existing financial systems.

5.4 Limitations and Further Scope

Although this study is informative, it is not without limitation. One of the significant limitations concerns the application of self-reported survey data, which is prone to social desirability bias or lack of information on green banking ideas. Subsequent research can circumvent this limitation by utilizing observational data or experimental designs to confirm consumer action in actual environments.

Second, this study is primarily focused on youth in India and thus limits generalizability to other age groups and other regions. Future research could expand coverage by performing cross-country and region-wise comparative analysis across various populations, regions, and countries to identify trends in the adoption of green banking at a broader level. Additionally, longitudinal studies would provide insights into changing patterns of green banking adoption over time with the passage of time and development in digital transformation and greater awareness regarding sustainability.

Another limitation of the study is that it is limited to the behavioural aspects, with no thorough investigation of the economic and policy aspects. Future studies may investigate the effects of monetary incentives, regulatory environments, and fiscal stability on the adoption of green banking practices. It would be fascinating to investigate the effects of technological advancements, including blockchain-based green finance, artificial intelligence-based sustainability monitoring, and digital carbon foot printing, to establish their possible implications on the adoption of green banking practices. This study adds significantly to the fundamental knowledge of determinants of green banking adoption among young adults in India. By overcoming the common obstacles and implementing the findings of this study, policymakers, researchers, and financial institutions can formulate targeted policies towards promoting the adoption of green banking and developing a greener financial system.

REFERENCES

Ajzen, I. (1991). The Theory of Planned Behaviour. *Organizational Behavior and Human Decision Processes, 50*(2), 179–211. DOI: 10.1016/0749-5978(91)90020-T

Ajzen, I. (2002). Perceived behavioural control, self-efficacy, locus of control, and the theory of planned behavior1. *Journal of Applied Social Psychology, 32*(4), 665–683. https://people.umass.edu/aizen/pubs/pbc.pdf. DOI: 10.1111/j.1559-1816.2002.tb00236.x

Anderson, J. C., & Gerbing, D. W. (1988). Structural equation modelling in practice: A review and recommended two-step approach. *Psychological Bulletin, 103*(3), 411–423. DOI: 10.1037/0033-2909.103.3.411

Annadurai, D. A. (2014). Effectiveness of green banking technology of the commercial banks in India. *International Journal of Research in Commerce and Management*. https://ijrcm.org.in/article_info.php?article_id=5016

Ashraf, M. A. (2023). "Go green" – evaluating the roles of environmental concerns, environmental social norms and green technology in fostering pro-green banking behaviours. *Journal of Financial Reporting and Accounting, 22*(1), 181–203. DOI: 10.1108/JFRA-05-2023-0232

Ashraf, M. A., Joarder, M. H. R., & Ratan, S. R. A. (2019). Consumers' anti-consumption behaviour toward organic food purchase: An analysis using SEM. *British Food Journal, 121*(1), 104–122. DOI: 10.1108/BFJ-02-2018-0072

Aslam, W., Farhat, K., & Arif, I. (2020). Regular to sustainable products: An account of environmentally concerned consumers in a developing economy. *International Journal of Green Energy, 18*(3), 243–257. DOI: 10.1080/15435075.2020.1854266

Bagozzi, R. P., & Yi, Y. (1988). On the Evaluation of Structural Equation Models. *Journal of the Academy of Marketing Science, 16*(1), 74–94. DOI: 10.1007/BF02723327

Bandura, A. (1982). *Self-Efficacy Mechanism in Human Agency*.

Bonett, D. G., & Wright, T. A. (2015). Cronbach's alpha reliability: Interval estimation, hypothesis testing, and sample size planning. *Journal of Organizational Behavior, 36*(1), 3–15. DOI: 10.1002/job.1960

Bose, S., Khan, H. Z., Rashid, A., & Islam, S. (2017). What drives green banking disclosure? An institutional and corporate governance perspective. *Asia Pacific Journal of Management, 35*(2), 501–527. DOI: 10.1007/s10490-017-9528-x

Bouteraa, M., Raja Hisham, R. R. I., & Zainol, Z. (2022). Challenges affecting bank consumers' intention to adopt green banking technology in the UAE: A UTAUT-based mixed-methods approach. *Journal of Islamic Marketing*, *14*(10), 2466–2501. DOI: 10.1108/JIMA-02-2022-0039

Bouteraa, M., Raja Hisham, R. R. I., & Zainol, Z.BOUTERAA. (2021). Exploring determinants of customers' intention to adopt green banking: qualitative investigation. *Journal of Sustainability Science and Management*, *16*(3), 187–203. DOI: 10.46754/jssm.2021.04.014

Bukhari, S. A. A., Hashim, F., & Amran, A. (2022). Pathways towards Green Banking adoption: Moderating role of top management commitment. *International Journal of Ethics and Systems*, *38*(2), 286–315. DOI: 10.1108/IJOES-05-2021-0110

Bukhari, S. A. A., Hashim, F., Amran, A. B., & Hyder, K. (2019). Green Banking and Islam: Two sides of the same coin. *Journal of Islamic Marketing*, *11*(4), 977–1000. DOI: 10.1108/JIMA-09-2018-0154

Campbell, D. T., & Fiske, D. W. (1959). Convergent and discriminant validation by the multigrain-multimethod matrix. *Psychological Bulletin*, *56*(2), 81–105. DOI: 10.1037/h0046016

Chan, K. H., Chong, L.-L., & Ng, T. H. (2022). Integrating extended theory of planned behaviour and norm activation model to examine the effects of environmental practices among Malaysian companies. *Journal of Entrepreneurship in Emerging Economies*, *14*(5), 851–873. Advance online publication. DOI: 10.1108/JEEE-08-2021-0317

Chatterjee, P. (2009). Green brand extension strategy and online communities. *Journal of Systems and Information Technology*, *11*(4), 367–384. DOI: 10.1108/13287260911002503

Cordano, M., & Frieze, I. H. (2000). Pollution reduction preferences of U.S. environmental managers: applying Ajzen's theory of planned behavior. *Academy of Management Journal*, *43*(4), 627–641. DOI: 10.2307/1556358

Coupland, C. (2006). Corporate social and environmental responsibility in web-based reports: Currency in the banking sector? *Critical Perspectives on Accounting*, *17*(7), 865–881. DOI: 10.1016/j.cpa.2005.01.001

do Paço, A., & Raposo, M. (2009). "Green" segmentation: An application to the Portuguese consumer market. *Marketing Intelligence & Planning*, *27*(3), 364–379. DOI: 10.1108/02634500910955245

Emekci, S. (2019). Green consumption behaviours of consumers within the scope of TPB. *Journal of Consumer Marketing*, *36*(3), 410–417. DOI: 10.1108/JCM-05-2018-2694

Evangelinos, K. I., & Nikolaou, I. E. (2009). Environmental accounting and the banking sector: A framework for measuring environmental-financial risks. *International Journal of Services Sciences*, *2*(3/4), 366. DOI: 10.1504/IJSSCI.2009.026547

Finger, M., Gavious, I., & Manos, R. (2018). Environmental risk management and financial performance in the banking industry: A cross-country comparison. *Journal of International Financial Markets, Institutions and Money*, *52*, 240–261. DOI: 10.1016/j.intfin.2017.09.019

Follows, S. B., & Jobber, D. (2000). Environmentally responsible purchase behaviour: A test of a consumer model. *European Journal of Marketing*, *34*(5/6), 723–746. DOI: 10.1108/03090560010322009

Fornell, C., & Larcker, D. F. (1981). Structural equation models with unobservable variables and measurement error: Algebra and statistics. *JMR, Journal of Marketing Research*, *18*(3), 382–388. DOI: 10.1177/002224378101800313

Hair, J. F., Black, W. C., & Babin, B. J. (2010). Multivariate Data Analysis: A Global Perspective. In *Google Books*. Pearson Education., https://books.google.co.in/books/about/Multivariate_Data_Analysis.html?id=SLRPLgAACAAJ&redir_esc=y

Henriques, I., & Sadorsky, P. (1999). The relationship between environmental commitment and managerial perceptions of stakeholder importance. *Academy of Management Journal*, *42*(1), 87–99. DOI: 10.2307/256876

Iqbal, U. P., Jose, S. M., & Tahir, M.Ubais Parayil Iqbal. (2024). Examining the demand side factors of green banking adoption – a study exploring the case of Oman. *International Journal of Islamic and Middle Eastern Finance and Management*, *17*(1), 213–231. DOI: 10.1108/IMEFM-12-2022-0483

Kaiser, H. F. (1974). An Index of Factorial Simplicity. *Psychometrika*, *39*(1), 31–36. DOI: 10.1007/BF02291575

Khanna, A. (2013, January 4). *Indian Banking Sector towards a Sustainable Growth: A Paradigm Shift*. ResearchGate; unknown. https://www.researchgate.net/publication/326175175

Khare, A. (2015). Antecedents to green buying behaviour: A study on consumers in an emerging economy. *Marketing Intelligence & Planning*, *33*(3), 309–329. DOI: 10.1108/MIP-05-2014-0083

Kumar, K., & Prakash, A. (2018). Developing a framework for assessing sustainable banking performance of the Indian banking sector. *Social Responsibility Journal, 15*(5), 689–709. Advance online publication. DOI: 10.1108/SRJ-07-2018-0162

Long, X., Chen, Y., Du, J., Oh, K., Han, I., & Yan, J. (2017). The effect of environmental innovation behaviour on economic and environmental performance of 182 Chinese firms. *Journal of Cleaner Production, 166*, 1274–1282. DOI: 10.1016/j.jclepro.2017.08.070

Malik, G., & Singh, D. (2022). Personality matters: does an individual's personality affect adoption and continued use of green banking channels? *International Journal of Bank Marketing, ahead-of-print*(ahead-of-print). DOI: 10.1108/IJBM-04-2021-0133

Milfont, T. L., & Duckitt, J. (2004). The structure of environmental attitudes: A first- and second-order confirmatory factor analysis. *Journal of Environmental Psychology, 24*(3), 289–303. DOI: 10.1016/j.jenvp.2004.09.001

Nisha, N., Iqbal, M., & Rifat, A. (2020). Green Banking Adoption. *International Journal of Technology and Human Interaction, 16*(2), 69–89. DOI: 10.4018/IJTHI.2020040106

Nizam, E., Ng, A., Dewandaru, G., Nagayev, R., & Nkoba, M. A. (2019). The impact of social and environmental sustainability on financial performance: A global analysis of the banking sector. *Journal of Multinational Financial Management, 49*(1), 35–53. DOI: 10.1016/j.mulfin.2019.01.002

Nunnally, J. C., & Bernstein, I. H. (1994). Psychometric Theory. In *Google Books*. McGraw-Hill Companies, Incorporated. https://books.google.com/books/about/Psychometric_Theory.html?id=r0fuAAAAMAAJ

Park, H. S. (2000). Relationships among attitudes and subjective norms: Testing the theory of reasoned action across cultures. *Communication Studies, 51*(2), 162–175. DOI: 10.1080/10510970009388516

Phau, I., & Ong, D. (2007). An investigation of the effects of environmental claims in promotional messages for clothing brands. *Marketing Intelligence & Planning, 25*(7), 772–788. DOI: 10.1108/02634500710834214

Podsakoff, P. M., MacKenzie, S. B., Lee, J.-Y., & Podsakoff, N. P. (2003). Common Method Biases in Behavioral research: A Critical Review of the Literature and Recommended remedies. *The Journal of Applied Psychology, 88*(5), 879–903. DOI: 10.1037/0021-9010.88.5.879

Podsakoff, P. M., & Organ, D. W. (1986). Self-Reports in Organizational Research: Problems and Prospects. *Journal of Management*, *12*(4), 531–544. DOI: 10.1177/014920638601200408

Qi, X., Lv, X., Li, Z., Yang, C., Li, H., & Ploeger, A. (2024). Factors influencing young adults' organic food purchase intention on fresh food e-commerce platforms. *British Food Journal*, *126*(12), 4277–4303. Advance online publication. DOI: 10.1108/BFJ-04-2024-0417

Rahbar, E., & Abdul Wahid, N. (2011). Investigation of green marketing tools' effect on consumers' purchase behavior. *Business Strategy Series*, *12*(2), 73–83. DOI: 10.1108/17515631111114877

Rehman, A., Ullah, I., Afridi, F.-A., Ullah, Z., Zeeshan, M., Hussain, A., & Rahman, H. U. (2021). Adoption of green banking practices and environmental performance in Pakistan: A demonstration of structural equation modelling. *Environment, Development and Sustainability*, *23*(9), 13200–13220. DOI: 10.1007/s10668-020-01206-x

Robichaud, Z., & Yu, H. (2021). Do young consumers care about ethical consumption? Modelling Gen Z's purchase intention towards fair trade coffee. *British Food Journal, ahead-of-print*(ahead-of-print). DOI: 10.1108/BFJ-05-2021-0536

Naveenan, R.V., Madeswaran, A., & R, A. K. (2021). Green banking practices in India-the customer's perspective. *Academy of Entrepreneurship Journal, 27*(4), 1–19. https://www.researchgate.net/publication/354761063

Sarkis, J., Gonzalez-Torre, P., & Adenso-Diaz, B. (2010). Stakeholder pressure and the adoption of environmental practices: The mediating effect of training. *Journal of Operations Management*, *28*(2), 163–176. DOI: 10.1016/j.jom.2009.10.001

Schultz, P. W. (2000). New Environmental Theories: Empathizing with Nature: The Effects of Perspective Taking on Concern for Environmental Issues. *The Journal of Social Issues*, *56*(3), 391–406. DOI: 10.1111/0022-4537.00174

Sehra, S. K., Godwin, B. J., & George, J. P. (2022). Are expensive decisions impulsive? Young adults' impulsive housing and real estate buying behavior in India. *International Journal of Housing Markets and Analysis*. DOI: 10.1108/IJHMA-06-2022-0090

Sharma, M., & Choubey, A. (2021). Green Banking initiatives: A Qualitative Study on Indian Banking Sector. *Environment, Development and Sustainability*, *24*(1), 293–319. Advance online publication. DOI: 10.1007/s10668-021-01426-9

Taylor, S., & Todd, P. A. (1995). Understanding Information Technology Usage: A Test of Competing Models. *Information Systems Research*, *6*(2), 144–176. DOI: 10.1287/isre.6.2.144

Thomas, S. S., George, J. P., Godwin, B. J., & Siby, A. (2022). Young adults' default intention: influence of behavioral factors in determining housing and real estate loan repayment in India. *International Journal of Housing Markets and Analysis*. DOI: 10.1108/IJHMA-01-2022-0012

Yadav, R., & Pathak, G. S. (2016). Young consumers' intention towards buying green products in a developing nation: Extending the theory of planned behavior. *Journal of Cleaner Production*, *135*, 732–739. DOI: 10.1016/j.jclepro.2016.06.120

Zahidul Islam, Md., Ahmed, S., & Hasan, I. (2012, February 5). *Corporate Social Responsibility and Financial Performance Linkage: Evidence from the Banking Sector of...* ResearchGate; unknown. https://www.researchgate.net/publication/228273307_Corporate_Social_Responsibility_and_Financial_Performance_Linkage_Evidence_from_the_Banking_Sector_of_Bangladesh

Zhang, H., & Yang, F. (2016). On the drivers and performance outcomes of green practices adoption. *Industrial Management & Data Systems*, *116*(9), 2011–2034. DOI: 10.1108/IMDS-06-2015-0263

Chapter 9
Fintech Meets Behavior:
How AI-Powered Tools Are Reshaping Financial Decision-Making

Tarika Singh Sikarwar
Prestige Institute of Management and Research, India

Nidhi Jain
http://orcid.org/0000-0003-0535-8733
Prestige Institute of Management and Research, India

Harshita Mathur
http://orcid.org/0009-0003-4130-9821
Prestige Institute of Management and Research, India

Seema Mehta
John Hopkins University, USA & Institute of Health Management and Research, India

Senthil Kumar A. V.
http://orcid.org/0000-0002-8587-7017
Nehru Institute of Information Technology and Management, India

ABSTRACT

The study was done to check the effect of financial beliefs, attitudes, and goals on the financial behavior of investors in changing digital contexts. Improvements in financial behavioral theory show that changing contexts, also called "evolving settings," can powerfully affect financial behavior. Our study shows that in the changing Artificial Intelligence (AI) contexts, beliefs affect financial behavior insig-

DOI: 10.4018/979-8-3373-5047-9.ch009

nificantly in the manifestation of attitude and goals. This study is an advancement over the previous studies as the results are not in line with the previous results of different studies done in the area and provide implications for a financial therapist for counseling and portfolio designing. The study has implications for society and individuals, as there are grave negative and long-term consequences to individuals and society if one fails to manage finances in today's AI age.

BACKGROUND

Recent research highlights how financial behavior is changing in the context of digitization. (Acquisti et al., 2016) examined how digital tools influence financial attitudes and objectives, for example, and found that access to technology modifies conventional behavioral patterns. Their research highlights the complex relationship between technology and financial judgment, a topic that needs more investigation.

Nevertheless, disparities in results point to the necessity of context-specific research. While some studies, such as (Aggarwal et al., 2016), highlight the importance of financial literacy in enhancing behavior, others contend that psychological elements like objectives and attitudes should get more attention, particularly in quickly evolving digital contexts (Ameliawati & Setiyani, 2018)

Financial behavior determines saving behavior, which is the key determinant of financial success. It benefits the individual as well as the economy (Ammerman et al., 2019). attitude toward money shapes financial behavior, but this relationship is further determined depending on the type of financial behavior (Andrews & Bategeka, 2013). Financial problems (Andrews & Bategeka, 2013) may be associated with financial attitude. Self-efficacy understood in terms of an individual's beliefs, is another factor determining financial behaviour (Andrews et al., 2017) Financial belief is the financial belief about the self to change self-financial behavior (Anthony et al., 2011). Difficult financial tasks are dealt with more confidence if an individual's self-belief is strong. With a stronger belief, financial behavior changes in a positive direction. The financial behavior of an individual is formed, keeping in mind (Antonides et al., 2011) and harmonizing with the overall financial goal (Antonides et al., 2011). People with an internal locus of control are goal-driven (Ballara, 2023). Financial security is also related to having goals (Ballara, 2023).

References also change the financial behavior for any decision (Barber & Odean, 2001) References may shift daily as well (Bikhchandani & Sharma, 2000) or even in hours. (Camerer et al., 1997) also recorded changes in interest rates on credit cards and the response. Poor mathematical abilities result in different financial behaviors of individuals. (Chandra & Kumar, 2011) identified income, higher education learning, financial knowledge, financial literacy, financial attitude, and the locus of control as determinants of financial behavior. Other factors include income (Crawford & Meng, 2010), financial management (Dholakia et al., 2016), financial knowledge (DiFonzo & Bordia, 1997) financial attitude, confidence, self-esteem, and self-belief (Dolan et al., 2012).

The proposed research aims to contribute to a growing body of studies concerning financial beliefs, attitudes, goals, and financial behavior in changing AI contexts. The social and financial systems changed because of the growth of digitalization in the global economy. This change is visible from the changes and consequences of complications and increased usage of technology in products and services of a financial nature. These questions the traditional association should be re-checked and connections should be re-drawn. Hence, this generates the necessity for the present work.

Studies done in different nations, in different sets of populations, and at different times, have not focused on these determinants together and individually do not lead to a common conclusion. Furthermore, fewer studies are done on Indian investors, leaving the area unexplored. Last, ten years give proof of changes in the economic environment. Globalization and digitalization of the Indian economy, technology-based trading, online transactions, and more information availability for financial products, and services have changed the way investors think and act.

The study starts with an explanation of the theoretical concepts used in the work and an understanding of the current research work available. Based on this, research hypotheses are formulated and checked using the appropriate methodology. The results and discussion part describes the statistical tests applied and the inferences drawn. Further presented are the conclusion, limitations, and implications of the study.

Financial Behavioral Theory: Key Concepts

In order to comprehend how people make financial decisions, a great deal of research has been done in the field of financial behavioral theory. Prospect Theory was first presented in early research by (Duflo & Saez, 2003), emphasizing that people are impacted by cognitive biases and risk perception and do not always act rationally. By highlighting the deviation from conventional economic models that presumed rational decision-making, this theory established the foundation for behavioral finance.

Later research expanded the understanding of financial behavior by incorporating psychological factors, including beliefs, attitudes, and aspirations. (Farber, 2008), for instance, examined how self-efficacy and financial attitudes influence prudent financial practices, such as debt management and saving. Their results highlight the indirect impact of beliefs, indicating that attitudes serve as a mediator between financial literacy and behavior.

Furthermore, the idea that intentions, which are influenced by attitudes, subjective norms, and perceived behavioral control are important determinants of behavior was first presented in Ajzen 's Theory of Planned Behavior (1991). Many financial behaviors, including debt repayment and investment decisions, have been explained by this approach (Furnham, 1984).

With a focus on the environmental and psychological aspects that affect financial decision-making, financial behavioral theory has seen substantial development. The prospect theory was first presented in early research, including that of Kahneman and Tversky (1979). It emphasizes how people assess possible advantages and costs in uncertain situations. This seminal study challenged the conventional economic models' presumption of rational conduct by demonstrating how biases and heuristics significantly influence financial decisions.

Building on this, the behavioral portfolio theory was put out by Shefrin and Statman (2000), who claimed that investors build their portfolios using layered goals that represent their fears and ambitions. These layers highlight the interplay between psychological and environmental aspects and are influenced by their financial ideas, attitudes, and ambitions.

The influence of changing environments, including digitization, on financial behavior has been the subject of recent studies. (Gupta, 1970), for example, showed how financial tools and digital platforms affect people's spending and saving behaviors. Their results highlight how, since technology offers real-time feedback and information availability, AI environments enhance the impact of financial objectives while reducing the influence of beliefs.

In contrast to these observations, (Hastings et al., 2013) discovered that financial education initiatives that aim to modify beliefs have varying degrees of success because, in the absence of a congruence between attitudes and objectives, behavior tends to remain constant. This demonstrates how environmental, emotional, and cognitive aspects interact while making financial decisions.

Moreover, (Hayhoe & Wilhelm, 1998) found in their meta-analysis that financial literacy is not enough to influence meaningful behavioral changes on its own. Instead, especially in technologically sophisticated contexts, goal-setting and attitude changes are important mediators.

Together, these studies show that a mix of external (technical and cultural) and internal (beliefs, attitudes, and aspirations) elements affects financial behavior. More research is still required to fully understand how digital transitions in terms of AI alter these interactions and provide fresh perspectives for financial behavioral theory.

Building a Theoretical Framework

Financial behavior is defined in terms of, "the capability to capture of understand overall impacts of financial decisions on one's (i.e., Person, family....) circumstances and to make the right decisions related to the cash management, precautions and opportunities for budget planning" (Henager & Cude, 2016).

Appropriate financial behavior is required to have the capability to manage finances. Individuals and family members exhibit different financial behavior at different points of time (Kahneman & Tversky, 1979) as per need, priorities, and level of skills. Financial behavior is a broad term, and several theories are proposed, to explain the financial behavior of the people (Kahneman, 2003). Some of the noteworthy among these theories specifically, psychological theories/models are cited as: "Transtheoretical Model of Change/ Stages of Change (TTM)," "Health Belief Model (HBM)," "The Theory of Reasoned Action/ Planned Financial behavior (TRA)," "Risk Reduction Model (RRM)," "Social Cognitive/Learning Theory (SCT)" and "Relapse Prevention Model (RPM)."Analysts have studied the fundamental knowledge of social, and financial matters put forward about the behavior of humans for over an era (Kahneman et al., 1997).

Investors in India, just like any other investor, do not act rationally because of cognitive and emotional weaknesses (Kaur & Shukla, 2016). Behavioral biases are the reasons for this irrational behavior. (Kaur & Vohra, 2014) recognized thirteen mental predispositions and seventeen logical variables influencing speculation behavior driving financial behavior in India. The financial behavior differed in rural and urban households (Kemp, 2018) and was influenced by the head of the family and its members (Kumar & Goyal, 2023). Further, there is a contradiction between modern financial theories with traditional behavioral theories (Kumar et al., 2020). Critical advancements in procedures, frameworks, and limits can, what is more, be made. However, there has been little change in results impacted by those frameworks. As cited by (Lusardi & Mitchell, 2007), "A great deal of behavior has not changed radically in territories where frameworks were created." This shows that structure is changing; however, work is not, which has been the expansive finish of numerous onlookers (Andrews et al., 2017; Crawford & Meng, 2010; Madrian & Shea, 2001)

A sound financial behavior is visualized from the mentality of an individual in allocating the forthcoming and outgoing cash, overseeing advances, and ventures. Money-related financial behavior might be impacted by a person's financial proficiency, as well. Financial proficiency can be deciphered as money-related information to secure reserves. A person with high monetary proficiency will impact their money-related behavior toward a constructive way. In this work, financial behavior relates to money behavior in terms of investments.

Beliefs

(Montford & Goldsmith, 2016) defined belief as "Belief is the state of mind in which a person thinks something to be the case with or without there being empirical evidence to prove that something is the case with factual certainty." In India, beliefs about money are related to religion too. Every religion guides individuals to saving, and they believe in future savings. As per an article published in Economic Times dated April 20 in the year 2008, "religion is a huge money spinner in India." Similarly, culture plays a crucial role in making beliefs about money. In this research, belief means money belief.

Beliefs about money affect financial behavior (Nofsinger, 2005). Money is considered a status symbol (Norvilitis et al., 2003), and people have a sense of money anxiety. Traditional research focused on change in financial behavior through the change in belief only (Odean, 1998). The financial behavioral expectation in terms of social and cultural norms governs society. Individuals comprehend these standards from the behavior of others. Some norms may affect the financial behavior of someone strongly while others may not (Oehler et al., 2020).

Hence, based upon above mentioned discussion, the hypothesis proposed is:

Ha1: There is a prevalence of affiliation amongst beliefs and financial behavior.

Attitude

According to Prominent psychologist Gordon Allport (1979), "Attitude is a psychological construct, a mental and emotional entity that inheres in, or characterizes a person". Attitude is eccentric and learned using experiences (Thaler, 1980). Attitudes can be positive or negative. The money attitude of an individual can be defined as "a means of influence and protection and reflects a personal dependence on money that leads to ongoing concern about money (Kahneman, 2003). Growing westernization in India has led to a change in the money attitude with people becoming more focused towards money and hence indicating changed financial behavior (Weber, 1999). Traditionally, people are more inclined towards savings in India, and the difference is visible between males and females too (Weber & Zuchel, 2005). In this research, attitude means money attitude.

Attitude has a noteworthy positive association with financial behavior (Heckman, 1976). Culture also plays a unique role in developing money attitudes and hence affects Financial behavior (Goldstein et al., 2008). There is a relationship between objective and subjective money attitudes (Shiller, 2003). People with substantial financial attitudes are less inclined to use credit cards (Ritter, 2003). In married individuals, financial attitude leads to better financial satisfaction and hence leads to more responsible financial behavior (Baker & Wurgler, 2007). Similar research

(Thaler, 1999) has proved financial attitude and financial behavior as determining factors of financial satisfaction. Hence the hypothesis can be proposed as-is:

- Ha2: There is a prevalence of affiliation between attitude and financial behavior.

Goals

According to the Merriam-Webster dictionary, "A goal is an idea of the future or desired result that a person or a group of people envisions, plans and commits to achieve people endeavor to reach goals within a finite time by setting deadlines." A goal is an explanation of the expected outcome guiding a reaction that has inherent worth. Goal-based planning for finances has become much more visible in recent times. Investors set goals for increasing wealth. As defined by (Olsen, 2002), "Financial goals are the personal, big-picture objectives you set for how you'll save and spend money". Social research likewise recommends that speculators get a feeling of inspiration and fulfilment with their monetary plans when consultants centre on a customer's close-to-home goals versus discretionary benchmarks. A study done by (Camerer & Loewenstein, 2004) has quoted that the investment horizon of Indians is short-term, and they do not set long-term goals for investing, but they do save for contingency. In this research, the goal means financial goals.

There are numerous studies quoted depicting that long-term financial goals are determining factors for the kind of financial behavior an individual shows (Fama, 1970) and noteworthy influence on the financial behavior of individuals (Kahneman et al., 1990). Goals keep motivating individuals and hence lead to changed financial behavior (Kahneman & Tversky, 1984).

Impact on Financial Goals and Decision-Making

Financial planning and goal-setting have also changed in AI environment. For example, by offering visual feedback on investing and savings goals, the gamification of financial apps encourages user involvement. But according to studies, these characteristics can occasionally result in a short-term concentration that undermines long-term financial stability (Laibson, 1997). Additionally, new financial pressures brought about by the AI era, such as cybersecurity threats and privacy issues, have an impact on people's financial attitudes and actions (Thaler & Johnson, 1990).

Hence, a hypothesis is proposed:

Ha3: There is a prevalence of affiliation between change in goals and Financial behavior.

Summing up the above review, conclusively, the following hypothesis is framed:

Ha4: There is a prevalence of affiliation amongst change in belief, attitude, and goal with financial behavior.

Influence of AI Contexts on Financial Decision-Making

AI technology's rapid growth has fundamentally changed how financial decisions are made. For individual investors, digital settings like as social media, financial applications, and online trading platforms have produced a dynamic environment (Bresciani et al., 2021). Real-time decision-making has been made easier by these changing circumstances, but they have also added complexity because of information overload and biases brought on by AI interfaces (Tversky & Kahneman, 1991).

The availability of financial data is one of the main effects of digital environments. The availability of financial data on digital platforms enables investors to make well-informed choices, claim (Simon, 1955). On the other hand, cognitive overload brought on by too much knowledge might result in mistakes or delays in decision-making. The automated curation of information, which frequently intensifies confirmation bias, makes this situation worse (Ariely et al., 2003).

AI tools and interfaces that are easy to use may have a big impact on how people behave financially. For instance, it has been demonstrated that gamified investing platforms boost investor involvement while also increasing impulsive decision-making (Friedman & Savage, 1948). Additionally, investors tend to prioritize short-term rewards over long-term strategy due to the transparency and immediacy of digital technologies (Simon, 1956).

Role of Social Media and Peer Influence

In the AI era, social media platforms play a crucial role in influencing financial decisions. Ausat (2023) claims that social networks encourage herd behavior, in which people imitate their peers' or influencers' financial moves without doing a careful examination. As seen by the GameStop stock spike, this behavior is more noticeable at times of market turbulence (Thaler, 2000).

Behavioral Shifts in the Digital Age

By facilitating quicker and more frequent transactions, the digitalization of money has changed conventional behavioral patterns. Convenience-driven behavior thus becomes more prevalent, frequently at the price of careful financial preparation (Antonides et al., 2011). Furthermore, as people depend more on peer reviews and social evidence when selecting financial goods, AI platforms have increased the impact of social networks on financial decision-making (Crawford & Meng, 2010).

Behavioral biases like loss aversion and overconfidence are exacerbated in AI environments. According to research by Kahneman and Tversky (1979), these biases make it likely for investors to make less-than-ideal choices. These inclinations can be made worse in a AI environment by the instantaneous nature of trades and alerts (Hayhoe & Wilhelm, 1998).

Ethical Concerns and Financial Well-Being

Ethical questions about privacy and manipulation are also brought up by the AI world. According to Acquisti et al. (2016), financial service providers frequently utilize behavioral data to influence consumers toward particular products that might not be in line with their financial objectives. Particularly for those with little financial literacy, this behavior can jeopardize financial well-being (Aggarwal et al., 2016; Henager & Cude, 2016).

Importance of Financial Behavior in the AI Age

The financial landscape has changed dramatically in the AI era, and personal financial behavior has been greatly impacted. Financial services are now more widely available due to technological advancements, including digital payment systems, smartphone apps, and internet banking. But these developments have also brought up new difficulties in the areas of security, decision-making, and financial literacy.

AI Contexts and Their Influence on Financial Behavior

Investor behavior has been significantly impacted by the growing integration of AI technology into financial systems. AI settings, such as financial applications, robo-advisors, and online banking systems, have changed how people deal with their money. In addition to providing comfort, transparency, and easier access to financial data, these technological developments also present drawbacks such as decision fatigue and an excessive dependence on automation (Hastings et al., 2013).

AI platforms have made financial services more accessible to everybody, allowing people to manage their money more effectively. Financial literacy is essential for people to make wise decisions in increasingly complicated financial contexts, claim Lusardi and Mitchell (2014). People can monitor and manage their money in the AI age with the help of technologies like online investing platforms and budgeting applications, but they also need a solid grasp of financial principles.

Because online transactions are so convenient, financial behaviour in the AI era is characterized by a greater degree of impulsivity and immediacy. When using AI payment methods, people are more likely to engage in emotional spending and quick gratification, according to research by (Furnham, 1984). Furthermore, the rise in online financial services has made it more important than ever for people to practice responsible money management to prevent bad things like overspending or being victims of fraud.

Digital technologies provide many potential benefits, but they also present formidable obstacles. For example, (Antonides et al., 2011) emphasized that people with less financial literacy are more prone to abuse digital financial services, and that AI tools by themselves cannot replace financial literacy. Furthermore, behavioral biases like loss aversion and overconfidence are exacerbated in digital environments, which results in less-than-ideal financial choices (Kaur & Shukla, 2016).

Investors may make judgments instantly thanks to digital platforms that provide them with quick access to financial markets. But because of the abundance of information, this accessibility may also result in rash decisions (Madrian & Shea, 2001). Due to the abundance of data available, investors frequently suffer from cognitive biases like overconfidence. For example, research indicates that regular access to stock market data raises the risk of speculative trading, which might have negative long-term financial effects (Norvilitis et al., 2003).

Investment procedures have been made more efficient by automation in financial services, such as robo-advisors and algorithmic trading. Although these technologies lessen human biases and mistakes, they also run the danger of lowering individual responsibility and financial decision-making comprehension (Oehler et al., 2020) . The development of financial literacy and autonomous decision-making may be impeded by automated systems' tendency to promote a passive attitude to money management (Ritter, 2003).

OBJECTIVES

The objectives include:

- Find out underlying factors for beliefs, attitudes, goals, and financial behavior;
- To learn how beliefs affect financial behavior.
- To learn how the attitude affects financial behavior,
- To learn how the goals of financial behavior
- To learn how beliefs, attitudes, and goals together affect financial behavior.

THE STUDY

Data and Variables

The personal characteristics and behavior shown by investors make them hard to measure and use in the research. The availability of historical investment data of such investors is tough to obtain. Hence, the inclusion of all such variables in the study model is not possible. The study was completed on the population of investors. Any person who has invested in any of the financial instruments in the last ten years (April 2014-December 2024) is an investor in the research. Here, a single cross-sectional study is conducted to capture the information related to the investment behavior of different investors during December 2024. The investors belonged to different age groups, genders, educational backgrounds, income levels, and cultures. The work hence helps to understand the general characteristics of the investor population and the prevalence of association between different variables of the study measured through the survey. Approximately 450 investors contacted various financial institutions in December 2024, and they were given questionnaires on their beliefs, attitudes, goals, and financial behavior, to fill. Out of these, 319 questionnaires were received back. Only 309 questionnaires were found to be filled and usable for the research.

With the end goal of information assortment, the following questionnaires were used: for beliefs (based on Klontz et al., 2011), attitude (Source: Financial Planning Association based on), Goals (based on Family Wealth Planning Questionnaire), and Financial behavior (Jeffrey Dew,2013). These questionnaires were easy to fill and hardly took 12-15 minutes. The data-filling phase was completed in December 2024. After that, the initial screening of the questionnaires for duplicity and incomplete data was done.

DATA ANALYSIS

The Chronbach's Alpha method was used to establish the reliability of the instruments, and the face validity method confirmed the validity of the instruments. EFA identified contributing factors of beliefs, attitudes, goals, and financial behavior in the AI era. The linear regression method checked the causatives between attitudes and financial behavior, goals and financial behavior, beliefs, and financial behavior, as well as between belief, attitude, and goal taken together with financial behavior to understand the prevalence of affiliation.

Consistency

Consistency assessment checked the uniformity coefficients of the different constructs used in the current study. Table 1 cites the outcomes (refer to Table 1).

Table 1. Consistency Statistics

Variables	Cronbach's Alpha	Number of Objects
Beliefs	.784	10
Attitudes	.788	15
Goals	.715	16
Financial behavior	.756	18

The outcome presented in the table1 indicates the high consistency of questionnaires of beliefs, attitudes, goals, and financial behavior as 0.784, 0.788,0.715, and 0.756, respectively, which is better than the standard value, which is 0.70 (Nunnally,1978).

Sample Appropriateness

KMO strategy checked the typical conveyance, and Bartlett tested the character grid to see if the information was reasonable for factor analysis or not. Table 2 summarizes the results.

Table 2. Sample appropriateness summary

Variable	"_Kaiser-Meyer-Olkin Measure of Sampling Adequacy_"	"_Bartlett's Test of Sphericity Approx. Chi-Square_"	_Df	_Significance
Beliefs	.774	742.364	45	.000
Attitudes	.772	1037.130	105	. 000
Goals	.739	1179.374	120	.000
Financial behavior	.739	1179.374	120	.000

Table 2 indicates the result of the Bartlett test for Belief, Attitude, Goals, and Financial Behaviour. A value higher than 0.7 for KMO indicates adequate respondents for identifying factors of the variables. The chi-square value is noteworthy at 0%, showing the response matrix is a non-identity matrix.

Factor Description

Exploratory factor analysis using the principal component method was applied to get a pattern of variance and covariance among responses given on the items of the scales used for different variables. The next part explains the amount of variation in a broad set of test items in each collection of a variable obtained by exhibiting them with calculations built on some limited hidden constituents.

Variable Belief: All ten statements for the variable converged on a single factor named Belief with a total variance of 29.496% and Eigenvalue of 2.950.

Variable: Attitude: Five elements emerged after dimension reduction (refer to Figure 1).

Figure 1. Factors of Variable Attitude

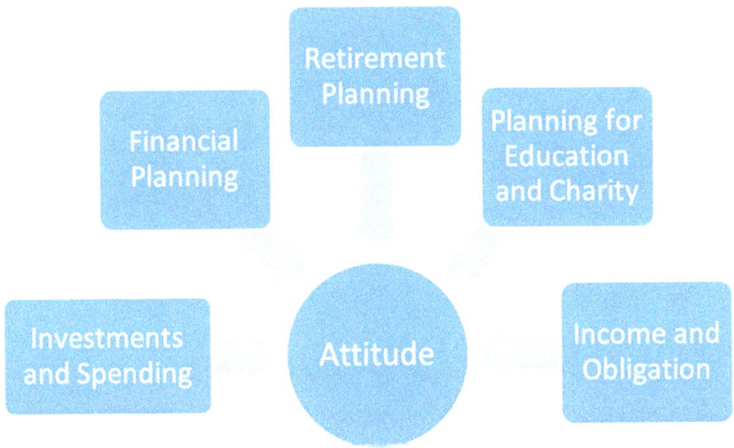

These elements are:

(1) Investments and Spending: With an eigenvalue of 3.347 and a total variance of 22.316%. Four statements converged on this factor.
(2) Financial Planning: With an eigenvalue of 1.313 and a total variance of 8.753%. Five statements converged on this factor.
(3) Retirement Planning: With an eigenvalue of .759 and a total variance of 5.063%. Two statements converged on this factor.
(4) Planning for Education and Charity: With an eigenvalue of .475 and a total variance of 3.164%. Two statements converged on this factor.

(5) Income and Obligation: With eigenvalue of .462 and total variance of 3.083%. Two statements converged on this factor.

Variable: Goals: Five factors emerged out after dimension reduction (refer to Figure 2).

Figure 2. Factors of variable Goals

These factors are:

(6) Working and Retirement Goals: With eigenvalue of 3.107 and a total variance of 19.419%. Six statements converged on this factor.
(7) Charity and Future Generation's Education: With eigenvalue of 1.802 and a total variance of 11.265%. Two statements converged on this factor.
(8) Cost Minimization and Career Choice: With eigenvalue of .939 and total variance of 5.868%. Four statements converged on this factor.
(9) Contingency Planning: With an eigenvalue of .726 and a total variance of 4.539%. Two statements converged on this factor.
(10) Distribution of Estate and Cutting Healthcare Cost: With eigenvalue of .546 and total variance of 3.410%. Two statements converged on this factor.

Regression

Linear regression analysis assessed the causatives between the variables—the outcomes presented in Table 3.

Table 3. Causation results

Dependent Variable	Independent Variable	R square Value	F value and Sig	Unstandardized Coefficient Beta	Standardized Coefficients	T value and Significance	Hypothesis testing
Financial behavior	Belief	.310	138.218 @0%	.761	.557	11.757@0%	Ha1:Not Rejected
Financial behavior	Attitudes	.406	210.002@0%	.701	.637	14.491@0%	Ha2:Not Rejected
Financial behavior	Goal	.384	191.474@0%	.664	.620	13.837@0%	Ha3: Not Rejected
Financial behavior	Belief, Attitudes and Goal	.517	110.842@0%	Beliefs total:- .149	-.109	-1.091@27.6%	Ha4: Not Rejected
				Attitudes total: .587	.534	5.095@0%	
				Goals total: .418	.391	8.391@0%	

Association for Financial Behavior and Belief

The R-squared value, in this case, is .310. The financial beliefs and financial behavior tested for causation fit with the F-statistic value of 138.218, noteworthy at 0% (refer to Table 3), indicating a high fit. The coefficient value of financial beliefs is .761, implying one component modification in belief leading to a .761-unit variation in financial behavior. The β value is 0.557, and the t-test value is 11.757, noteworthy at a 0% level of significance. Hence, hypothesis (Ha1) of the prevalence of affiliation amongst beliefs and financial behavior is not rejected.

Association for Financial Behavior and Attitudes

Referring to table_3, the R-squared value, in this case, is 0.406. The financial attitudes and financial behavior were tested for causation with an F-value of 210.002, noteworthy at 0% (refer to Table 3), indicating a high fit. The coefficient value of financial beliefs is .761, implying one component modification in attitude leading to. Seven hundred sixty-one units change in financial behavior. Further, the β value is 0.637, and the t-test value is 14.491 at a 0% level of significance. Hence, hypothesis (Ha2) of the prevalence of affiliation amongst attitudes and financial behavior is not rejected.

Association for Financial Behavior and Goals

The R-squared value, in this case, is 0.384. The financial goals and financial behavior were tested for causation with the F-value of 191.474, noteworthy at 0% (refer to table_ 3), indicating high fit. The coefficient value of financial goals is .664, implying one component modification in attitude leading to 664 units' changes in Financial behavior. The β value is 0.620, and the t-value is 13.837, noteworthy at a 0% level of significance. Hence, hypothesis (Ha3) of the prevalence of affiliation amongst goals and financial behavior is not rejected.

Association for Financial Behavior, Beliefs, Attitudes, and Goals

After an individual variable-wise causality check, the combined effect of beliefs, attitudes, and Goals on financial behavior is checked to understand if financial behavior alters because of the combined effect. Referring to table_3, the adjusted R-squared value, in this case, is 0.517. The financial beliefs, attitudes, and financial goals tested for causation fit with financial behavior with an F-test value of 110.842, noteworthy at 0% (refer to Table 3), indicating a high fit. Coefficient values for financial beliefs, attitudes, and goals are -.149, .587, .418, respectively, indicating a unit change in financial beliefs, attitudes, and goals would lead to -.149, .587, .418 units change in financial behavior, respectively, by each. Further, it was found that the β values of -.109, .534, and .391 tested through t-test values -1.091, 5.095, 8.391 were noteworthy at 0.276, 0.000, 0.000 level of significance. Hence, hypothesis (Ha4) of the prevalence of affiliation amongst attitudes, beliefs, goals, and financial behavior is not rejected for goals and attitudes.

DISCUSSION

The study was done with a heterogeneous sample of 309 respondents who belonged to different backgrounds, and ages, differing in level of education, profession, the experience of investment as well as belonging to different genders. Exploratory factor analysis resulted in a single factor for belief. Belief has a noteworthy association with financial behavior and further on the thinking of the individual, in turn, affecting the financial behavior of an individual (Bikhchandani & Sharma, 2000) Beliefs likewise contribute to the formation of the attitude of an individual toward money and, in turn, lead to the healthy financial status of a person (Henager & Cude, 2016). The present study found a constructive connotation between beliefs and financial behavior (Kaur & Shukla, 2016). Thus, for investors, their financial belief is a definite determiner of their financial behavior.

A variable-naming attitude resulted in five factors (mentioned above) and has a positive affiliation with financial behavior. Good financial behavior is developed through an upright and appropriate financial attitude. Causality tests resulted in a positive connection between attitude and financial behavior. The results are homogenous to the work done by (Dolan et al., 2012).

The variable naming Goals has five factors, namely: "budgeting, saving, investing, debt management, and other aspects related to personal money," following which personal goals are achieved (Kahneman et al., 1997). Financial goals play a crucial part in deciding the personal finances of an individual. These elements show the dynamics of the beliefs, attitudes, goals, and financial behavior of investors (Andrews & Bategeka, 2013; Dolan et al., 2012; Kaur & Shukla, 2016)

The joint effect of financial belief, attitude, and goals on financial behavior showed that beliefs have an adverse and less noteworthy impact on financial behavior. However, attitude and goals still have a substantial impact on finances, suggesting that even if one has the right attitude towards finances and has financial goals set, beliefs can act as a hindrance in displaying correct financial behavior.

CONCLUSION

The study in question focused on financial behavior in 309 respondents, thus was an attempt at a cross-sectional and heterogeneous study population in terms of age, education level, professional activity, level of experience in investment, and gender. The study situates beliefs, attitudes, and financial goals at the helm of financial behavior with special regard to the AI era.

To start with, why was the present research required? Initially, existing assumptions and techniques (Kahneman, 2003) leave a substantial extent of the behavior change, past the impact of rational expectations (Baker & Wurgler, 2007). Human decisions are affected by the restrained ups and downs going on in the surroundings. These changes are to be incorporated into the research work. Hence, the present research is done to come up with novel dimensions of belief, attitude, financial goals, and financial behavior, which are valid in the current AI times' thought processes and perspectives.

This article joins proof from scholarly research (discussed below), and contextual analyses to show that it is feasible to make modifications in the attitudes, goals, and beliefs in the surroundings wherein choices are taken in such a manner as to make financial ability. The results of the work are applied to the broader group of investor population.

There is less clarity in information on the financial behavior of investors, it makes it hard to detect, measure, and find directly.

Simple linear regression results show individually that each variable, belief, goal, and attitude, noticeably affects the financial behavior of an investor. It's found that taking all variables of the study together for effect, belief has a negative and an in-noteworthy impact on the behavior of investors. The rest two variables, i.e., goals and attitude, have a remarkable effect on financial behavior. The causation test result shows that financial behavior is dependent upon the beliefs, attitudes, and goals of the investors. Beliefs, attitudes, and goals help in developing a positive financing activity at times. Financial knowledge of a high level, flexibility, and attitude toward the goals, as per the previous researchers, are all significant factors contributing to positive financial behavior, which leads to positive financial activity, dealing, and understanding, respectively (Camerer & Loewenstein, 2004).

The time of the AI global era has numerous progressions of nations; the world has constructive and antagonistic effects on individuals' monetary behavior to supply their everyday necessities of life (Kahneman & Tversky, 1984). Earlier, financial decisions were taken considering perceived information rather than objective information (Hastings et al., 2013). In the present context, the results are apt as investors are literate, and they have a focused attitude toward financial decisions and set specific goals, affecting financial behavior. Financial advice shapes Attitudes (Kahneman et al., 1997). However, a low level of financial knowledge may also lead to attitudinal bias (Kumar & Goyal, 2023). Hence, attitudes are more influential rather beliefs. Financial goals keep changing in the current AI world.

The goals that had something on a priority may not be in the present (van Raaij, 2016). Individuals make sound money-related choices; individuals ought to the furnished with great budgetary information and attitudes (Ritter, 2003). Attitude determines the accepted financial behavior. Hence, the outcomes have inferences for individuals to understand his/her financial behavior and for therapists to understand the roles of beliefs, goals, and attitudes as determinants of financial behavior. It will help them to design the investment portfolio of an individual as well as develop convincing strategies for investment. Analysts ought to perceive that every individual's financial history, beliefs, attitudes, as well as goals influence how they consider cash, which can impact their capacity to allocate funds to a accomplice. Counselors help individuals mitigate monetary pressure, improve budgetary connections, and eventually upgrade conjugal quality. They have a role in shaping the attitude of the investors by increasing financial awareness.

In a domain where the range and the intricacy of financial items keep on expanding, people create a proper comprehension of the universe of the fund to have the option to make decisions that are generally suitable to their financial objectives and needs. This comprehension is mentioned as financial literacy.

Using the articles in the review as the base, we have summed up the experiences built up by the researchers in different works done in approximately two decades of research, which have supported the inferences drawn in the present work and the relationship developed here. The results add to the theoretical literature available on investors' financial goals, attitudes, beliefs, and financial behavior. The scholars have emphasized the association of these variables.

Even in the age of throwaway financial tools and applications, nevertheless, cognitions involving beliefs, attitudes, and goals have a marked bearing on financial behavior. In contrast, what has been referred to as beliefs may sometimes be a hindrance to healthier financial practice in the sense of its contribution to the variable. Therefore, while designing and implementing financial education and AI literacy, it is crucial to pay special attention to attitudes toward financial behavior and establish realistic financial objectives regarding financial plans and financial choices.

LIMITATIONS & IMPLICATIONS

There has been little research on when and how investors secure information on money and the monetary framework by and large, or how much beliefs and attitudes continue into utilization exercises as adults. The answers to the questions related to family financial choices. Individuals' age & their cash engagement, participation in money-related exercises, and socialization operators significantly affect individuals' cash convictions, beliefs, attitudes, and money goals, all remain almost unexplored or less explored. The subject of how these examples have changed throughout the years should be to. No investigations have investigated if individuals relate to any of the recommended money characters. Also, little thought about purchasing practices and how they have changed over the years.

This study is a useful contribution for various financial institutions, researchers, and investors as it evaluates the impact of three major contributors, beliefs, attitudes, and goals, on financial behavior in the AI era. It provides additional support to the works done previously on beliefs, attitudes, goals, and financial behavior (Singh & Gupta, 2015; Ammerman, Stueve, & Hayward, 2019; Nelson, Smith, Shelton, & Richards, 2015; Klontz and Klontz, 2009; Sabri and Zakaria, 2015; Seijts et al., 2004). This study is a useful contribution for various financial institutions, researchers, and investors as it evaluates the impact of beliefs, attitudes, and goals on financial behavior in the present times.

From financial advocates, money-related specialists, and budgetary mentors, it appears that investors may hold potentially dangerous beliefs about money. This may impact their capacity to accomplish money-related objectives and autonomous budgetary security. As per the results, it is beyond the realm of imagination to expect to decide if money beliefs go before financial education and salary accomplishment, or whether the training at lower levels and income leads to specific convictions and demeanors about money. One of the fundamental attitudes that individuals must get to work is to manage cash. There has been little research on when and how investors secure information on money and the monetary framework by and large, or how much beliefs and attitudes continue into utilization exercises as behavior formation as adults.

The items (factors of belief, attitudes, goals, and financial behavior) found in the study may be good starting points for researchers, academicians, and experts who are very keen on this research area. They may engage their clients in counseling and the therapeutic process by focusing on these factors. Such money beliefs, attitudinal factors, goal-related aspects, and behavioral determinants can act as a useful resource for them to use for investors facing problems in financial management. They may help their clients to find out and develop habits consistent with strong beliefs, reinforcing positive money attitudes, setting achievable money goals, and showing appropriate financial behavior.

The research work is descriptive research, done with a sample of 309 respondents who have invested in one or the other financial instruments. The area can be explored initially by conducting experimental research, which may explain the behavior described above in terms of causative association. Further, descriptive research can get real-world results. The present work involves checking of reliability of instruments and establishing face validity. Further, the research advancement can be done by the involvement of finding construct reliability and discriminant validity. Further, manipulation checks and taking care of heterogeneous population samples may improve the results of the study as the respondents belonged to different ages, genders, and education levels, were located at different places, and were inattentive to respondents while filling data. The work can be replicated in different countries to see the new associations of the variables as investors of different nations may differ in beliefs, attitudes, goals, and behavior formation.

REFERENCES

Acquisti, A., Taylor, C., & Wagman, L. (2016). The economics of privacy. *Journal of Economic Literature*, *54*(2), 442–492.

Aggarwal, R., Faccio, M., Guedhami, O., & Kwok, C. C. (2016). Culture and finance: An introduction. *Journal of Corporate Finance*, *41*, 466–474.

Ameliawati, M., & Setiyani, R. (2018). The influence of financial attitude, financial socialization, and financial experience to financial management behavior with financial literacy as the mediation variable. *KnE Social Sciences*, *3*(10), 811–823. DOI: 10.18502/kss.v3i10.3174

Ammerman, D. A., Stueve, C., & Hayward, S. (2019). Debt, religious beliefs, and life satisfaction. *Journal of Financial Therapy*, *10*(2). Advance online publication. DOI: 10.4148/1944-9771.1195

Andrews, M., & Bategeka, L. "Overcoming the limits of institutional reform in Uganda," SSRN *Electronic Journal*, 2013. doi: DOI: 10.2139/ssrn.2209465

Andrews, M., Pritchett, L., & Woolcock, M. (2017). *Building State Capability: Evidence, Analysis, Action*. Oxford Univ. Press.

Anthony, R., Ezat, W. S., Junid, S. A., & Moshiri, H. (2011). Financial management attitude and practice among the medical practitioners in public and private medical service in Malaysia. *International Journal of Business and Management*, *6*(8), 105–113.

Antonides, G., de Groot, I. M., & van Raaij, W. F. (2011). Mental budgeting and the management of household finance. *Journal of Economic Psychology*, *32*(4), 546–555.

Ariely, D., Loewenstein, G., & Prelec, D. (2003). Coherent arbitrariness: Stable demand curves without stable preferences. *The Quarterly Journal of Economics*, *118*(1), 73–106.

Baker, M., & Wurgler, J. (2007). Investor sentiment in the stock market. *The Journal of Economic Perspectives*, *21*(2), 129–152.

Ballara, N. B. (2023). The power of social validation: A literature review on how likes, comments, and shares shape user behavior on social media. *International Journal of Research Publication and Reviews*, *4*(7), 3355–3367.

Barber, B. M., & Odean, T. (2001). Boys will be boys: Gender, overconfidence, and common stock investment. *The Quarterly Journal of Economics*, *116*(1), 261–292.

Bikhchandani, S., & Sharma, S. (2000). Herd behavior in financial markets. *IMF Staff Papers*, *47*(3), 279–310.

Camerer, C., Babcock, L., Loewenstein, G., & Thaler, R. (1997). Labor supply of New York City cabdrivers: One day at a time. *The Quarterly Journal of Economics*, *112*(2), 407–441.

Camerer, C., & Loewenstein, G. (2004). *Behavioral economics: Past, present, future*. Advances in Behavioral Economics.

Chandra, A., & Kumar, R. (2011). "Determinants of individual investor behaviour: An orthogonal linear transformation approach," *Munich Personal RePEc Archive (MPRA)*, Paper No. 29722, [Online]. Available: https://mpra.ub.uni-muenchen.de/29722

Crawford, V. P., & Meng, J. "New York City cabdrivers' labor supply revisited: Reference-dependent preferences with rational-expectations targets for hours and income," SSRN *Electronic Journal*, 2010.

Dholakia, U., Tam, L., Yoon, S., & Wong, N. (2016). The ant and the grasshopper: Understanding personal saving orientation of consumers. *The Journal of Consumer Research*, *43*(1), 134–155.

DiFonzo, N., & Bordia, P. (1997). Rumor and prediction: Making sense (but losing dollars) in the stock market. *Organizational Behavior and Human Decision Processes*, *71*(3), 329–353.

Dolan, P., Hallsworth, M., Halpern, D., King, D., Metcalfe, R., & Vlaev, I. (2012). Influencing behaviour: The mindspace way. *Journal of Economic Psychology*, *33*(1), 264–277.

Duflo, E., & Saez, E. (2003). The role of information and social interactions in retirement plan decisions: Evidence from a randomized experiment. *The Quarterly Journal of Economics*, *118*(3), 815–842.

Fama, E. (1970). Efficient capital markets: A review of theory and empirical work. *The Journal of Finance*, *25*(2), 383–417.

Farber, H. S. (2008). Reference-dependent preferences and labor supply: The case of New York City taxi drivers. *The American Economic Review*, *98*(3), 1069–1082.

Friedman, M., & Savage, L. (1948). The utility analysis of choices involving risk. *Journal of Political Economy*, *56*(4), 279–304.

Furnham, A. (1984). Many sides of the coin: The psychology of money usage. *Personality and Individual Differences*, *5*(5), 501–509.

Goldstein, D. G., Johnson, E. J., & Sharpe, W. F. (2008). Choosing outcomes versus choosing products: Consumer-focused retirement investment advice. *The Journal of Consumer Research*, *35*(3), 440–456.

Gupta, K. L. (1970). Personal saving in developing nations: Further evidence. *The Economic Record*, *46*(2), 243–249.

Hastings, J. S., Madrian, B. C., & Skimmyhorn, W. L. (2013). Financial literacy, financial education, and economic outcomes. *Annual Review of Economics*, *5*(1), 347–373. PMID: 23991248

Hayhoe, C. R., & Wilhelm, M. S. (1998). Modeling perceived economic well-being in a family setting: A gender perspective. *Financial Counseling and Planning*, *9*, 21–34.

Heckman, J. J. (1976). The common structure of statistical models of truncation, sample selection, and limited dependent variables and a simple estimator for such models. *Annals of Economic and Social Measurement*, *5*(4), 475–492.

Henager, A., & Cude, C. R. (2016). Financial literacy and long- and short-term financial behavior in different age groups. *Financial Counseling and Planning*, *27*(1), 3–19.

Kahneman, D. (2003). Maps of bounded rationality: Psychology for behavioral economics. *The American Economic Review*, *93*(5), 1449–1475.

Kahneman, D. (2003). A perspective on judgment and choice: Mapping bounded rationality. *The American Psychologist*, *58*(9), 697–720. PMID: 14584987

Kahneman, D., Knetsch, J. L., & Thaler, R. (1990). Experimental tests of the endowment effect and the Coase theorem. *Journal of Political Economy*, *98*(6), 1325–1348.

Kahneman, D., & Tversky, A. (1979). Prospect theory: An analysis of decision under risk. *Econometrica*, *47*(2), 263–292.

Kahneman, D., & Tversky, A. (1984). Choices, values, and frames. *The American Psychologist*, *39*(4), 341–350.

Kahneman, D., Wakker, P. P., & Sarin, R. (1997). Back to Bentham? Explorations of experienced utility. *The Quarterly Journal of Economics*, *112*(2), 375–405.

Kaur, M., & Vohra, T. (2014). Understanding individual investor's behavior: A review of empirical evidences. *Pacific Business Review International*, *6*(6), 37–47.

Kaur, S., & Shukla, M. A. (2016). Behavioral finance: A review. *International Journal of Management and Applied Science*, *2*(11), 104–107.

Kemp, C. (2018). Money attitudes, financial literacy, and financial behaviour. *Journal of Financial Education, 44*(1–2), 1–14.

Kumar, R., & Goyal, A. (2023). Behavioral biases in investment decision making–a systematic literature review. *Qualitative Research in Financial Markets, 15*(1), 1–24.

Kumar, S., Charles, M. R., & Goyal, P. (2020). Financial literacy, behavioral biases, and investor performance: Evidence from India. *Journal of Behavioral and Experimental Finance, 28*, 100414.

Laibson, D. (1997). Golden eggs and hyperbolic discounting. *The Quarterly Journal of Economics, 112*(2), 443–477.

Lusardi, A., & Mitchell, O. S. (2007). Financial literacy and retirement preparedness: Evidence and implications for financial education. *Business Economics (Cleveland, Ohio), 42*(1), 35–44.

Madrian, S., & Shea, D. (2001). The power of suggestion: Inertia in 401(k) participation and savings behavior. *The Quarterly Journal of Economics, 116*(4), 1149–1187.

Montford, J., & Goldsmith, C. (2016). How gender and financial self-efficacy influence investment risk-taking. *International Journal of Consumer Studies, 40*(1), 101–106.

Nofsinger, J. (2005). Social mood and financial economics. *Journal of Behavioral Finance, 6*(3), 144–160.

Norvilitis, M., Szablicki, M., & Wilson, S. (2003). Factors influencing levels of credit-card debt in college students. *Journal of Applied Social Psychology, 33*(5), 935–947.

Odean, T. (1998). Are investors reluctant to realize their losses? *The Journal of Finance, 53*(5), 1775–1798.

Oehler, D., Horn, M., & Wedlich, U. (2020). Young adults' use of mobile payment services: An empirical analysis of the moderating influence of consumer financial knowledge. *Journal of Behavioral and Experimental Finance, 28*, 100404.

Olsen, J. P. (2002). The many faces of Europeanization. *Journal of Common Market Studies, 40*(5), 921–952.

Ritter, J. R. (2003). Behavioral finance. *Pacific-Basin Finance Journal, 11*(4), 429–437.

Shiller, R. (2003). From efficient markets theory to behavioral finance. *The Journal of Economic Perspectives, 17*(1), 83–104.

Simon, H. (1955). A behavioral model of rational choice. *The Quarterly Journal of Economics*, *69*(1), 99–118.

Simon, H. (1956). Rational choice and the structure of the environment. *Psychological Review*, *63*(2), 129–138. PMID: 13310708

Thaler, R. (1999). Mental accounting matters. *Journal of Behavioral Decision Making*, *12*(3), 183–206.

Thaler, R. H. (1980). Toward a positive theory of consumer choice. *Journal of Economic Behavior & Organization*, *1*(1), 39–60.

Thaler, R. H. (2000). From homo economicus to homo sapiens. *The Journal of Economic Perspectives*, *14*(1), 133–141.

Thaler, R. H., & Johnson, E. J. (1990). Gambling with the house money and trying to break even: The effects of prior outcomes on risky choice. *Management Science*, *36*(6), 643–660.

Tversky, A., & Kahneman, D. (1991). Loss aversion in riskless choice: A reference-dependent model. *The Quarterly Journal of Economics*, *106*(4), 1039–1061.

Weber, M. (1999). Stock market participation and investors' risk-taking behavior. *Journal of Banking & Finance*, *23*(1), 27–56.

Weber, M., & Zuchel, H. (2005). How do prior outcomes affect risk attitude? Comparing escalation of commitment and the house-money effect. *Decision Analysis*, *2*(1), 30–43.

Compilation of References

Acquisti, A., Taylor, C., & Wagman, L. (2016). The economics of privacy. *Journal of Economic Literature*, *54*(2), 442–492.

Adams, C. A., & Abhayawansa, S. (2022). Connecting the COVID-19 pandemic, sustainable development, and responsible corporate reporting. Sustainability Accounting. *Management and Policy Journal*, *13*(1), 1–16. DOI: 10.1108/SAMPJ-05-2021-0196

Adams, J. C., Nishikawa, T., & Rao, R. P. (2018). Mutual fund performance, management teams, and boards. *Journal of Banking & Finance*, *92*, 358–368. DOI: 10.1016/j.jbankfin.2016.09.006

Adhav, M. S. M., & Chauhan, P. M. (2015). Comparative study of mutual funds of selected Indian companies. *International Journal of Science. Technology & Management*, *4*(2), 2394–1537.

Affandi, H., & Malik, Q. (2020). Financial inclusion and financial literacy in low income group in emerging economy. *Journal of Accounting and Finance in Emerging Economies*, *6*(4), 1005–1013. DOI: 10.26710/jafee.v6i4.1451

Aggarwal, R. (2000). Stabilization activities by underwriters after initial public offerings. *The Journal of Finance*, *55*(3), 1075–1103. DOI: 10.1111/0022-1082.00241

Aggarwal, R., Faccio, M., Guedhami, O., & Kwok, C. C. (2016). Culture and finance: An introduction. *Journal of Corporate Finance*, *41*, 466–474.

Agrawal, M., Goyal, A., Akhtar, A., & Abbas, H. (2024). Green Bond: A Government Initiative Towards Sustainable Finance. In *Issues of Sustainability in AI and New-Age Thematic Investing* (pp. 124–137). IGI Global Scientific Publishing. DOI: 10.4018/979-8-3693-3282-5.ch008

Agrawal, A. (2024). IPO performance anomaly: Evidence from new-aged ventures and loss-making listings in India. *Journal of Advances in Management Research, 21*(3), 421–448. DOI: 10.1108/JAMR-07-2023-0197

Aguinis, H., & Glavas, A. (2012). What We Know and Don't Know About Corporate Social Responsibility: A Review and Research Agenda: A Review and Research Agenda. *Journal of Management, 38*(4), 932–968. DOI: 10.1177/0149206311436079

Ahen, F., & Amankwah-Amoah, J. (2018). Institutional voids and the philanthropization of CSR practices: Insights from developing economies. *Sustainability (Basel), 10*(7), 2400. DOI: 10.3390/su10072400

Ahmed, S., Alshater, M. M., El Ammari, A., & Hammami, H. (2022). Artificial intelligence and machine learning in finance: A bibliometric review. *Research in International Business and Finance, 61*, 101646. DOI: 10.1016/j.ribaf.2022.101646

Ajayi, A. D., Hayo, L., Iliya, J. P., & Hasegawa, H. (2025). Exploring voluntary carbon markets as a tool for sustainable agriculture in Nigeria: Opportunities and challenges. *Scientific African, 29*, e02923. DOI: 10.1016/j.sciaf.2025.e02923

Ajzen, I. (1991). The Theory of Planned Behaviour. *Organizational Behavior and Human Decision Processes, 50*(2), 179–211. DOI: 10.1016/0749-5978(91)90020-T

Ajzen, I. (2002). Perceived behavioural control, self-efficacy, locus of control, and the theory of planned behavior1. *Journal of Applied Social Psychology, 32*(4), 665–683. https://people.umass.edu/aizen/pubs/pbc.pdf. DOI: 10.1111/j.1559-1816.2002.tb00236.x

Albuquerque, R., Koskinen, Y., & Zhang, C. (2019). Corporate social responsibility and firm risk: Theory and empirical evidence. *Management Science, 65*(10), 4451–4469. DOI: 10.1287/mnsc.2018.3043

Allen, F., & Faulhaber, G. R. (1989). Signaling by underpricing in the IPO market. *Journal of Financial Economics, 23*(2), 303–323. DOI: 10.1016/0304-405X(89)90060-3

Alonso, A., & Marqués, J. M. (2019). Financial innovation for a sustainable economy. Banco de España Occasional Paper, (1916).

Aloysius, J. E., & Tamilmaran, D. J. C. (2023). A study on the performance of Indian IPOs during 2012–2022. In *Studies in Systems* (pp. 725–732). Decision and Control., DOI: 10.1007/978-3-031-42085-6_62

Alshareef, M. N. (2025). Artificial intelligence-enhanced environmental, social, and governance (ESG) disclosure quality and financial performance. *Sustainability, 17*(16), 7421. DOI: 10.3390/su17167421

Ameliawati, M., & Setiyani, R. (2018). The influence of financial attitude, financial socialization, and financial experience to financial management behavior with financial literacy as the mediation variable. *KnE Social Sciences, 3*(10), 811–823. DOI: 10.18502/kss.v3i10.3174

Ammerman, D. A., Stueve, C., & Hayward, S. (2019). Debt, religious beliefs, and life satisfaction. *Journal of Financial Therapy, 10*(2). Advance online publication. DOI: 10.4148/1944-9771.1195

Anderson, B., & Bernauer, T. (2016). How much carbon offsetting and where? Implications of efficiency, effectiveness, and ethicality considerations for public opinion formation. *Energy Policy, 94*, 387–395. DOI: 10.1016/j.enpol.2016.04.016

Anderson, J. C., & Gerbing, D. W. (1988). Structural equation modelling in practice: A review and recommended two-step approach. *Psychological Bulletin, 103*(3), 411–423. DOI: 10.1037/0033-2909.103.3.411

Andrews, M., & Bategeka, L. "Overcoming the limits of institutional reform in Uganda," SSRN *Electronic Journal*, 2013. doi: DOI: 10.2139/ssrn.2209465

Andrews, M., Pritchett, L., & Woolcock, M. (2017). *Building State Capability: Evidence, Analysis, Action*. Oxford Univ. Press.

Anindyastri, R., Lestari, W. D., & Sholahuddin, M. (2022). The influence of financial technology (fintech) on the financial performance of Islamic banking (Study on Islamic Banking listed on the Indonesia Stock Exchange Period 2016-2020). *Benefit: Jurnal Manajemen Dan Bisnis, 7*(1), 80–92. DOI: 10.23917/benefit.v7i1.18051

Annadurai, D. A. (2014). Effectiveness of green banking technology of the commercial banks in India. *International Journal of Research in Commerce and Management*. https://ijrcm.org.in/article_info.php?article_id=5016

Anthony, R., Ezat, W. S., Junid, S. A., & Moshiri, H. (2011). Financial management attitude and practice among the medical practitioners in public and private medical service in Malaysia. *International Journal of Business and Management, 6*(8), 105–113.

Antonides, G., de Groot, I. M., & van Raaij, W. F. (2011). Mental budgeting and the management of household finance. *Journal of Economic Psychology, 32*(4), 546–555.

Ariely, D., Loewenstein, G., & Prelec, D. (2003). Coherent arbitrariness: Stable demand curves without stable preferences. *The Quarterly Journal of Economics, 118*(1), 73–106.

Arvidsson, S. (2018). How are stakeholder relations communicated in sustainability reports? A longitudinal and cross-country focus* (book chapter). In *Challenges in Managing Sustainable Business (Chap. 1).DOI: 10.1007/978-3-319-93266-8_1

Arya, U., Tiwari, R., & Jain, A. (2024). Sustainability of IPO returns in the Indian equity market. In *Advances in Business Strategy and Competitive Advantage* (pp. 57–70). https://doi.org/DOI: 10.4018/979-8-3693-9117-4.ch004

Ashaley-Nikoi, J., & Abbey, E. (2023). Determinants of the level of informality amongst female street food vendors in sub-Saharan Africa: Evidence from two regions in Ghana. *Cities (London, England), 138*, 104359. DOI: 10.1016/j.cities.2023.104359

Ashrafi, M., Magnan, G. M., Adams, M., & Walker, T. R. (2020). Understanding the conceptual evolutionary path and theoretical underpinnings of corporate social responsibility and corporate sustainability. *Sustainability (Basel), 12*(3), 760. DOI: 10.3390/su12030760

Ashraf, M. A. (2023). "Go green" – evaluating the roles of environmental concerns, environmental social norms and green technology in fostering pro-green banking behaviours. *Journal of Financial Reporting and Accounting, 22*(1), 181–203. DOI: 10.1108/JFRA-05-2023-0232

Ashraf, M. A., Joarder, M. H. R., & Ratan, S. R. A. (2019). Consumers' anti-consumption behaviour toward organic food purchase: An analysis using SEM. *British Food Journal, 121*(1), 104–122. DOI: 10.1108/BFJ-02-2018-0072

Aslaksen, H. M., Hildebrandt, C., & Johnsen, H. C. G. (2021). The long-term transformation of the concept of CSR: Towards a more comprehensive emphasis on sustainability. *International Journal of Corporate Social Responsibility, 6*(11), 11. Advance online publication. DOI: 10.1186/s40991-021-00063-9

Aslam, W., Farhat, K., & Arif, I. (2020). Regular to sustainable products: An account of environmentally concerned consumers in a developing economy. *International Journal of Green Energy, 18*(3), 243–257. DOI: 10.1080/15435075.2020.1854266

Atayah, O. F., Najaf, K., Ali, M. H., & Marashdeh, H. (2024). Sustainability, market performance and FinTech firms. *Meditari Accountancy Research, 32*(2), 317–345. DOI: 10.1108/MEDAR-08-2021-1405

Atkinson, A., & Messy, F. (2013). Promoting financial inclusion through financial education:

Atlantic Council. (2024). *How digital public infrastructure can support financial inclusion*. Atlantic Council.

Aureli, S., Magnaghi, E., & Salvatori, F. (2020). The role of regulation in sustainability reporting quality: Evidence from the EU directive. *Accounting in Europe*, *17*(3), 223–250. DOI: 10.1080/17449480.2020.1768929

Azimi, M. (2022). New insights into the impact of financial inclusion on economic growth: A global perspective. *PLoS One*, *17*(11), 17. DOI: 10.1371/journal.pone.0277730 PMID: 36395150

Badgley, G., Freeman, J., Hamman, J. J., Haya, B., Trugman, A. T., Anderegg, W. R. L., & Cullenward, D. (2021). Systematic over crediting in California's forest carbon offsets program. *Global Change Biology*, *28*(4), 1433–1445. DOI: 10.1111/gcb.15943 PMID: 34668621

Bagozzi, R. P., & Yi, Y. (1988). On the Evaluation of Structural Equation Models. *Journal of the Academy of Marketing Science*, *16*(1), 74–94. DOI: 10.1007/BF02723327

Baker, M., Bergstresser, D., Serafeim, G., & Wurgler, J. (2022). The Pricing and Ownership of US Green Bonds. *Annual Review of Financial Economics*, *14*(Volume 14, 2022), 415–437. DOI: 10.1146/annurev-financial-111620-014802

Baker, M., & Wurgler, J. (2007). Investor sentiment in the stock market. *The Journal of Economic Perspectives*, *21*(2), 129–152.

Ballara, N. B. (2023). The power of social validation: A literature review on how likes, comments, and shares shape user behavior on social media. *International Journal of Research Publication and Reviews*, *4*(7), 3355–3367.

Bandura, A. (1982). *Self-Efficacy Mechanism in Human Agency.*

Barajas, A., Beck, T., Belhaj, M., & Ben Naceur, S. (2020). *Financial inclusion: What have we learned so far? What do we have to learn?* (IMF Working Paper No. 2020/157). International Monetary Fund.

Barber, B. M., & Odean, T. (2001). Boys will be boys: Gender, overconfidence, and common stock investment. *The Quarterly Journal of Economics*, *116*(1), 261–292.

Barbu, C., Florea, D., Dabija, D., & Barbu, M. (2021). Customer experience in Fintech. *Journal of Theoretical and Applied Electronic Commerce Research*, *16*(5), 1415–1433. DOI: 10.3390/jtaer16050080

Barney, J. (1991). Firm resources and sustained competitive advantage. *Journal of Management*, *17*(1), 99–120. DOI: 10.1177/014920639101700108

Baron, D. P. (1982). A model of the demand for investment banking, advising, and distribution services for new issues. *The Journal of Finance*, *37*(4), 955–976. DOI: 10.1111/j.1540-6261.1982.tb03591.x

Barua, S. K., Varma, J. R., & Venkiteswaran, N. (1991). A regulatory framework for mutual funds. *Economic and Political Weekly*, •••, M55–M59.

Ben-Amar, W., Chang, M., & McIlkenny, P. (2017). Board gender diversity and corporate response to sustainability initiatives. *Journal of Business Ethics*, *142*(2), 369–383. DOI: 10.1007/s10551-015-2759-1

Berg, F., Kölbel, J. F., Pavlova, A., & Rigobon, R. (2022). *ESG confusion and stock returns: Tackling the problem of noise (No. w30562)*. National Bureau of Economic Research. DOI: 10.3386/w30562

Berg, F., Kölbel, J. F., & Rigobon, R. (2022). Aggregate confusion: The divergence of ESG ratings. *Review of Finance*, *26*(6), 1315–1344. DOI: 10.1093/rof/rfac033

Bhatia, S., & Singh, S. (2019). Empowering women through financial inclusion: A study of urban slum. *Vikalpa*, *44*(4), 182–197. DOI: 10.1177/0256090919897809

Bhowmik, S. K. (2012). *Street vendors in the global urban economy*. Routledge. DOI: 10.4324/9780203150542

Bhullar, P. S., Grover, K. L., & Tiwari, R. (2024). IPO underpricing: A comparative analysis of risk factor disclosures in the financial and non-financial sectors. *The Bottom Line (New York, N.Y.)*, *37*(3), 332–350. DOI: 10.1108/BL-04-2023-0123

Bhutta, U. S., Tariq, A., Farrukh, M., Raza, A., & Iqbal, M. K. (2022). Green bonds for sustainable development: Review of literature on development and impact of green bonds. *Technological Forecasting and Social Change*, *175*, 121378. DOI: 10.1016/j.techfore.2021.121378

Bikhchandani, S., & Sharma, S. (2000). Herd behavior in financial markets. *IMF Staff Papers*, *47*(3), 279–310.

Bin-Humam, Y., Braunmiller, J., & Elsaman, M. (2023). Emerging Trends in National Financial Inclusion Strategies that Support Women's Entrepreneurship.

Birindelli, G., Dell'Atti, S., Iannuzzi, A. P., & Savioli, M. (2018). Composition and activity of the board of directors: Impact on ESG performance in the banking sector. *Sustainability (Basel)*, *10*(12), 4699. DOI: 10.3390/su10124699

Bissoondoyal-Bheenick, E., Bennett, S., Lehnherr, R., & Zhong, A. (2024). ESG rating disagreement: Implications and aggregation approaches. *International Review of Economics & Finance*, *96*, 103532. DOI: 10.1016/j.iref.2024.103532

Bolognesi, E., Burchi, A., Goodell, J. W., & Paltrinieri, A. (2025). Stakeholders and regulatory pressure on ESG disclosure. *International Review of Financial Analysis*, *103*, 104145. DOI: 10.1016/j.irfa.2025.104145

Bolton, P., & Kacperczyk, M. (2021). Do investors care about carbon risk? *Journal of Financial Economics*, *142*(2), 517–549. DOI: 10.1016/j.jfineco.2021.05.008

Bonett, D. G., & Wright, T. A. (2015). Cronbach's alpha reliability: Interval estimation, hypothesis testing, and sample size planning. *Journal of Organizational Behavior*, *36*(1), 3–15. DOI: 10.1002/job.1960

Bose, S., Khan, H. Z., Rashid, A., & Islam, S. (2017). What drives green banking disclosure? An institutional and corporate governance perspective. *Asia Pacific Journal of Management*, *35*(2), 501–527. DOI: 10.1007/s10490-017-9528-x

Bouattour, A., Kalai, M., & Helali, K. (2024). The non-linear relationship between ESG performance and bank stability in the digital era: New evidence from a regime-switching approach. *Humanities & Social Sciences Communications*, *11*(1), 1–17. DOI: 10.1057/s41599-024-03876-8

Boulton, T. J., Smart, S. B., & Zutter, C. J. (2010). IPO underpricing and international corporate governance. *Journal of International Business Studies*, *41*(2), 206–226. DOI: 10.1057/jibs.2009.38

Bouteraa, M., Raja Hisham, R. R. I., & Zainol, Z. (2022). Challenges affecting bank consumers' intention to adopt green banking technology in the UAE: A UTAUT-based mixed-methods approach. *Journal of Islamic Marketing*, *14*(10), 2466–2501. DOI: 10.1108/JIMA-02-2022-0039

Bouteraa, M., Raja Hisham, R. R. I., & Zainol, Z.BOUTERAA. (2021). Exploring determinants of customers' intention to adopt green banking: qualitative investigation. *Journal of Sustainability Science and Management*, *16*(3), 187–203. DOI: 10.46754/jssm.2021.04.014

Bowen, H. R. (1953). *Social responsibilities of the businessman*. Harper & Row.

Broekhoff, D., Gillenwater, M., Colbert-Sangree, T., & Cage, P. (2019). *Securing climate benefit: A guide to using carbon offsets*. Stockholm Environment Institute & Greenhouse Gas Management Institute. https://www.offsetguide.org

Bromley, R. (2000). Street vending and public policy: A global review. *The International Journal of Sociology and Social Policy*, *20*(1/2), 1–28. DOI: 10.1108/01443330010789052

Brown, S. J., & Warner, J. B. (1985). Using daily stock returns. *Journal of Financial Economics*, *14*(1), 3–31. DOI: 10.1016/0304-405X(85)90042-X

Buallay, A. (2019). Is sustainability reporting (ESG) associated with performance? Evidence from the European banking sector. *Management of Environmental Quality*, *30*(1), 98–115. DOI: 10.1108/MEQ-12-2017-0149

Buchak, G., Matvos, G., Piskorski, T., & Seru, A. (2018). Fintech, regulatory arbitrage, and the rise of shadow banks. *Journal of Financial Economics*, *130*(3), 453–483. DOI: 10.1016/j.jfineco.2018.03.011

Bukhari, S. A. A., Hashim, F., & Amran, A. (2022). Pathways towards Green Banking adoption: Moderating role of top management commitment. *International Journal of Ethics and Systems*, *38*(2), 286–315. DOI: 10.1108/IJOES-05-2021-0110

Bukhari, S. A. A., Hashim, F., Amran, A. B., & Hyder, K. (2019). Green Banking and Islam: Two sides of the same coin. *Journal of Islamic Marketing*, *11*(4), 977–1000. DOI: 10.1108/JIMA-09-2018-0154

Busch, T., Bauer, R., & Orlitzky, M. (2016). Sustainable development and financial markets: Old paths and new avenues. *Business & Society*, *55*(3), 303–329. DOI: 10.1177/0007650315570701

Busse, C. (2016). Doing well by doing good? The self-interest of buying firms and sustainable supply chain management. *The Journal of Supply Chain Management*, *52*(2), 28–47. DOI: 10.1111/jscm.12096

Calel, R., & Dechezleprêtre, A. (2016). Environmental policy and directed technological change: Evidence from the European carbon market. *The Review of Economics and Statistics*, *98*(1), 173–191. DOI: 10.1162/REST_a_00470

Camerer, C., Babcock, L., Loewenstein, G., & Thaler, R. (1997). Labor supply of New York City cabdrivers: One day at a time. *The Quarterly Journal of Economics*, *112*(2), 407–441.

Camerer, C., & Loewenstein, G. (2004). *Behavioral economics: Past, present, future*. Advances in Behavioral Economics.

Cames, M., Harthan, R. O., Füssler, J., Lazarus, M., Lee, C. M., Erickson, P., & Spalding-Fecher, R. (2016). *How additional is the Clean Development Mechanism? Analysis of the application of current tools and proposed alternatives* (Study prepared for DG CLIMA). Öko-Institut. https://ec.europa.eu/clima/system/files/2017-04/clean_dev_mechanism_en.pdf

Campbell, D. T., & Fiske, D. W. (1959). Convergent and discriminant validation by the multigrain-multimethod matrix. *Psychological Bulletin, 56*(2), 81–105. DOI: 10.1037/h0046016

Campbell, J. L. (2007). Why would corporations behave in socially responsible ways? An institutional theory of corporate social responsibility. *Academy of Management Review, 32*(3), 946–967. DOI: 10.5465/amr.2007.25275684

Carlini, F., Del Gaudio, B. L., Porzio, C., & Previtali, D. (2022). Banks, Fintech and stock returns. *Finance Research Letters, 45*, 102252. DOI: 10.1016/j.frl.2021.102252

Carroll, A. B. (1999). Corporate Social Responsibility: Evolution of a Definitional Construct. *Business & Society, 38*(3), 268–295. DOI: 10.1177/000765039903800303

Carroll, A. B., & Shabana, K. M. (2010). The business case for corporate social responsibility: A review of concepts, research and practice. *International Journal of Management Reviews, 12*(1), 85–105. DOI: 10.1111/j.1468-2370.2009.00275.x

Casey, R. J., & Grenier, J. H. (2015). Understanding and contributing to the enigma of corporate social responsibility (CSR) assurance in the United States. *Auditing, 34*(1), 97–130. DOI: 10.2308/ajpt-50736

CCS. (2022). *Street vendors Act Compliance Index 2022*. Centre for Civil Society.

Chaddha, S., & Jain, S. (2024). Digital transformation of financial sector in India: Evolution, issues and challenges. *International Journal of Advanced Research in Science. Tongxin Jishu, 4*(5), 107–111.

Chakrabarty, K. C. (2013). Financial inclusion in India: Journey so far and way forward. *Address delivered at the Finance Inclusion Conclave*, New Delhi.

Chan, G. (2024). *EY global IPO trends Q2 2024* [Report]. EY. https://www.ey.com/content/dam/ey-unified-site/ey-com/de-de/insights/ipo/documents/ey-global-ipo-trends-report-q2-2024.pdf

Chandra, A., & Kumar, R. (2011). “Determinants of individual investor behaviour: An orthogonal linear transformation approach,” *Munich Personal RePEc Archive (MPRA)*, Paper No. 29722, [Online]. Available: https://mpra.ub.uni-muenchen.de/29722

Chang, E., Chen, C., Chi, J., & Young, M. (2008). IPO underpricing in China: New evidence from the primary and secondary markets. *Emerging Markets Review, 9*(1), 1–16. DOI: 10.1016/j.ememar.2007.06.004

Chan, K. H., Chong, L.-L., & Ng, T. H. (2022). Integrating extended theory of planned behaviour and norm activation model to examine the effects of environmental practices among Malaysian companies. *Journal of Entrepreneurship in Emerging Economies*, *14*(5), 851–873. Advance online publication. DOI: 10.1108/JEEE-08-2021-0317

Charfeddine, L., & Zaouali, S. (2022). The effects of financial inclusion and the business environment in spurring the creation of early-stage firms and supporting established firms. *Journal of Business Research*, *143*, 1–15. DOI: 10.1016/j.jbusres.2022.01.014

Chatterjee, P. (2009). Green brand extension strategy and online communities. *Journal of Systems and Information Technology*, *11*(4), 367–384. DOI: 10.1108/13287260911002503

Chen, H. L., Jegadeesh, N., & Wermers, R. (2000). The value of active mutual fund management: An examination of the stockholdings and trades of fund managers. *Journal of Financial and Quantitative Analysis*, *35*(3), 343–368. DOI: 10.2307/2676208

Cheung, A. W., Evans, E., & Wright, S. (2022). Mandatory ESG disclosure and market pricing of sustainability. *Accounting and Finance*, *62*(4), 5117–5149.

Cheung, H. (2023). Non-monetary double-entry carbon accounting method for entities in emission trading systems. *Journal of Cleaner Production*, *422*, 138475. DOI: 10.1016/j.jclepro.2023.138475

Chitra, V., & Hemalatha, T. (2018). Risk and return analysis of performance of mutual fund schemes in India. *International Journal of Applied Research*, *4*(1), 279–283.

Choi, S. U., & Lee, W. J. (2024). Financial statement comparability and environmental, social, and governance (ESG) performance. *Sustainability (Basel)*, *16*(18), 7993. DOI: 10.3390/su16187993

Christensen, H. B., Hail, L., & Leuz, C. (2021). Mandatory sustainability reporting and firm behavior. *Review of Accounting Studies*, *26*, 1176–1248. DOI: 10.1007/s11142-021-09609-5

Chueca Vergara, C., & Ferruz Agudo, L. (2021). Fintech and sustainability: Do they affect each other? *Sustainability (Basel)*, *13*(13), 7012. DOI: 10.3390/su13137012

Clarkson, P. M., Li, Y., Richardson, G. D., & Vasvari, F. P. (2008). Revisiting the relation between environmental performance and environmental disclosure: An empirical analysis. *Journal of Accounting and Economics*, *45*(1), 116–135. DOI: 10.1016/j.jacceco.2007.02.003

Climate Case Chart. (2025). *Deutsche Umwelthilfe v. Adidas*. Retrieved December 14, 2025, from https://www.climatecasechart.com/non-us-case/deutsche-umwelthilfe-v-adidas

Conca, L., Manta, F., Morrone, D., & Toma, P. (2021). The impact of direct environmental, social, and governance reporting: Empirical evidence in European-listed companies in the agri-food sector. *Business Strategy and the Environment*, *30*(4), 1080–1093. DOI: 10.1002/bse.2672

Cordano, M., & Frieze, I. H. (2000). Pollution reduction preferences of U.S. environmental managers: applying Ajzen's theory of planned behavior. *Academy of Management Journal*, *43*(4), 627–641. DOI: 10.2307/1556358

Cornelli, F., Goldreich, D., & Ljungqvist, A. (2006). Investor sentiment and pre-IPO markets. *The Journal of Finance*, *61*(3), 1187–1216. DOI: 10.1111/j.1540-6261.2006.00870.x

Costa-Climent, R., & Martínez-Climent, C. (2018a). Sustainable finance and the Fintech revolution. *Sustainability*, *10*(8), 1–18.

Costa-Climent, R., & Martínez-Climent, C. (2018b). Sustainable profitability of ethical and conventional banking. *Contemporary Economics*, *12*(4), 519–531.

Coupland, C. (2006). Corporate social and environmental responsibility in web-based reports: Currency in the banking sector? *Critical Perspectives on Accounting*, *17*(7), 865–881. DOI: 10.1016/j.cpa.2005.01.001

Crawford, V. P., & Meng, J. "New York City cabdrivers' labor supply revisited: Reference-dependent preferences with rational-expectations targets for hours and income," SSRN *Electronic Journal*, 2010.

Danisman, G., & Tarazi, A. (2020). Financial inclusion and bank stability: Evidence from Europe. *European Journal of Finance*, *26*(18), 1842–1855. DOI: 10.1080/1351847X.2020.1782958

de Villiers, C., Kuruppu, S., & Dissanayake, D. (2021). A (new) role for business in society and the emergence of CSR accounting. *Journal of Business Research*, *131*, 598–609. DOI: 10.1016/j.jbusres.2020.11.066

Deb, S. G., & Marisetty, V. B. (2010). Information content of IPO grading. *Journal of Banking & Finance*, *34*(9), 2294–2305. DOI: 10.1016/j.jbankfin.2010.02.016

Del Gesso, C., & Lodhi, R. N. (2024). Theories underlying environmental, social and governance (ESG) disclosure: A systematic review of accounting studies. *Journal of Accounting Literature*. Advance online publication. DOI: 10.1108/JAL-08-2023-0143

Delmas, M. A., & Burbano, V. C. (2011). The drivers of greenwashing. *California Management Review, 54*(1), 64–87. DOI: 10.1525/cmr.2011.54.1.64

Delmas, M. A., & Grant, L. E. (2014). Eco-labeling strategies and price-premium: The wine industry puzzle. *Business & Society, 53*(1), 6–44. DOI: 10.1177/0007650310362254

Deloitte. (2023). *Heads up — Global sustainability disclosure standards converge: ISSB finalizes IFRS S1 and S2.* Deloitte Accounting Research Tool. Retrieved December 17, 2025, from

Demirgüç-Kunt, A., Klapper, L., & Singer, D. (2017). Financial inclusion and inclusive growth: A review of recent empirical studies. *The World Bank Research Observer, 32*(2), 238–264.

Deore, P., & Lathia, S. (2019). Streets as Public Spaces: Lessons from Street Vending in Ahmedabad, India. *Urban Planning, 4*(2), 138–153. DOI: 10.17645/up.v4i2.2058

Devine, A., Sanderford, A., & Wang, C. (2024). Sustainability and private equity real estate returns. *The Journal of Real Estate Finance and Economics, 68*(2), 161–187. DOI: 10.1007/s11146-022-09914-z

Dhaliwal, D. S., Li, O. Z., Tsang, A., & Yang, Y. G. (2011). Voluntary nonfinancial disclosure and the cost of equity capital: The initiation of corporate social responsibility reporting. *The Accounting Review, 86*(1), 59–100. DOI: 10.2308/accr.00000005

Dhaliwal, D. S., Radhakrishnan, S., Tsang, A., & Yang, Y. G. (2014). Nonfinancial disclosure and analyst forecast accuracy. *The Accounting Review, 87*(3), 723–759. DOI: 10.2308/accr-10218

Dholakia, U., Tam, L., Yoon, S., & Wong, N. (2016). The ant and the grasshopper: Understanding personal saving orientation of consumers. *The Journal of Consumer Research, 43*(1), 134–155.

Di Vaio, A., Zaffar, A., Chhabra, M., & Balsalobre-Lorente, D. (2024). Carbon accounting and integrated reporting for net-zero business models towards sustainable development: A systematic literature review. *Business Strategy and the Environment, 33*(7), 7216–7240. DOI: 10.1002/bse.3863

DiFonzo, N., & Bordia, P. (1997). Rumor and prediction: Making sense (but losing dollars) in the stock market. *Organizational Behavior and Human Decision Processes, 71*(3), 329–353.

DiMaggio, P. J., & Powell, W. W. (1983). The iron cage revisited: Institutional isomorphism and collective rationality in organizational fields. *American Sociological Review, 48*(2), 147–160. DOI: 10.2307/2095101

Ding, T., Zhou, Y., & Chen, L. (2025). Non-financial factors and financial returns: The impact of linking ESG metrics to executive compensation on corporate financial performance. *Sustainability (Basel), 17*(22), 10220. DOI: 10.3390/su172210220

do Paço, A., & Raposo, M. (2009). "Green" segmentation: An application to the Portuguese consumer market. *Marketing Intelligence & Planning, 27*(3), 364–379. DOI: 10.1108/02634500910955245

Dolan, P., Hallsworth, M., Halpern, D., King, D., Metcalfe, R., & Vlaev, I. (2012). Influencing behaviour: The mindspace way. *Journal of Economic Psychology, 33*(1), 264–277.

Dowling, J., & Pfeffer, J. (1975). Organizational Legitimacy: Social Values and Organizational Behavior. *Pacific Sociological Review, 18*(1), 122–136. DOI: 10.2307/1388226

Dranev, Y., Frolova, K., & Ochirova, E. (2019). The impact of Fintech M&A on stock returns. *Research in International Business and Finance, 48*, 353–364. DOI: 10.1016/j.ribaf.2019.01.012

Drishti IAS. (2022, October 16). *75 new Digital Banking Units in India*. Drishti IAS.

Duflo, E., & Saez, E. (2003). The role of information and social interactions in retirement plan decisions: Evidence from a randomized experiment. *The Quarterly Journal of Economics, 118*(3), 815–842.

Du, P., Huang, S., Hong, Y., & Wu, W. (2022). Can FinTech improve corporate environmental, social, and governance performance? - A study based on the dual path of internal financing constraints and external fiscal incentives. *Frontiers in Environmental Science, 10*, 1061454. DOI: 10.3389/fenvs.2022.1061454

Dyck, A., Lins, K. V., Roth, L., & Wagner, H. F. (2019). Do institutional investors drive corporate social responsibility? *Journal of Financial Economics, 131*(3), 693–714. DOI: 10.1016/j.jfineco.2018.08.013

Dzage, E. J., & Szabados, G. N. (2024). The relationship of corporate social responsibility with business performance—A bibliometric literature review. *Sustainability (Basel), 16*(7), 2637. DOI: 10.3390/su16072637

East & Partners. (2021, July 12). *"Project Carbon" offset platform launched by global bank consortium*. Retrieved December 17, 2025, from https://eastandpartners.com/news/project-carbon-offset-platform-launched-by-global-bank-consortium/

Eccles, R. G., Ioannou, I., & Serafeim, G. (2014). The impact of corporate sustainability on organizational processes and performance. *Management Science*, *60*(11), 2835–2857. DOI: 10.1287/mnsc.2014.1984

Eccles, R. G., & Klimenko, S. (2019). The investor revolution. *Harvard Business Review*, *97*(3), 106–116.

El Ghoul, S., Guedhami, O., Kwok, C. C. Y., & Mishra, D. R. (2011). Does corporate social responsibility affect the cost of capital? *Journal of Financial Economics*, *102*(1), 79–96. DOI: 10.1016/j.jfineco.2011.10.009

El Khoury, R., Nasrallah, N., Hussainey, K., & Assaf, R. (2023). Spillover analysis across Fintech, ESG, and renewable energy indices before and during the Russia-Ukraine war: International evidence. *Journal of International Financial Management & Accounting*, *34*(2), 279–317. DOI: 10.1111/jifm.12179

Elton, E. J., Gruber, M. J., & Blake, C. R. (1996). The persistence of risk-adjusted mutual fund performance. *The Journal of Business*, *69*(2), 133–157. DOI: 10.1086/209685

Emekci, S. (2019). Green consumption behaviours of consumers within the scope of TPB. *Journal of Consumer Marketing*, *36*(3), 410–417. DOI: 10.1108/JCM-05-2018-2694

Equations. (2012). *Women Street vendors and Tourism: Negotiating Lives and Spaces*. Bangalore: Equations, Equitable Tourism.

European Commission. (2011, October 7). *Progress towards achieving the Kyoto objectives* (COM(2011) 624 final; SEC(2011) 1151 final). Retrieved December 18, 2025, from https://eur-lex.europa.eu/legal-content/EN/TXT/?uri=CELEX%3A52011DC0624

European Commission. (2023). *Green claims: New criteria to stop companies from making misleading claims about environmental merits of their products and services*. Directorate-General for Environment. Retrieved December 18, 2025, from https://environment.ec.europa.eu/topics/circular-economy/green-claims_en

Evangelinos, K. I., & Nikolaou, I. E. (2009). Environmental accounting and the banking sector: A framework for measuring environmental-financial risks. *International Journal of Services Sciences*, *2*(3/4), 366. DOI: 10.1504/IJSSCI.2009.026547

EY. (2024). *EY global IPO trends 2024*. https://www.ey.com/content/dam/ey-unified-site/ey-com/en-gl/insights/ipo/documents/ey-gl-ipo-trends-v1-12-2024.pdf

Fama, E. (1970). Efficient capital markets: A review of theory and empirical work. *The Journal of Finance*, *25*(2), 383–417.

Farber, H. S. (2008). Reference-dependent preferences and labor supply: The case of New York City taxi drivers. *The American Economic Review*, *98*(3), 1069–1082.

FASB. (2024). *Proposed Accounting Standards Update: Environmental credits and environmental credit obligations (Topic 818) [Exposure draft]*. FASB. https://www.fasb.org

Favara, G., Ivanov, I., & Rezende, M. (2021). GSIB surcharges and bank lending: Evidence from US corporate loan data. *Journal of Financial Economics*, *142*(3), 1426–1443. DOI: 10.1016/j.jfineco.2021.06.026

FERROUHI. E. M. (2018, April 1). *Determinants of banks' profitability and performance: An overview* [MPRA Paper]. https://mpra.ub.uni-muenchen.de/89470/

Feyen, E., Natarajan, H., & Saal, M. (2023). *Fintech and the future of finance: Market and policy implications*. World Bank Publications. DOI: 10.1596/978-1-4648-1914-8

Finger, M., Gavious, I., & Manos, R. (2018). Environmental risk management and financial performance in the banking industry: A cross-country comparison. *Journal of International Financial Markets, Institutions and Money*, *52*, 240–261. DOI: 10.1016/j.intfin.2017.09.019

Flammer, C., Hong, B., & Minor, D. (2019). Corporate governance and the rise of integrating ESG metrics into CEO incentive contracts. *Management Science*, *65*(12), 5501–5525. DOI: 10.1287/mnsc.2018.3094

Follows, S. B., & Jobber, D. (2000). Environmentally responsible purchase behaviour: A test of a consumer model. *European Journal of Marketing*, *34*(5/6), 723–746. DOI: 10.1108/03090560010322009

Fornell, C., & Larcker, D. F. (1981). Structural equation models with unobservable variables and measurement error: Algebra and statistics. *JMR, Journal of Marketing Research*, *18*(3), 382–388. DOI: 10.1177/002224378101800313

Frankel, R., Kothari, S. P., & Raghunandan, A. (2025). The economics of ESG disclosure regulation. *Review of Accounting Studies*, *30*(4), 3218–3253. DOI: 10.1007/s11142-025-09900-9

Freeman, R. E. (1984). *Strategic management: A stakeholder approach*. Pitman (book).

Freeman, R. E., & McVea, J. (2005). A stakeholder approach to strategic management. The Blackwell handbook of strategic management, 183-201. doi:DOI: 10.2139/ssrn.263511

Friede, G., Busch, T., & Bassen, A. (2015). ESG and financial performance: Aggregated evidence from more than 2000 empirical studies. *Journal of Business Ethics*, *137*(2), 197–227. DOI: 10.1007/s10551-015-2878-6

Friede, G., Busch, T., & Bassen, A. (2015). ESG and financial performance: Aggregated evidence. *Journal of Sustainable Finance & Investment*, *5*(4), 210–233. DOI: 10.1080/20430795.2015.1118917

Friedman, M., & Savage, L. (1948). The utility analysis of choices involving risk. *Journal of Political Economy*, *56*(4), 279–304.

Furnham, A. (1984). Many sides of the coin: The psychology of money usage. *Personality and Individual Differences*, *5*(5), 501–509.

Galeone, G., Ranaldo, S., & Fusco, A. (2024). ESG and Fintech: Are they connected? *Research in International Business and Finance*, *69*, 102225. DOI: 10.1016/j.ribaf.2024.102225

Gallego-Álvarez, I., Martínez-Ferrero, J., & Cuadrado-Ballesteros, B. (2016). Accounting treatment for carbon emission rights. *Systems*, *4*(1), 12. DOI: 10.3390/systems4010012

Gholami, A., Sands, J., & Rahman, H. U. (2022). Environmental, social and governance disclosure and value generation: Is the financial industry different? *Sustainability (Basel)*, *14*(5), 2647. DOI: 10.3390/su14052647

Gillenwater, M. (2012). *What is additionality? Part 1: A long-standing problem* (Discussion Paper No. 001). Greenhouse Gas Management Institute. Retrieved December 20, 2025, from https://ghginstitute.org/wp-content/uploads/2015/04/AdditionalityPaper_Part-1ver3FINAL.pdf

Global Partnership for Financial Inclusion. (2017). *G20 financial inclusion action plan*.

Gober, P. (2017). Big data and financial service efficiency. Working paper.

Gogoi, M., & Bhattacharyya, M. (2022). Work security and other challenges for Street vendors in Guwahati City, Assam. *The Asia Pacific Journal of Anthropology*, *23*(3), 250–265. DOI: 10.1080/14442213.2022.2056912

GOI. (2023). *Government of India Report on Street vendors*. Ministry of Housing and Urban Affairs.

Goldstein, D. G., Johnson, E. J., & Sharpe, W. F. (2008). Choosing outcomes versus choosing products: Consumer-focused retirement investment advice. *The Journal of Consumer Research*, *35*(3), 440–456.

Gomber, P., Kauffman, R. J., Parker, C., & Weber, B. W. (2018). On the fintech revolution: Interpreting the forces of innovation, disruption, and transformation in financial services. *Journal of Management Information Systems*, *35*(1), 220–265. DOI: 10.1080/07421222.2018.1440766

Gomber, P., Koch, J. A., & Siering, M. (2017). Digital Finance and FinTech: Current research and future research directions. *Journal of Business Economics*, *87*(5), 537–580. DOI: 10.1007/s11573-017-0852-x

Goswami, S., Sharma, R., & Chouhan, V. (2022). *Impact of Financial Technology (Fintech) on Financial Inclusion(FI) in Rural India*. Universal Journal of Accounting and Finance. DOI: 10.13189/ujaf.2022.100213

GPFI. (2017). *G20 Global Partnership for Financial Inclusion*. Financial Stability Board.

Grewal, J., Hauptmann, C., & Serafeim, G. (2020). Material sustainability information and stock price informativeness. *Journal of Business Ethics*, *167*(3), 513–533. DOI: 10.1007/s10551-020-04451-2

Guerrero-Baena, M. D., Castilla-Polo, F., & Rodríguez-Gutiérrez, P. (2024). Motivations for social and environmental reporting in SMEs: Evidence and drivers. *Sustainability-related journal* / SBIR. DOI: 10.1002/bsd2.29

Gupta, K. L. (1970). Personal saving in developing nations: Further evidence. *The Economic Record*, *46*(2), 243–249.

Hair, J. F., Black, W. C., & Babin, B. J. (2010). Multivariate Data Analysis: A Global Perspective. In *Google Books*. Pearson Education., https://books.google.co.in/books/about/Multivariate_Data_Analysis.html?id=SLRPLgAACAAJ&redir_esc=y

Han, R., & Melecky, M. (2013). *Financial inclusion for financial stability: Access to bank deposits and the growth of deposits in the global financial crisis* (Policy Research Working Paper No. 6577). World Bank.

Haney, P. (2021). *Comparative analysis of mutual funds with reference to public and private sector funds*.

Haque, F., & Ntim, C. G. (2018). Environmental policy, environmental performance, and board ESG oversight. *Business Strategy and the Environment*, *27*(3), 1–17. DOI: 10.1002/bse.1993

Haque, S., & Islam, M. A. (2017). Stakeholder pressures on corporate climate change-related accountability and disclosures: Australian evidence. *Business and Politics*, *17*(2), 355–390. DOI: 10.1017/S1369525800001674

Hastings, J. S., Madrian, B. C., & Skimmyhorn, W. L. (2013). Financial literacy, financial education, and economic outcomes. *Annual Review of Economics*, *5*(1), 347–373. PMID: 23991248

Hatalis, M. (2024). Greenwashing or going green? An empirical analysis of the drivers and the effects of carbon offsets and renewable energy certificates on firm performance. *American Journal of Management*, *24*(2), 7108. Advance online publication. DOI: 10.33423/ajm.v24i2.7108

Hawaldar, I. T., Kumar, K. R. N., & Mallikarjunappa, T. (2021). Pricing and performance of Indian IPOs in the free-pricing era: An empirical study. *Journal of Legal, Ethical and Regulatory Issues, 24*(Special Issue 6), 1–63. https://www.abacademies.org/articles/pricing-and-performance-of-indian-ipos-in-the-freepricing-era-an-empirical-study.pdf

Haya, B. K., Alford-Jones, K., Anderegg, W. R. L., Beymer-Farris, B., Blanchard, L., Bomfim, B., Chin, D., Evans, S., Hogan, M., Holm, J. A., McAfee, K., So, I. S., West, T. A. P., & Withey, L. (2023). *Quality assessment of REDD+ carbon credit projects*. Berkeley Carbon Trading Project. Retrieved December 17, 2025, from https://gspp.berkeley.edu/research-and-impact/centers/cepp/projects/berkeley-carbon-trading-project/REDD+

Hayhoe, C. R., & Wilhelm, M. S. (1998). Modeling perceived economic well-being in a family setting: A gender perspective. *Financial Counseling and Planning*, *9*, 21–34.

Hearn, B. (2014). The impact of institutional infrastructure on IPO firm prospectus information and performance: Evidence from sub-Saharan Africa. *Research in International Business and Finance*, *31*, 296–323. DOI: 10.1016/j.ribaf.2014.01.003

Heckman, J. J. (1976). The common structure of statistical models of truncation, sample selection, and limited dependent variables and a simple estimator for such models. *Annals of Economic and Social Measurement*, *5*(4), 475–492.

He, M. D., Leckow, M. R. B., Haksar, M. V., Griffoli, M. T. M., Jenkinson, N., Kashima, M. M., & Tourpe, H. (2017). *Fintech and financial services: Initial considerations*. International Monetary Fund.

Henager, A., & Cude, C. R. (2016). Financial literacy and long- and short-term financial behavior in different age groups. *Financial Counseling and Planning*, *27*(1), 3–19.

Hendriks, S. (2019). The role of financial inclusion in driving women's economic empowerment. *Development in Practice*, *29*(8), 1029–1038. DOI: 10.1080/09614524.2019.1660308

Henriques, I., & Sadorsky, P. (1999). The relationship between environmental commitment and managerial perceptions of stakeholder importance. *Academy of Management Journal*, *42*(1), 87–99. DOI: 10.2307/256876

He, P., Chen, Q., & Chen, L. (2025). The impact of ESG on corporate value under the 'Dual Carbon' goals: Empirical evidence from Chinese energy listed companies. *Energies*, *18*(18), 4811. DOI: 10.3390/en18184811

Hsu, A. W., Lee, S., & Chen, H. (2021). ESG-linked compensation and corporate sustainability performance. *Journal of Business Ethics*, *170*(1), 15–35. DOI: 10.1007/s10551-020-04525-0

Huang, P.-C., Mirza, N., Umar, M., & Horobet, A. (2025). Impact of environmental double materiality on firm valuation: Evidence from the EU. *International Review of Economics & Finance*, *103*, 104461. DOI: 10.1016/j.iref.2025.104461

Huang, X., & Watson, L. (2015). Corporate social responsibility research in accounting. *Journal of Accounting Literature*, *34*(1), 1–16. DOI: 10.1016/j.acclit.2015.03.001

Huber, E., Bach, V., & Finkbeiner, M. (2024). A qualitative meta-analysis of carbon offset quality criteria. *Journal of Environmental Management*, *352*, 119983. DOI: 10.1016/j.jenvman.2023.119983 PMID: 38183915

Hummel, K., & Schlick, C. (2016). The relationship between sustainability performance and sustainability disclosure — Reconciling voluntary disclosure theory and legitimacy theory. *Journal of Accounting and Public Policy*, *35*(5), 455–476. DOI: 10.1016/j.jaccpubpol.2016.06.001

Hussain, A., Endut, N., Das, S., Chowdhury, M., Haque, N., Sultana, S., & Ahmed, K. (2018). Does financial inclusion increase financial resilience? Evidence from Bangladesh. *Development in Practice*, *29*(6), 798–807. DOI: 10.1080/09614524.2019.1607256

Huynh, Q. (2023). Street vendors in Vietnam: Short Cultural and Economic Insight. *International Journal of Culture and Education.*

Ibbotson, R. G. (1975). Price performance of common stock new issues. *Journal of Financial Economics*, *2*(3), 235–272. DOI: 10.1016/0304-405X(75)90015-X

IBEF. (2024). *Digital loans up 49% in FY24 by value.* India Brand Equity Foundation.

ICAEW. (2023). *ISSB issues first sustainability disclosure standards. ICAEW Insights.* Retrieved December 17, 2025, from https://www.icaew.com/insights/viewpoints-on-the-news/2023/jun-2023/issb-issues-first-sustainability-disclosure-standards

ICAR. (2024). *Sustainability of vegetable Street vendors in India.* ICAR-National Academy of Agricultural Research Management.

IFRS Foundation. (2023). IFRS S1 & IFRS S2 Sustainability Standards. https://www.ifrs.org

IFRS Foundation. (2023). *IFRS Sustainability Disclosure Standards S1 and S2.* IFRS Foundation. Retrieved December 21, 2025, from https://www.ifrs.org/news-and-events/news/2023/06/issb-issues-ifrs-s1-ifrs-s2/

ILO. (2020). *Women and men in the informal economy: A statistical picture* (3rd ed.). International Labour Organization.

IMF & World Bank. (2019). *The Bali Fintech Agenda.* Policy Papers, 2019.

India Forum. (2025, October 29). *Closing India's gender gap in financial inclusion.* The India Forum.

Intelligence, G. S. M. A. (2024). *The mobile economy: Asia Pacific 2024.* GSMA.

International Monetary Fund. (2023). Digital public infrastructure and financial inclusion. In *Digital finance: Opportunities and risks* (pp. xx–xx). International Monetary Fund.

Ioannou, I., & Serafeim, G. (2012). What drives corporate social performance? The role of nation-level institutions. *Journal of International Business Studies*, *43*(9), 834–864. DOI: 10.1057/jibs.2012.26

Ioannou, I., & Serafeim, G. (2014). The impact of corporate social responsibility on investment recommendations: Analysts' perceptions and shifting institutional logics. *Strategic Management Journal*, *36*(7), 1053–1081. DOI: 10.1002/smj.2268

IPCC. (2022). *Climate Change 2022: Mitigation of Climate Change.* Cambridge University Press., DOI: 10.1017/9781009157926

IPO data – Jay R. Ritter. (2025, May 16). https://site.warrington.ufl.edu/ritter/ipo-data/

Ippolito, R. A. (1993). On studies of mutual fund performance, 1962–1991. *Financial Analysts Journal*, *49*(1), 42–50. DOI: 10.2469/faj.v49.n1.42

Iqbal, U. P., Jose, S. M., & Tahir, M.Ubais Parayil Iqbal. (2024). Examining the demand side factors of green banking adoption – a study exploring the case of Oman. *International Journal of Islamic and Middle Eastern Finance and Management*, *17*(1), 213–231. DOI: 10.1108/IMEFM-12-2022-0483

Isayas, Y. N. (2022). Determinants of banks' profitability: Empirical evidence from banks in Ethiopia. *Cogent Economics & Finance*, *10*(1), 2031433. DOI: 10.1080/23322039.2022.2031433

Itan, I., Sylvia, S., Septiany, S., & Chen, R. (2025). The influence of environmental, social, and governance disclosure on market reaction: Evidence from emerging markets. *Discover Sustainability*, *6*(1), 347. DOI: 10.1007/s43621-025-01085-0

Jacolin, L., Massil, J. K., & Noah, A. (2021). Informal sector and mobile financial services in emerging and developing countries: Does financial innovation matter? *World Economy*, *44*(5), 1292–1328. DOI: 10.1111/twec.13093

Jaffer, S., Dales, M., Ferris, P., Swinfield, T., Sorensen, D., Message, R., Keshav, S., & Madhavapeddy, A. (2024). Global, robust and comparable digital carbon assets *(arXiv:2403.14581v2)* [Computer science—Cryptography and security]. DOI: 10.1109/ICBC59979.2024.10634343

Jamir, C., & Pongen, M. (2022). Income and Employment Generation in Informal Sector: A case study of the Street vendors of Kohima and Dimapur district of Nagaland, India. *International Journal of Engineering Business Management*, *6*(4), 52–63.

Jayadev, M. (1996). Mutual fund performance: An analysis of monthly returns. *Finance India*, *10*(1), 73–84.

Jensen, M. C., & Meckling, W. H. (1976). Theory of the firm: Managerial behavior, agency costs and ownership structure. *Journal of Financial Economics*, *3*(4), 305–360. DOI: 10.1016/0304-405X(76)90026-X

Jungo, J., Madaleno, M., & Botelho, A. (2022). The Effect of Financial Inclusion and Competitiveness on Financial Stability: Why Financial Regulation Matters in Developing Countries? *Journal of Risk and Financial Management*, *15*(3), 122. DOI: 10.3390/jrfm15030122

Kabulova, J., & Stankevičienė, J. (2020). Valuation of FinTech innovation based on patent applications. *Sustainability (Basel)*, *12*(23), 10158. DOI: 10.3390/su122310158

Kahneman, D. (2003). A perspective on judgment and choice: Mapping bounded rationality. *The American Psychologist*, *58*(9), 697–720. PMID: 14584987

Kahneman, D. (2003). Maps of bounded rationality: Psychology for behavioral economics. *The American Economic Review*, *93*(5), 1449–1475.

Kahneman, D., Knetsch, J. L., & Thaler, R. (1990). Experimental tests of the endowment effect and the Coase theorem. *Journal of Political Economy*, *98*(6), 1325–1348.

Kahneman, D., & Tversky, A. (1979). Prospect theory: An analysis of decision under risk. *Econometrica*, *47*(2), 263–292.

Kahneman, D., & Tversky, A. (1984). Choices, values, and frames. *The American Psychologist*, *39*(4), 341–350.

Kahneman, D., Wakker, P. P., & Sarin, R. (1997). Back to Bentham? Explorations of experienced utility. *The Quarterly Journal of Economics*, *112*(2), 375–405.

Kaiser, H. F. (1974). An Index of Factorial Simplicity. *Psychometrika*, *39*(1), 31–36. DOI: 10.1007/BF02291575

Kallbekken, S., & Sælen, H. (2011). Public acceptance for environmental taxes: Self-interest, environmental and distributional concerns. *Energy Policy*, *39*(5), 2966–2973. DOI: 10.1016/j.enpol.2011.03.006

Kalyan, N. B., & Gautami, S. (2018). A study on risk and return analysis of the selected mutual fund schemes in India. *International Journal of Research in Social Sciences*, *8*(5), 212–221.

Kanagaretnam, K., Lobo, G. J., & Whalen, D. J. (2023). Cultural dimensions and corporate environmental disclosure. *Journal of Business Ethics*, *184*, 529–558.

Kan, C., & Delina, L. L. (2025). Unlocking the transformative potential of blockchain to enhance transparency and efficiency in voluntary carbon markets for a sustainable energy transition. *Energy Research & Social Science*, *126*, 104177. DOI: 10.1016/j.erss.2025.104177

Kandpal, V. (2014). *Comparative study of selected public and private sector equity diversified mutual fund schemes in India.*

Kaur, M., & Vohra, T. (2014). Understanding individual investor's behavior: A review of empirical evidences. *Pacific Business Review International*, *6*(6), 37–47.

Kaur, S., & Shukla, M. A. (2016). Behavioral finance: A review. *International Journal of Management and Applied Science*, *2*(11), 104–107.

Kedla, S., Nandini, B., & Chethan, S. (2025). Street Food Culture and Culinary Tourism: Economic Drift for the Tourism Industry. *European Journal of Arts, Humanities and Social Sciences.*

Kemp, C. (2018). Money attitudes, financial literacy, and financial behaviour. *Journal of Financial Education*, *44*(1–2), 1–14.

Kend, M., & Nguyen, L. A. (2020). Big data analytics and other emerging technologies: The impact on the Australian audit and assurance profession. *Australian Accounting Review*, *30*(4), 269–282. DOI: 10.1111/auar.12305

Khan, M., Serafeim, G., & Yoon, A. (2016). Corporate sustainability: First evidence on materiality. *The Accounting Review*, *91*(6), 1697–1724. DOI: 10.2308/accr-51383

Khanna, A. (2013, January 4). *Indian Banking Sector towards a Sustainable Growth: A Paradigm Shift*. ResearchGate; unknown. https://www.researchgate.net/publication/326175175

Khare, A. (2015). Antecedents to green buying behaviour: A study on consumers in an emerging economy. *Marketing Intelligence & Planning*, *33*(3), 309–329. DOI: 10.1108/MIP-05-2014-0083

Kharrat, H., Trichilli, Y., & Abbes, B. (2024). Relationship between FinTech index and bank's performance: A comparative study between Islamic and conventional banks in the MENA region. *Journal of Islamic Accounting and Business Research*, *15*(1), 172–195. DOI: 10.1108/JIABR-03-2022-0081

Khatri, I., Giskås, P. E., Kyrrø, A. K., & Kjærland, F. (2025). Corporate governance mechanisms and non-financial disclosure quality: Evidence from sustainability committee, external CSR assurance, and stakeholder engagement. *International Review of Financial Analysis*, *107*, 104645. DOI: 10.1016/j.irfa.2025.104645

Klassen, R. D., & Vereecke, A. (2012). Social issues in supply chains. *Journal of Operations Management*, *30*(1–2), 7–23. DOI: 10.1016/j.jom.2011.06.004

Kochar, R., Kalsie, A., & Deka, N. (2025). Voluntary carbon markets (VCMs) in a nutshell: A systematic review based on the empirical evidence from across the globe. *Journal of Cleaner Production*, *522*, 146261. DOI: 10.1016/j.jclepro.2025.146261

Koh, K., Li, H., & Tong, Y. H. (2023). Corporate social responsibility (CSR) performance and stakeholder engagement: Evidence from the quantity and quality of CSR disclosures. *Corporate Social Responsibility and Environmental Management*, *30*(2), 504–517. DOI: 10.1002/csr.2370

Kolk, A. (2016). The social responsibility of international business. *Journal of World Business*, *51*(1), 23–34. DOI: 10.1016/j.jwb.2015.08.010

Kothari, S. P., & Warner, J. B. (2007). Econometrics of event studies. In Eckbo, B. E. (Ed.), *Handbook of empirical corporate finance* (Vol. 1, pp. 3–36). Elsevier., DOI: 10.1016/B978-0-444-53265-7.50015-9

Kotsantonis, S., Pinney, C., & Serafeim, G. (2016). ESG integration in investment management: Myths and realities. *The Bank of America Journal of Applied Corporate Finance*, *28*(2), 10–16. DOI: 10.1111/jacf.12169

Kour, M. (2022). COMPARATIVE RISK-RETURNS ANALYSIS OF STOCKS IN THE INDIAN STOCK MARKET. *Journal of Commerce & Accounting Research*, *11*(3).

Kour, M., Taneja, S., Özen, E., Sood, K., & Grima, S. (Eds.). (2025). *Financial Landscape Transformation: Technological Disruptions*. Emerald Publishing Limited. DOI: 10.1108/9781837537501

Krishnamurti, C., & Kumar, P. (2002). The initial listing performance of Indian IPOs. *Managerial Finance*, *28*(2), 39–51. DOI: 10.1108/03074350210767681

Krishnan, D., Brahmi, M., & Archana, K. (2025). Examining the sector-specific ramifications of initial public offering (IPO) underpricing in the Indian stock market. In *Advances in Finance, Accounting, and Economics* (pp. 59–82). https://doi.org/ DOI: 10.4018/979-8-3693-5723-1.ch003

Krueger, P., Sautner, Z., & Starks, L. (2023). Climate risk and institutional investors. *Review of Financial Studies*, *36*(1), 456–505. DOI: 10.1093/rfs/hhac035

Krueger, P., Sautner, Z., & Starks, L. T. (2020). The importance of climate risks for institutional investors. *Review of Financial Studies*, *33*(3), 1067–1111. DOI: 10.1093/rfs/hhz137

Kumar, K. R., & Rani, S. (2025). Social Inclusion of Street vendors In Market Economy: A Study with Reference to Visakhapatnam District, Andhra Pradesh, India. *International Journal for Multidisciplinary Research*, *7*(1).

Kumar, K., & Prakash, A. (2018). Developing a framework for assessing sustainable banking performance of the Indian banking sector. *Social Responsibility Journal*, *15*(5), 689–709. Advance online publication. DOI: 10.1108/SRJ-07-2018-0162

Kumar, R., & Goyal, A. (2023). Behavioral biases in investment decision making–a systematic literature review. *Qualitative Research in Financial Markets*, *15*(1), 1–24.

Kumar, R., & Sah, S. K. (2025). Socioeconomic dynamics of Street vendors in a globalized urban context: A case study of Bihar. *International Journal of Advanced Academic Studies*, *7*(3), 144–147. DOI: 10.33545/27068919.2025.v7.i3b.1426

Kumar, S., Charles, M. R., & Goyal, P. (2020). Financial literacy, behavioral biases, and investor performance: Evidence from India. *Journal of Behavioral and Experimental Finance*, *28*, 100414.

La Porta, R., & Shleifer, A. (2008). The unofficial economy and economic development. *Brookings Papers on Economic Activity*, •••, 275–352.

Laibson, D. (1997). Golden eggs and hyperbolic discounting. *The Quarterly Journal of Economics*, *112*(2), 443–477.

Lakhani, L., & Herbert, S. L. (2022). Theoretical frameworks applied in integrated reporting and sustainability reporting research. *Suid-Afrikaanse Tydskrif vir Ekonomiese en Bestuurswetenskappe*, *25*(1), a4427. DOI: 10.4102/sajems.v25i1.4427

Lebbar, H., & El-Aroui, M.-A. (2025). CSR performance in global context: Institutional determinants in developed, developing, and emerging economies. *Social Responsibility Journal*, 1–23. DOI: 10.1108/SRJ-04-2025-0386

Lee, M. T., & Raschke, R. L. (2023). Stakeholder legitimacy in firm greening and financial performance: What about greenwashing temptations? *Journal of Business Research, 155*(Part B), 113393. DOI: 10.1016/j.jbusres.2022.113393

Lee, M.-D. P. (2008). A review of the theories of corporate social responsibility: Its evolutionary path and the road ahead. *International Journal of Management Reviews*, *10*(1), 53–73. DOI: 10.1111/j.1468-2370.2007.00226.x

Lehmann, B. N., & Modest, D. M. (1987). Mutual fund performance evaluation: A comparison of benchmarks and benchmark comparisons. *The Journal of Finance*, *42*(2), 233–265. DOI: 10.1111/j.1540-6261.1987.tb02566.x

Levis, M. (1993). The long-run performance of initial public offerings: The UK experience 1980–1988. *Financial Management*, *22*(1), 28–41. DOI: 10.2307/3665972

Lewis, L., & Tietenberg, T. (2020). *Environmental economics and policy* (7th ed.). Routledge.

Liang, H., & Renneboog, L. (2020). Corporate social responsibility and sustainable finance: A review. European Corporate Governance Institute Working Paper.

Li, B., Liu, S., Liu, D., Fan, Z., Qu, Z., Yao, S., Su, X., & Wang, L. (2025). Using Sentinel-2A and Landsat 8 imagery to assess changes in forest carbon storage. *Scientific Reports*, *15*(1), 37489. DOI: 10.1038/s41598-025-21607-0 PMID: 41145783

Li, J., & Sasaki, M. (2024). Political embeddedness and corporate social responsibility (CSR) in a state-led developing country: Evidence from China. *Asian Business & Management*, *23*(4), 597–621. DOI: 10.1057/s41291-023-00256-z

Li, L., & Zhang, D. (2024). Forest carbon offset protocols in compliance carbon markets. *Forest Policy and Economics*, *165*, 103253. DOI: 10.1016/j.forpol.2024.103253

Lins, K. V., Servaes, H., & Tamayo, A. (2017). Social capital, trust, and firm performance during the financial crisis: The value of corporate social responsibility. *The Journal of Finance*, *72*(4), 1785–1824. DOI: 10.1111/jofi.12505

Liu, M., Tripe, D. W. L., & Jiang, W. (2017). *Does fintech increase or reduce commercial banks' risk-taking? Evidence from China's banking sector*. Econfin. Massey. Ac. Nz.

Liu, Y., Saleem, S., Shabbir, R., Shabbir, M. S., Irshad, A., & Khan, S. (2021). The relationship between corporate social responsibility and financial performance: A moderate role of fintech technology. *Environmental Science and Pollution Research International*, *28*(16), 20174–20187. DOI: 10.1007/s11356-020-11822-9

Li, Y., Zheng, Y., Li, X., & Mu, Z. (2024). The impact of digital transformation on ESG performance. *International Review of Economics & Finance*, *96*, 103686. DOI: 10.1016/j.iref.2024.103686

Lo, K. Y., & Kwan, C. L. (2017). The effect of environmental, social, governance and sustainability reporting on financial performance: An empirical study in Hong Kong. *Journal of Business Research*, *71*, 185–191. DOI: 10.1016/j.jbusres.2017.02.020

Long, X., Chen, Y., Du, J., Oh, K., Han, I., & Yan, J. (2017). The effect of environmental innovation behaviour on economic and environmental performance of 182 Chinese firms. *Journal of Cleaner Production*, *166*, 1274–1282. DOI: 10.1016/j.jclepro.2017.08.070

Loo, M. K. L. (2019). Enhancing financial inclusion in ASEAN: Identifying the best growth markets for Fintech. *Journal of Risk and Financial Management*, *12*(4), 181. DOI: 10.3390/jrfm12040181

Loughran, T., & Ritter, J. (2004a). Why has IPO underpricing changed over time? *Financial Management*, *33*(1), 5–37. https://site.warrington.ufl.edu/ritter/files/2015/06/Why-Has-IPO-Underpricing-Changed-Over-Time-2004.pdf

Loughran, T., & Ritter, J. R. (2004b). Initial public offering: International insight? *Financial Management*, *33*(3), 5–37. DOI: 10.1111/j.1755-053X.2004.tb00018.x

Lusardi, A., & Mitchell, O. S. (2007). Financial literacy and retirement preparedness: Evidence and implications for financial education. *Business Economics (Cleveland, Ohio)*, *42*(1), 35–44.

Macchiavello, E., & Siri, M. (2022). Sustainable finance and Fintech: Can technology contribute to achieving environmental goals? A preliminary assessment of 'green Fintech' and 'sustainable digital finance'. *European Company and Financial Law Review, 19*(1), 128–174. DOI: 10.1515/ecfr-2022-0005

Madrian, S., & Shea, D. (2001). The power of suggestion: Inertia in 401(k) participation and savings behavior. *The Quarterly Journal of Economics, 116*(4), 1149–1187.

Majhi, S. (2025). *Signalling quality through underpricing: A Bayesian game-theoretic analysis of Indian startup IPOs (2020–2024).* IIM Calcutta. https://ir.iimcal.ac.in:8443/jspui/handle/123456789/6305

Malik, G., & Singh, D. (2022). Personality matters: does an individual's personality affect adoption and continued use of green banking channels? *International Journal of Bank Marketing, ahead-of-print*(ahead-of-print). DOI: 10.1108/IJBM-04-2021-0133

Manning, S., Boons, F., & von Hagen, O. (2019). Governance and sustainability standards. *Journal of Business Ethics, 154*(2), 361–383.

Marques, P., Rodrigues, L. L., & Oliveira, A. (2020). The relevance of CSR practices in the healthcare sector. *Journal of Business Ethics, 162*, 379–396.

Martielli, F., Battisti, E., Gonzalez-Cruz, T. F., & Salvi, A. (2025). Carbon credits and financial performance: Exploring the moderating role of CSR strategy and corporate governance practices. *Research in International Business and Finance, 77*(Part B), 102919. DOI: 10.1016/j.ribaf.2025.102919

Martínez-Ferrero, J., & García-Sánchez, I. (2017). Sustainability assurance and cost of capital. *Journal of Business Ethics, 140*(2), 353–367.

Masila, M.. (2024). *ESG transparency and profitability.* Sustainability Accounting Journal.

Matten, D., & Moon, J. (2008). "Implicit" and "explicit" CSR: A conceptual framework for a comparative understanding of corporate social responsibility. *Academy of Management Review, 33*(2), 404–424. DOI: 10.5465/amr.2008.31193458

Mazumder, M. S. (2025). *PM SVANidhi: Street vendors' digital journey.* Ministry of Housing and Urban Affairs.

McDonald, J. G. (1974). Objectives and performance of mutual funds, 1960–1969. *Journal of Financial and Quantitative Analysis, 9*(3), 311–333. DOI: 10.2307/2329866

Megginson, W. L., & Weiss, K. A. (1991). Venture capitalist certification in initial public offerings. *The Journal of Finance, 46*(3), 879–903. DOI: 10.1111/j.1540-6261.1991.tb03770.x

MeitY. (2024). *Annual Report 2023-24*. Ministry of Electronics and Information Technology, Government of India.

MicroSave Consulting. (2023). *Account inactivity in India: Is there a problem?* MicroSave Consulting.

Milfont, T. L., & Duckitt, J. (2004). The structure of environmental attitudes: A first- and second-order confirmatory factor analysis. *Journal of Environmental Psychology*, *24*(3), 289–303. DOI: 10.1016/j.jenvp.2004.09.001

Ministry of Housing & Urban Poverty Alleviation. (2009). *National Policy on Urban Street vendors, 2009*. Government of India.

Mishra, A. K. (2005). Aftermarket performance of initial public offerings in India. *Vikalpa*, *30*(1), 27–38. DOI: 10.1177/0256090920050103

Mishra, D., Kandpal, V., Agarwal, N., & Srivastava, B. (2024). Financial inclusion and its ripple effects on socio-economic development: A comprehensive review. *Journal of Risk and Financial Management*, *17*(3), 105. DOI: 10.3390/jrfm17030105

Mitra, S., & Karathanasopoulos, A. (2020). Fintech revolution: The impact of management information systems upon relative firm value and risk. *Journal of Banking and Financial Technology*, *4*(2), 175–187. DOI: 10.1007/s42786-020-00023-0

Mittal, V., & Koh, L. (2024). The fintech nation: excellence unlocked in Singapore.

MoF. (2024). *Stand Up India Scheme: Ministry of Finance*. Government of India.

Mohan, D. M. M., Rao, D. M. A., Chakravarthi, D. P., & Rao, P. V. L. (2021). Risk and return analysis with performance evaluation of selected mutual fund schemes: An empirical study. *International Journal of Aquatic Science*, *12*(2), 2676–2692.

Mohanty Committee. (2015). *Report of the Committee on Medium-term Path on Financial Inclusion*. Reserve Bank of India.

MoHUA. (2023). *Number of Street vendors identified by states*. Ministry of Housing and Urban Affairs.

Mokhtar, N. B., & Alam, A. (2023). The Mediating Role of Fintech on ESG and Bank Performance. In *Fintech and Sustainability: How Financial Technologies Can Help Address Today's Environmental and Societal Challenges* (pp. 191–218). Springer Nature Switzerland. DOI: 10.1007/978-3-031-40647-8_10

Montford, J., & Goldsmith, C. (2016). How gender and financial self-efficacy influence investment risk-taking. *International Journal of Consumer Studies*, *40*(1), 101–106.

Moro-Visconti, R., Cruz Rambaud, S., & López Pascual, J. (2020). Sustainability in FinTechs: An explanation through business model scalability and market valuation. *Sustainability (Basel), 12*(24), 10316. DOI: 10.3390/su122410316

Moura-Leite, R. C., & Padgett, R. C. (2011). Historical background of corporate social responsibility. *Social Responsibility Journal, 7*(4), 528–539. DOI: 10.1108/17471111111117511

Munishi, E., Songa, P., & Kirumirah, M. (2021). Challenges to Accessing Credit Financing from Financial Institutions by the Urban Based Street vendors: Experience from Dar Es Salaam – Tanzania. *International Journal of Business and Management, 17*(1), 65. DOI: 10.5539/ijbm.v17n1p65

Murthy, K., & Kumar, G. P. (2025). Initial public offerings and long-term returns: A sector-based evaluation. *International Journal of Innovative Research in Engineering & Management, 12*(1), 75–81. DOI: 10.55524/ijirem.2025.12.1.12

NAFIS. (2024). *All India Rural Financial Inclusion Survey*. NABARD.

Narayanan, S. (2021). *A comparative analysis of performance of mutual funds between private and public sector* (Doctoral dissertation, Institute of Management, NU).

National Institute of Rural Development and Panchayati Raj. (2019). *An evaluation of the SHG-BLP with special reference to its loan portfolio and asset quality*.

Naveenan, R.V., Madeswaran, A., & R, A. K. (2021). Green banking practices in India-the customer's perspective. *Academy of Entrepreneurship Journal, 27*(4), 1–19. https://www.researchgate.net/publication/354761063

NBK. (2025). *Green Bond Allocation & Impact Report 2025*. NBK. Retrieved December 17, 2025, from https://www.nbk.com/dam/jcr%3A0c178f5f-223a-407f-8656-a14be484f8e2/green-bond-report-2025.pdf

Neaime, S., & Gaysset, I. (2017). Financial inclusion and stability in MENA: Evidence from poverty and inequality. *Finance Research Letters, 24*, 230–237. DOI: 10.1016/j.frl.2017.09.007

Neri, L.. (2021). Sustainability and innovation in the tech sector. *Technovation, 102*, 102214. DOI: 10.1016/j.technovation.2020.102214

Newman, S., Wyrobisch, S., & PwC Global IPO Centre. (2024). *Global IPO watch 2023 and outlook for 2024*. PwC. https://www.pwccn.com/en/audit-assurance/publication/global-ipo-watch-jan2024.pdf

Nigerian Central Bank. (2024). *Financial inclusion and digital payments statistics 2024*. Central Bank of Nigeria.

Niinimäki, J. P. (2018). Collateral in credit rationing in markets with asymmetric information. *The Quarterly Review of Economics and Finance*, *68*, 97–102. DOI: 10.1016/j.qref.2017.10.001

NIRDP et al. (2019). *Status of Self Help Group Bank Linkage Programme in India: A radical shift*. National Institute of Rural Development and Panchayati Raj.

Nisha, N., Iqbal, M., & Rifat, A. (2020). Green Banking Adoption. *International Journal of Technology and Human Interaction, 16*(2), 69–89. DOI: 10.4018/IJTHI.2020040106

Nizam, E., Ng, A., Dewandaru, G., Nagayev, R., & Nkoba, M. A. (2019). The impact of social and environmental sustainability on financial performance: A global analysis of the banking sector. *Journal of Multinational Financial Management, 49*(1), 35–53. DOI: 10.1016/j.mulfin.2019.01.002

Nofsinger, J. (2005). Social mood and financial economics. *Journal of Behavioral Finance*, *6*(3), 144–160.

Norvilitis, M., Szablicki, M., & Wilson, S. (2003). Factors influencing levels of credit-card debt in college students. *Journal of Applied Social Psychology*, *33*(5), 935–947.

NPCI. (2025). *Aadhaar-enabled Payments Data*. National Payments Corporation of India.

Nunnally, J. C., & Bernstein, I. H. (1994). Psychometric Theory. In *Google Books*. McGraw-Hill Companies, Incorporated. https://books.google.com/books/about/Psychometric_Theory.html?id=r0fuAAAAMAAJ

Odean, T. (1998). Are investors reluctant to realize their losses? *The Journal of Finance*, *53*(5), 1775–1798.

OECD/INFE evidence, policies and practice. *OECD Working Papers on Finance, Insurance and Private Pensions*, 34.

Oehler, D., Horn, M., & Wedlich, U. (2020). Young adults' use of mobile payment services: An empirical analysis of the moderating influence of consumer financial knowledge. *Journal of Behavioral and Experimental Finance*, *28*, 100404.

Öhman, P., Nourallah, M., & El Kalak, I. (2025). Guest Editorial: Navigating Contemporary FinTech Solutions: Revealing Potential and Challenges. *Financial Services Review*, *33*(3), i–v. DOI: 10.61190/fsr.v33i3.4352

Olsen, J. P. (2002). The many faces of Europeanization. *Journal of Common Market Studies*, *40*(5), 921–952.

Omar, M. A., & Inaba, K. (2020). Does financial inclusion reduce poverty and income inequality in developing countries? A panel data analysis. *Journal of Economic Structures*, *9*(1), 37. DOI: 10.1186/s40008-020-00214-4

Onodugo, V., Ezeadichie, N., Onwuneme, C., & Anosike, A. (2016). The dilemma of managing the challenges of street vending in public spaces: The case of Enugu City, Nigeria. *Cities (London, England)*, *59*, 95–101. DOI: 10.1016/j.cities.2016.06.001

Ortiz-de-Mandojana, N.. (2016). Board independence and environmental innovation. *Business Strategy and the Environment*, *25*(4), 272–289.

Ozili, P. K. (2018). Impact of digital finance on financial inclusion and stability. *Borsa Istanbul Review*, *18*(4), 329–340. DOI: 10.1016/j.bir.2017.12.003

Palmaccio, M., Dicuonzo, G., & Belyaeva, Z. S. (2021). The internet of things and corporate business models: A systematic literature review. *Journal of Business Research*, *131*, 610–618. DOI: 10.1016/j.jbusres.2020.09.069

Pande, A., & Vaidyanathan, R. (2007). *Determinants of IPO underpricing in the National Stock Exchange of India. SSRN.* https://papers.ssrn.com/sol3/papers.cfm?abstract_id=1081272

Pandow, B. A., & Butt, K. A. (2017). Risk and return analysis of mutual fund industry in India. *Journal of Banking and Financial Dynamics*, *1*(1), 54–65. DOI: 10.20448/journal.525.2017.11.54.65

Panigrahi, M. S. (1996). Mutual funds: Growth, performance and prospects. *Economic and Political Weekly*, •••, 765–775.

Panwar, S., & Madhumathi, R. (2006, January). Characteristics and performance evaluation of selected mutual funds in India. In *Proceedings of the 9th Capital Markets Conference*, Indian Institute of Capital Markets. DOI: 10.2139/ssrn.876402

Park, H. S. (2000). Relationships among attitudes and subjective norms: Testing the theory of reasoned action across cultures. *Communication Studies*, *51*(2), 162–175. DOI: 10.1080/10510970009388516

Pata, U. K., Si Mohammed, K., Serret, V., & Kartal, M. T. (2024). Assessing the influence of climate risk, carbon allowances, and technological factors on the ESG market in the European Union. *Borsa Istanbul Review*, *24*(4), 828–837. DOI: 10.1016/j.bir.2024.04.013

Patel, R., & Koshy, A. (2023). Gender inclusivity of India's digital financial revolution for the poor: A critical review. *Journal of Global Health Reports*, *7*, e2023025.

Petria, N., Capraru, B., & Ihnatov, I. (2015). Determinants of Banks' Profitability: Evidence from EU 27 Banking Systems. *Procedia Economics and Finance, 20*, 518–524. DOI: 10.1016/S2212-5671(15)00104-5

Phau, I., & Ong, D. (2007). An investigation of the effects of environmental claims in promotional messages for clothing brands. *Marketing Intelligence & Planning, 25*(7), 772–788. DOI: 10.1108/02634500710834214

Philippon, T. (2016). *The FinTech opportunity*. NBER Working Paper No. 22476.

Pillay, S. KPMG in India, NASSCOM, & Roy, S. (2022). *BFSI GCCS: The road ahead* [Report]. KPMG. https://assets.kpmg.com/content/dam/kpmg/in/pdf/2022/01/bfsi-gccs-the-road-ahead-a-nasscom-kpmg-in-itiative.pdf

Pizzi, S., Rosati, F., Venturelli, A., & Bosetti, L. (2022). The moderating role of corporate governance in the relationship between sustainability performance and financial performance. *Business Strategy and the Environment, 31*(4), 1714–1730. DOI: 10.1002/bse.3000

Pizzi, S., Venturelli, A., & Bosetti, L. (2023). Digital transformation and ESG reporting. *Technological Forecasting and Social Change, 187*, 122160.

Planning Commission. (2009). *Report of the Expert Group on Financial Inclusion in India*. Government of India.

Podsakoff, P. M., MacKenzie, S. B., Lee, J.-Y., & Podsakoff, N. P. (2003). Common Method Biases in Behavioral research: A Critical Review of the Literature and Recommended remedies. *The Journal of Applied Psychology, 88*(5), 879–903. DOI: 10.1037/0021-9010.88.5.879

Podsakoff, P. M., & Organ, D. W. (1986). Self-Reports in Organizational Research: Problems and Prospects. *Journal of Management, 12*(4), 531–544. DOI: 10.1177/014920638601200408

Pomeroy, R., Arango, C., Lomboy, C., & Box, S. (2020). Financial inclusion to build economic resilience in small-scale fisheries. *Marine Policy, 118*, 103982. DOI: 10.1016/j.marpol.2020.103982

Porter, M. E., & Kramer, M. R. (2006). Strategy and society: The link between competitive advantage and corporate social responsibility. *Harvard Business Review, 84*(12), 78–92. PMID: 17183795

Post, C., Rahman, N., & Rubow, E. (2011). Board gender diversity and corporate social responsibility. *Journal of Business Ethics, 102*(2), 179–196. DOI: 10.1007/s10551-011-0902-1

Potharla, S. (2025). *Unlocking value through IPOs: A two-decade review of India's corporate listings and capital market dynamics. SSRN.* https://papers.ssrn.com/sol3/papers.cfm?abstract_id=5392297

Pratama, A., Dewi, N., Sofia, P., Muhammad, K., & Megawati, L. R. (2024). Sustainability reporting ecosystem and IFRS S1 and S2: How accounting research can assist its implementation. *Journal of Ecohumanism, 3*(4), 3101–3129. DOI: 10.62754/joe.v3i4.3830

Press Information Bureau. (2022, October 15). *PM dedicates 75 Digital Banking Units across 75 districts to the nation*. Government of India.

Press Trust of India. (2025, March 31). Women's share in digital transactions doubled from 14% to 28% in last 7 years: Government. *The Hindu BusinessLine*.

Progress Report, C. C. S. (2020). *Progress Report 2020: Implementing the Street vendors Act*. Centre for Civil Society.

Putri, W. H., Nurwiyanta, N., Sungkono, S., & Wahyuningsih, T. (2019). The emerging fintech and financial slack on corporate financial performance. *Investment Management & Financial Innovations, 16*(2), 348–354. DOI: 10.21511/imfi.16(2).2019.29

Qi, X., Lv, X., Li, Z., Yang, C., Li, H., & Ploeger, A. (2024). Factors influencing young adults' organic food purchase intention on fresh food e-commerce platforms. *British Food Journal, 126*(12), 4277–4303. Advance online publication. DOI: 10.1108/BFJ-04-2024-0417

Qi, Y., Yue, L., Guo, T., Zhou, D., Ren, Y., Wang, M., Liu, Y., & Yang, Y. (2024). A Study on the Perception of Local Characteristics in Cultural Street Vending Spaces, Taking Xi'an Baxian Temple as an Example. *Buildings (Basel, Switzerland), 14*(1), 192. DOI: 10.3390/buildings14010192

Qureshi, N. (2025). The growing significance of corporate social responsibility: From ethical obligation to strategic imperative. *International Journal for Multidisciplinary Research, 7*(3), 1–5. DOI: 10.36948/ijfmr.2025.v07i03.48259

Rahbar, E., & Abdul Wahid, N. (2011). Investigation of green marketing tools' effect on consumers' purchase behavior. *Business Strategy Series, 12*(2), 73–83. DOI: 10.1108/17515631111114877

Rangarajan Committee. (2008). *Report of the Committee on Financial Inclusion*. Government of India.

Rao, S., & Nair, L. (2019). Aadhaar: A digital identity for the unorganized. *Information Technology for Development, 25*(4), 797–815.

Rastogi, S., Singh, K., & Kanoujiya, J. (2023). Do countries capture their inclusive growth, sustainability, and poverty correctly? A study on statistical performance indicators defined by World Bank. *Social Responsibility Journal*, *19*(10), 1935–1951. DOI: 10.1108/SRJ-12-2022-0553

RBI. (2021). *Master Circular – Mobile Banking Transactions in India*. Reserve Bank of India.

RBI. (2025). *Financial Inclusion Index Report*. Reserve Bank of India.

Reddy, K. S. M. (2015). The aftermarket pricing performance of initial public offers: Insights from India. *International Journal of Commerce and Management*, *25*(1), 84–107. https://core.ac.uk/download/pdf/213970008.pdf

Rehman, A., Ullah, I., Afridi, F.-A., Ullah, Z., Zeeshan, M., Hussain, A., & Rahman, H. U. (2021). Adoption of green banking practices and environmental performance in Pakistan: A demonstration of structural equation modelling. *Environment, Development and Sustainability*, *23*(9), 13200–13220. DOI: 10.1007/s10668-020-01206-x

Rehmani, A. (2018). Performance evaluation of select mutual funds: A public–private comparison. *Indian Journal of Finance*, *12*(9), 41–55. DOI: 10.17010/ijf/2018/v12i9/131563

Rehmani, A., & Khan, M. A. (2018). Growth of Indian mutual fund industry: An empirical analysis. *International Journal of Social Science and Economic Research*, *3*(8), 3763–3777.

Ren, X., Zeng, G., & Zhao, Y. (2023). Digital finance and corporate ESG performance: Empirical evidence from listed companies in China. *Pacific-Basin Finance Journal*, *79*, 102019. DOI: 10.1016/j.pacfin.2023.102019

RGGI. (2023). *CO_2 allowance program overview*. Retrieved December 24, 2025, from https://www.rggi.org/

Ritter, J. R. (1991). The long-run performance of initial public offerings. *The Journal of Finance*, *46*(1), 3–27. DOI: 10.1111/j.1540-6261.1991.tb03743.x

Ritter, J. R. (2003). Behavioral finance. *Pacific-Basin Finance Journal*, *11*(4), 429–437.

Ritter, J. R., & Welch, I. (2002). A review of IPO activity, pricing, and allocations. *The Journal of Finance*, *57*(4), 1795–1828. DOI: 10.1111/1540-6261.00478

Robichaud, Z., & Yu, H. (2021). Do young consumers care about ethical consumption? Modelling Gen Z's purchase intention towards fair trade coffee. *British Food Journal, ahead-of-print*(ahead-of-print). DOI: 10.1108/BFJ-05-2021-0536

Rock, K. (1986). Why are new issues underpriced? *Journal of Financial Economics, 15*(1–2), 187–212. DOI: 10.1016/0304-405X(86)90054-1

Roever, S., & Skinner, C. (2016). Street vendors and cities. *Environment and Urbanization, 28*(2), 359–374. DOI: 10.1177/0956247816653898

Romānova, I., & Kudinska, M. (2016). Banking and Fintech: A challenge or opportunity? Contemporary issues in finance: Current challenges from across [). Emerald Group Publishing Limited.]. *Europe, 98*, 21–35.

Romero, R., Paulino, E., Tan, R., & Cortez, D. (2024). Urban entrepreneurship on the fringe: Action research on the challenges of Street vendors in Manila. *Journal of Business and Management Studies.*

Ruseva, T., Marland, E., Szymanski, C., Hoyle, J., Marland, G., & Kowalczyk, T. (2017). Additionality and permanence standards in California's Forest Offset Protocol: A review of project and program level implications. *Journal of Environmental Management, 198*, 277–288. DOI: 10.1016/j.jenvman.2017.04.082 PMID: 28477569

Sadhak, H. (2003). *Mutual funds in India: Marketing strategies and investment practices.*

Sahay, R., von Allmen, U. E., Lahreche, A., Khera, P., Ogawa, S., Bazarbash, M., & Beaton, K. (2020). *The promise of fintech: Financial inclusion in the post COVID-19 era* (Departmental Paper No. 20/09). International Monetary Fund.

Sahoo, S., & Rajib, P. (2010). After-market pricing performance of initial public offerings (IPOs): Indian IPO market 2002–2006. *Vikalpa, 35*(4), 27–44. DOI: 10.1177/0256090920100403

Saini, A., Fariya, 2., Agarwal, M., Kumar, P., Chauhan, R., Surendra, L., & Singh, P. (2024). Unveiling awareness and perception patterns: A comprehensive analysis of PM SVA Nidhi for Street vendors in Meerut. *Journal of Social Economics Research.*

Sakariya, S. M. (2014). *Financial inclusion: A study of commercial banks in India* [Doctoral dissertation, Saurashtra University].

Salah Mahdi, I. B., Bouaziz, M., & Boujelbène Abbes, M. (2025). The moderating effect of fintech on the relationship between CSR and banks' financial stability: Baron and Kenny's approach analysis. *EuroMed Journal of Business, 20*(2), 300–324. DOI: 10.1108/EMJB-03-2023-0082

Salguero, R. A. F. (2025). *Effectiveness of carbon pricing and compensation instruments: An umbrella review of the empirical evidence* (arXiv:2512.06887) [Preprint]. arXiv. 2512.06887

Salvi, A., Martielli, F., Battisti, E., Forliano, C., & Kumar, S. (2025). Climate change management and companies' financial performance: Exploring the moderating role of carbon credits. *Research in International Business and Finance, 75*, 102785. DOI: 10.1016/j.ribaf.2025.102785

Sangeetha, P., & Menaka, S. (2022). Study on livelihood of street food vendors. *International Journal of Agricultural Sciences, 18*(CIABASSD), 47–53. DOI: 10.15740/HAS/IJAS/18-CIABASSD/47-53

Sapar, N. R., & Madava, R. (2003). Performance evaluation of Indian mutual funds. SSRN *Electronic Journal*. https://ssrn.com/abstract=433100 DOI: 10.2139/ssrn.433100

Sarkis, J., Gonzalez-Torre, P., & Adenso-Diaz, B. (2010). Stakeholder pressure and the adoption of environmental practices: The mediating effect of training. *Journal of Operations Management, 28*(2), 163–176. DOI: 10.1016/j.jom.2009.10.001

Satyasai, K. J. S. (2020). NAFINDEX: A measure of financial inclusion based on NABARD All India Rural Financial Inclusion Survey. *Rural Pulse, 33*, 1–4.

SBTi. (2024). *Corporate Net-Zero Standard: Updated guidance.* Retrieved December 22, 2025, from https://sciencebasedtargets.org/net-zero

Schimanski, T., Reding, A., Reding, N., Bingler, J., Kraus, M., & Leippold, M. (2024). Bridging the gap in ESG measurement: Using NLP to quantify environmental, social, and governance communication. *Finance Research Letters, 61*, 104979. DOI: 10.1016/j.frl.2024.104979

Schmuck, D., Andersson, H., & Mark-Herbert, C. (2025). Corporate motives for financing carbon offsets: A case study of Swedish corporations. *Journal of Cleaner Production, 520*, 146049. DOI: 10.1016/j.jclepro.2025.146049

Schneider, L., Duan, M., Stavins, R., Kizzier, K., Broekhoff, D., Jotzo, F., Winkler, H., Lazarus, M., Howard, A., & Hood, C. (2019). Double counting and the Paris Agreement rulebook. *Science, 366*(6462), 180–183. DOI: 10.1126/science.aay8750 PMID: 31601755

Schultz, P. W. (2000). New Environmental Theories: Empathizing with Nature: The Effects of Perspective Taking on Concern for Environmental Issues. *The Journal of Social Issues, 56*(3), 391–406. DOI: 10.1111/0022-4537.00174

SEBI. (2023). *Annual report 2022–23.* https://www.sebi.gov.in/reports-and-statistics/publications/aug-2023/annual-report-2022-23_74990.html

SEBI. (n.d.). *Primary market initial public offerings (IPOs)*. https://www.bseindia.com/downloads1/PPT3_HowtoinvestinIPO.pdf

Sehgal, S., & Singh, B. (2008). Determinants of initial and long-run performance of IPOs in the Indian stock market. *Asia Pacific Business Review, 4*(4), 24–37. DOI: 10.1177/097324700800400403

Sehra, S. K., Godwin, B. J., & George, J. P. (2022). Are expensive decisions impulsive? Young adults' impulsive housing and real estate buying behavior in India. *International Journal of Housing Markets and Analysis*. DOI: 10.1108/IJHMA-06-2022-0090

Sekhar, G. (2014). *The Indian mutual fund industry: A comparative analysis of public vs. private sector performance*. Springer. DOI: 10.1057/9781137407993

Serafeim, G. (2020). How to build enduring commitment to long-term goals. *Harvard Business Review*.

Shahzad, F.. (2020). The role of sustainability reporting in tech innovation. *Journal of Cleaner Production, 263*, 121367.

Shahzad, U., Asl, M. G., & Tedeschi, M. (2023). Is there any market state-dependent contribution from Blockchain-enabled solutions to ESG investments? Evidence from conventional and Islamic ESG stocks. *International Review of Economics & Finance, 86*, 139–154. DOI: 10.1016/j.iref.2023.03.001

Shakil, A. K. M. A. Z., Hossain, M. M., Khan, M. M., Noyon, S. I., & Ripon, M. B. (2025). A systematic review of corporate social responsibility practices in emerging markets. *Business and Social Sciences, 3*(1), 1–9. DOI: 10.25163/business.3110211

Sharma, A., Das, N., & Singh, S. P. (2023). Causal association of the entrepreneurship ecosystem and financial inclusion. *Heliyon, 9*(3), e14596. DOI: 10.1016/j.heliyon.2023.e14596 PMID: 36950562

Sharma, M., & Choubey, A. (2021). Green Banking initiatives: A Qualitative Study on Indian Banking Sector. *Environment, Development and Sustainability, 24*(1), 293–319. Advance online publication. DOI: 10.1007/s10668-021-01426-9

Sharma, R. G. (2013). A comparative study on public and private sector mutual funds in India. *Journal of Research in Humanities and Social Sciences, 1*(6), 23–25.

Sharpe, W. F. (1966). Mutual fund performance. *The Journal of Business, 39*(1), 119–138. DOI: 10.1086/294846

Shiller, R. (2003). From efficient markets theory to behavioral finance. *The Journal of Economic Perspectives, 17*(1), 83–104.

Shmelev, S. E., & Gilardi, E. (2025). Corporate environmental, social, and governance performance: The impacts on financial returns, business model innovation, and social transformation. *Sustainability (Basel), 17*(3), 1286. DOI: 10.3390/su17031286

Siddique, M. A., Karim, S., Haque, M. R., & Mia, P. (2026). The truth behind sustainability claims: Examining carbon risk, ESG disclosures, and greenwashing. *International Review of Financial Analysis, 109*, 104735. DOI: 10.1016/j.irfa.2025.104735

Sierra, L., Zorio, A., & García-Benau, M. (2013). Sustainability report assurance. *Business Strategy and the Environment, 22*(7), 484–500. DOI: 10.1002/bse.1764

Sila, V., & Cek, K. (2017). The impact of ESG on firm value. *Journal of Applied Accounting Research, 18*(2), 208–225.

Simon, H. (1955). A behavioral model of rational choice. *The Quarterly Journal of Economics, 69*(1), 99–118.

Simon, H. (1956). Rational choice and the structure of the environment. *Psychological Review, 63*(2), 129–138. PMID: 13310708

Simoni, L., Bini, L., & Bellucci, M. (2020). Effects of social, environmental and institutional factors on sustainability report assurance: Evidence from European countries. *Meditari Accountancy Research, 28*(6), 1059–1087. DOI: 10.1108/MEDAR-03-2019-0462

Singh, A. K., Kalra, S., Jain, K., & Soni, K. (n.d.). IPO pricing and performance: Market insights with a green lens. *Management Dynamics, 26*(1). https://managementdynamics.researchcommons.org/journal/vol26/iss1/1/

Singh, P. (2022). Implementation of Street vendors Act in India. *Urban Development Journal, 18*(2), 134–152.

Singh, U. V., & Shrivastava, M. K. (2024). POLICY BRIEF ACCELERATING. *Growth.*

Sinha, P. (2025). Street vendors in India, estimated at over 15 million, make up roughly 10% of urban workers. *Hindustan Times*. https://www.hindustantimes.com/opinion/urban-renewal-with-street vendors-haats-101735836890911.html

Sisodiya, A. S. (2004). Mutual fund industry in India: Coming of age. *Chartered Financial Analyst*, (July), 17–22.

Son, B., & Jang, H. (2023). Economics of blockchain-based securities settlement. *Research in International Business and Finance, 64*, 101842. DOI: 10.1016/j.ribaf.2022.101842

Srivastava, A. (2022). Digital Financial Inclusion. *International Journal of Innovation in the Digital Economy*, *13*(1), 1–12. DOI: 10.4018/IJIDE.303611

Stolz, N., & Probst, B. (2025). The negligible role of carbon offsetting in corporate climate strategies. *Nature Communications*, *16*(1), 7963. Advance online publication. DOI: 10.1038/s41467-025-62970-w PMID: 40931031

Street vendors Act. (2014). *The Street vendors (Protection of Livelihood and Regulation of Street Vending) Act, 2014*. Government of India.

Subramanyam, P., & Kalyan, N. B. (2018). A study on risk and return analysis of selected securities in India. *International Journal of Engineering Technologies and Management Research*, *5*(4), 79–86. DOI: 10.29121/ijetmr.v5.i4.2018.211

Suchman, M. C. (1995). Managing legitimacy: Strategic and institutional approaches. *Academy of Management Review*, *20*(3), 571–610. DOI: 10.2307/258788

Sudhakar, A., & Sasi Kumar, K. (2005). Performance evaluation of mutual funds: A case study. *Southern Economist*, *44*(13), 19–23.

Sufi, A. (2007). Information asymmetry and financing arrangements: Evidence from syndicated loans. the Journal of Finance, 62(2), 629-668.

Swarmy, V. (2014). Financial inclusion, gender dimension, and economic impact on poor households. *World Development*, *56*, 1–15. DOI: 10.1016/j.worlddev.2013.10.019

Syam, M. A., Djaddang, S., Adam, A., Merawati, E. E., & Roziq, M. (2024). Carbon accounting: Its implications on accounting practices and corporate sustainability reports. *International Journal of Economics and Financial Issues*, *14*(4), 178 187. DOI: 10.32479/ijefi.16333

Takeda, A., & Ito, Y. (2021). A review of Fintech research. *International Journal of Technology Management*, *86*(1), 67–88. DOI: 10.1504/IJTM.2021.115761

Tang, D. Y., & Zhang, Y. (2020). Do shareholders benefit from green bonds? *Journal of Corporate Finance*, *61*, 101427. DOI: 10.1016/j.jcorpfin.2018.12.001

Tao, R., Su, C. W., Naqvi, B., & Rizvi, S. K. A. (2022). Can Fintech development pave the way for a transition towards low-carbon economy: A global perspective. *Technological Forecasting and Social Change*, *174*, 121278. DOI: 10.1016/j.techfore.2021.121278

Tay, C., Jovani-Sancho, A. J., Yulianti, L., Evans, C., Callaghan, N., Jaya, A., Salman, R., Zheng, Y., Susilo, S., Dohong, S., & Yun, S.-H. (2025). Satellite radar advances carbon emissions accountability over tropical peat. *Communications Earth & Environment*, *6*(1), 971. DOI: 10.1038/s43247-025-02926-6

Taylor, S., & Todd, P. A. (1995). Understanding Information Technology Usage: A Test of Competing Models. *Information Systems Research*, *6*(2), 144–176. DOI: 10.1287/isre.6.2.144

Tetteh, G. K., Goedhuys, M., Konte, M., & Mohnen, P. (2025). Mobile money use and entrepreneurs' access to trade credit in the informal sector. *Review of Development Economics*, *29*(4), 2311–2331. DOI: 10.1111/rode.13223

Thakuria, A., & Kashyap, S. (2017). Comparative performance analysis of public sector sponsored and private sector sponsored mutual funds in India. *European Journal of Economics and Business Studies*, *3*(1), 7–16. DOI: 10.26417/ejes.v7i1.p7-16

Thaler, R. (1999). Mental accounting matters. *Journal of Behavioral Decision Making*, *12*(3), 183–206.

Thaler, R. H. (1980). Toward a positive theory of consumer choice. *Journal of Economic Behavior & Organization*, *1*(1), 39–60.

Thaler, R. H. (2000). From homo economicus to homo sapiens. *The Journal of Economic Perspectives*, *14*(1), 133–141.

Thaler, R. H., & Johnson, E. J. (1990). Gambling with the house money and trying to break even: The effects of prior outcomes on risky choice. *Management Science*, *36*(6), 643–660.

Thamara, S. D., Andriani, N., & Syarif, M. (2025). Integration of CSR and ESG into corporate strategies in realizing social-environmental accountability: Systematic literature review. *East African Journal of Multidisciplinary Research*, *4*(11), 5407–5416. DOI: 10.55927/eajmr.v4i11.461

Tharsika, K. (2025). *A systematic review of IFRS sustainability standards*. Institute of Certified Management Accountants of Sri Lanka. Retrieved December 27, 2025, from http://repo.lib.jfn.ac.lk/ujrr/handle/123456789/11599

The impact of green bonds on corporate environmental and financial performance | Managerial Finance | Emerald Publishing. (n.d.). Retrieved November 19, 2025, from https://www.emerald.com/mf/article-abstract/47/10/1486/289997/The-impact-of-green-bonds-on-corporate?redirectedFrom=fulltext

Thomas, S. S., George, J. P., Godwin, B. J., & Siby, A. (2022). Young adults' default intention: influence of behavioral factors in determining housing and real estate loan repayment in India. *International Journal of Housing Markets and Analysis*. DOI: 10.1108/IJHMA-01-2022-0012

Tok, Y. W., & Heng, D. (2022). *Fintech: Financial inclusion or exclusion?* International Monetary Fund.

Trencher, G., Nick, S., Carlson, J., & Johnson, M. (2024). Demand for low-quality offsets by major companies undermines climate integrity of the voluntary carbon market. *Nature Communications, 15*(1), 6863. Advance online publication. DOI: 10.1038/s41467-024-51151-w PMID: 39127784

Troshani, I., & Rowbottom, N. (2021). Digital corporate reporting: Research developments and implications. *Australian Accounting Review, 31*(3), 213–232. DOI: 10.1111/auar.12334

Tut, D. (2020). *FinTech and the COVID-19 pandemic: Evidence from electronic payment systems* (SSRN Working Paper No. 3660987). SSRN.

Tversky, A., & Kahneman, D. (1991). Loss aversion in riskless choice: A reference-dependent model. *The Quarterly Journal of Economics, 106*(4), 1039–1061.

UNFCCC. (2020). *The Paris Agreement and carbon markets.* Retrieved December 19, 2025, from https://unfccc.int/process-and-meetings/the-paris-agreement

UNFCCC. (2024). *What is offsetting?* UN Climate Neutral Now. Retrieved December 19, 2025, from https://offset.climateneutralnow.org/aboutoffsetting

United Nations. (2015). *Transforming our world: The 2030 Agenda for Sustainable Development* (Resolution A/RES/70/1). United Nations General Assembly.

UNSGSA. (2011). *Financial inclusion: Advancing the global agenda* (Máxima trans.). Office of the United Nations Secretary-General's Special Advocate for Inclusive Finance for Development.

Utgård, J., & Gaustad, T. (2024). Carbon emission reductions and offsets: Consumer perceptions of firm environmental sustainability. *Journal of Cleaner Production, 470*, 143300. DOI: 10.1016/j.jclepro.2024.143300

Vaihekoski, M., & Yahya, H. (2025). Environmental, social, and governance (ESG) and firm valuation: The moderating role of audit quality. *Journal of Risk and Financial Management, 18*(3), 148. DOI: 10.3390/jrfm18030148 van Wyk, M., & Els, G. (2023). The relevance of integrated reporting in future standard setting of the International Sustainability Standards Board. *Frontiers in Sustainability, 4*, 1218985. Advance online publication. DOI: 10.3389/frsus.2023.1218985

Van, L., Vo, A., Nguyen, N., & Vo, D. (2019). Financial Inclusion and Economic GROWTH: An International Evidence. *Emerging Markets Finance & Trade, 57*(1), 239–263. DOI: 10.1080/1540496X.2019.1697672

Veena, M.Dr. Veena M. (2022). Conceptual Evolution of Financial Inclusion. *EPRA International Journal of Economic and Business Review, 10*(7), 1–7. DOI: 10.36713/epra10762

Velte, P. (2021). Meta-analyses on corporate social responsibility (CSR) and firm performance: A literature review. *Sustainability, 13*(12), 7269. DOI: 10.3390/su13137269

Vidani, J. (2024). Revolutionizing finance: Unveiling the digital banking terrain in India with a focus on ICICI Bank. SSRN *Electronic Journal*. DOI: 10.2139/ssrn.4848084

Vinayak. (2025, May 21). Why carbon offsets matter: Understanding the science behind credible credits. *Switch Climate Tech*. Retrieved December 17, 2025, from https://switchclimatetech.com/blog/why-carbon-offsets-matter

Vishnu, M., Praveen Raj, R., & Ananthi, R. (2024). Risk–return analysis of special mutual fund schemes: An empirical study in the Indian context with special reference to solution-oriented mutual funds and ESG funds. In *Harnessing AI, machine learning, and IoT for intelligent business* (Vol. 1, pp. 1161–1176). Springer Nature Switzerland.

Vives, X. (2019). Digital disruption in banking. *Annual Review of Financial Economics, 11*(1), 243–272. DOI: 10.1146/annurev-financial-100719-120854

Waked, S. S., Alturki, K. H., & Yamani, A. (2025). How governance and CSR reporting shape emission outcomes: A firm-level study from BRICS countries. *Sustainability (Basel), 17*(17), 8040. DOI: 10.3390/su17178040

Walls, J. L., Berrone, P., & Phan, P. H. (2012). Corporate governance and environmental performance. *Strategic Management Journal, 33*(8), 885–913. DOI: 10.1002/smj.1952

Wang, D., Peng, K., Tang, K., & Wu, Y. (2022). Does FinTech development enhance corporate ESG performance? Evidence from an emerging market. *Sustainability (Basel), 14*(24), 16597. DOI: 10.3390/su142416597

Wang, Y., Xiuping, S., & Zhang, Q. (2021). Can Fintech improve the efficiency of commercial banks? An analysis based on big data. *Research in International Business and Finance*, *55*, 101338. DOI: 10.1016/j.ribaf.2020.101338

Wan, S., Lee, Y. H., & Sarma, V. J. (2023). Is Fintech good for green finance? Empirical evidence from listed banks in China. *Economic Analysis and Policy*, *80*, 1273–1291. DOI: 10.1016/j.eap.2023.10.019

Weber, O., & Saravade, V. (2019). *Current Development and Their Future Olaf Weber and Vasundhara Saravade. 210.*

Weber, M. (1999). Stock market participation and investors' risk-taking behavior. *Journal of Banking & Finance*, *23*(1), 27–56.

Weber, M., & Zuchel, H. (2005). How do prior outcomes affect risk attitude? Comparing escalation of commitment and the house-money effect. *Decision Analysis*, *2*(1), 30–43.

Wen, Q., & Kang, H. (2025). Research on the impact of carbon information disclosure on corporate ESG performance: Evidence from China's manufacturing industry. *Sustainability (Basel)*, *17*(20), 9272. DOI: 10.3390/su17209272

Wermers, R. (2000). Mutual fund performance: An empirical decomposition into stock-picking talent, style, transaction costs, and expenses. *The Journal of Finance*, *55*(4), 1655–1695. DOI: 10.1111/0022-1082.00263

Widyawati, L. (2020). A systematic literature review of socially responsible investment and environmental, social and governance (ESG) criteria. *Journal of Business Ethics*, *175*(2), 323–341. DOI: 10.1007/s10551-019-04143-y

WIEGO. (n.d.). *Street vendors and Market Traders*. Retrieved from https://www.wiego.org/

World Bank Global Findex Database. (2021). *Global Findex Database 2021: Financial Inclusion, Digital Payments, and Resilience in the Age of COVID-19*. World Bank.

World Bank Global Findex Database. (2025). *Global Findex Database 2025*. World Bank.

World Bank. (2014). *Global financial development report 2014: Financial inclusion*. World Bank Publications.

World Bank. (2023). *World Bank (IBRD) Green Bonds — FY22 Impact Report*. Retrieved December 19, 2025, from https://treasury.worldbank.org/en/about/unit/treasury/impact/impact-report

World Bank. (2024). *Financial inclusion overview*. Retrieved from https://www.worldbank.org/en/topic/fi nancialinclusion

Yadav, R., & Pathak, G. S. (2016). Young consumers' intention towards buying green products in a developing nation: Extending the theory of planned behavior. *Journal of Cleaner Production*, *135*, 732–739. DOI: 10.1016/j.jclepro.2016.06.120

Yang, D., & Park, H. (2025). Integrity challenges in carbon markets: Comparing UNFCCC and voluntary REDD+ verification in the Amazon Biome. *Environmental Science & Policy*, *169*, 104080. DOI: 10.1016/j.envsci.2025.104080

Yang, S. S., Huang, J.-W., Chen, H.-Y., & Tsay, M.-H. (2025). Detecting corporate ESG performance: The role of ESG materiality in corporate financial performance and risks. *The North American Journal of Economics and Finance*, *76*, 102370. DOI: 10.1016/j.najef.2025.102370

Yao, T., & Song, L. (2021). Examining the differences in the impact of Fintech on the economic capital of commercial banks' market risk: Evidence from a panel system GMM analysis. *Applied Economics*, *53*(23), 2647–2660. DOI: 10.1080/00036846.2020.1864275

Yong, O. (2011). Winner's curse and bandwagon effect in Malaysian IPOs: Evidence from 2001–2009. *Jurnal Pengurusan*, *32*, 21–35. DOI: 10.17576/pengurusan-2011-32-03

Yu, H., Zhao, Y., Liu, Z., Liu, W., Zhang, S., Wang, F., & Shi, L. (2021). Research on the financing income of supply chains based on an E-commerce platform. *Technological Forecasting and Social Change*, *169*, 120820. DOI: 10.1016/j.techfore.2021.120820

Zahidul Islam, Md., Ahmed, S., & Hasan, I. (2012, February 5). *Corporate Social Responsibility and Financial Performance Linkage: Evidence from the Banking Sector of...* ResearchGate; unknown. https://www.researchgate.net/publication/228273307_Corporate_Social_Responsibility_and_Financial_Performance_Linkage_Evidence_from_the_Banking_Sector_of_Bangladesh

Zairis, G., Liargovas, P., & Apostolopoulos, N. (2024). Sustainable finance and ESG importance: A systematic literature review and research agenda. *Sustainability (Basel)*, *16*(7), 2878. DOI: 10.3390/su16072878

Zavolokina, L., Dolata, M., & Schwabe, G. (2016). The FinTech phenomenon: Antecedents of financial innovation perceived by the popular press. *Financial Innovation*, *2*(1), 1–16. DOI: 10.1186/s40854-016-0036-7

Zdolšek, D., & Taškar Beloglavec, S. (2023). *"The 2023's new and the fresh": The International Sustainability Disclosure Standards*. In *Proceedings of the International Scientific Conference on Economy, Management and Information Technologies (ICEMIT 2023)* (Vol. 1, No. 1). DOI: 10.46793/ICEMIT23.205Z

Zetterberg, L., Johnsson, F., & Möllersten, K. (2021). Incentivizing BECCS—A Swedish case study. *Frontiers in Climate*, *3*, 685227. Advance online publication. DOI: 10.3389/fclim.2021.685227

Zhang, A., Wang, S., Liu, B., & Liu, P. (2022). How fintech impacts pre-and post-loan risk in Chinese commercial banks. *International Journal of Finance & Economics*, *27*(2), 2514–2529. DOI: 10.1002/ijfe.2284

Zhang, D., Wang, C., He, Y., & Vigne, S. A. (2024). Does Fintech efficiently hamper manipulating ESG data behavior? *The British Accounting Review*, •••, 101494. DOI: 10.1016/j.bar.2024.101494

Zhang, H., & Yang, F. (2016). On the drivers and performance outcomes of green practices adoption. *Industrial Management & Data Systems*, *116*(9), 2011–2034. DOI: 10.1108/IMDS-06-2015-0263

Zhou, X., Wang, X., Fei, X., Liu, W., Xie, B.-C., & Zhao, J. (2025). Carbon disclosure effect, corporate fundamentals, and net-zero emission target: Evidence from China. arXiv. 2508.17423

About the Contributors

Maizaitulaidawati Md Husin (PhD) is a dedicated academic with a profound passion for Islamic banking and finance. With over 12 years of teaching and supervisory experience, she is recognized for her expertise in the field. Mai earned her PhD in Islamic Economics from the University of Malaya, alongside an MSc in Banking and a BBA in Finance. She is also a Certified Islamic Financial Planner in Malaysia. Currently, Mai serves as the Director of Business Administration at Azman Hashim International Business School, Universiti Teknologi Malaysia. In this role, she oversees the strategic and operational direction of the institution's academic and administrative functions. Her leadership is underscored by her involvement in more than 30 consultancy and research projects, collectively valued at over RM10 million. A prolific writer, Mai has authored over 100 scholarly works, including research papers, book chapters, and journal articles, with a primary focus on financial management. Beyond her professional endeavors, she finds joy in spending quality time with family and friends, enjoying music, reading, traveling, and exploring the outdoors.

Muslim Amin is an Associate Professor at Azman Hashim International Business School, Universiti Teknologi Malaysia. He holds PhD and MBA from National University of Malaysia (UKM) and BBA from Faculty of Economic and Business, University of Syiah Kuala, Aceh, Indonesia. His current research interests include service quality, customer satisfaction, customer loyalty, electronic commerce and interactive marketing, and entrepreneurship marketing. He is the author of more than 50 international refereed journal papers and international conference papers. His recent publications have appeared in journals such as The Service Industries Journal, International Journal of Bank Marketing, Services Marketing Quarterly, Clinical Governance: An International Journal, The TQM Journal, International Journal of Retail & Distribution Management, Journal of Hospitality Marketing &

Management, Journal for Global Business Advancement and International Journal of Islamic Middle Eastern Finance and Management.

Haliyana Khalid is an Associate Professor in Digital Experience Transformationand currently serves as the Deputy Dean of Research and Innovation at theAzman Hashim International Business School, UTM. She holds a PhD inComputing, specializing in Human-Computer Interaction (HCI) from LancasterUniversity, UK, and is a professional member of the Association for ComputingMachinery (ACM) and IEEE She also holds a Certified Professional Marketer(CPM, Asia) certification, reflecting her expertise in integrating User Experience(UX), Information Systems (IS), and marketing. With a strong focus on digitaltransformation, Dr. Haliyana actively leads industry and community-driveninitiatives that leverage UX design, data-driven insights, and emergingtechnologies to enhance digital experiences. Her research spans digitalmarketing, information systems and big data, with a particular emphasis oncrafting seamless, user-centric digital ecosystems. As an advocate for human-centered design, she employs Design Thinking as the foundation of herteaching pedagogy, fostering problem-solving, creativity, and empathy-driveninnovation in her students. Through her consultancy work and research grants,she continues to shape the future of digital experience transformation, bridgingthe gap between technology, business, and user needs.

Nor Aiza Mohd Zamil is an Associate Professor at Azman Hashim International Business School, Universiti Teknologi Malaysia (UTM). She holds a Ph.D. in Accounting and Finance from Cardiff Business School, UK, and has extensive expertise in accounting, Islamic finance, corporate governance, and banking performance. With over two decades of academic and industry experience, she has contributed significantly to research on Islamic banking, Shariah governance, and financial institutions. Nor Aiza has led and participated in multiple international and national research projects, including Erasmus+ initiatives on family business, green entrepreneurship, and research performance. These projects have strengthened international academic collaboration and contributed to policy discussions on governance and entrepreneurship. She has published widely in reputable journals and serves on editorial boards of academic publications. Beyond academia, she is involved in industry collaborations, consultancy work, and community projects, particularly focusing on digital empowerment, financial literacy and corporate sustainability. Her expertise and leadership continue to shape discussions on Islamic finance and corporate governance both in Malaysia and internationally.

Mustafa Nourallah, PhD, works as an Assistant Professor at Mid Sweden University and Digital Banking and Finance Project Manager at the Centre for Research on Economic Relations (CER), where his focus is on exploring how financial technology can be leveraged to enhance the personal finance landscape of households. Dr Nourallah published his work in international peer-reviewed journals such as the Journal of Business Research, reviewed assignments for various journals, served as Associate Editor for the Financial Services Review, and he the Vice President-International member of Board of Directors of Academy of Financial Services (USA) and member of advisory board of (CER) at Mid Sweden University.

***

A.V. Senthil Kumar is working as a Professor and Principal, Nehru Institute of Information Technology and Management, Coimbatore, India. He has worked as Professor and Director, PG and Research Department of Computer Applications, Hindusthan College of Arts & Science, Coimbatore, Tamilnadu for 15 years and as Senior Grade Lecturer in CMS College of Science and Commerce for 14 years. To his credit he has industrial experience for five years and teaching experience of 29 years. He has also received his Doctor of Science (D.Sc in Computer Science). He has to his credit 86 Book Chapters, 234 papers in International and National Journals, 85 papers in International Conferences in International and National Conferences, and edited 17 books and 3 Text books. He is as Associate Editor of IEEE Access. He is an Editor-in-Chief for many journals and Key Member for India, Machine Intelligence Research Lab (MIR Labs). He is an Editorial Board Member and Reviewer for various International Journals. He is also a Committee member for various International Conferences. He has guided 16 Ph.D scholars and guiding 3 Ph. D scholars now.

Arshika B is a student of Bachelor of Commerce with a specialization in Financial Analytics. With a keen interest in sustainability and sustainable financing, she is passionate about exploring the intersection of finance and environmental responsibility. Her academic pursuits reflect a commitment to promoting green financial practices and contributing to research that supports sustainable development goals.

B. Raghava Reddy, MBA, Ph.D. is a seasoned academician and finance expert with over 21 years of teaching and research experience in management education. Currently serving as a Professor at Mohan Babu University, Tirupati, he holds a Ph.D. in Management (Finance) from Rayalaseema University. His expertise spans Capital Markets, Mutual Funds, Financial Derivatives, and Technical & Fundamental

Analysis. He has served in various academic roles, including Associate Professor, HOD, and Assistant Professor at reputed institutions across Andhra Pradesh. He is also a certified NISM trainer and has actively contributed as a Resource Person for SEBI, conducting over 120 financial literacy programs. His research contributions include multiple publications in national and international journals, and he has presented papers at several seminars and conferences. A passionate educator and researcher, he aims to bridge the gap between academia and industry through innovative teaching and applied research in finance.

Naresh Choppari is having 16 years of rich academic excellence in teaching and 1 year industry experience in NBFC. He is expertise in training with research software's i.e., SPSS, AMOS and SMART PLS for Management students and Research scholars (HR and Marketing). He holds certifications in Data Science from NISM, Agent of Life Insurance (Life Planner) from IRDA, SPSS (Udemy), Data Analytics using Excel (Great Learning) and Published articles in Scopus Journal (04), 12 UGC – Care and Peer reviewed journals (9). He attended 12 National and International conferences at reputed institutions.such as IIM Sambalpur, Jaipuria Institute of Management, Pune Institute of Business Management and Govt Degree (City) College, Hyderabad.

Blesson James, Head, Department of Commerce at CHRIST (Deemed to be University) Pune Lavasa, specializes in Accounting, Investments, Finance, and Taxation. With a decade of teaching experience and UGC NET qualification, he has served as adjunct faculty at prestigious institutions. His academic journey includes B.Com and M.Com from Savitribai Phule Pune University, and he has contributed to research with publications in esteemed national and international journals.

Manjit Kour is working as Professor at University Business School at Chandigarh University. She holds a PhD in Business Management from IK Gujral Punjab Technical University, India. She has a good research record with several research papers published in reputed journals. She is an editorial board member and reviewer of many reputed journals including Scopus and ABDC-indexed journals. Her areas of interest include sustainability, green practices, Fintech, online marketing trends and business ethics.

Divya Mathur is a dynamic management professional and Ph.D. scholar in Commerce at the University of Mysore, with over 14 years of academic experience. She holds an MBA and M.Com from Jiwaji University and is UGC-NET (Commerce) qualified. Currently serving as an Assistant Professor at NSB, Bangalore, she brings a strong passion for teaching Finance and Economics, coupled with exceptional research and pedagogical skills.

Soleiman Mohammadi Limaei is an Associate Professor in Industrial Engineering and Management, and a member of the Centre for Research on Economic Relations (CER) at Mid Sweden University (MIUN). He holds a Ph.D. in Economics (Forest Economics) from the Swedish University of Agricultural Sciences (SLU). Additionally, Limaei has served as a Professor of Forest Economics at the University of Guilan in Iran. He also serves as a reviewer and editorial board member for several journals.

Chokkamreddy Prakash MBA., M. Com., DTS., Ph.D., is working as an Assistant Professor, at School of Management Studies, Guru Nanak Institutions Technical Campus, Ibrahimpatnam, R.R. Dist., Telangana. He had pursued Ph.D in Andhra University, Andhra Pradesh. He did his MBA from Anna University and M. Com, University of Madras, Tamilnadu. He had completed Diploma in Tourism Studies (DTS) from IGNOU. He is holding 19 years of teaching experience in various reputed colleges. 3 years he worked as Head of the department (HOD) for MBA department. He is a Review member for 6 peer review journals (ABCD index, ASTESJ, IJCS, IJRAR). He had published 19 patents and 53 research papers in various national and international journals like Peer review, Referred Journal, ABDC and Scopus Journals. He had attended 6 national and international conferences. He had also published 4 Text books titled "Project Management for Beginners" and "Research Methodology and Statistical Analysis" and also published 11 chapter books. His areas of interest are Finance, Marketing Management, Research Methodology and Project Management.

T. Praveen Kumar is an Assistant Professor at Guru Nanak Institutions Technical Campus, with a Ph.D. in Finance from SV University, Tirupati (2020) and an MBA. With over a decade of teaching experience since 2012 across Andhra Pradesh and Telangana, his areas of expertise include Business Statistics, Quantitative Analysis, International Finance, Financial Derivatives, Risk Management, and Financial Strategy. His research interests lie in Finance and Banking. He has published in ABDC, UGC Care, and ISSN-listed journals, coordinated national seminars, and conducted Faculty Development Programmes. Dr. Kumar also serves on the Review Board of International Research Stars and is a lifetime member of the Indian Science Congress Association (ISCA).

Merin K. Varghese is an Assistant Professor of Economics at Christ College, Pune. She is currently pursuing doctoral research in Economics at Savitribai Phule Pune University. With a strong passion for teaching and research, Merin has been actively engaged in academia, fostering critical thinking and analytical skills among her students. Her research interests include environmental economics and international trade. Through her work, Merin aims to contribute meaningfully to the field of economics and inspire future generations of scholars.

Index

T

Y

www.ingramcontent.com/pod-product-compliance
Lightning Source LLC
LaVergne TN
LVHW081529300926
849161LV00006B/1360
* 9 7 9 8 3 3 7 3 5 0 4 7 9 *